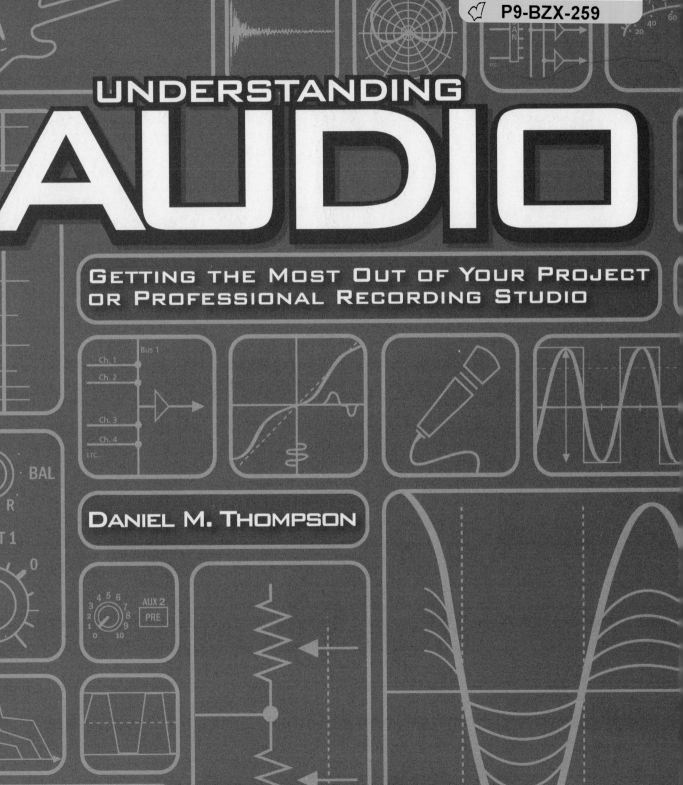

UNDERSTANDING AUDIO

GETTING THE MOST OUT OF YOUR PROJECT OR PROFESSIONAL RECORDING STUDIO

DANIEL M. THOMPSON

Edited by Jonathan Feist

Berklee Media

Vice President: Dave Kusek
Dean of Continuing Education: Debbie Cavalier
Director of Business Affairs: Robert Green
Associate Director of Technology: Mike Serio
Marketing Manager, Berkleemusic: Barry Kelly
Senior Graphic Designer: David Ehlers

Berklee Press

Senior Writer/Editor: Jonathan Feist
Writer/Editor: Susan Gedutis Lindsay
Production Manager: Shawn Girsberger
Marketing Manager, Berklee Press: Jennifer D'Angora
Product Marketing Manager: David Goldberg
Production Assistant: Louis O'choa

ISBN 978-0-634-00959-4

1140 Boylston Street
Boston, MA 02215-3693 USA
(617) 747-2146

Visit Berklee Press Online at
www.berkleepress.com

DISTRIBUTED BY

HAL•LEONARD®
CORPORATION
7777 W. BLUEMOUND RD. P.O. BOX 13819
MILWAUKEE, WISCONSIN 53213

Visit Hal Leonard Online at
www.halleonard.com

for
Anaïs and Gavril
never stop wondering and asking questions

Contents

Preface

It is a funny business that we are in, this music business. Whether producers, recording engineers, or recording musicians, our common bond is that we love music and we love recording music. We have come a long way from the days in which audio engineers wore lab coats, and musicians were not allowed to enter the control room. In part, we have artists like the Beatles to thank for that. By insisting on being involved in the technical aspects of the recording and production process, and by applying to it their own musical and artistic sensibilities, they, and countless other creative artists, producers, and engineers, helped give birth to a process that is eminently creative on both sides of the glass.

Since then, we have seen the advent of digital recording, MIDI, MDMs (modular digital multitracks), the project studio, hard-disk recording, desktop mastering, and home CD and DVD-burning. These developments have made music recording increasingly accessible to all.

But in the process of jumping into the audio soup, we often take it upon ourselves to know everything about everything related to making music—composition, songwriting, arranging, production, acoustics, recording engineering, mixing and mastering, and perhaps even marketing, sales, and distribution. In trying to do the job of ten people, it is easy for us to lose some fundamentals along the way. The intent of this book is to try to fill in some of those gaps in our understanding of audio and the recording process. This is not a book about recording techniques *per se*—there are several good titles currently available. It is also not a book about circuit design, architectural acoustics, or how to design, build, and operate your own studio, integrating MIDI, hard-disk recording, and analog multitrack tape with synchronization for video postproduction. However, if you plan to do any of these things, read this book first.

Understanding Audio explores the fundamentals of audio and acoustics that impact every stage of the music-making process. Whether you are a musician setting up your first Pro Tools project studio, or you are a seasoned professional recording engineer or producer eager to find one volume that will fill the gaps in your understanding of audio, this book is for you.

The intent of this text is to give anyone interested or involved in audio a thorough understanding of the underlying principles of sound, acoustics, psychoacoustics, and basic electronics, as well as recording studio and console signal flow. It is meant to be of use as a reference, but the topical flow should also allow the reader to proceed straight through, from beginning to end, and hopefully come out with a much deeper understanding of audio and how it relates to sound and the recording process.

Do not be put off by any of the mathematical formulae. They are included to deepen your understanding of the concepts being discussed, and are thoroughly explained and worked through to be accessible to even the uninitiated. We have attempted, to the extent possible, to include graphical representations of each of the concepts discussed. The old cliché "a picture is worth a thousand words" certainly applies here, and the reader is strongly encouraged to take the time to understand each picture or graph; within them is encapsulated a wealth of information. We have also taken care to follow each topical discussion with practical studio applications, as well as occasional end-of-chapter problems to work through for additional reinforcement of concepts learned.

Where mathematical discussions are necessary, especially with respect to the decibel, we have tried to give the reader enough background and additional information to make the discussion accessible to all. Mathematics, as a language, has the advantage of being extremely succinct while simultaneously being capable of generalizing a truth to a broad range of possible situations. To take an extreme view, Lord Kelvin once wrote that until you can explain something mathematically, in numbers, your understanding of that concept is "of a meager and unsatisfactory kind . . . [only] the beginning of knowledge." Food for thought.

Chapter ① The Recording Studio
A Brief History and Overview

To better understand audio in the context of recording and the recording studio, we must understand the process first. What is it that we are trying to accomplish? To appreciate this fully, it is beneficial to look at how we have gotten to the point at which we are today. Technology and recording has always been a two-way street, from the point of view of development. The emergence of new technologies, such as multitrack recording, MIDI, and digital audio workstations (DAWs), not only radically change the way we do things but also open up new creative possibilities previously unimagined. At the same time, the drive for new creative directions and for easier, faster ways to do what we need to do often inspire and spawn new technologies. Let's take a brief look at how recording has evolved over the last century.

Early Recording

Recording Through the 1920s

At the beginning of the twentieth century, recordings were all made "direct to disc." The storage/playback media were either wax cylinders or shellac discs that were cut live, one at a time. These discs were then played back on one form or another of phonograph (predecessors to the "modern" turntable). The recording studio setup consisted of a room in which musicians were arranged around a horn. This horn gathered sound and fed it acoustically to a vibrating diaphragm and cutting stylus (figure 1.1). As the musicians played, the disc or cylinder rotated and a pattern was

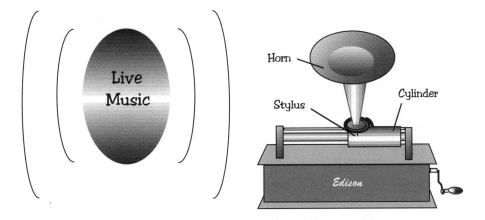

Fig. 1.1. *Audio recording setup through the 1920s. By the turn of the century, the flat disc coexisted with, and then eventually replaced, the cylinder.*

cut into the wax or shellac corresponding to the acoustic pressure changes of the original signal. The cylinder could then be loaded onto a phonograph with a lighter *stylus* (needle) and the process reversed. The pattern on the cylinder caused the needle and diaphragm assembly to vibrate, and the resulting air pressure changes were amplified by the horn. From beginning to end, this was a fully acoustic process, with no electronics involved.

Making multiple copies consisted of having several horn-loaded cutting machines lined up and run simultaneously, as well as having the musicians play the piece multiple times (each time resulting in a slightly different performance, of course). Thus, one could say that the recording, mixing, mastering, and manufacturing processes were all rolled into one; it all happened simultaneously at the initial recording session. "Mixing" simply consisted of arranging the musicians and instruments at varying distances (and heights) from the main recording horn(s). Further development of the Emile Berliner's flat disc as well as Thomas Edison's cylinder did allow for the manufacture of multiple copies from the one master. The flat disc eventually won out commercially in the 1910s.

Mid 1920s to 1950

With the development of the vacuum tube amplifier and the condenser microphone in the 1920s came a new setup, shifting away from a purely acoustical recording process to an electrical one. The microphone could *transduce* (convert one form of energy into another) the acoustical vibrations of the source into an alternating electrical current. This current would then feed a drive amp and a cutting stylus (figure 1.2). The development of the moving coil loudspeaker allowed for the playback process to also be electrified. Before long, working in the electrical realm would allow for the possibility of having a setup that included multiple micro-

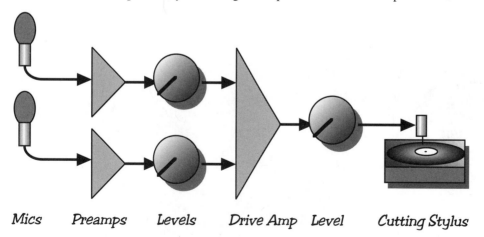

Mics   Preamps   Levels   Drive Amp Level   Cutting Stylus

Fig. 1.2. *Audio recording setup through the 1940s. Mics feed individual preamps and level controls, which collectively feed a drive amp and cutting stylus. Still direct-to-disc and mono.*

phones, each accenting a different portion of the ensemble, each feeding its own dedicated preamplifier and associated circuitry, and collectively feeding the drive amp and cutting stylus. This development in turn gave rise to the need for, or usefulness of, one device or platform that might group together all level controls and switches—namely, the *mixer* or *recording console* (figure 1.3). It also gave rise to the development of a two-room studio setup—the studio where the musicians and mics are set up, and the control room where the engineer can monitor the performance through the console and through speakers under more critical conditions. Note that in the late 1940s, magnetic tape recording took hold in the United States and began to be used initially as a safety backup to direct-to-disc recording, and as the standard for prerecorded radio broadcast.

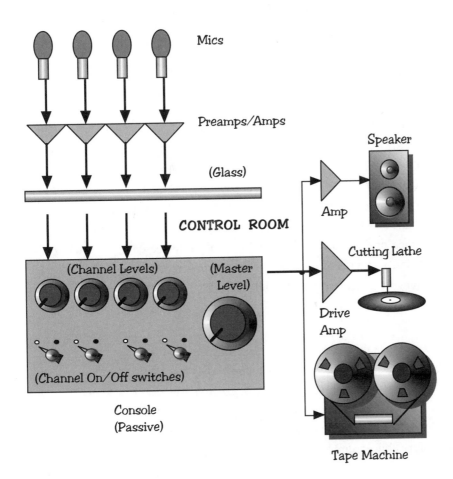

Fig. 1.3. *Audio recording setup through the early 1950s. Mics feed preamps and amps through a passive console with level controls (stepped resistor networks) and cutting lathe direct to disc (and/or tape after 1946).*

1950 to 1960

Up through the early 1950s, the console consisted of a black box the size of a large book, with four large rotary knobs (with level markings 1 to 10) for respective input levels, one larger knob for overall level, and a few switches. The tube amplifiers for each channel were located in racks accessible via a patch bay. *Equalization* (EQ) originally consisted of self-contained plug-in cassettes made up of passive resistors tailored to specific microphones. Rather than being used for creative purposes, they were meant to flatten out the peaks and roll-offs inherent in the sonic characteristics of specific microphones. These equalizations would result in a signal "more equal" to the original sound source being captured. Eventually, EQ would make it into the console as a series of stepped switches that could be manipulated as desired. Magnetic tape recording had arrived after the war (WWII) and coexisted with direct-to-disc recording for about a decade, sometimes playing the role of backup for the main disc master. The great advantage of tape, of course, was that it could be rerecorded as well as edited. Thus, the best segments of several performances could be cut together and presented as a single performance. This practice remains with us to this day, even for classical music, which is often thought to be presented as a live unedited performance. This is, in fact, rarely the case.

Artificial reverb was generally added to the final tape rather than to individual signals, and was in the form of an acoustical *echo chamber* (both "echo" and "chamber" are words that linger today on some consoles and patch bays to designate reverb). The signal from the original tape was sent to the chamber via speaker lines, allowed to reverberate in the chamber, and the result was captured using mics, and recorded onto the final tape or disc. Before long, because of its increased fidelity, decreased surface noise, and ease of editing (not to mention rerecordability), magnetic tape recording replaced direct-to-disc altogether.

Late 1950s to 1980

With the advent of stereo recording in the 1950s came the need for *ganged* (stereo) faders and equalizers, and of course, stepped *panpots*, which direct a signal towards the left or right channel. These last—consisting of two levels controls (resistors) ganged in inverse proportion (as one level is increased the other decreases proportionally)—were employed mainly to direct individual spot mics, placed to enhance instrument groups within orchestral ensembles, to coincide with their physical placement within the stereo field. Before the end of the decade, legendary musician and audio pioneer Les Paul had conceived of recording using multiple tracks, giving rise to the practice of *overdubbing*—recording new parts to coincide with and enhance previously recorded tracks (as heard in Les Paul's classic recordings with Mary Ford). This new technology marks the beginnings of the modern recording studio. With the widespread adoption of 4-track recording in the 1960s (with 8-tracks soon to follow), a whole new approach to music production was born, as is evinced in the Beatles classic *Sergeant Pepper's Lonely Hearts Club Band*, a seminal album whose intricate production was astoundingly all done using 4-track recording. Monitoring was typically accomplished using four speakers, tracks 3 and 4 being sent to the inner pair of speakers. The possibility of sending more than one input signal to a given track necessitated the use of combining networks, or *busses*, which allowed the operator to combine input signals and assign them to a given destination track. Busses were also now used to send signals from each channel via individual level controls to the reverb chamber, the output of which returned to the console and could be mixed in with the final 2-track (stereo) mix.

The emergence of the transistor as a much smaller alternative to the tube for amplification made it easier for the console to include all level or gain stages internally, first in cassette plug-in form, and ultimately in either discrete or integrated circuit (IC) chip form. (Few consoles exist with all tube rather than transistor stages.)

Because of overdubbing, it became necessary for the musician in the studio to hear what had previously been recorded so as to know when and what to play. This necessitated the inclusion of a *"fold-back"* or *cue* system, which generally consisted of an on-off switch on each channel (including the reverb return channel). This switch allowed that channel's signal to be sent back into the studio for the musician(s) to hear. At this point, level controls were also gradually moving away from stepped *rotary pots* (circular knobs) and towards linear faders and (continuously) variable-resistor rotary pots.

With the advent of 8-track recording, and given the implausibility of using eight speakers, it was found that virtually any position could be reproduced using just two speakers through *phantom imaging*.[1] It is really at this point that the modern studio setup and recording console were born in earnest (figure 1.4). We see the emergence of the monitor mix path for the return of tape track outputs. Here, every level control, mute, and solo of the record path is duplicated in a path independent of the recording, for the sole purpose of creating a preview mix for the producer or engineer. This development allows for significant experimental manipulation during the recording session without disturbing the actual recording to multitrack. At this point, equalization also became available in both the record and the monitor path, as did reverb. Foldback switches became *cue mix* rotary controls, and as tracks multiplied so did the complexity of the cue mix system. And just like that, glossing over a few developmental details along the way, we arrive at the modern recording studio.

1. Through psychoacoustics, a sound reaching both ears simultaneously (from two equidistant loudspeakers, for instance) will be perceived by the listener as emanating from a *phantom* source between the two speakers directly in front of the listener. This is the principle upon which two-speaker stereo playback is based. More on this in a later chapter.

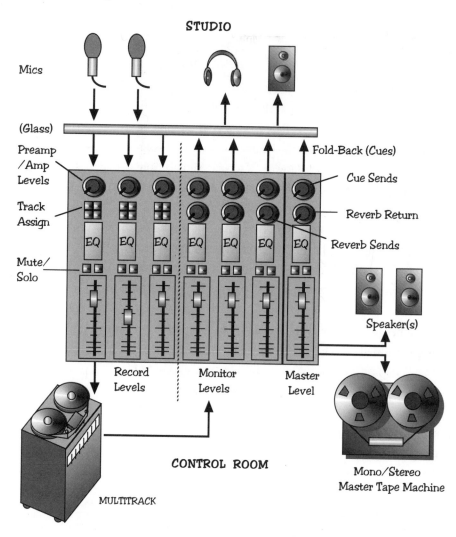

Fig. 1.4. The emergence of the modern studio in the 1960s

The Modern Recording Studio

Figure 1.5 shows what a standard multitrack recording session setup might look like in a modern-era studio. The *console* or *desk* is the heart of the studio. Through it, all signals pass to be properly balanced, processed, and routed to the appropriate destination. (In a more modest setup such as a home or small project studio, a smaller-format *mixer* or *control surface* might replace the console.) It also provides a means of communication between the studio and the control room. The engineer communicates with the musicians in the studio via a *talkback mic* or *engineer's mic* on the console. This mic is routed either through the musicians' *cues* (headphones) or to the studio speakers. A *communications mic* is also set up in the studio and routed through the console to the control room speakers to allow the musicians to talk to the engineer or producer.

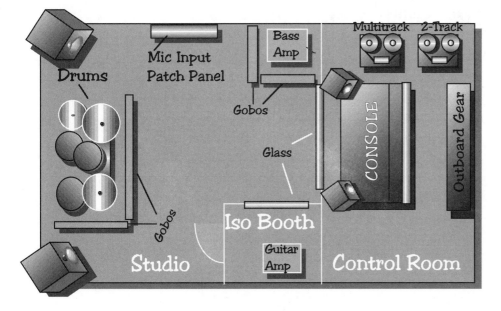

Fig. 1.5. *Bird's-eye view of a typical multitrack recording session layout in a modern-era recording studio*

Instruments can be acoustically isolated from one another using movable barriers called *baffles* or *gobos*. Microphones positioned on individual instruments in the studio are patched into the mic input patch panel, which is connected by cables running through the wall, to the mic inputs on the console. Within the console, each low-level mic signal is boosted to a usable line level by a *mic preamplifier*. The signals can then be processed using *equalizers* or "EQs" to adjust tone or "timbre," *compressors* for dynamic level control and "punch," *noise gates* to eliminate unwanted sounds, and *faders* and *panpots*, respectively used for level balancing and stereo (or surround) placement or "imaging." These effects can be part of the console or can be accessed as *outboard* gear, along with artificial reverberation, delay, and other effects, via a *patch bay,* or as computer-based software *plug-ins*. The destination for signals can be either individual tracks of the *multitrack machine*, or the *2-track stereo mixdown machine* (or, more recently, multiple channels of the *multitrack surround mixdown machine* for 5.1 surround mixes). These machines can take the form of analog reel-to-reel tape machines (as pictured), digital reel-to-reel (DASH) or cassette-based *modular digital multitracks* (MDMs, such as ADATs or DA88s), or stand-alone or computer-based hard-disk recorder systems (such as Pro Tools). In addition, the main output signal from the console or mixer feeds power amplifiers that boost the signal level enough to drive the control room speakers or *monitors*.

Basic Recording Studio Signal Flow

A simplified global studio signal flow is shown in figure 1.6. Input signals are grouped and routed to the multitrack via the *track busses*, where bus 1 out is *normalled* to track 1 in, bus 2 to track 2, etc. A *bus* is a signal path where audio signals can be combined and are jointly routed to a particular destination. A *normal* is a connection that has been set up between an audio source and destination and does not require repeated patching. The outputs of the multitrack are normalled to the line-level inputs of the console. The main stereo output of the console is normalled to the 2-track machine and to the control room outputs (speakers). The specifics of the signal flow will depend on the type of session occurring. Sessions break down into four general categories: *basics*, *overdubs*, *mixdown*, and *live-to-2* (excluding preproduction, postproduction, or mastering).

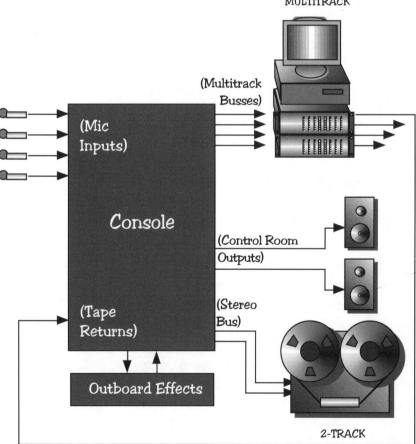

Fig. 1.6. *Basic modern-era recording studio flow. Inputs are routed to the multitrack via the track busses, track outputs are* normalled *(appear automatically without having to be patched) to the line inputs of the console, and the main stereo bus is normalled to the inputs of the 2-track and feeds control room outputs to the speakers.*

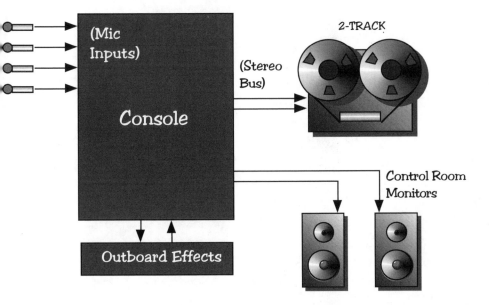

Fig. 1.7. *"Live-to-2" session signal flow. Mic is the source, 2-track (and monitors) the destination.*

The most straightforward of these sessions is the *live-to-2* (figure 1.7). This type of session is reminiscent of pre-multitrack productions of the '50s and '60s. Essentially, all musicians are in the studio at the same time, microphones are routed directly to the main stereo mix bus, and the music is recorded to the 2-track stereo master recorder live, as it happens (hence the term "live-to-2"). All level adjustments, effects, and other production decisions are made in real-time. Figure 1.7 shows the basic flow for a live-to-2 session. The idea is to make the flow as direct as possible from source to 2-track, as if it were a mixdown session; the difference is that the source signals are from live microphones rather than prerecorded tracks.

The advantage of this type of session is that it tends to be very time-efficient, has a definite immediacy, and captures the natural and spontaneous interaction between the musicians that is sometimes lost in the course of lengthy isolated overdubs. For this reason, it is probably the most common recording situation for jazz as well as classical music. The downside is that decisions about sounds, effects, and levels, once made, cannot easily be changed. A common alternative, live-to-multitrack, overcomes this limitation.

The *basics session* (figure 1.8) is the initial recording session in a multitrack production project where the basic rhythm section (drums, bass, and perhaps guitar or piano) is often recorded. In this case, our source is still the microphone, but our destination is now the multitrack (as well as the control-room speakers, so that we can hear what we are doing). Individual microphones are generally routed to individual tracks or subgrouped to individual tracks or pairs of tracks. Outboard effects at this point are not generally recorded, but rather included in the monitor mix only, as a preview.

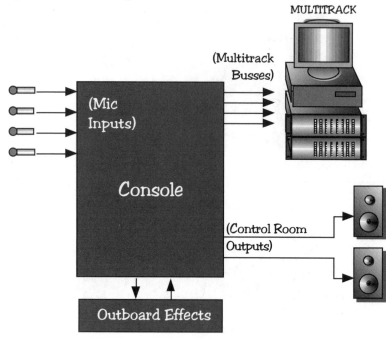

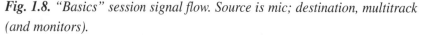

Fig. 1.8. "Basics" session signal flow. Source is mic; destination, multitrack (and monitors).

The *overdub* session(s) occurs once the basics session is completed. Tracks are added one by one, in isolation, to fill out and complete the production. In this case, we have two different sources. On the one hand, we have the live mic (or alternatively, a line input) for the signal currently being recorded; on the other hand, we have the previously recorded tracks, which must be monitored and performed to. We also have two different destinations: the live mic is routed to the multitrack to be recorded (and control room monitors to be heard), while the previously recorded tracks are arranged in a rough mix to be sent to the control room monitors (as well as headphones for the musician). The principal flow for an overdub session is shown in figure 1.9.

The mixdown session occurs once all material has been recorded (hopefully). The source is the multitrack, the final destination is the 2-track machine, whether it is a 1/2-inch reel-to-reel or, increasingly, a computer-based or stand-alone hard disk destination. At this point, final effects are added and will be recorded as part of the final mix to the stereo master. Several passes may be performed with minor alterations, such as vocal slightly up (louder) and vocal slightly down, or an instrumental version with no vocals. Additional editing may follow to create a composite or "comp" mix using favorite sections from the various "passes," as well as a shorter "radio edit" version, etc. The principal mixdown session flow is shown in figure 1.10.

The *mastering* session is usually done in a studio specializing in this type of work. It consists of taking all of the final 2-track stereo mixes for the entire project (or multi-channel mixes, in the case of surround-sound masters), and making global sonic refinements, including global EQ, compression, level matching, and song sequencing.

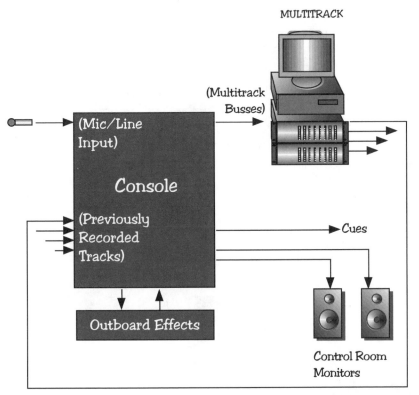

Fig. 1.9. *"Overdub" session signal flow. Source is mic and previously recorded tracks, destination is multitrack for the mic only (and monitors) as well as headphone mix (cues).*

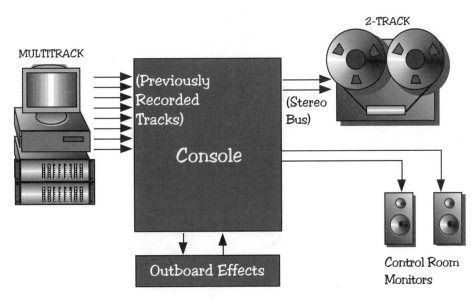

Fig. 1.10. *Mixdown session signal flow. Source is multitrack, destination is 2-track master recorder (generally 1/2-inch reel-to-reel analog tape, DAW, or CD-R) as well as control room monitors. Outboard effects are finally recorded along with the mix.*

While *DATS* (digital audio tapes) are sometimes used as masters, the more common professional 2-track stereo master format is still ½-inch 2-track analog tape. A common format for multi-channel surround masters is the *digital tape recording system* (DTRS) or "Hi-8" 8-mm tape used in 8-track digital multitracks such as the Tascam DA-78. Other options include mixing down to two tracks (or multiple, for surround tracks) of a hard disk recorder, or mixing directly to CD or DVD. Mastering can be done in the analog realm, but more commonly, it is done on a *digital audio workstation* (DAW, figure 1.11). Any analog master tape is transferred onto hard disk through a hardware *analog-to-digital (A/D) converter*, sometimes preceded by choice analog processing equipment such as vintage EQs and compressors. It is then manipulated entirely in the digital domain, digitally signal-processed, edited, and finally "burned" directly to a CD or DVD master by means of a CD or DVD recorder.

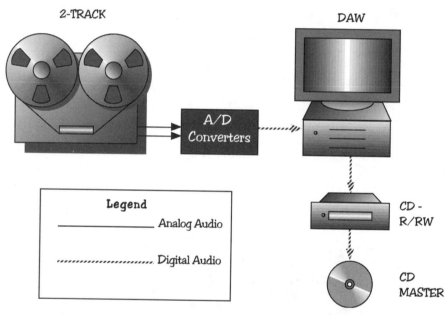

Fig. 1.11. Mastering session signal flow. Source is 2-track, destination is generally CD or DVD master, by way of a digital audio workstation *(DAW).*

While the technology of recording changes at a sometimes furious pace, particularly in recent years, the basic underlying principles of session and signal flow, signal level management, acoustics, mic placement technique, and problem solving remain relatively unchanged. *[It is interesting to note that as far as we have come, we still often refer to recording as "cutting" tracks, to reverb as "chamber" or "echo," and to the multitrack recorder as "tape."]* It is only through the development and mastery of these fundamental skills that we are able to adapt to the rapid changes in technology. These principles form the basis of all good past and future recordings (as do creativity, experience, experimentation, and love of music); they are the basis of this book. The following chapters will explore each of these topics in great detail, and hopefully lead the reader to a better understanding and a greater ability to make the best recordings under the available conditions.

Chapter **2** The Modern Studio
Recording Studio Basics

As an overview, let's start by taking a quick look at a typical scenario encountered in the recording studio. We will touch on the elements used in most modern recordings, as they appear in typical order in the recording chain, from source to destination. In every case, the scenario can be broken down into three general elements: a sound source or signal to be recorded, a series of stages to modify that signal in various ways, and a number of possible destinations for the modified signal. Each of these elements will be discussed in much greater detail throughout the book. The concept of source and destination is fundamental to understanding audio and the recording process, and to becoming a functional participant in that process. We will return to it often.

This chapter will provide a foundation for the reader who may be relatively new to the process. The advanced reader with previous recording session experience may still find this a helpful source for review, as well as the starting point for subsequent topics discussed.

Sound Source

The first step is to look at the sound source to be recorded. A typical basics session for rock or pop may consist of drums, bass, keyboard, and *scratch* vocal. (A scratch vocal is simply a vocal track that is recorded along with the rhythm section, ultimately to be replaced during a later overdub session by the final vocal performance; it is there merely as a guide for the rhythm section, so that the players are better able to respond to the subtleties of the song's melody and phrasing.) For simplicity's sake, let's look at a single element such as the vocal. Most sound sources, musical or otherwise, contain a vibrating or rotating element, such as the string on a guitar or the head on a drum. This element, when struck, vibrates, generating fluctuations in pressure in the air around it. In the case of our vocal, it is the vocal cords that vibrate to generate pressure fluctuations in air.

We hear this as "sound" when our ear drum responds to these pressure changes and vibrates sympathetically. Our hearing mechanism *transduces* the vibrations into electrical impulses that are sent back and forth between the brain and the inner ear, and are eventually interpreted as sound. A *transducer* is any element that converts energy from one form into another, in this case from mechanical energy (vibrating eardrum) to electrical energy (impulses sent between the inner ear and brain).

In the recording process, we need a mechanical, magnetic and/or electrical transducer to take the place of the ear in order to be able to store these fluctuations. The two most common types of transducers used are the *microphone* and the *pickup*. Thus, our process begins with placing the sound source in a room and locating a transducer (mic or pickup) near the source in such a way as to best capture the instrument's sound.

Fig. 2.1. *Recording vocals*

Microphone

As part of the setup process, one of the first choices encountered by the engineer in the signal chain is selecting the proper microphone to best capture the sound source. All microphones contain a moving element called a *diaphragm*, which picks up fluctuations in air pressure around it, not unlike the eardrum. When our vocalist sings into the microphone (figure 2.1), the diaphragm is set into motion and its movements are converted into an electrical waveform. This electrical waveform or current is an *analog*, or copy, of the original sound wave. It travels down the microphone cable and can now be recorded in various ways. Microphone choices include *dynamic (moving coil), ribbon,* and *condenser (capacitor).*

Dynamic: Moving Coil

Perhaps the most common microphone is the so-called *dynamic* microphone. A dynamic mic requires no external power to work. Most dynamic mics contain a plastic diaphragm attached to a coil of wire (figure 2.2). This type of mic is called a *moving-coil microphone.* The coil sits inside a magnet. When the diaphragm moves, the coil also moves within the magnetic field. This motion creates an electrical current within the coil proportional to the original acoustical waveform. The current is fed to the output of the microphone via wire leads. This process of converting mechanical and magnetic energy to electrical energy is called *electro-magnetic induction.*

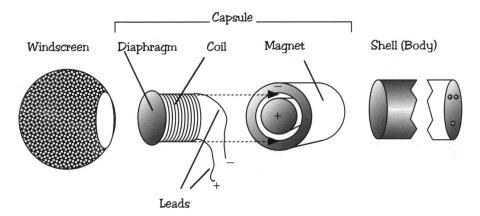

Fig. 2.2. *Simplified details of a moving-coil microphone*

Moving-coil microphones are known for being ruggedly built. They can handle high sound-pressure levels (SPL) as are generated by electric guitar amps or kick and snare drums. They tend to exhibit a *roll-off* (attenuation) in the higher frequencies (above 10 kHz) as well as a boost in attack range frequencies (2 to 5 kHz, sometimes called "presence peak"). For this reason, they are often used on drums and are popular for live sound and touring because of their dependability and ability to take abuse, as well as their low handling noise. Some of the most popular dynamic moving coil mics include the Shure SM57 (figure 2.3) and SM58, as well as the Electrovoice (EV) RE20 and Sennheiser MD421. In the studio, moving-coil microphones are simply referred to as "dynamic mics." If we choose a moving-coil microphone for our vocal, it will tend to be fairly aggressive, somewhat sibilant, and not overly detailed or shimmery sounding. While moving-coil mics are often used for live vocals on stage, they are not generally a first choice for recording vocals, unless a particularly aggressive sound is desired, or the vocalist insists on holding the mic while recording.

Dynamic: Ribbon

A more particular type of dynamic mic is the *ribbon microphone*. Instead of a coil, the ribbon mic uses a very thin piece of corrugated metal suspended within a magnetic field (figure 2.4). This ribbon acts as both the diaphragm to capture sound energy and vibrate sympathetically, and the transducer itself, taking the place of the coil. Otherwise, the function is exactly the same as that of the moving coil.

Fig. 2.3. *Shure SM57 dynamic (moving coil) microphone*

(© 2003 Shure Incorporated. Used by permission.)

However, ribbons are less *sensitive* than moving coils and therefore will need more gain from the external mic preamplifier. Sensitivity is a measure of output voltage generated given a reference input sound-pressure level.

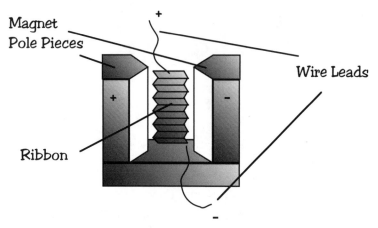

Fig. 2.4. *Simplified details of a ribbon microphone*

Because of its tiny mass, the ribbon is extremely susceptible to damage and tearing. Thus, special care must be taken never to drop or hit ribbon mics at all. For this reason, they are rarely used for live sound reinforcement applications. It is also generally not a good idea to place a ribbon in front of a loud sound source that generates high SPLs, such as an electric guitar amp or a kick drum, although newer ribbon mics are more rugged and better able to handle high SPLs. In addition, because of their construction, ribbon mics *must NOT* receive any external power. The thin ribbon element is likely to overheat and burn up. While moving-coil mics also do not need external power, under most circumstances, they will be unaffected by it.

At the same time, ribbon mics tend to exhibit a warm low end, and gentle roll-off of high frequencies. For this reason, they are especially pleasing when used on certain bright-sounding sources such as horns, piano, and certain vocals. Some classic ribbon mics include the RCA 44 BX and 77-DX (figure 2.5), as well as mics by Coles and Royer. In the studio, ribbon microphones are typically not referred to as dynamic but simply as "ribbon mics." A ribbon mic could be a good choice for our vocal, although these mics are somewhat less common and less likely to be encountered in every studio situation.

Fig. 2.5. *RCA 77-DX ribbon microphone*
(Courtesy Rob Jaczko)

Condenser / Capacitor

Unlike dynamic microphones, *condenser* microphones require some form of external power in order to work, generally in the form of *phantom power* (+48 V DC) from the console or mixer. Rather than having an *element* (coil or ribbon) suspended in a magnetic field, condensers use an electrical element called a *capacitor*. A capacitor is made up of two metal plates that hold a charge. In a condenser microphone, these take the form of a metallic diaphragm (often metal foil) and fixed backplate (figure 2.6). Phantom power supplies the polarizing voltage to the element and powers the internal preamp in the microphone. The *capacitance* (a form of electrical resistance) of the element is determined by the distance between the two plates and the voltage across them. When our vocalist sings into the microphone, the diaphragm vibrates, moving alternately closer then further from the backplate. This motion causes a commensurate fluctuation in capacitance, which

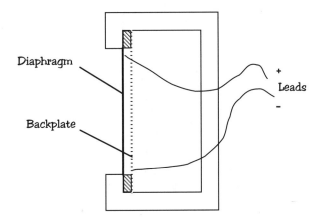

Fig. 2.6. *Simplified details of a capacitor microphone capsule*

in turn yields a variation in electrical current. The varying current is an electrical analog of the original acoustical waveform.

Tube condenser mics, which use vacuum tubes instead of transistors for power, come with their own proprietary power supply and should not be fed with the console's phantom power, unless it is expressly permitted in the mic's technical documentation.

Condenser microphones are the most sensitive of microphones (highest output voltage for same reference pressure), and also tend to exhibit a much "truer" sonic characteristic than dynamic mics, extending well into both the low and high ends of the spectrum. For this reason, they are often used to capture detailed and nuanced sound sources, such as acoustic guitar, vocals, and cymbals. They also exhibit the best *transient* ("attack") response of all microphone types. Most modern condensers can also handle fairly high SPLs and thus may be used for virtually any sound

Fig. 2.7. Neumann
U47 tube condenser
microphone

*(Courtesy Georg Neumann
GmbH, Berlin)*

source. Special care must be taken with them, however, as they are generally more fragile than moving-coil mics. Classic examples of condenser microphones include the Neumann U47 (figure 2.7) and U67, AKG C12, and more recently Brüel & Kjaer (B&K) and Earthworks microphones. A condenser would probably be the first choice for our vocalist, and can be expected to yield a warm, nuanced, and even shimmery sound.

Electret Condenser

A special kind of condenser, the *electret condenser*, was developed that does not require a polarizing voltage. Instead, the diaphragm itself is treated at the factory with a permanent charge (like a magnet). This type of microphone still needs power for the internal preamp, but power can be provided for by an internal AA battery (or alternatively by phantom power). In the studio, phantom power is generally preferred to avoid the sad occurrence of the batteries running out during the perfect take. They can be a convenient alternative, however, where phantom power is not easily accessible, such as during on-location or live-sound recording.

Polar Patterns

In addition to transducer type, microphones must be chosen according to their directional sensitivity characteristics, or *polar patterns* (figure 2.8). These describe how a microphone responds to sound emanating from different directions. Microphone directional sensitivities range from *omnidirectional*, which responds to sound equally from all directions; to various *unidirectional* types (cardioid, supercardioid, and hypercardioid), which are most sensitive to sounds directly *on-axis* (in front of the mic) while generally rejecting sound from the sides and rear (180°); and to *bidirectional*, which respond equally to sounds directly in front of or at the rear of the mic (0° and 180°), while rejecting sound from the sides (90° and 270°).

Polar patterns chart microphone sensitivity versus *angle of incidence* of a single frequency, with the 0 dB reference being on-axis (0°) response. All other angles and resulting voltages are referenced to this level. Sometimes, response to several frequencies are superimposed. Note that omnidirectional mics are equally sensitive at all angles of incidence (although at high frequencies they become more directional). Cardioids are about 6 dB less sensitive at the sides and 15 to 25 dB less sensitive at the rear. Supercardioids are about 8.7 dB less sensitive at the sides and

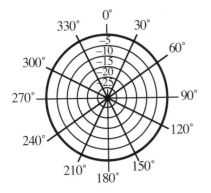

Omnidirectional

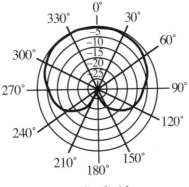

Cardioid

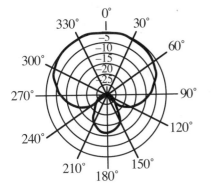

Supercardioid

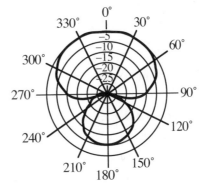

Hypercardioid

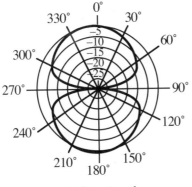

Bidirectional

Fig. 2.8 *Microphone polar patterns*

have two points of maximum rejection at ± 125°, while hypercardioids are about 12 dB down at the sides with points of maximum rejection at ± 110°.

Omnidirectional mics, because they pick up sound equally from all directions, will pick up sounds other than the principal source, such as room *reverberation* (reflections) and other nearby instruments. Thus, they must generally be placed relatively closer to the source. At the same time, they tend to introduce less off-axis coloration, as well as exhibit extended low-frequency response. For this reason, they are a good choice for use as a stereo pair to record ensembles, particularly in reverberant spaces such as concert halls. The more directional the mic, the better it is at rejecting unwanted sounds, but the more off-axis coloration it introduces. Therefore, directional mics such as hypercardioids should mainly be used when their rejection properties are essential, such as when using multiple mics on individual elements of a drum set. They also exhibit *proximity effect*, which is an exaggerated low-frequency response from nearby sources. This property can sometimes actually be helpful in making a source, such as a vocal or kick drum, sound more full. For our vocal, a cardioid makes the most sense, as a compromise between the other two extremes. An omni may pick up excessive room reflections; a hypercardioid will sound less natural, and its added directionality is unnecessary.

Pickup

In the case of the electric guitar or bass, the instrument's pickups (figure 2.9), rather than a microphone, are used to generate an electrical sound wave (although they are often recorded plugged into an amplifier, which is in turn miked). The pickups can be either *electromagnetic* or *piezoelectric*. *Piezo* pickups—based on the piezoelectric principle discovered near the turn of the 20th century—use the fact that certain materials, such as crystal, when physically stressed, emit a very controllable electrical current. When the guitar string is plucked over a piezo pickup, the pickup's element is slightly physically distorted and emits a voltage proportional to the motion of the string. An electromagnetic pickup uses magnetic pole pieces to set up a magnetic field in which the strings are suspended. Plucking a string results in motion that upsets the field and generates an electrical current in the coils

surrounding the pole pieces.[2] As with the microphone, this current is fed via wire leads to the output of the guitar.

Fig. 2.9. *Seymour Duncan SSL-1 single-coil pickup*

2. Because of the susceptibility of the coil in a typical single-coil pickup to outside electromagnetic interference (EMI, heard as hum or buzz), a special pickup was devised called a *Humbucker*. This uses a dual-coil construction with the two coils wired in opposite polarity (+/–). Thus, any outside interference is induced equally in both coils but in opposite polarity, canceling itself out when the signals from the two coils are combined at the guitar's output. The audio signal, on the other hand, is actually boosted. Thus, humbucking pickups tend to have a greater output signal level as well as lower noise level. On the other hand, single-coil pickups are characterized by a brighter, "clearer," and more "attacky" sound.

Direct Injection (DI) Box

Sometimes it is desirable to record electric instruments, such as guitar and bass, directly without passing through an instrument amp and microphone. We would plug the instrument into a *DI box* (figure 2.10) to convert the instrument's line-level signal to a microphone-level signal to address the mic input of the console or mixer. DI boxes are often used for their particular sonic characteristic, and are generally a much better, cleaner way to record an instrument's direct signal rather than trying to plug its cable directly into the mixer. More on this later.

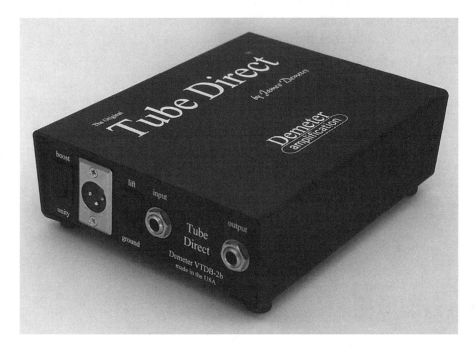

Fig. 2.10. *DI box (Courtesy Demeter)*

Mic Preamp

Coming back to our vocal recording, we have selected a cardioid condenser microphone. The next step is to plug the microphone into a mic preamp (figure 2.11). The level of the electrical signal coming out of the microphone is extremely low (on the order of 1 mV) and unusable as such. In order to be manipulated and recorded, this signal must be boosted to *line level* (closer to 1 V); this is the primary function of the *mic preamp* (or "mic pre," for short), which is the first stage at the mic input to the mixer or console. Line level is the optimum average signal level at which all audio equipment operates (specifically +4 dBu, or 1.228 V, for professional equipment, –10 dBV or dBu for semi-pro and consumer gear).

Often, an external mic preamp will be used instead for its superior sonic characteristics, particularly if it is tube-based or "vintage." The mic preamp consists of a mic input, a mic *trim* or level control that determines the amount of signal boost, and a line-level output. It generally also contains a phantom power circuit that feeds +48 V DC (or other proprietary voltage) back up the microphone cable to the microphone for use with condensers. Because our microphone is a condenser, we would engage phantom power *after* having plugged in the mic cable. In addition, the preamp may have an optional *high-pass filter* (HPF) to eliminate low-frequency rumble picked up through the mic stand, as well as a *pad*. The pad reduces the incoming signal by an additional 10–20 dB; we would use this when recording a sound source such as the kick drum, which is particularly loud and may distort at the very input of the mic pre. For our vocal we should not need it.

Fig. 2.11. *Microphone preamp (Courtesy Universal Audio)*

Recording Console/Mixer

The *console* or *mixer*, the heart of most recording studios, is the one device through which all signals pass at one time or another. It allows incoming signals, whether mic or line, to be effectively submixed, grouped, and/or routed to various destinations (including recorders, outboard effects, musicians' headphones, and main studio monitors). Our vocal signal would come in through the mic preamp and mic trim level *pot* (potentiometer) of one channel of the console, pass through that channel's recording level pot or fader, and be routed to one input of the multitrack recorder. For best results, the channel level should be set to *unity gain* (0), which allows the signal to pass unaffected. The mic trim would be used to boost the signal to the proper level for recording. The vocal signal being recorded would also be routed through the console's monitor path, master section, and control room section to the monitor speakers for monitoring by the engineer. It would also be sent, via auxiliary sends, to the musicians' headphones.

The console may contain *onboard* effects (internal to the desk itself) such as compressors and noise gates on every channel. This is typical of both large-format analog consoles, such as a Neve (figure 2.12) or SSL (Solid State Logic), as well as small-format digital consoles such as the Yamaha DM2000. Digital consoles add other onboard digital effects such as reverb, delay, and chorus. These effects are more likely to be used during mixdown than at this stage of the recording, although they may be added to the monitor mix to give all involved a better sense of what the final mix might sound like. However, certain effects, such as compression and EQ, are sometimes used on the signal at the input stage—particularly if they are available as vintage or tube-based outboard analog gear ahead of a digital recording platform to take advantage of this outboard gear's sonic stamp.

Fig. 2.12. *Large-format analog recording/mixing console (Courtesy Neve)*

Outboard Effects

Outboard effects, or *signal processors*, are used to manipulate a signal in various ways, often to make it sound unique or different from the original source, or to bring out a particular characteristic in the source. The choice of outboard effect is often made based on the sonic characteristics of the specific piece of equipment, as well as the musical context of the material being recorded. Most of these effects are now available as software plug-ins that are often modeled on their hardware cousins.

Compressor / Limiter

A *compressor* is a device that allows the engineer to control the swing in the level of a signal, reducing, for instance, the difference in signal level between the softest and loudest notes of a vocal performance. This allows for greater flexibility in recording the signal to tape or hard-disk while avoiding distortion and noise (although when misused, it can actually add both of these). Even more often, a compressor is used to change the sound of a signal, adding "punch" or "tightness" to the sound, rather than just to control the signal's *dynamics* (difference between highest and lowest signal levels, or colloquially, "loudest and softest sounds"). If we are using an outboard mic preamp for the vocal, we will probably feed the output of the preamp into an outboard compressor previous to recording the signal, sometimes bypassing the console entirely and going directly to the recorder. This is especially common during overdubs, when only one or two mics are typically being used at a time to capture a single instrument.

Fig. 2.13. Teletronix LA2A single-channel compressor (Courtesy Universal Audio)

More recently, single-channel processors that include a mic preamp, compressor, and an EQ have gained great popularity, especially such devices that are tube-based. They are particularly useful when a great-sounding, classic, large-format console is not available, such as in the home or project studio environment. As is often the case with home audio equipment, such integrated designs run the potential risk of compromising the audio fidelity of each individual element. Nevertheless, excellent models exist.

Noise Gate

A *noise gate* (figure 2.14) is a device that allows the engineer to automatically mute and unmute (or simply lower) a given track, channel, or instrument signal, based on a desired threshold level. They may allow a noisy track, for instance, to be automatically muted whenever there is no music or audio signal present. This is usually done to clean up a mix in the final stages, although there are also many creative uses for gates. Simple noise gates are often combined with compressors, but full-featured gates exist as stand-alone units. On large-format consoles, each channel is often equipped with a noise gate along with a compressor. During recording, it is not a good idea to gate signals, as any mis-setting may result in a desired portion of the signal not being recorded. During mixdown, on the other hand, noise gates can help to clean up noisy tracks or remove bleed-through from adjacent tracks or musicians' headphones.

Fig. 2.14. *Two-channel noise gate (Courtesy Drawmer)*

EQ

Equalizers (figure 2.15) are tone-shaping controls that are typically found on a console or mixer and are grouped in ranges of frequency bands; for example: high (above 10 kHz), high mid (1 kHz–10 kHz), low mid (100 Hz–1 kHz), and low (below 100 Hz), although bands generally overlap substantially for greater flexibility of use. They generally consist of variable resistors in the form of rotary pots, or occasionally sliders (on graphic EQs), to control frequency, amount of boost or cut, and *bandwidth* or *Q* (range of frequencies to be affected). EQ is an essential tool for the engineer, particularly when working with complex music mixes, to carve out space in the frequency spectrum, high to low, for all elements to coexist without obscuring one another. At the same time, again, an outboard EQ is often used for its particular sonic characteristics or fine-tunability.

Fig. 2.15. *Vintage Pultec single-channel EQ (Courtesy Brian Charles)*

Time-Based Digital Effects

Time-based *digital effects*—such as delay, chorus, and flanging—are often added to vocals, guitars, and other instruments to add interest or to "fatten" the sound of a given element. Usually these are not added until the final mix, and while they are not generally recorded during basics and overdubs, they are often temporarily added in the monitor mix during these sessions, to give the engineer, producer, and artist a better idea of what the final mix may ultimately sound like. *Digital reverb*, of course, is an artificial method of simulating various live acoustic spaces. It allows sound sources to be recorded "dry," largely isolated from their acoustic environment, and later "placed" within the desired acoustical space. While it is certainly not a substitute for a great-sounding live performance space or studio, it does afford the engineer and producer added flexibility, particularly during overdubs and final mix.

These digital effects are found on all digital consoles, but also exist either as prized outboard hardware multi-effects processors (figure 2.16), or as software-based plug-ins. Their analog counterparts have been largely relegated to specialty uses, such as an analog reel-to-reel tape machines being used for Elvis-style "slapback" echo or delay. Some notable exceptions exist. Analog plate reverbs are still found in many of the top recording studios, and are prized for their particular bright and shimmery sonic signature.

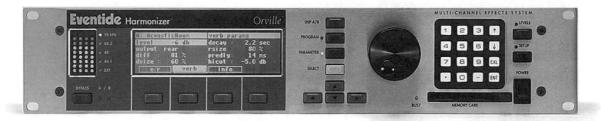

Fig. 2.16. *Digital multi-effects processor (Courtesy Eventide)*

Signal Destinations

Multitrack Recorders

Once our vocal signal is properly leveled and processed, it is routed to one track of the multitrack recorder. This can take the form of a traditional analog 2-inch 24-track machine (figure 2.17-a), a stand-alone hard-disk recorder such as the Tascam MX2424, or a computer-based hard-disk recording system such as Digidesign Pro Tools (figure 2.17-b). Other options may include a reel-to-reel digital tape-based DASH machine (such as the Sony 3348) or digital MDM machines (such as the

Alesis ADAT or the Tascam DA78. Each instrument to be recorded will typically be assigned to its own track for later balancing and mixing during the mixdown session.

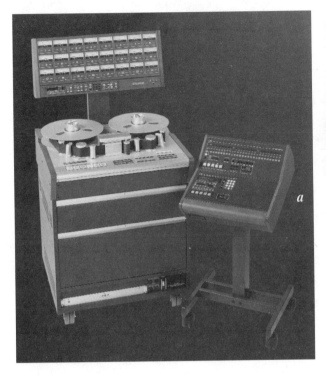

Fig. 2.17. *(a) Studer 24-track analog recorder, and (b) Pro Tools HD digital multitrack recording system (Courtesy Studer; Digidesign)*

Amplifier

After our audio signal has passed through microphone, preamp, console, and effects (and recorder, if it is being recorded), it is sent via the main control room outputs of the console or mixer to the *power amplifiers(s)* (figure 2.18). This amplifier's job is to boost the line-level signal output from the console to a signal strong enough to drive the speakers or monitors. Monitors are notoriously inefficient devices, which need much electrical power input for modest acoustical power output (3% efficiency ratio between input and output power is typical). Power amplifiers use wall line voltage (120 V AC) and large internal transformers to boost the input audio signal from around a volt to tens of volts (typically up to a maximum of 70.7 V_{rms}).[3] Output power varies greatly, but 100 W to 500 W is typical of power amps found in recording studios. Live sound applications typically require much greater power output ratings.

3. Gear generating voltages greater than this (which corresponds to a peak voltage of 100 V) are considered a potential shock hazard and are therefore subject to strict regulation and more expensive internal construction. For this reason, most amplifier manufacturers design their amps for a maximum peak operating voltage of 100 V (70.7 V_{rms}) regardless of ultimate output power.

Fig. 2.18. *Power amp (Courtesy Bryston)*

While too often an afterthought, the power amplifier can have a dramatic impact (negative or positive) on the overall sound of the audio system, perhaps second only to the monitors themselves. It is responsible for correctly reproducing the waveform ultimately fed to the speaker, and must be both fast enough to respond to the onset of the waveform's attack (slew rate), as well as powerful enough to reproduce it properly and drive the speaker correctly with minimum distortion.

Headphone Amp

In addition to being sent to the main monitors, the signal is also sent to the musicians' headphones, typically via an *auxiliary send*. In order to drive the headphones' tiny speaker elements, an amplifier less powerful than the main monitor's amp must be used. This either takes the form of an individual *headphone amp* (figure 2.19), or a *headphone distribution amplifier system* that allows multiple headphones to be fed from the same signal, to allow for use by multiple musicians simultaneously. If the console or mixer has a headphone jack built in, it is preceded internally by such an amp as well.

Fig. 2.19. *Headphone amp (Courtesy Grado)*

Monitors (Speakers)

The vocal signal that has been boosted to speaker level by the power amplifier is then fed from the amp outputs to the monitor speaker inputs, to be heard. A *monitor* consists of a box-like enclosure or *baffle* containing several *drivers*, each reproducing a different portion of the audio spectrum. The most common driver used in monitors is the *moving-coil driver* (figure 2.20). The principle is identical to that of the moving coil microphone, but in reverse. The input electrical audio signal is fed to a *voice coil* suspended within a magnetic field. (The large magnet is what makes most speakers so heavy.) The voice coil and *former* (the cylinder around which the coil is wound) are attached to the back of the speaker cone and suspended within the magnet's *annular gap*. It is held in place by the rubber or foam *surround* and the corrugated cloth *spider*. The changing audio signal generates a changing magnetic field around the coil and forces the whole assembly, cone and all, to move in and out of the magnet in response.

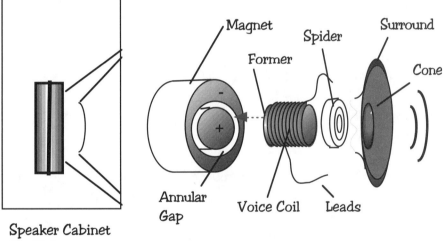

Fig. 2.20. *Moving-coil speaker driver details*

As with the microphone, it is possible to build a speaker element made of corrugated ribbon rather than coil. The problem is that because of its low mass, it is incapable of moving much air. Therefore, ribbon elements are generally relegated to use as *tweeters* for reproducing high frequencies (where much less air movement is needed) and occasionally as midrange drivers. In this capacity, however, they can exhibit tremendous detail and imaging, and are often used in high-end audiophile speakers as well as select studio monitors. The tweeter is responsible for reproducing the high frequencies, the *midrange driver* for the midrange frequencies, and the *woofer* for the lows. A *crossover network*, generally inside the speaker cabinet, splits up the signal to feed each portion of the signal's frequency range to the appropriate driver. A monitor containing three driver elements as described above is know as a *three-way* speaker. A *two-way* speaker would only have a tweeter and woofer. A classic example of a two-way moving coil speaker is the venerable Yamaha NS10M, equally loved and reviled by professional engineers and musicians everywhere.

Often there will be an additional tunnel-like hole or *port* on the front from which the lowest frequencies will emanate. A ported enclosure, called a *bass reflex* design (figure 2.21), allows for a small enclosure to reproduce lower frequencies than it might otherwise be capable of (generally speaking, the larger the speaker, the lower the frequency it might be able to reproduce—all other things being equal). It accomplishes this by creating a longer path for a low frequency to travel inside the cabinet and emerge back from the front in phase with the low-frequency driver output.

An alternative to the moving-coil speaker is the *electrostatic* speaker. Based on the same principle as the capacitor microphone but engineered in reverse, the electrostatic speaker uses a large, flat metal diaphragm and two perforated metal backplates, one on either side of the diaphragm. The backplates also serve as the speaker's outer grill, protecting the diaphragm from damage and protecting the listener from the charged diaphragm. The diagram is charged with a large polarizing voltage. The signal is applied to the backplates, causing the diaphragm to vibrate in response to the input signal and generate a commensurate acoustical waveform.

Because of their awkward size as well as expense, electrostatic speakers are rarely found in recording studios but are more common in home audiophile setups. Also, because of their inability to reproduce very low frequencies, they are often designed in combination with a woofer, or even a subwoofer.

Fig. 2.21. *Vented powered monitors (Courtesy KRK)*

Powered Monitors

It is possible for a monitoring setup not to include a separate power amplifier, but rather to use *powered* monitors. Powered monitors, which include the power amp built right into the enclosure, have become extremely popular. They receive a line-level input, rather than a speaker-level input, directly from the console or mixer's main output. They have the benefit of being easy to set up and of having the two elements (amp and speaker) optimized for use together. They are also often less expensive than the two components sold separately. While it is hard to generalize, powered monitors tend to exhibit an overall brighter and punchier sound than traditional non-powered speakers (although this is not necessarily always desirable for an accurate representation of the mix).

Satellite / Subwoofer

Satellite/subwoofer speaker systems (figure 2.22) have become increasingly common in home setups, especially with the advent of surround sound and home theater. The idea is to create small "satellite" speakers that take up much less physical space but also only reproduce the high and midrange frequencies. A *subwoofer*, a square or rectangular speaker enclosure with only a port for low frequencies, is then solely responsible for reproducing the low end. The system's *crossover frequency* determines at which point in the frequency spectrum the satellites roll off and the subwoofer takes over (generally somewhere around 80 Hz).

Fig. 2.22. 5.1 satellite and subwoofer speaker system (Courtesy Genelec)

While satellite/subwoofer systems can be found in certain smaller home studios where there is not enough physical space for full-size monitors, they tend to be avoided by many studios, as the transition point from low to midrange frequencies can be pronounced and problematic for detailed work and sonic accuracy. On the other hand, with the advent of 5.1 surround-sound mixing, which calls for five full-frequency speakers plus a sub (the ".1", as in $\frac{1}{10}$ of the bandwidth of full-range speakers) for the lowest frequencies, subwoofers are becoming a more common occurrence in all studios.

Computer/MIDI/DAW

In addition to the elements discussed above, most recording setups include a computer loaded with sequencing, sampling, and/or audio recording software programs. A *MIDI interface* allows all external MIDI gear, such as keyboards, drum pads, or other MIDI controllers, to communicate with the computer. MIDI is also used internally for software-based synthesizers and samplers. These elements will be dealt with in a later chapter. With the growing presence of computer-based *digital audio workstations* (DAWs) in the recording studio, there are also software analogs to most of the elements thus far discussed, from compressor and EQ plug-ins for Pro Tools, to mixers found in all sequencing and hard-disk recording pro-grams. These are often used in tandem with their hardware counterparts, to best harness the strongest and most useful aspects of each. However, in some setups, the entire recording environment may be based in and around the computer. Even for such setups, our fundamental discussions of setup, levels, signal flow, and process translate directly and remain largely unchanged.

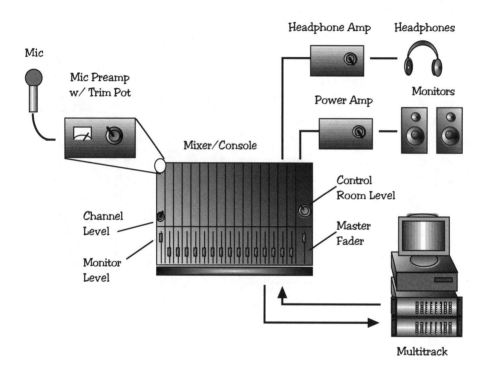

Fig. 2.23. *Basic pictorial signal flow for a vocal recording session*

Summary

The signal-flow chain for our vocal recording, then, is as pictured above (figure 2.23): the vocal, acoustically, feeds the microphone; electrically, it travels down the microphone cable through the mic preamp and mic trim; it continues through the console's channel (recording) path and channel-level control, and is routed to one track of the multitrack recorder. It is also routed through the console's monitor path and is output via the console's master section and control room output section to the power amp and monitors. In addition, it is sent via auxiliary sends to the singer's headphones. We will return to this example vocal-recording scenario throughout the following chapters as an easy illustration of the concepts to be discussed.

Chapter ❸ Basic Symbols and Signal Flow
The Audio Map

To take the next step towards understanding how audio systems work, we must become familiar with some of the conventions used to communicate truths about audio technology. These truths include recording console and mixer operation, studio setup and signal flow, proper level management, and gain-staging. One of the most succinct and versatile tools we have at our disposal is the block diagram or signal flowchart. By using certain standard symbols and flowchart conventions, we can represent relatively complex electronic systems, such as mixing consoles or entire studio setups, in an easy-to-read diagram. In this chapter, we will review the types of switches and devices encountered in a typical audio signal flow and learn the conventions for representing them in a standard flowchart.

Once we learn these basic conventions, we unlock a very powerful tool. As a studio musician or engineer, being able to read and interpret, or even create, a flowchart allows for the ability to walk into a studio for the first time and begin to work on a previously unfamiliar mixing console simply by having looked over the console signal flow ahead of time. Creating a flowchart can also be a very useful learning tool, a way to narrow in on and identify uncertainties in our own understanding. For instance, as a musician/engineer who operates a project studio, you might create a signal flowchart of the studio setup, how each device is connected and functions within the larger system. By finding the stumbling blocks in creating the flow, you can then zero in on those areas where you are uncertain precisely how the signal is proceeding, and can then investigate it further to clear up the confusion. Once completed, this flowchart will henceforth serve as a good reference for the recording studio setup and signal flow.

Flowchart Basics

The most basic type of flowchart is called a *block diagram*. A block diagram consists of blocks representing stages or devices, connected by lines representing the flow between devices. As a rule, convention shows the flow moving from left to right and from top to bottom (source to destination) across the page. Thus, at the most basic level, the block diagram for a guitar and amp setup would consist of two blocks representing the guitar and the amplifier, connected by a single line or arrow (representing the guitar cable), with the guitar as signal source and the amp as destination (figure 3.1). This simple example effectively illustrates the conventions that we can then translate to more complex setups. For instance, a block

Fig. 3.1. *A simple block diagram of audio flow between a guitar and a guitar amp*

diagram of our basic vocal recording signal flow from chapter 2 might appear as in figure 3.2 below.

Notice that the blocks representing stages in the process are arranged from left to right corresponding to a source-to-destination flow. While the main source-destination flow may be from the mic to the monitors, within that flow we can find individual or subset sources to destinations, such as mic to multitrack, or multitrack to headphones. This is very much akin to a road map. The map contains many different internal destinations. At any given time, the user should be able to trace a clear path within the map from the current source location to the desired destination (with perhaps a few one-way signs built in) and find the best path to follow. Also note that smaller individual steps could be inserted within the flow, such as channel or monitor levels, EQ, master fader, aux sends, and outboard gear. The level of detail used is dictated by the intended purpose for the flowchart.

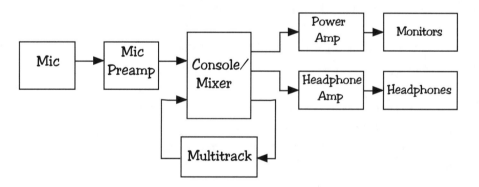

Fig. 3.2. *A simple block diagram of the vocal-recording signal flow*

This type of flowchart can be used not only for audio signal flow but for any type of process that is completed in stages. For instance, we could create a flowchart to describe a song's structure (figure 3.3). Again, note that individual steps could be inserted within the existing flow, such as a 4-bar interlude, prechorus, or 2-bar modulation. The path from chorus 1 to verse 2 could be detailed down to the bar, chord change, or beat if necessary, such as when studying a complex arrangement for performance. Similarly, an electrical engineer's schematic detailing every circuit, capacitor, and transformer in a mixing console's design is necessary for the purposes of repair or maintenance. However, this level of detail would be overkill for the purposes of recording, and would in fact be a distraction to the work at hand: understanding the *function* of each switch and pot and being able to effectively guide and manipulate the flow of audio during a recording session.

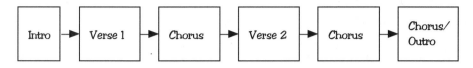

Fig. 3.3. *Simplified flowchart for a song. A flowchart can be made more or less detailed depending on the requirements and purpose.*

Before exploring the internal flow of audio devices, such as mixing consoles, we must first be able to read and produce simple block diagrams representing the external flow of audio systems made up of multiple devices, such as a studio setup or a home theater setup. Again, the key to this kind of flow is to think "source to destination," going from left to right. It also helps to begin to identify and differentiate between *input devices* and *output devices*. An input device, such as a microphone, is one that provides input signal to the system; an output device, such as a loudspeaker, allows for output signal from the system. We can also identify *input-output devices* (I/O), which both receive input signals and either pass those signals to the outputs of the system or become a source for signal fed to the output. Such a device would be, for instance, a recorder, which can record input signals and also play back those signals (or other prerecorded signals) to be fed to the output of the system (figure 3.4). A computer CPU (central processing unit) also acts as the main I/O for a computer system.

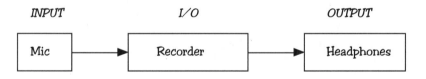

Fig. 3.4. *Basic block diagram flowchart of a desktop computer system setup*

As an example, let's generate a flowchart describing the interaction of the various components of a computer system. We might begin by identifying input devices. These would include the mouse, QWERTY keyboard (named after the arrangement of the first six letters that appear on the keyboard), scanner, and microphone. These all feed different input signals to the CPU. Output devices might include the computer monitor, printer, and speakers. Additionally, we might have other I/O devices besides the main CPU, such as a fax/modem and an external hard drive. There are a number of ways to represent this setup in a flow. Figure 3.5 shows one possible solution. Notice that the flow, as much as possible, is kept in a left-to-right, source-to-destination, configuration, with input devices lined up on the left, and output devices together on the right. The actual physical orientation of the equipment in the setup plays little part and should not affect the block diagram. Also, note the avoidance of diagonal (and if possible, crossed) lines; they tend to be more visually confusing. The idea here is to create as clear and legible a road map as possible. To this end, label all inputs and outputs accordingly.

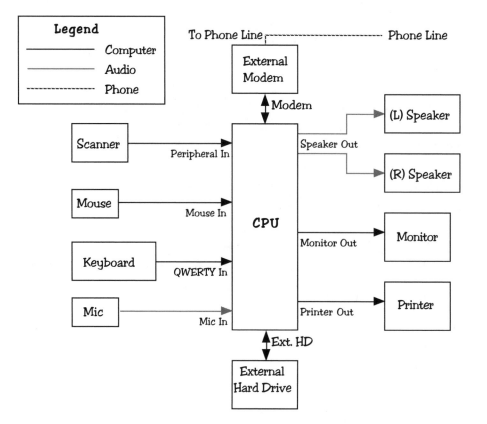

Fig. 3.5. *Basic block diagram flowchart of a desktop computer system setup*

When dealing with different types of signals within the flow, it is important to differentiate between them using either different colors or different line patterns. In this particular case we might differentiate between audio signals (from the mic and to the speakers), and other binary computer-based signals (from the scanner and to the printer). An explanation should also accompany the flow in the form of a *legend* or key to the symbols used. Finally, instead of simple boxes, block diagrams sometimes use pictures more closely representing the physical appearance of the devices in question (figure 3.6). This is especially common in owner's manuals meant to help the end-user with system setup. The flow itself should be the same; only the physical representation changes.

Notice that for this type of block diagram, we are principally interested in signal flow. Therefore, AC connections are routinely left out and considered separately. (AC does not constitute a *signal* because it does not carry any information.) On the other hand, control signals such as MIDI and others are often included in this type of flow, and are generally differentiated from audio signals and designated with some sort of dashed line. Control signals typically carry and send information about, or otherwise affect, how the system functions but do not directly carry audio information.

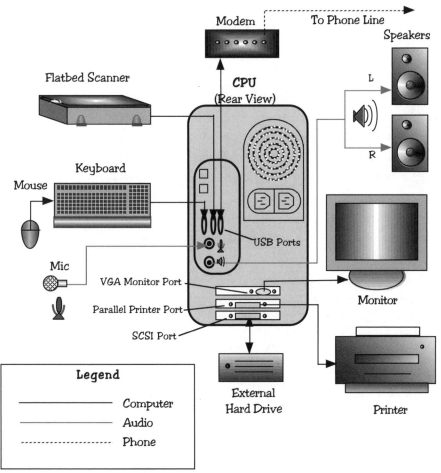

Fig. 3.6. *Pictorial block diagram flowchart of a desktop computer system setup. Flow remains principally from left to right. Connections are shown more literally.*

EXERCISE Create a block diagram of your own computer setup. Include any MIDI peripherals that may be connected, such as keyboards or other controllers, sound modules, and MIDI interface. Differentiate between MIDI, audio, and other non-audio signal flow (such as between the computer and printer) using a separate color for each.

Symbols

Now that we have a sense of what flowcharting is all about, let's look at the various devices, switches, and pots that we are likely to encounter in the studio, on consoles and other recording equipment, in the way they are most typically represented in flowcharts. This will enable us to both interpret and create flows that describe the function of our audio systems and devices.

Signal Paths

As we have already seen, the basic building block for signal flow is the solid line, which represents the actual flow of audio signals (figure 3.7a). Often, a device will also contain non-audio paths for *control* voltages. These *control paths* allow switches to be linked in such a way that toggling a single external switch triggers a series of internal switches to alter the signal flow (grouping faders, or switching from "record" to "mix" status on a console, for instance). These are designated by dashed or broken rather than solid lines (figure 3.7b).

In a complex flowchart, lines often need to crisscross (figure 3.7), so it is necessary to make a differentiation between lines that cross because there is an audio connection (c) designated by a dot at the crossing point (implying one source and multiple destinations, such as aux sends), and lines that cross simply by drawer's necessity (d) designated either by no dot or by a hump. While use of a hump to designate lack of connection seems clearer, it is unfortunately less frequently encountered in flowcharts.

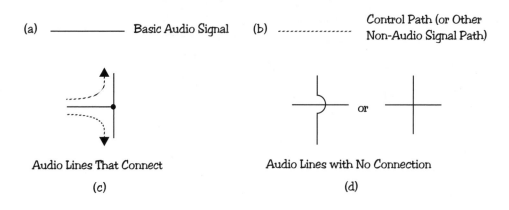

(a) ——————— Basic Audio Signal   (b) ----------------- Control Path (or Other Non-Audio Signal Path)

Audio Lines That Connect

(c)

Audio Lines with No Connection

(d)

Fig. 3.7. *Flowcharts often contain audio lines that crisscross, some out of necessity due to spatial concerns (d), and others because an audio connection exists (c).*

Switches

Most other symbols used in a flow represent a device or element over which we will have physical control, such as a *switch*, *pot* (potentiometer), or *pan pot* (panoramic potentiometer). A switch can be an on/off or *momentary* switch (a), such as a channel mute on a console or mixer (figure 3.8a). It could also be an A/B or *toggle* switch (b), which selects between two (or more) sources or destinations, such as a mic/line selection switch that selects between a mic input signal and a line input source signal for a given channel. It acts as a kind of router for the signal, the way a rail switch might redirect a train to a different set of tracks. A *ganged* switch (c) is a switch that simultaneously affects more than one path (often left and right) by means of a single physical switch, such as a stereo control-room mute switch.

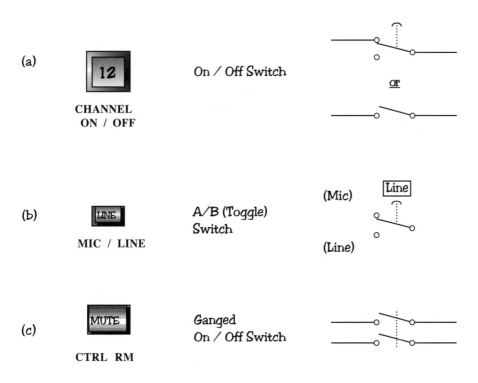

Fig. 3.8. *Switch types (left) and their associated symbology (right)*

A switch can also be used to engage a *pad* or a *dim* function, typically found on consoles and some mixers (figure 3.9). For instance, if the mic signal coming into the console's mic preamp is too great in level (as is often the case when miking a kick or snare drum), we may need to engage an additional resistance circuit, called a *pad*, to bring the level down by a fixed amount (generally –10 to –20 dB) to avoid distortion. Like the pad, the dim function reduces the overall level by a fixed amount (generally around –30 dB), but only on the way to the monitors. This allows you to globally dim the monitoring level in the control room, for conversation or to check the mix at a lower level, without losing your reference monitoring level.

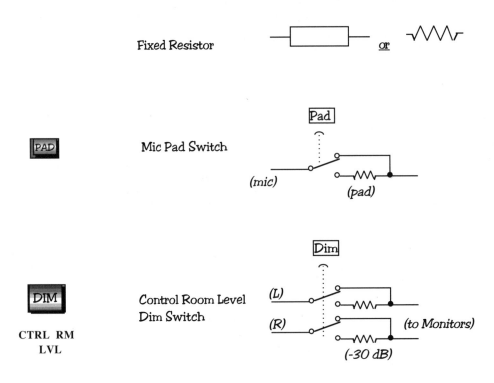

Fig. 3.9. *Fixed resistors used in pad and dim switches*

Pots and Faders

A *potentiometer*, or *pot*, is simply a knob that, when turned, changes the level of the audio signal passing through it by varying the electrical resistance in its path. The greater resistance, the lower the level of the audio signal allowed to pass through it. For this reason, it is called a *variable resistor*. Simply stated, a variable resistor is a level control, such as a volume knob (figure 3.10b). Other types of variable resistors include *linear* (or *long-throw*) *faders* (c). Note that the generic symbol for a variable resistor is the same as that for a resistor, but with an arrow through it. Also note both the generic symbols, which give no indication as to the

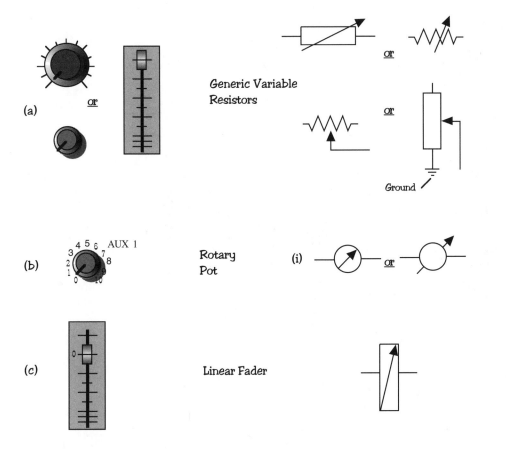

Fig. 3.10. *Variable resistors used in level pots and faders*

physical appearance of the component (a), as well as the physically specific symbols for pots and faders (b, c). Functionally these are all the same. They allow the user to adjust signal level, and thus represent what we would call a *gain stage* in the signal flow. A gain stage is any point in the flow where the user can adjust the level of the signal passing through that point.

However, a gain stage can either be *active* or *passive*. An active gain stage generally is tied to an internal amplifier, allowing the user to either boost or attenuate the level of a signal arriving at the stage (figure 3.11a). The triangle is the generic flowchart symbol for an amplifier. A passive gain stage (b) consists of the variable resistor alone; the most the user can do is either allow the full signal through without attenuation, or attenuate the signal. The generic variable resistor symbols are more specific with respect to active or passive status than are the physically specific fader and pot symbols (which generally give no indication of active or passive status). In this case, looking at the actual device would give us clarification; the numbering scheme on level controls marks 0 as the point where the gain stage is neither adding to nor reducing the level of the signal passing through it. If

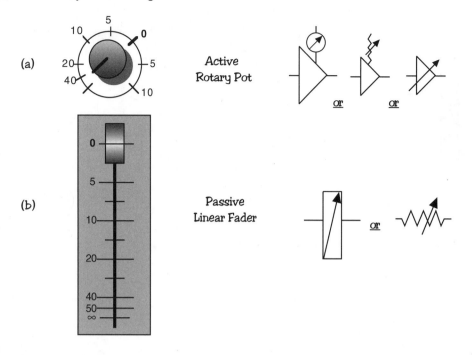

(a)

Active
Rotary Pot

_or_   _or_

(b)

Passive
Linear Fader

_or_

Figure 3.11. *An active gain stage allows the user to boost or cut the signal level; a passive gain stage allows for attenuation only. Both rotary and linear faders can be either active or passive.*

there is room above 0, the gain stage must be active; if 0 is the highest point on the fader or pot, then it must be passive. The point where the signal is passed without being either attenuated or boosted (0) is called *unity gain*. Pushing the fader

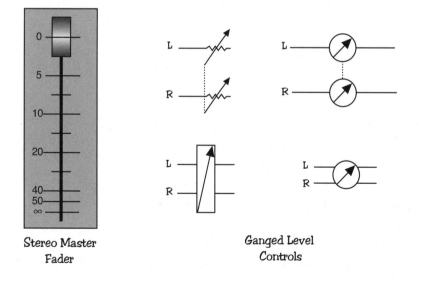

Stereo Master
Fader

Ganged Level
Controls

3.12. *Various schematic representations of a ganged level control such as a stereo master fader, or a stereo control room level pot*

or pot beyond this point activates the additional *operational amplifier* (*op amp*) for added gain. Note: Added gain, in this case, also means added noise, so it is best to avoid pushing the fader into this region except when absolutely necessary. Also, notice the logarithmic numbering scale used on the level controls. This is the most common level scale for faders because it corresponds most closely to the way we perceive level change. (A logarithmic or exponential change sounds linear to the ear.)

There are also *stereo level* controls, such as the console's *master fader*, which would be used during a mixdown session to fade the overall two-track stereo mix at the end of a song. A stereo level control consists of two *ganged* variable resistors that affect both left and right signal paths simultaneously, in direct proportion, using a single physical control (figure 3.12).

Pan Pots

A *panoramic potentiometer*, or *pan pot*, allows the user to send the source signal more or less to either the left or the right (or possibly rear) destination channels, thus altering that instrument's apparent location (or *imaging*) within the stereo field. Physically, a pan pot is a type of rotary pot that affects two paths (typically left and right) simultaneously but in inverse proportion. In other words, as level is increased to one channel, it is reduced proportionally to the other (figure 3.13).

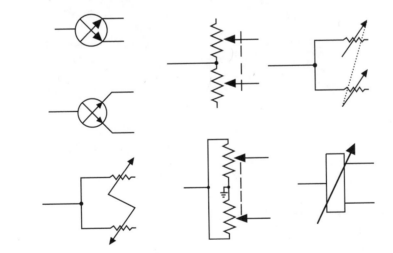

Pan Pot

Fig. 3.13. *Various schematic representations of a pan pot, which allows a signal to be panned between two (or more) channels*

Patch Bay

Within the signal flow, it is useful to be able to insert the actual signal, as well as have access to that signal at different points along its travels. This allows one to process the signal using outboard equipment such as compressors and gates or even outboard equalizers. *Outboard* refers to any device that is not physically part of the main mixing console (or *board*) and, as a result, must be patched into the flow using patch cords and *jacks*. Jacks or *patch points* are what allow us to either extract a signal from the console flow, or insert a signal into the flow, in order to compress the vocal using an outboard vintage tube compressor, for instance. These patch points are generally spread in pairs (output paired with input) throughout the flow, and are physically grouped together in a *patch bay* (figure 3.14). Horizontal rows of patch points are set up in pairs on a patch bay in such a way that the upper row consists entirely of outputs, while the row below it is all inputs.

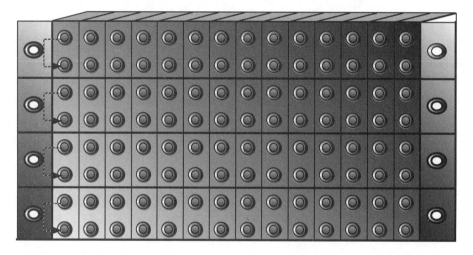

Fig. 3.14. Typical patch bay used to access signals at different points within the audio flow. Horizontal rows are arranged in pairs with outputs in the row above normalled to inputs in the row directly below it.

The most common type of patch bay is called a *TT* (or *tiny telephone*—as once used by the phone company before electronic switching) patch bay (figure 3.15a). The older style, larger ¼-inch or *phone* patch bays (b) are still occasionally found in the recording studio. Because this type of patch bay is generally cheaper, but contains fewer patch points within the same amount of space, it is more often found in semi-pro installations. As of this writing, nearly every pro studio relies on an analog TT patch bay for much of its audio routing.

The input and output patch points are drawn into the flowchart using the schematic symbols shown below (c).

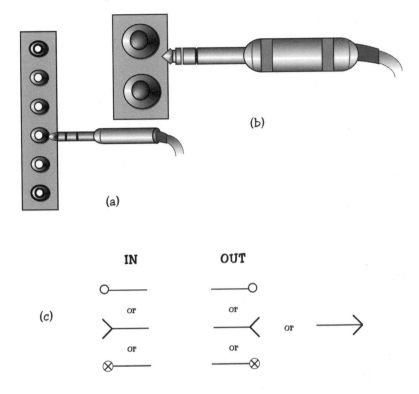

Fig. 3.15. *(a) TT (tiny telephone) patch bay and patch cord; (b) ¹/₄-inch phone patch bay and patch cable; (c) generic input and output patch point symbols*

Normalled Connections

By far the most common wiring scheme for these patch points is what is known as *half-normalled* (figure 3.16). A *normalled* connection simply means that a source signal (output) is wired through the patch bay to a destination (input) without it having to be patched every time it is used. For example, the outputs of the multi-track recorder are "normalled" to the inputs of the mixing board. Just bring up the faders, and there are your signals—no patching necessary (figure 3.17). Having them pass through the patch bay, however, allows for the track output signals to be accessed before they reach the console inputs, to insert outboard compression, gating, etc.

HALF-NORMAL

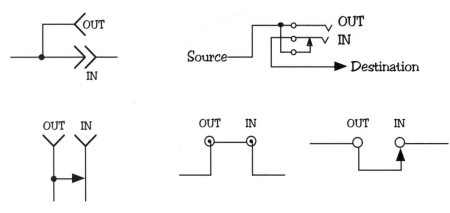

Fig. 3.16. *Possible flow symbols for a half-normalled pair of patch points. Note that the output does not break the normal; the input breaks the normal from source to destination.*

A *half-normalled* connection implies a pair of patch points in which the outputs are normalled to the inputs such that when a patch cord is inserted into the output patch point, the normal is not broken. This means that this output signal is split and can now be patched elsewhere while still getting to the normalled input as well. However, if we patch a different signal into the *input*, the normal is broken and the new signal takes its place. For instance, if we wanted to compress the vocal signal coming back from the multitrack, track 10, we could patch out of Multitrack Out 10 to the compressor (figure 3.18). The flow is as yet undisturbed. However, as soon as we patch the compressor output into the line input of the console, we break the normal of the original flow, replacing the output of track 10 with the compressed version of the track. We have extended the flow, so to speak, to include the outboard compressor.

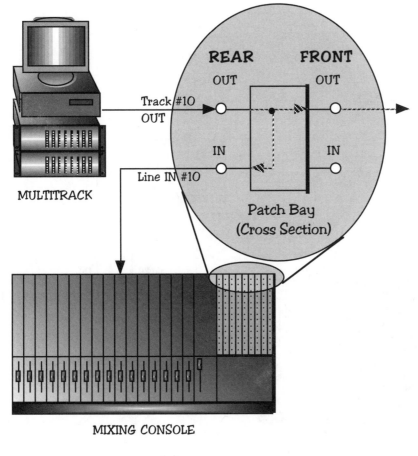

MULTITRACK

MIXING CONSOLE

(a)

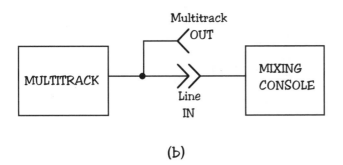

(b)

Fig. 3.17. *Half-normalled connection between multitrack outputs and line inputs of recording/mixing console. Output can be accessed (patched out) without interrupting the normal connection. Pictorial (a) and schematic (b) representation.*

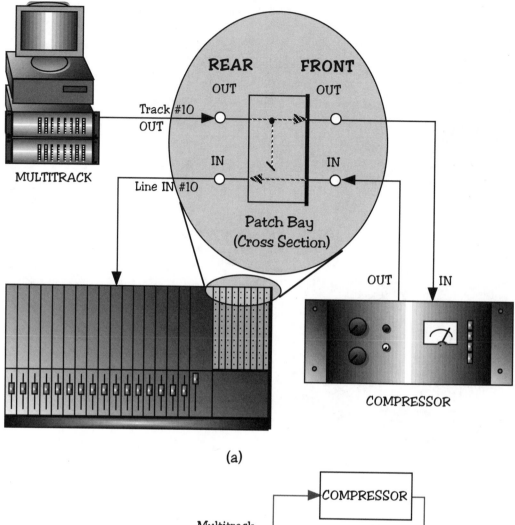

(a)

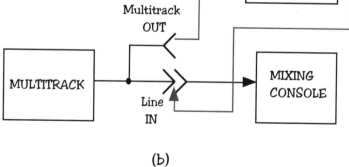

(b)

Fig. 3.18. *Inserting a compressor between the half-normalled track output and console line input. The normal is not broken until the output of the compressor is patched into the flow, thus replacing the direct output from the multitrack.*

To sum up: half-normalled means output does not break the normal, input breaks the normal. By contrast, a *fully-normalled* connection would be broken as soon as a patch cord were insert into *either* the output or the input. This last scheme is much less flexible and not often employed, except in the case of mic level signals.

Figure 3.19 shows the details of a half-normalled patch bay connection employing a switching jack for the connections. With no plug inserted, signal from the source is routed directly to the destination. The output jack does not disturb the normal; the input switching jack, however, interrupts normalled connection by physically separating the contact points.

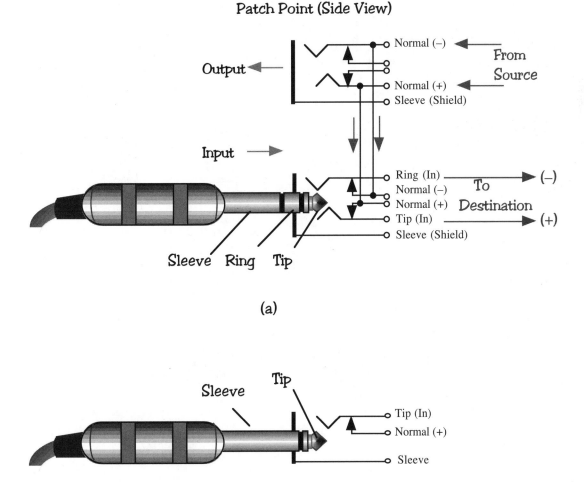

Fig. 3.19. *(a) Details of half-normalled connection; (b)* unbalanced *switching input*

Mic and Line Inputs

Besides patch points, flowcharts generally include the main inputs to the console, namely the mic and line inputs. These are found on the back of the console or mixer and will generally be in the form of XLR balanced jacks and/or ¼-inch balanced (or occasionally unbalanced) jacks. (Balanced and unbalanced connections will be discussed in a later chapter.) These are often represented in a more hardware-specific form, shown below (figure 3.20), than the generic patch-point symbols shown above. Principal outputs, such as headphone outs, may be similarly treated as well.

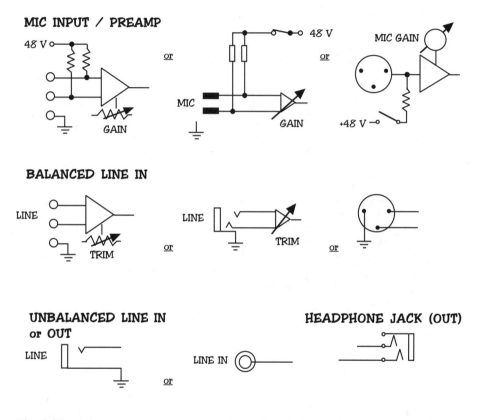

Fig. 3.20. *Schematic representations of console mic inputs (with preamp gain trim) and balanced/unbalanced console line inputs*

Applied Signal Flow

Now that we know some of the standard symbols used in flowcharts, we can use them to create the internal signal flow for an audio device. Let's take, for instance, an analog multitrack recorder (figure 3.21). A 24-track recorder has twenty-four inputs and outputs, three head stacks—erase, record, and play—as well as a monitor switching system. This last allows the user to monitor signal (including metering) either directly from the input, off of the playback head (called *repro*—for repro-duce—mode), or off of the record head (called *sel rep* or *sel sync*—for selective reproduce or selective synchronization, respectively).

Input mode is typically used during initial recording, since nothing is on tape yet. Repro mode is used to listen to playback of prerecorded material, such as during mixdown. Sel rep (sel sync) mode is used for *overdubbing*—recording new tracks that are being added to previously recorded tracks. Monitoring using the playback head would be problematic in this situation because the record and play-back heads are physically separated by a small distance. This introduces a delay between signal being read off of the playback head and signal currently being recorded at the record head. To eliminate the delay, prerecorded tracks are set to be monitored in sel-rep mode off of the record head, while newly recorded tracks are set to be monitored in input mode, which corresponds to the signal at the record head.

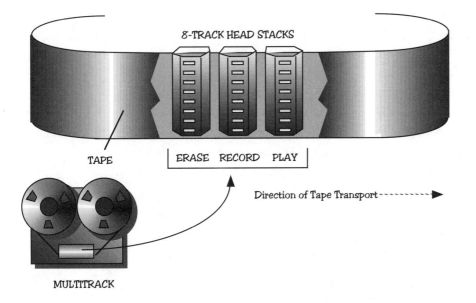

Fig. 3.21. An 8-track multitrack head assembly, with erase, record, and play head stacks (a 24-track would be similar but with twenty-four heads per stack).

The head stacks consist of twenty-four individual heads grouped into a single stack and separated from each other by a track guard, which minimizes bleed from one channel to the adjacent channels. For any device that has multiple channels with all controls duplicated in each channel, the flow for a single channel is generally drawn out. Thus, we need only include one input, one output, and one set of heads and related circuitry.

As a first step, let's list the elements we need to include in our flow. We will need the following:

(1) line input (of 24)	(1) erase head
(1) line output	(1) record head
(1) record switch	(1) play head
(1) 3-way output monitor switch	(1) VU meter
(input, sel rep, and repro options)	

We can begin by aligning our input (source) to the left and output (destination) to the right. We also recognize that the heads (and tape) themselves can be an intermediate source (play) and destination (record). When thinking about where each element should be placed, think of the flow as a stream. If an element such as a level control or a switch affects the signal at another point in the flow, such as at a meter, it must occur upstream in the flow from that point (just as adding green dye at a point in a stream will only affect points downstream—water upstream will remain clear). The monitor switch, therefore, must come *before* the output but *after* the heads. Conversely, the VU meter must come *after* the switch to properly reflect the signal appearing at the output of the machine. Figure 3.22 shows a possible signal-flow solution.

Now, if we have more information about our tape machine we could flesh out the flow even further. For instance, all magnetic tape machines contain a *bias oscillator*, which is used to feed a high-amplitude, high-frequency sine wave to the erase head. This signal fully erases the tape before it reaches the record head. A small amount of that signal is also fed to the record head and mixed in with the input signal to overcome crossover distortion inherent in the recording process. Adjusting the *bias level* (amount of bias signal fed to the record head) is a necessary part of the maintenance process to prepare a machine for recording. Additional calibrations for each track include playback level, playback EQ (to overcome a very skewed

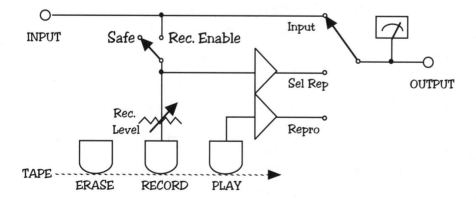

Fig. 3.22. *Signal flow for one channel of a 24-track multitrack recorder*

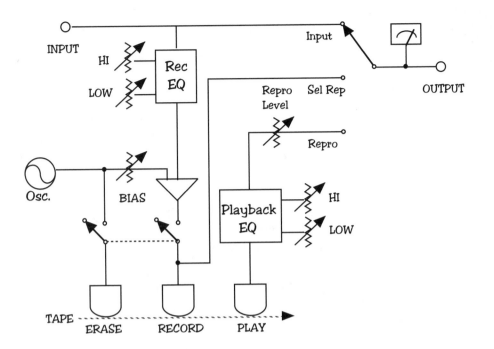

Fig. 3.23. *Signal flow for one channel of a 24-track multitrack recorder*

frequency response inherent in the physics of the playback process), record EQ, and record level. Adding these elements to the flow would yield the result shown in figure 3.23.

Note the inclusion of a *summing amp*, which combines the input signal and the bias signal to be fed to the record head. Any time we combine signals, we need some kind of combining stage (or summing amp) to properly regulate the process. This is the case with multitrack and send busses (as depicted in chapter 4, figure 4.7b). The summing stage includes resistors configured in such a way as to prevent the signals from interacting with each other in unpredictable ways.

The specifics of analog tape recording will be covered in greater detail in chapter 13.

PROJECTS

1. Create a basic block diagram of your studio setup. Include all devices, and label all inputs and outputs. Test the flow by passing a source signal from input to final destination, verifying signal presence at each stage in between.

2. Pick one simple device, such as an outboard EQ or a guitar amp, and create a basic flowchart of the device. Be sure to include every physical control (knob, fader, switch) accessible to the user, except for power. Use a source signal to problem-solve the flow, keeping in mind that signal flow moves from left to right, source to destination.

Chapter **4** Advanced Signal Flow
The Recording Console

Now that we have discussed how to interpret and create signal flowcharts, as well as a gained a grasp of recording studio signal flow and function, let's look more closely at the heart of the recording studio: the recording console itself. As we saw in chapter 1, the console is essential for grouping and balancing incoming signals to be recorded. It also helps to facilitate communication between the control room and the musicians in the studio (figure 4.1). Virtually every project and professional studio has some sort of console or mixer through which all signals are routed and monitored. Every console has unique options and nomenclature, but because they are all meant to perform the same type of functions, consoles have a lot more in common than not.

The following discussion should apply to most professional consoles and mixers across the board (no pun intended). It should serve as a good primer for what to expect functionally on any console or mixer with which you might be faced. This will be true even for digital consoles and mixers, or digitally-controlled analog consoles. The platform may look different, the options may be multiplied, but the basic functionality remains the same. There are also some differences between consoles geared towards recording, and, for instance, consoles meant for live-performance mixing. However, the differences tend to be in magnitude rather than architecture. A live-sound console might have more options for subgrouping and matrixing (which signals are sent where) to help manage the rigors of live mixing, and less of a developed dual-path (recording/monitoring) architecture found on recording consoles. Mixers, on the other hand, tend to have slightly less functionality and fewer features, but the basic principles remain the same. On-screen computer-based mixers are also modeled on the paradigm of the traditional console. Once you understand this functionality and associated flow, you will be ready to tackle anything.

Console Architecture

As we have already seen, the main function of the console is to receive input signals from various sources such as our vocal signal, level (and process) them, and group and/or route them to destinations such as multitrack recorder tracks and monitor speakers, as well as headphones for the musicians' mix. The following discussion will focus on the specifics of how to accomplish these tasks on any console. For most of this discussion, we will focus on *in-line* architecture. This is perhaps the most common large-format console architecture in the United States. *Split architecture*, which preceded it, is still widely in use, however, especially in Europe, as well as in "mix-to-pix" or audio postproduction (sound for film and television). We will deal with this a bit later in the chapter.

Fig. 4.1. *A day in the life of the recording studio*

The recording console can be broken down into three physical sections: the *I/O (input/output) modules*, the *master (center) section*, and the *patch bay* (figure 4.2). Let's look at the I/O section first.

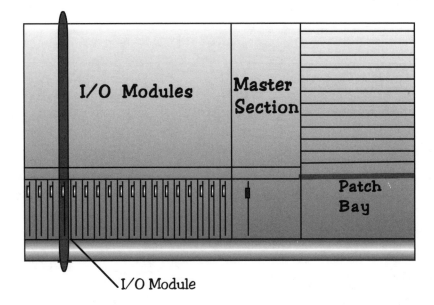

Fig. 4.2. *The in-line console consists of three principal sections: the I/O modules, the master section, and the patch bay.*

I/O Modules

Perhaps the most frequently posed question by the novice to the engineer is "How do you know what all of those buttons do?" This section of the console, which boasts the most "buttons," becomes quickly less intimidating once one realizes that each module or *channel strip* is identical (bar the occasional added option). Once you have learned the functioning of one module, you have learned virtually the entire board. Earlier console designs, which we explored in the first chapter, expanded by necessity. Once the number of tracks that could be recorded separately began to grow, the natural tendency was to mic every element individually, to be recorded on its own track. More mics meant more input channels; more tracks meant more tape returns and more inputs to the mix.

Each I/O module or "channel strip" (figure 4.3) contains three basic sections: the *input* section (A), the *output* section (B), and the *monitor* section (C). The *input* section provides for inputs to the console. Generally, these consist of a mic input with preamp and trim (level pot), to boost the very low level mic signal up to line level; a line input for the return signal from multitrack, and occasionally a third line input to accommodate an alternate signal such as a synthesizer or other line-level

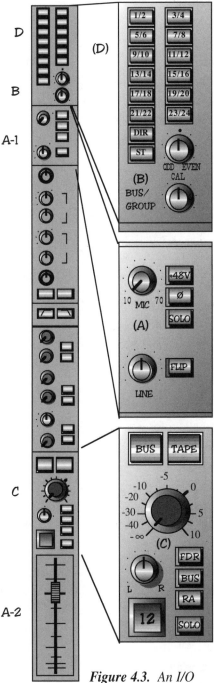

Figure 4.3. *An I/O module consists of an input section—mic input with preamp and trim (A-1)—feeding the channel fader (A-2), an output section (B) with bus assignment network (D), and a monitor section (C).*

source. For our vocal recording, the mic signal would come in through the input section first. With the channel-level fader set at 0, the mic trim at the preamp would be boosted until proper level was attained.

The *output* section (B) contains the *busses* that group signals and send them out to the multitrack via the normalled connections (bus 1 to track 1, etc.). A *bus* is simply a circuit for combining or "summing" signals going to a particular destination, not unlike a conventional bus does with people. If we were recording drums, for instance, we might have a separate mic on each drum, with each mic feeding a separate channel. The busses would allow us to group all of those individual drum mic signals to a stereo pair of tracks, such as tracks 1 and 2. This would be done by selecting busses 1 and 2 on each drum mic channel and using the bus pan pots to place each drum in the stereo image. Also included in the output section is a master group or bus level control for all of the signals assigned to that particular numbered bus (output section of module 1 contains all signals assigned to bus 1, output 2 corresponds to bus 2, etc.). Thus, the overall level of stereo drums to tracks 1 and 2 could be adjusted at the bus trim of channels 1 and 2.

The *bus assignment network* (D) is where the routing occurs (figure 4.3). This allows you to send the input signal from any module to any of the track output busses. It is always located between the input and output sections in the signal flow. Thus the vocal signal coming in on channel input 10, after passing through the mic preamp, mic trim, and channel level of module 10 (the *channel path*), might be assigned to track 7 for recording by selecting the bus 7 switch.

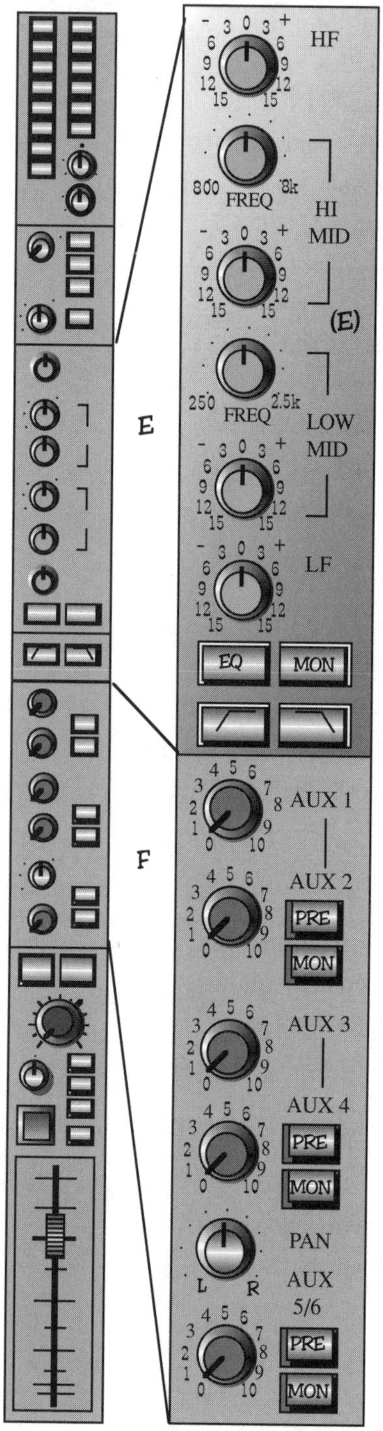

Figure 4.4. *The I/O module also includes an EQ (E) and an aux send (F) section.*

The *monitor* section (C), or *monitor* path, takes the return from the multitrack recorder (monitor or line input) and feeds it, via an individual level control, to the console's main stereo bus to be monitored in the control room. Alternatively, monitor switching (the BUS/TAPE switch) allows for the engineer to monitor the signal on its way to the multitrack (the bus or group) instead of the signal returning from multitrack.

The I/O module is rounded out by the EQ section (E) for timbre shaping, and the *auxiliary* or *aux send* (F) section for adding effects such as reverb or delay—usually to the tracks being monitored (figure 4.4). To EQ our vocal signal on its way to tape (or disk), we would make sure the EQ was routed to the channel path (using the MON/CHAN switch set to CHAN), engage the EQ switch, and adjust EQ to taste.

Each of these sections is generally color-coded or otherwise demarcated to allow for easy identification. Many consoles also include a dynamics section on every channel with compression and noise gating. This is true for both large-format analog consoles as well as small-format digital consoles.

Console configurations are often described by numbers such as "48 × 24 × 2." The first number refers to the number of input channels (input section), the second refers to the number of multitrack busses (output section), and the third refers to the number of main output busses. The example above describes a 48-input, 24-bus stereo mixing console. A console built for surround sound might have six (or eight) main output busses instead of two, to feed each of six separate channels of a surround mix recording—left front, center, right front, left and right surrounds, and subwoofer. The surround-capable console would be designated by a final number of 6 (or 8). Surround panning is also often facilitated by a joystick control rather than a traditional pan pot.

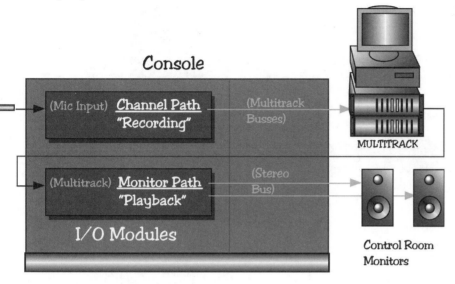

Fig. 4.5. *The I/O module contains two paths: the channel path—from mic to multitrack busses—and the monitor path—from multitrack return to stereo bus.*

Channel Path/Monitor Path

There are two basic paths through the I/O module: the *channel path* and the *monitor path* (figure 4.5). These emerged from the historic development of the console and the need for a recording path and a separate path for monitoring. In general, the *channel path* means mic input (source) to multitrack (destination), and *monitor path* means multitrack return to stereo mix bus and monitors. The monitor path is used to set up a rough mix of signals being recorded. However, many consoles allow the user to reconfigure the console depending on the session at hand. For instance, while *tracking* (recording basics and overdubbing), the channel path is used as the record path. The monitor path carries the rough mix derived from the multitrack returns. When the time comes for the mixdown session, the console can be reconfigured to use the channel path for mixing, with the multitrack returns feeding the channel path to the stereo bus and 2-track recorder. The channel-level control is almost always a linear fader, which is easy to mix on, while the monitor level control is often a rotary fader or a smaller linear fader located higher up in the channel strip and thus farther from the engineer. The console can often be configured to have both the channel and monitor paths accessible at mix time, thus allowing for double the number of inputs to the mix.

Channel Path

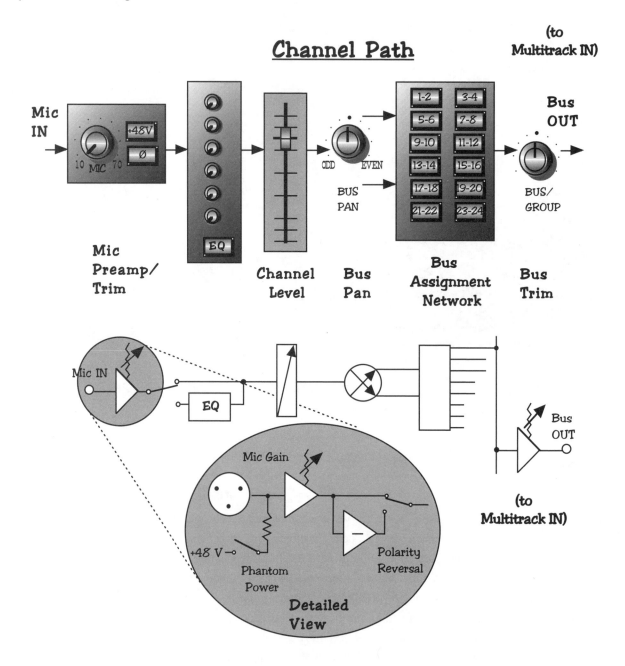

Fig. 4.6a. The basic channel path through an I/O module, when the console is set up for recording

Monitor Path

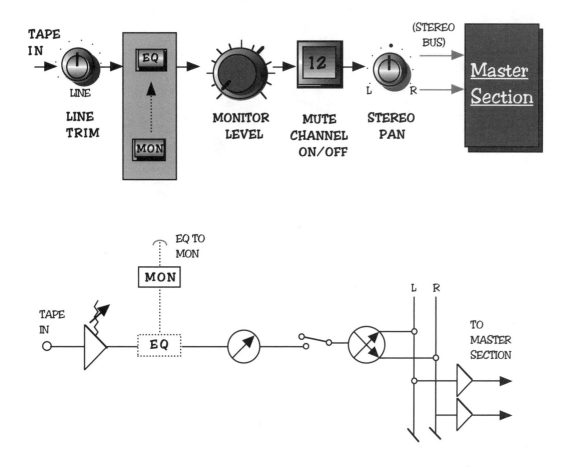

Fig. 4.6b. *The basic monitor path through an I/O module, when the console is set up for recording*

Note that convention has switches, such as the EQ-enable switch, drawn according to how the flow is when the switch is physically in the "up" (generally off) position. Also, the schematic representation of a bus (figure 4.7a) is a compromise to allow for more practical flowcharting. In the actual bus (figure 4.7b), all signals assigned to each bus are combined at the summing stage, rather than before it. Note the use of resistors in the summing stage, configured so as to prevent the signals that are being combined from interacting in unpredictable or undesirable ways. An attempt to combine signals without this electronic summing stage can result in loss of signal, frequency cancellations, or other anomalies.

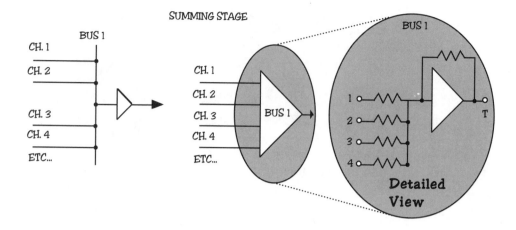

Fig. 4.7. *(a) Schematic convention for drawing a bus, and (b) more accurate depiction of a bus*

Figures 4.6a,b give us a closer look at the signal flow through a typical I/O module for both channel path (a) and monitor path (b) when set up for recording, accompanied by the schematic representation typical of console signal flow. This type of representation is what you will see in the console's flowchart and documentation. It represents a standard and clear approach that gives very specific and accurate information about each of the devices' functions and resulting signal flow. It is much more succinct and complete than a verbal description of said functions could ever be.

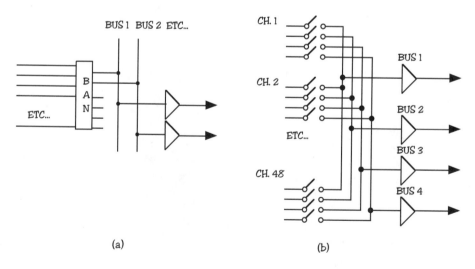

(a)   (b)

Fig. 4.8. *(a) Schematic convention for drawing a bus assignment network, and (b) more detailed depiction of a 4-bus multichannel assignment network*

Also, compare the conventional representation of the bus assignment network in figure 4.8a with the more detailed view of figure 4.8b. Note that each channel has access to all busses, so that any signal or group of signals can be sent to any destination. This is a very flexible setup, but also a slightly noisy one (on the order of +3 to +6 dB of noise). Whenever the combining power and flexibility of the bus is not needed, for instance, while overdubbing a single vocal to a single track, it is a better idea to use the direct (DIR) switch to route a source signal directly to a destination track, bypassing the bus entirely. If the destination track is of a different number than the input channel, the signal can still be patched directly via the patch bay (Direct Out 5 to Multitrack In 7, for instance).

Figure 4.9 shows the possible signal flow for a console reconfigured for mixing using the channel path. The monitor path, in this case, can be used for additional inputs to the mix, from an additional multitrack source (a second 2-inch 24-track machine or additional Pro Tools or other hard disk tracks, or from synth or sampler outputs), by assigning it directly to the stereo mix bus (ST or MIX assignment switch).

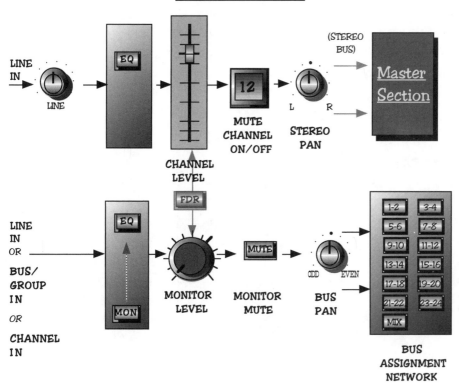

Fig. 4.9. *Possible signal flow for a console reconfigured for mixing using the channel path. The monitor path can act as extra inputs feeding the stereo mix, or as additional aux sends or groups.*

Monitor vs. Channel Fader

Most consoles allow for the swapping of functions of the channel and monitor fader, generally called *fader flip*, or FDR here (figure 4.9). This is most often done when recording on a console with VCA (*voltage controlled amplifier*) channel faders, to remove the VCA fader from the record path. Some engineers feel that because VCAs generate more self-noise than other gain stages, removing it from the record path yields a cleaner recording. Thus, if our vocal were passing through a VCA channel fader in the recording path, we would select FDR to swap the large VCA fader and the non-VCA small or rotary fader; the large fader would then be in the less-crucial monitor path.

Sometimes this fader swap is accomplished globally in the master section by means of a switch, which might be named "Channel to Monitors." This would generally be done during a basics session, since multiple mics will need to be fed through the non-VCA level control to the busses. Faders can still be flipped back individually to override this global function on a given module if needed. The advantage of the VCA fader is that it is voltage controlled (figure 4.10) and therefore easily grouped (as well as automatable). The voltage from a single fader can be fed to each fader in a group, such as background vocals or drums. This allows for global level control of the entire group by a single fader. For this reason, and because it is the largest fader and closest to the operator, it is always designated as the principal fader during mixdown on a VCA-based console.

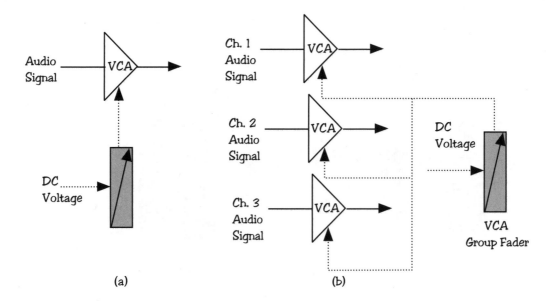

(a)   (b)

Fig. 4.10. *A VCA (voltage controlled amplifier) fader (a) controls the audio level passing through the gain stage by adjusting the level of DC control voltage sent to the amp. Because the gain stage is DC voltage controlled, VCA faders can easily be grouped (b) as well as automated.*

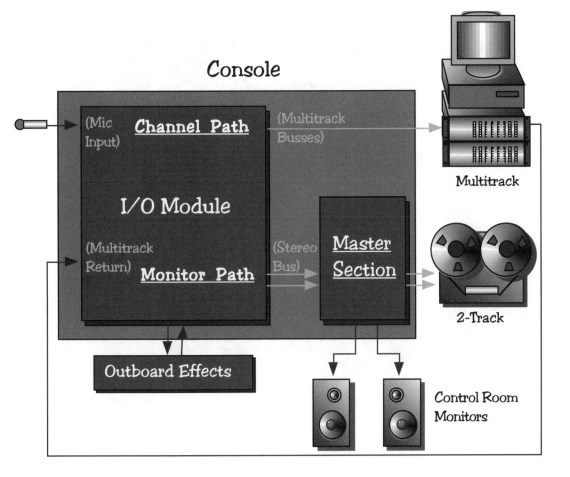

Fig. 4.11. *All signals pass through the master section on their way to the*
control room speakers and 2-track stereo mixdown machine

Master Section

All signals must pass through the center section of the console, or *master section*,
in order to be heard and to be recorded to the main 2-track mixdown machine
(figure 4.11).

There are two principal functions for the console or mixer's *master section*. The
first is to provide master or global level controls (figure 4.12): master aux send
levels (A) for global level to headphone (*cue*) mixes and *effects sends* (reverb, delay,
etc.), *aux* or *echo* returns (B) for reverb and other effects levels added back into
the main mix, and master fader (C) for overall level and fades to the console's main
output. All of these functions affect the signal flow to the main stereo bus outputs
and to the 2-track mixdown recorder. The second principal function of the master
section is to provide source selection and levels for control room and studio monitor
speakers (D). This second function is principally *non-destructive*, meaning that

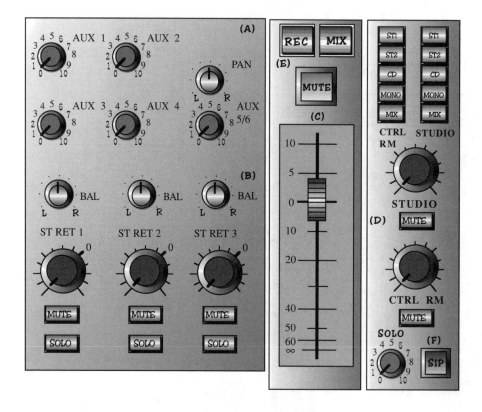

Fig. 4.12. A typical console master (center) section, with master aux send levels (A), stereo aux returns (B), master stereo mix fader (C), control room and studio routing and signal level (D), global I/O flow switching (E), and master solo level and function (F)

changes that are made here only affect the feed to the monitors (speakers) but do not affect the signal being recorded to the 2-track. Therefore, dimming or muting the control room speaker level, for instance, does not affect the mix being recorded to the 2-track. Note also that various sources besides the stereo mix, such as CD or other 2-track source, can be selected for monitoring over either the control room or the studio speakers. (This assumes speakers are also set up in the studio's live space, as is often the case.)

The master section can, however, also contain some *destructive* global signal-flow switching that affects both multitrack as well as 2-track recording. Although certain consoles are focused primarily on mixing while others may be geared principally towards recording or broadcasting, the norm has become to provide facility for all of these different functions in a single console. This is often done by way of a master switching scheme (E), which might reconfigure the signal flow for recording mode or mixing mode, for instance.

In the case of our vocal recording session, we would select Record mode in the master section, in which the channel path is designated as the recording path. Mic inputs feed the channel faders on the way to the multitrack busses. EQ and processing are placed in this path on the way to tape or disk, and the monitor faders simply carry the multitrack returns for setting up a rough mix in the control room. Once all recording is done and we are ready to mix, we would select Mix mode, whereby the channel path is reassigned to be the mix path; the multitrack outputs feed the main channel faders on the way to the stereo bus.

Also located in the master section are the engineer's talkback mic and the oscillator or sine wave generator (figure 4.13). The talkback mic allows the engineer to communicate with the musicians in the studio, and can also be routed to the multitrack and stereo mix busses for the purposes of *slating*. Slating is the act of recording spoken information before a take to identify the recorded material to follow, such as "'Missed the Boat'—Take 5."

Fig. 4.13. *The engineer's talkback mic in the master section can be routed to the cues (headphones) to communicate with the musicians, or to the multitrack or stereo mix busses for the purpose of "slating" the recording. The built-in oscillator can also be routed to the multitrack or 2-track as well as accessed at the patch bay.*

The oscillator can be routed to the multitrack busses to record reference level tones at the beginning of a multitrack session, or to the stereo bus for recording reference tones at the head of the 2-track analog tape. These reference tones are essential to ensure proper playback of prerecorded tracks when brought to a different studio or played on a different machine. The oscillator section, which often contains a pink- and white-noise generator as well, is also accessible at the patch bay for use as a test signal source for all other equipment in the studio. Tones and pink/white noise are known, measurable signals that can be used to troubleshoot audio connections and signal flow, and calibrate studio equipment and metering.

Console

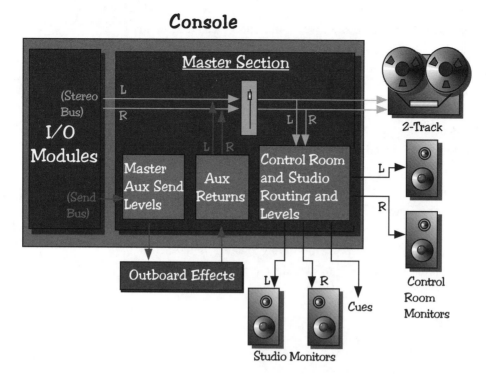

Fig. 4.14. *Basic signal flow through the master section of the console*

Figure 4.14 shows the basic signal flow through the master section. Notice that the aux sends fed from individual modules pass through the master section's master aux send levels and to the outboard effects (or cues). The output of the effects are then returned in stereo to the aux returns in the master section. The aux returns are simply additional line inputs to the mix, which are generally reserved for effects returns. These returns feed the stereo mix bus along with the mix outputs (either channel or monitor) from all I/O modules. The mix bus passes through the master fader and on to the main outputs (to the 2-track) and also to the control room/monitor section to be routed to the control room monitors as well as cues and/or studio speakers.

Advanced Console Flow

Let's integrate what we have learned so far into a traditional console signal-flow chart using the symbols that we have learned. No need to panic! We will walk through this in stages, progressively adding more advanced functions as we go. Remember that each of these diagrams simply represents real switches and pots on the console or mixer and their associated function and signal flow. Figure 4.15 shows a typical I/O module recording path, from mic to multitrack out, passing through channel path, channel fader, and bus assignment network. The FLIP switch allows switching between mic and tape/line input. (Line in could be used in conjunction with an external mic pre.)

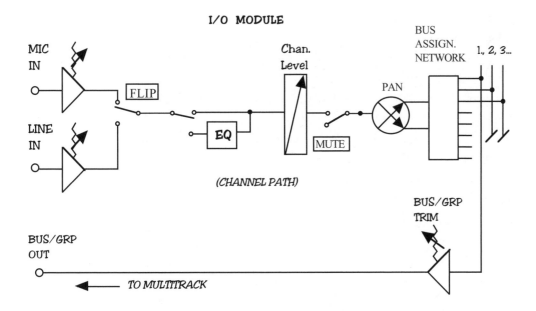

Fig. 4.15. *Basic console I/O signal flow from mic in to bus out*

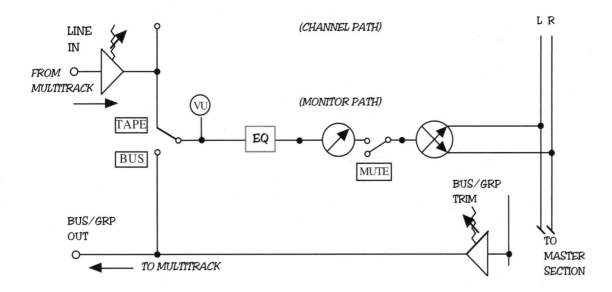

Fig. 4.16. *Basic console signal flow from monitor path to stereo mix bus*

Figure 4.16 picks up the signal flow at the bus output as it feeds out to the multitrack and into the monitor path on its way to the stereo mix bus. The stereo bus feeds the master section. Note that the signal feeding the monitor path and fader could be taken either directly off of the bus on its way to the multitrack, or back from the multitrack through the tape return (as shown), depending on the position of the BUS/TAPE switch. In general, we want to monitor the signal being recorded in *tape* mode to ensure that the signal has indeed reached the multitrack recorder and is being passed through without issue. In *bus* mode, the recorder could be completely off and signal would still be passed on to the monitor path and stereo bus. This function, while common on large-format consoles, is generally not found on mixers.

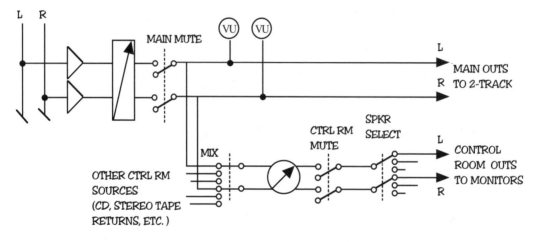

Fig. 4.17. *Basic console signal flow from stereo mix bus through the master section*

Figure 4.17 picks up the signal from the stereo bus on its way to the master section. Note that the master fader affects the 2-track recording, allowing for a master fade at the end of a mix on a given song, for instance. The control room selections and level, on the other hand, do not affect the 2-track recording. These only affect the control-room outputs to the speakers, allowing the engineer to dim the control-room level, or switch between a reference CD and the mix, without affecting the recording.

Adding EQ and fader swapping (MON and FDR respectively) between the channel path and the monitor path as discussed yields figure 4.18.

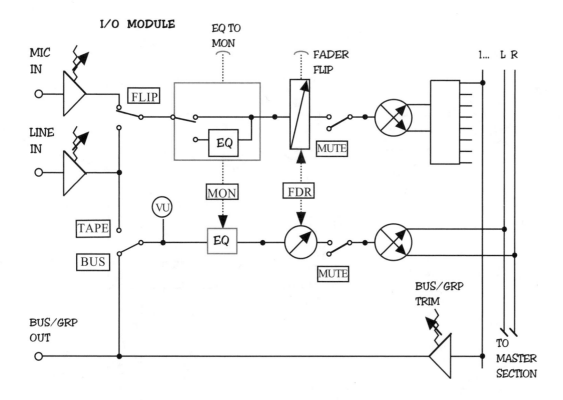

Fig. 4.18. *The MONITOR and FADER switches allow the EQ and faders to be swapped between the channel and monitor paths.*

Putting all of these individual flows into one module signal flow yields figure 4.19. This flowchart sums up all of the functions of the console's I/O module(s).

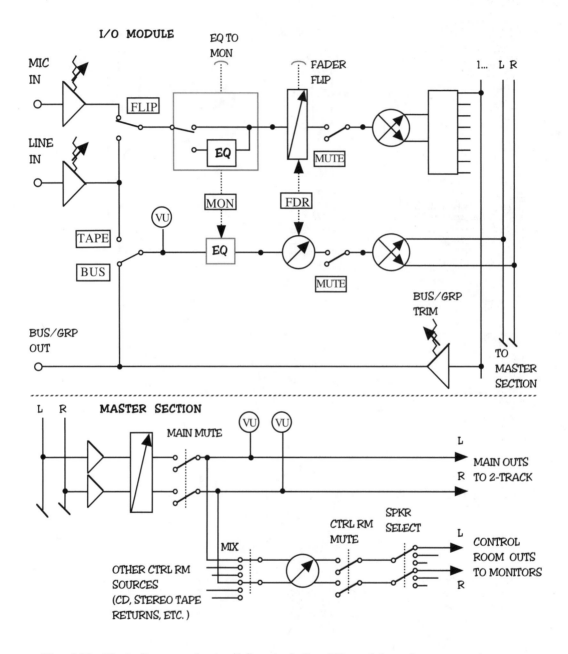

Fig. 4.19. *The in-line console signal flow, including I/O module and master section*

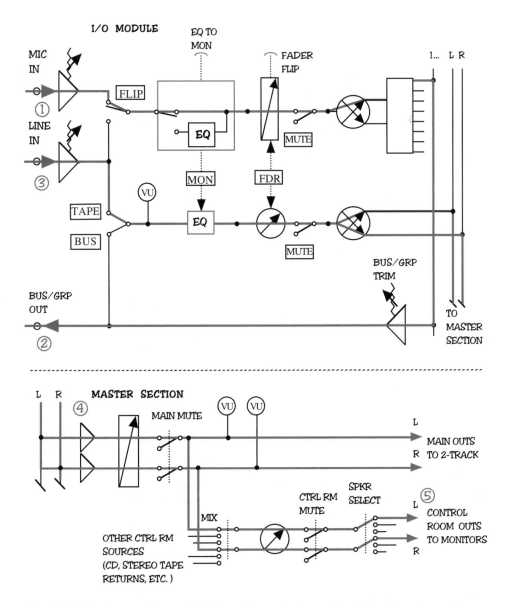

Fig. 4.20. *Tracing vocal recording flow, from mic input to multitrack and control-room monitors*

If we trace our vocal recording flow through the I/O module, from mic input to multitrack and control-room monitors, we would get figure 4.20. We can trace the signal from the mic input (1) through the channel path, out to the multitrack via the multitrack bus (2), back in through the tape return (3) to the monitor section, over to the master section via the stereo mix bus (4), and through to the 2-track and control room output (5).

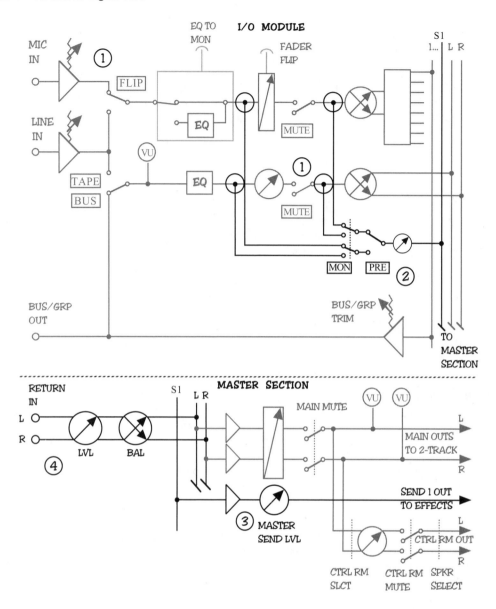

Fig. 4.21. *Adding aux sends and returns to the console flow. In this particular flow, just one aux send of several possible is included.*

Aux Sends and Returns

As discussed previously, the *aux sends* are used to send signals such as our vocal to effects processors, such as reverbs and delays, as well as to create cue (headphone) mixes for the musicians. Adding aux/effects sends and returns to our flow yields figure 4.21. The flow for adding reverb to our vocal signal, for instance, consists of taking the (dry) source signal (1) and sending it via the aux send level control (2) to the aux send bus. From there, it passes through the master section and master send level (3) to the reverb device. The output of the reverb device would then be returned to the console via a stereo aux return (4) in the master section, and be mixed into the main stereo mix bus along with the original dry vocal as well as all other signals in the mix. Alternatively, the reverb may be returned to a free pair of line inputs instead. The advantage of doing this is that the reverb may then be equalized and even easily recorded via the busses to the multitrack, if so desired. It also allows for automation of reverb levels.

Note that there are four possible sources for the send: pre- or post-channel fader and pre- or post-monitor fader. Which of these options is chosen will depend on the desired function and current session setup. To add reverb to our vocal signal, for instance, the aux send used is almost always sourced post-fader. This allows for the vocal fader to be adjusted without disrupting the wet/dry balance that has been established between the source vocal signal and its reverb. The first step is to turn up the master level of the aux send that is normalled to the desired reverb, as well as the reverb return level (aux return or line input returns). The individual aux send on the vocal channel, sourced from the monitor path, is then turned up until the desired reverb level is achieved. Now any changes made to the vocal fader level in the mix will also be reflected in the level sent to reverb, thus maintaining the wet/dry balance. An exception to this might be when a special effect is desired whereby the source is meant to appear to be moving closer or further from the listener. This perception is largely dependent on the wet/dry balance. If we were to send the vocal to reverb pre-fader and then gradually bring down the source signal's fader level, the dry signal would be decreased, while the wet signal would be unaffected (since it is sourced before the fader in the flow). As the signal becomes increasingly "wet" (the wet/dry ratio leans in the direction of wet), the resulting perception is of the vocalist moving into the distance, away from the listener.

Besides pre- and post-fader, the send can also be sourced either from the channel or the monitor path. During a mixdown, since the channel path is being used to mix, this is the path containing the source signal; therefore, the channel path is also the source for the reverb. During recording, however, either the channel or monitor path may be used as the source. Since the reverb at this stage is only for rough-mix purposes, it is generally fed from the monitor path.

In addition to effects, aux sends are also used to set up cue mixes for the musicians in the studio. In this case, the sends are always sourced pre-fader. This allows for the cue mix to be set up completely independent from the rough mix levels in the control room; and if sourced pre-channel, even independent from the recording levels. Thus, if the drummer wants more bass guitar, the engineer can increase the send level from the bass channel while maintaining a reasonable level both to disk and in the control room. The advantage of sourcing cues pre-*channel* fader as opposed to pre-*monitor* fader is that any on-the-fly recording (channel path) level adjustments made by the engineer while recording or setting levels (with the exception of the mic gain) will not affect or disrupt any of the musicians' headphone mixes that have been established. On the other hand, setting up a cue mix pre-*monitor* is generally easier, since mic groupings have already been accomplished going to the multitrack. For instance, drums may be miked using as many as thirteen or fourteen (or thirty-six!—ask noted engineer Frank Filipetti) mics and mic input channels, but may be grouped to as few as six tracks (such as kick, snare, L/R toms, and L/R overheads). This leaves fewer individual sources to deal with in setting up the cue mix post-multitrack.

Solos: AFL, PFL, SIP

Adding *AFL (after fade listen) solo* to the flow yields figure 4.22. The solo allows the engineer to monitor a single (or several) channel(s) in the absence of all others for more critical listening and adjustment purposes. There are actually three different possible types of solo functions in a console: AFL, PFL, and SIP. AFL is the most common type of solo. It is a non-destructive mono feed from either the channel or monitor path to the solo bus, which then replaces the main mix feeding the control-room speakers. The solo bus is a *bus* since several channels can be soloed simultaneously and therefore must be grouped. Because the feed is post-fader, it will be affected by both the fader level and mute.

PFL (pre-fader listen), on the other hand, is a solo feed taken *before* the fader and sent to the PFL bus. The PFL bus often feeds a small, separate PFL speaker built into the console or otherwise close to the engineer. PFL allows the engineer to preview signals on channels that are currently muted, without having to add them to or otherwise disrupt the current mix. This feature is especially useful in live sound reinforcement, where any changes made to the main stereo mix will immediately be heard by the audience. Using PFL allows the engineer to check an individual drum mic or vocal mic signal in isolation, without interrupting the performance and without the audience noticing.

SIP (solo in place), in contrast to the first two, is a destructive solo. This is because it uses the main stereo mix bus as the solo bus. This allows for solo monitoring of signals exactly as they appear in the stereo field with their panning and even their effects such as reverb. This type of solo is generally found on VCA-based consoles, because it involves remote muting of other channels. Instead of sending the soloed signal to a separate solo bus, the SIP command mutes all other channels from the main stereo mix bus, leaving only the signal in question, as well as its effects, intact. (If the effects are returning to a pair of modules, those modules can be "solo-isolated," making them immune to the SIP command). Obviously, this is destructive with respect to the stereo mix, and can only be done while rehearsing a mix or during multitrack recording where the 2-track stereo mix is not being

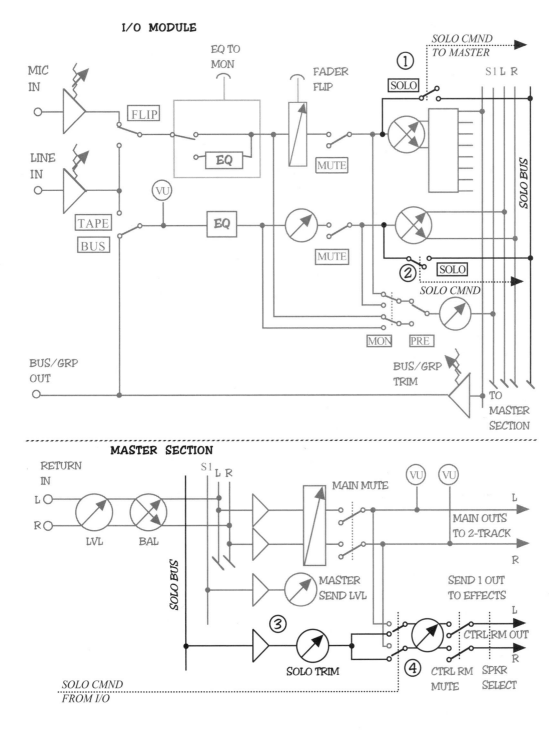

Fig. 4.22. *Adding AFL solo to the console flow. Selecting solo in the I/O (1, 2) also sends a solo command to the control-room switch (4), which overrides the previous selection and feeds the solo bus to the control room outputs via the solo trim in the master section (3). All AFL functions are non-destructive.*

recorded yet. On the other hand, because it is destructive, it could be used as a global or group mute function instead of a solo, for example to create a "break-down" section where all instruments but the drums and bass drop out in the middle of a mix. SIP is generally engaged in the master section (figure 4.12) as an option to AFL, making the normal AFL solo switches function as SIP instead.

To recap, the non-destructive mono AFL is used most of the time; the destructive SIP is used when stereo-panned groups need to be soloed "in-place"; and the non-destructive PFL is used for special applications, to preview muted tracks during a mix, or to preview individual signals through the PFL speaker without disrupting the monitor mix, such as during live sound reinforcement.

Patch Points

Patch points, which are grouped in pairs of rows in the patch bay, allow for signals to be extracted at various points in the flow, in order to insert outboard effects, for instance. Figure 4.23 shows the typical location of patch points within the console's flow. The idea is to allow the engineer as much flexibility as possible to extract and insert signals at different key points, such as pre- or post-equalization. At the same time, patch points allow for the insertion of new signals such as from another track, synthesizer, or additional recorder. It also allows for the insertion of outboard effects such as compression, noise-gating, or equalization to process signals already in the flow. As we have seen, patch points generally come in pairs, with an output half-normalled to an input. Let's look at some of the patch point pairs that can be expected.

There is generally a pair of patch points in both the channel path (1) and the monitor path (4) respectively, allowing early-on access to each in the flow. There is also an insert patch point (2) at the level of the EQ, which can generally be switched pre- or post-EQ as well as access either the channel path or monitor path. The insert patch point is generally accompanied by an insert switch, which allows the patch point (and associated signal processing device) to be inserted or removed from the flow at will. The decision to insert an effect pre- or post-EQ is somewhat complex and largely based on experience. Compression, for instance, will often be inserted pre-EQ, since it tends to color the sound in a way that the engineer may want to control with the EQ. If the compressor is inserted post-EQ, changes made at the EQ may in turn affect the functioning of the compressor, since they are both gain-based devices. However, even this situation represents something of a generalization; in some cases, this last is exactly the desired effect. Only experience and continued critical listening will teach one the advantage of one or the other option under a broad range of situations.

The next pair of patch points allows access to the grouped signal from the bus on its way to the multitrack (3). This allows for global compression or outboard EQ of a group on its way to tape or disk, or for cross-patching of a bus to a different

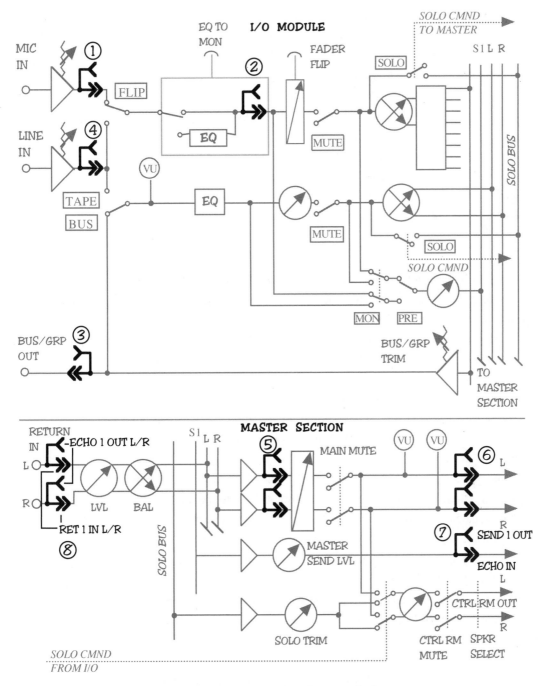

Fig. 4.23. *Typical patch point pair locations within the console flow*

number track. There will also be patch points across the main stereo bus, both pre-(5) and post-master fader (6). The post-fader patch point would be useful for making a copy of the main mix, including fade-outs, to a non-normalled 2-track recorder, or potentially for linking two consoles together. The pre-fader patch point would be essential for inserting global stereo compression to the mix. This is because a post-fader feed would be affected by master fader movements. In the case of a fade-out at the end of a song, as the master fader is pulled down, the drop in level would also cause a drop in amount of compression (since this effect is level-based) and eventually a complete elimination of compression. Since compression has a large impact on the overall sound, especially in popular music styles (rock, pop, rap, etc.), the mix would be perceived to fall apart sonically with the fade.

Finally, there is a set of patch points associated with the master section including all of the 2-track machines, as well as the normalled aux sends (7), reverbs, and aux returns (8). These patch points allow for cross-patching sends to non-normalled outboard effects as well as cross-patching reverb outputs to channel inputs for fader control and EQ (and possible automation).

Bouncing

One very important function not discussed thus far is *bouncing*. Bouncing consists of taking several prerecorded tracks, and submixing and grouping them to be recorded onto one or a pair of tracks (figure 4.24). This is generally done for the purpose of track-consolidation and economy, to allow for more new parts to be recorded to separate tracks, or to batch-process a group of tracks through a particular signal processor. Bouncing might be performed after having layered multiple performances of background vocals to individual tracks in order to achieve a rich, full sound. Once that has been achieved, a submix of those vocal tracks can be performed and recorded back in stereo to the multitrack on a pair of unused tracks. This frees up all of the previous vocal tracks for rerecording new material and/or allows for group processing. The submix is generally done in the mix path, which feeds the stereo mix bus. In order to send submixed tracks back to the multitrack, the mix path must gain access to the multitrack busses. Although there is more than one way to do this, it is generally accomplished by means of a switch on the individual I/O, generally named in such a way as to suggest its function (such as FLOAT, DUMP, or REASSIGN).

As an example, let's say we have recorded twelve tracks of background vocals. We want to bounce those tracks down to a stereo pair of tracks. In mix mode, we pan each of the tracks to the desired left/right position, and select RA (REASSIGN, or FLOAT, or DUMP, depending on the particular console) on each of the vocal channels. This feeds the mix path to the bus assignment network instead of (or sometimes as well as) to the stereo mix bus. We then assign each of these channels to the desired pair of busses, say 13 and 14, to route the stereo background vocal group to destination tracks 13 and 14. We can now monitor the group from the monitor path of I/O modules 13 and 14. This may involve muting the source tracks out of the stereo mix so that we do not hear them twice. This last step is either accomplished automatically as part of the REASSIGN or FLOAT function, or must be done manually using a 2-MIX MUTE switch on each vocal source channel individually.

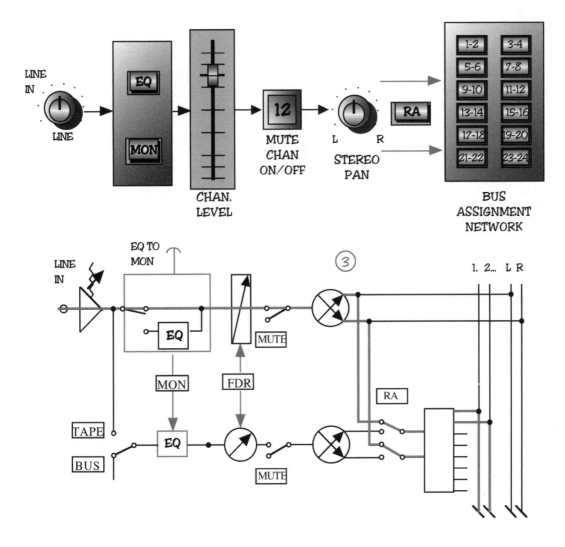

Fig. 4.24. *Signal flow for bouncing multiple tracks from the multitrack back to one or two tracks of the multitrack. Since the console is configured for mixing, the channel path normally feeds the stereo mix bus, while the monitor path has access to the busses. The REASSIGN switch allows the post-fader post-pan channel path access to the busses.*

In the realm of DAWS, a similar task can be accomplished within the computer using the "bounce to disk" function, although some engineers complain of sonic degradation introduced in the process.

EQ Section

The EQ section is used for signal tone shaping. It generally consists of a number of *peak/dip filters* (also called *band-reject* or *band-pass filters*), which cover different frequency ranges with some overlap: high (8 to 20 kHz), high mid (800 Hz to 10 kHz), low mid (125 Hz to 2 kHz), and low (20 to 250 Hz), for example. If *semi-parametric*, each band has a control to adjust center frequency and another for amount of boost or cut. A *fully parametric* EQ (figure 4.25) has an additional control for Q or *bandwidth*. Bandwidth determines the range of frequencies around the center frequency to be affected by a boost or cut—the narrower the bandwidth (in octaves), the fewer frequencies affected, and the more precise the adjustment. Q (which is unitless), on the other hand, is defined as center frequency divided by bandwidth ($Q = f_c/B$); so while the function is the same, the number markings for Q vs. bandwidth are exactly inversely proportional. Q = 1 indicates a broad bandwidth boost or cut, Q = 10 indicates a narrow bandwidth. If we wanted to remove the *sibilance* ("s" sound) from an overly sibilant vocal signal, we would need to dial in a high Q or narrow bandwidth so that only the sibilance range (centered around 5 kHz perhaps) would be affected.

High- and low-frequency bands often have the option of having a *shelving* response (figure 4.26), whereby all frequencies above (for the high band) or below (for the low band) the selected *turnover frequency* are boosted or cut by an equal

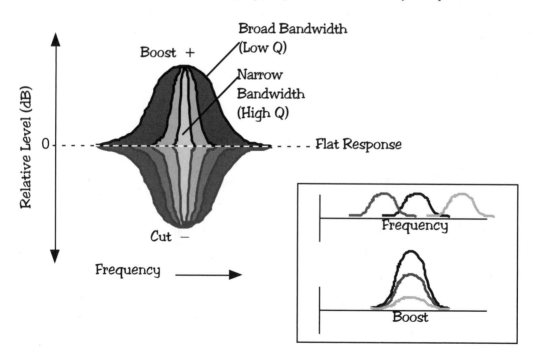

Fig. 4.25. *Peak/dip filter with bell curve response. Fully parametric EQ allows for variable bandwidth or Q (f_c/B), variable-center frequency, and amount of boost or cut.*

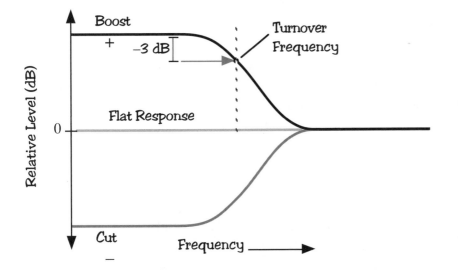

Fig. 4.26. *Low-frequency shelving filter*

amount. This is useful when an overall increase (or *attenuation*) in the high or low end is required, such as adding brilliance to the drum cymbals.

In addition to the peak/dip and shelving filters, the EQ section generally contains high-pass and low-pass filters (figure 4.27a, b). These are multi-pole filters, which allow only high and low frequencies respectively to pass while drastically attenuating frequencies in the stop band, with slopes on the order of 18 dB/octave. The *cut-off frequency* is defined as the frequency where the response is down by 3 dB from flat.

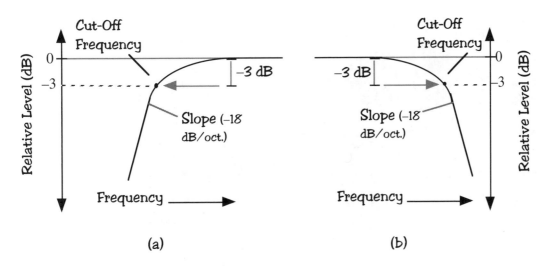

Fig. 4.27. *High-pass filter (a) and low-pass filter (b)*

Dynamics Section

For the sake of simplicity, we have left out from our flow any onboard dynamics signal processing, such as noise-gating and compression. More often than not, especially in this age of digital signal processing and the digital recording console, this feature is becoming a standard part of every channel in the modern recording console, including small-format digital consoles. For some time, onboard dynamics has also been a standard feature of many large-format analog consoles. As with outboard dynamics patched via an insert, the onboard dynamics section is generally switchable either pre- or post-EQ, into the channel or monitor path. In our flow, this would appear as a box similar to the EQ, switchable in or out of the flow. These dynamics are generally employed during mixdown rather than recording. Outboard compression is sometimes used during recording to capture the sonic characteristic of a particular favorite device, particularly on the way to a digital recording medium. Gating, on the other hand, is basically never used for recording because, if mis-set, it can cause parts of a live musical performance to be lost completely. For instance, if a drummer decides to play softer "ghost" notes, a gate set to open for strong snare hits would remain closed and those rhythms would never make it to the recording. Gating to remove unwanted leakage or noise can always be done later, during mixdown. If onboard dynamics are ever used during recording, perhaps to preview what the final mix might sound like, they would generally be placed in the monitor path.

At mixdown time, the onboard dynamics are inserted into the channel path, which is almost always the mixdown path. Compression and gating are most often inserted pre-EQ, and the processed signal is then EQ'ed to taste. Adjacent chan-

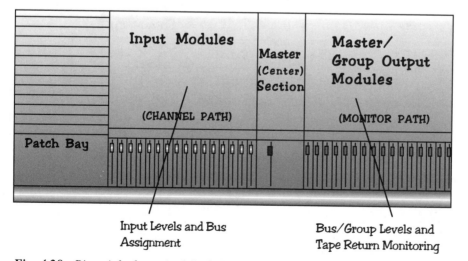

Fig. 4.28. *Pictorial of a typical "split" console. The three main sections are the input modules (channel path), master or group output modules (output section and monitor path), and the master (monitor/control-room) section.*

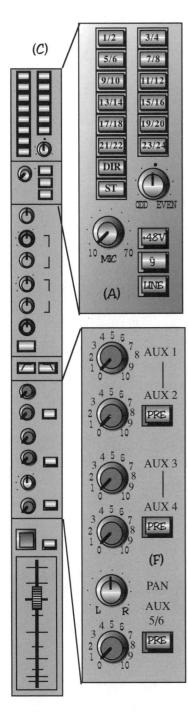

Fig. 4.29. *On a split console,*
the input section (A), channel
path and channel-level fader (B)
and bus assignment network (C)
are found on the input module.

nels are also generally linkable for stereo compression as well as external triggering (such as using a snare signal to open a gate on a reverb or white noise, for special effect).

Split Consoles

While our discussion has focused on the modern in-line recording console, there is an alternative architecture that is actually a predecessor to the in-line design: the *split console* (figure 4.28). The main difference here is that instead of having the input and output (busses) sections coexisting in a single module or channel strip along with both the channel and monitor paths, they are physically separated, located in two different sections on the console. The input section (A), channel path and channel level fader (B) are located on the *input module(s)* to the left of the master section along with the bus assignment network (C) (figure 4.29). Note that none of the in-line I/O's channel/monitor switches are included here since the input module carries only the channel path.

The actual output section (busses), as well as monitor path and monitor level (E), are located to the right of the master section in the *master/group output module(s)* (figure 4.30). The master/group output level fader (D) replaces the I/O's bus trim and determines group level to the multitrack.

These master/group output faders should not be confused with the VCA group faders that are sometimes found in the center section of in-line VCA-based consoles. The latter are generally eight to ten faders dedicated for use as remote level controls for VCA faders. The VCA faders are assigned to a group fader number by means of a thumb wheel at the base of each fader. The big difference is that

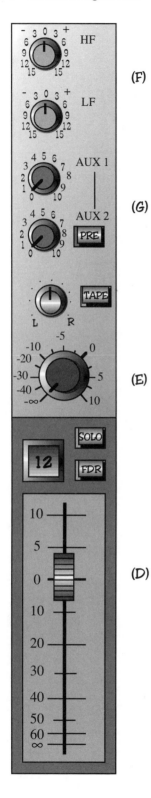

no audio passes through the VCA group fader; it simply sends a DC control voltage to each of the VCAs assigned to it (see figure 4.10). By contrast, the master/group faders in a split console are *the* principal level control for the bus signal passing through it and feeding the track of the same number on the multitrack. This fader corresponds to the bus/group trim on the I/O of the in-line console.

Also contained in the master/group output modules, coexisting with the output section, is the monitor path and monitor fader. This is generally a rotary fader whose function is the same as on the in-line console, namely to create a rough mix of the multitrack returns. As with the in-line console, the monitor path can be fed from either the tape returns or directly from the bus outputs going to the multi-track, selected by means of the TAPE switch, depending on what the engineer would prefer to monitor.

The output modules can contain some rudimentary EQ (F) and aux send (G) capability (figure 4.30) for cue mixes (or possibly reverb), as shown, with the bulk of these features contained in the input modules. Upon mixdown, the channel path may be used again as the mix path, now fed from multitrack returns. This is achieved by selecting the line input (via the *line* switch) as the source for the channel path, and then assigning the channel path to feed the stereo mix bus rather than to a multitrack bus (via the *mix* or *stereo* assignment switch). At this time, the output/group modules may be used as additional inputs to the mix or for creating subgroups to facilitate mixing. The faders can generally be swapped, using the FDR switch, so that the long-throw group fader can be used to feed the stereo mix bus. Figure

Fig. 4.30. *On a split console, the output section includes the monitor path and monitor level (E) and master/group output level fader (D). It can also include a rudimentary EQ (F), and aux sends (G).*

4.31 shows the split console signal flows for recording (a) and mixing (b). The function of the split and in-line consoles is largely the same, only the physical layout is different.

Recording Flow

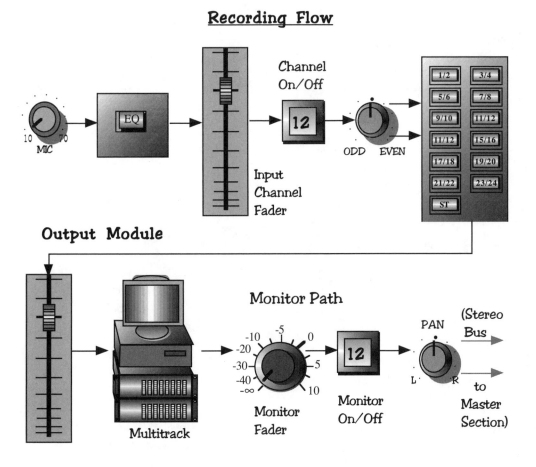

Fig. 4.31a. Recording signal flow for a split console

The advantage of the split-console architecture is greatly enhanced ergonomic clarity. There is no mistaking which signal is currently being manipulated, since the channel path and monitor path are physically separated on the console. Split architecture lends itself especially well to classical recording sessions where individual instrumental groups can easily be spot-miked and manipulated as a subgroup within the larger ensemble. Split consoles are also widely used in film, for recording and *stem mixing*. Because of the large number of potential sound sources in a film mix, the signals are grouped into *stems* or subgroups, where each stem is made up of smaller groupings of instruments, sound effects, and dialog. During mixdown, the multitrack returns feed the channel path and faders on the left of the console, which can then be grouped and controlled via the faders on the right. The natural group (bus) architecture with discrete level control through the output

Mixdown Flow

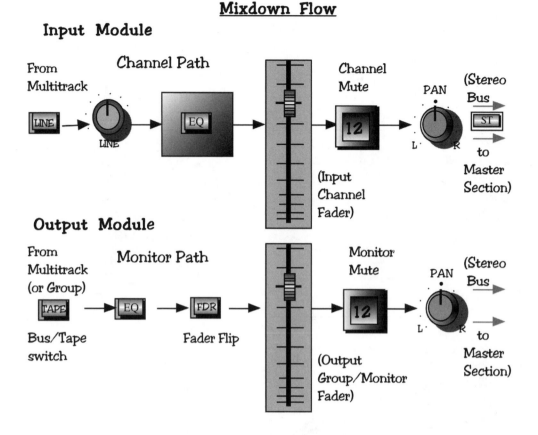

Fig. 4.31b. *Mixdown signal flow for a split console*

section's numerous group faders is perfectly suited for this treatment, especially since the final mix will not be 2-channel stereo but rather multichannel surround. As an example, an orchestral group might have individual pairs of mics on each of the string subsections (violin, viola, cello, and bass), as well as individual spot mics on soloists, and perhaps a stereo pair or two on the entire string section. This section alone may consist of fifteen or twenty mic inputs addressing the input modules. At the bus assignment network, however, these mic signals can be grouped in various ways, and appear at the output faders as more manageable subgroups (such as stereo violins/violas and stereo celli/basses, or even stereo string section), whose level to multitrack or mix can now be adjusted more easily.

The main disadvantage of the split console is that physically it takes up almost twice as much space as an in-line model with the same number of input channels. A 24-track (or 24-bus) console would have twenty-four master or group output modules *in addition* to the input modules, each feeding the associated track on the multitrack recorder. In fact, it is the rapid growth of tracks and input channels that led to the search for a space-saving alternative and the development of the in-line console.

In addition to the master group modules, there would be a master/monitor section similar to that found in the in-line console containing master levels and studio/control room signal routing and levels (see figure 4.12). Besides saving on space (often at a premium, especially in real-estate-starved metropolitan areas), the in-line console also has the advantage that signal processing blocks, such as EQ and compression, are easily shared and swapped between the two paths within a given module or channel strip. This also means economy of cost, by avoiding unnecessary duplication of electronics and associated hardware.

Mixers

Mixers are smaller variations on the larger-format console concept. Because of space and cost limitations, various features found on larger consoles are left out. To begin with, there are generally fewer aux sends and returns, fewer EQ options, and very often a single path rather than a dual-path architecture. The inputs (mic or line) address the main channel faders directly, and then are often patched directly to the multitrack recorder via direct outputs. The multitrack outputs must then be returned to a separate set of faders or patched back in for overdubs and mixing. This is how a small home studio setup might be arranged. Grouping is generally limited, as is bus assignment (often only four to eight busses). The master section is also very limited and often leaves out the bulk of the studio-/control-room routing options.

A particular breed of analog mixer, the *8-bus mixer*, works on very similar principles to the large-format console. It is often a hybrid of the split and in-line concepts, with eight group-output faders to the right in the master section, but the monitor section grouped with the input section on the left. While we won't go into great detail on varieties of mixer architecture, once the typical console flow has been understood, it is very easy to apply this understanding to mixer flow on a case-by-case basis, as well as to signal flow in a DAW recording/mixing program such as Pro Tools.

Digital Consoles/Mixers

With the rapid increase of processing power available through computer chip technology, digital consoles and mixers (figure 4.32) have fast been gaining in popularity. They open up, even within the home-studio realm, staggering possibilities in onboard signal processing and switching previously available only on the highest-end professional consoles. The most common implementation for a digital mixer is to have a master section that includes all of the surface controls (switches, pots, etc.) for configuration, switching, and signal processing. Individual channels, each with only a fader, mute, and select switch, can then be selected to access those

Fig. 4.32. The Sony DMX-R100 small-format console (Courtesy Sony)

physical controls for full processing power, either on an individual or group basis. This is what allows for a small-format console at a very reasonable price point to contain such powerful processing and functionality.

This same approach can be applied to larger-format analog consoles yielding the so-called "digitally-controlled analog console." This type of console takes advantage of the processing power and efficiency of digital circuits for switching and signal flow configuration. However, it maintains the sonic characteristic of analog circuits, as well as the appeal of having a physical control on every channel for each signal-processing function and some fundamental routing functions. Large-format, fully digital consoles (figure 4.33) tend to use similar layouts to classic large-format analog consoles, maintaining the single-control-for-single-function topology. However, because all signals at the console inputs are converted to digital signals, they can be routed and processed in the digital realm with great power and efficiency. Also, the console's routing can be reconfigured at the touch of a button, and all settings can be stored and recalled instantly for remix purposes.

Potential complications arise, however, particularly when interfacing such consoles with vintage analog signal processing gear. Every time a signal must be extracted from, and reinserted into the console flow, it must be converted from digital to analog and back again. This conversion process introduces real-time delay. In this case, manual delay offsets on individual channels are necessary to realign all signals back into proper time/phase relationship. More on analog-to-digital (A/D) and digital-to-analog (D/A) conversion in a later chapter.

Fig. 4.33. *Large-format digital production console (Courtesy Solid State Logic)*

PROJECTS

Signal Flow Exercises

For the following exercises, assume an in-line console architecture.

1. You have drums coming in on mic inputs 1 through 8 (individual mic signals would include kick, snare, toms, etc.), and being recorded as a stereo group to tracks 1 and 2. You would like to add reverb on the snare only, which is coming in on mic input 2. How would you set up the send for the reverb, pre or post, mon or chan, and from which module? Draw the signal flow for the above scenario using flowchart symbols.

2. Which modules would you use to monitor the stereo drum group?

3. You decide you would like to record the reverb along with the drums onto tracks 1 and 2. How would you accomplish this task? Be specific. Draw the flow for this scenario.

Project Answers

1. Each of these signals would feed individual mic inputs to separate channels of the console. Once these signals reach the bus assignment network, however, and are bussed to tracks 1 and 2, they proceed to exist only as a stereo grouped signal. They would feed the output section of modules 1 and 2 (busses 1 and 2) only, and the monitor path of modules 1 and 2 only. If we wanted to add reverb to the snare *alone*, we would have to source the send from the *channel* path of the source signal, the snare mic, that is, module 2. We would also want it to be post-fader so that any changes to the recorded snare level would also be reflected in the reverb level.

2. 1 and 2.

3. If the reverb is returning to a pair of modules, you would hit REASSIGN or FLOAT on those channels to feed the monitor path to the busses, and assign to busses 1 and 2. You would now monitor the reverb through the monitor path of modules 1 and 2 along with the drums, and 2-mix mute the original reverb returns if necessary so as not to hear it twice.

Before taking the next step in dealing with audio and recording systems in earnest, it is imperative for us to have a fundamental understanding of what it is that we call "sound." After all, it is through sound that we experience music, and it is from this musical perspective that we will approach audio. The audio that we record, whether in magnetic, mechanical, or optical form, is simply an *analog*, or copy, of sound that usually begins as acoustical energy. The concepts introduced here will be discussed further throughout the book.

Sound and Vibration

So, what is sound? If a guitar amp explodes in a forest and no one is there to hear it, does it make a sound? Let's look at what actually happens. All sound sources produce vibrations that create disturbances in the air (or other elastic medium, like water) around them. These disturbances spread away from the source as ever-expanding spheres, very much like ripples away from a stone dropped in a pond (figure 5.1).

Fig. 5.1. Sound spreads away from the source as an ever-expanding sphere.

If we think of the pond at rest (no disturbance), there is an *equilibrium*, which we could describe as a certain (large!) number of water molecules per unit area (ft^2, for instance). The dropped stone initially pushes the water molecules nearest to it down. Since water is not easily compressed, this downward push forces the water molecules directly surrounding the initial disturbance upwards. When these in turn fall back down, the original downward disturbance is mimicked and the pattern begins anew, with slightly decreased amplitude. Over time, this pattern of the upwards and downwards motion of water molecules spreads away from the initial disturbance in an outward circular motion, an ever-expanding sphere. Similarly, though invisibly, a vibrating sound source, such as a plucked guitar string, generates a disturbance in the air molecules around it that spreads out spherically away from the source (back-and-forth rather than up-and-down). With water, the result is a visible pattern of ripples on the surface of the pond moving outwardly from the initial point of disturbance. With the guitar string and air, we get sound.

Transverse Waves

This ripple phenomenon is known as a *transverse* wave: a wave in which the motion of the actual particles of matter is perpendicular to the motion of the wave moving through that matter. While the wave visibly moves away from the center of disturbance, the actual water molecules do not. They simply bob up and down around their steady-state position (figure 5.2).[4]

To visualize a transverse wave more easily, imagine holding a string fixed at one end and snapping it in a downwards motion (figure 5.3). While the wave moves away from you through the string, the vibration of the string is actually up and

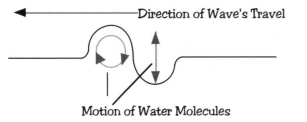

Fig. 5.2. *A transverse (or circular) wave motion traveling along the water's surface*

down, perpendicular to the direction of the wave's travel. Also, the actual string molecules do not travel away from you; only the wave passing through the string does. Similarly, in sound, air molecules do not move very far at all but simply vibrate and pass on the disturbance to adjacent molecules. While sound waves are not transverse in nature, the analogy of a transverse wave is often useful to help us better visualize the properties of sound waves.

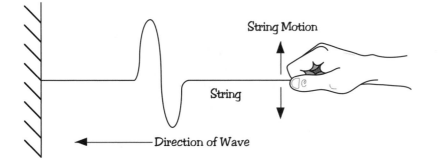

Fig. 5.3. *A transverse wave passing through a string*

4. Confusing matters somewhat, the water molecules within the water wave tend to have an overall circular motion, rather than just an up an down motion. Some would argue that this is not a transverse wave at all but a hybrid circular one.

Longitudinal Sound Waves

A similar though more invisible process occurs with sound in air, with some important differences. The equilibrium in air is known as *atmospheric pressure*, and is generally given as 14.7 lbs/in². We could also think of this equilibrium as a certain number of air molecules per unit area, although actually measuring this is a little more problematic and perhaps less informative. A vibrating sound source, such as a guitar string, causes minute disturbances in air that upset this equilibrium by pushing and pulling on the air molecules around it. The disturbance results in areas of greater or lesser pressures (figure 5.4), i.e., areas where molecules are bunched together (*compression*) and other areas where they are stretched thin (*rarefaction*).

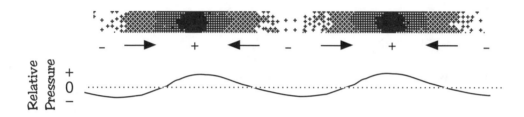

Fig. 5.4. *Sound vibrations result in alternating regions of over-pressures (compressions) and under-pressures (rarefactions).*

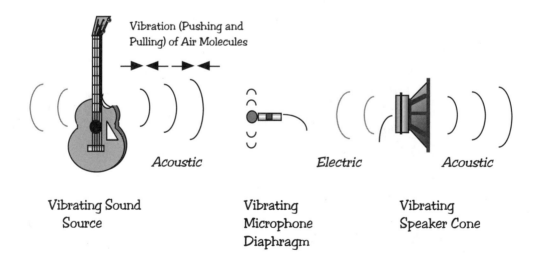

Fig. 5.5. *Longitudinal sound wave in air. Sound wave travels in same direction as air particles.*

These patterns of compressions and rarefactions repeat in direct proportion to the vibrating motion of the source, spreading away from the source in a wave-like motion. The major difference here is that the air molecules are pushed and pulled in the same direction as the sound wave's travel. This is called a *longitudinal* wave (figure 5.5). As with transverse waves, while the wave motion can travel a great distance, the actual molecules do not move very far at all. They simply move back and forth (vibrate) a very short distance around their steady-state position. To better visualize a longitudinal sound wave, imagine a slightly stretched out Slinky being tapped on one end (figure 5.6). You would notice that while the individual rings do not move far, a longitudinal wave travels through the length of the Slinky from one end to the other. If it were alternately pushed and pulled, you would notice first compressions and then rarefactions traveling through the coils.

Because longitudinal waves are somewhat less intuitive and harder to visualize than transverse waves, we often use transverse wave imagery to discuss sound waves. This is fine as long as we keep in mind the simple fact that sound waves push and pull rather that bob up and down.

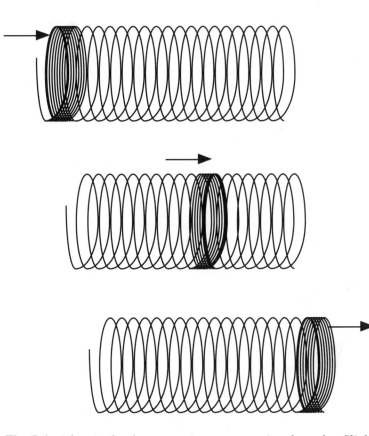

Fig. 5.6. A longitudinal compression wave passing through a Slinky. This is akin to a sound wave compression traveling through the air.

Simple Harmonic Motion

The simplest pattern of vibration is called *sinusoidal* motion. If you were to place a weight at the end of a spring and allow it to bounce up and down, that up and down motion would be sinusoidal (figure 5.7).[5] The mass would accelerate downward, slow to its point of furthest (or lowest) travel, come to a virtual stop and return in the opposite direction passing its point of rest and continuing upwards, following the same pattern of acceleration and deceleration. The point of *maximum velocity* is always the halfway point between the maximum upward and downward excursions (or "crests").

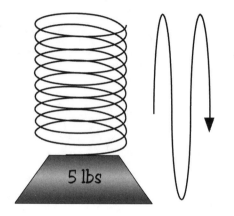

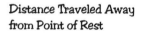

Fig. 5.7. Simple sinusoidal motion of a weight on a spring

If we were to graph that motion over time, it would look like figure 5.8 below:

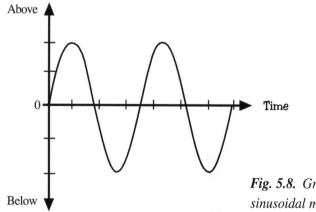

Fig. 5.8. Graph of simple sinusoidal motion

5. This assumes that the restoring force is linear, i.e., proportional to the amount of displacement—greater displacement, equally greater force pulling it back.

The simplest kind of sound, a sinusoidal (or sine) wave, follows this same pattern of motion or vibration, sometimes called *simple harmonic motion*. As we shall see later, this sine wave is the fundamental building block for all sounds no matter how complex. A sine wave can be created using an *oscillator*, an electronic wave generator that can be used to generate continuous waves of different kinds (sine, square, triangle, sawtooth, etc.). These are often used as test signals, and also form the basis of analog synthesis to generate synthesized sounds of various kinds. A tuning fork is also capable of generating a sine wave when struck—the prongs vibrate the air molecules around them in a sinusoidal back-and-forth motion (figure 5.9). Certain instruments, such as a flute, have simple enough vibrational patterns that they come close to producing a sinusoidal waveform.

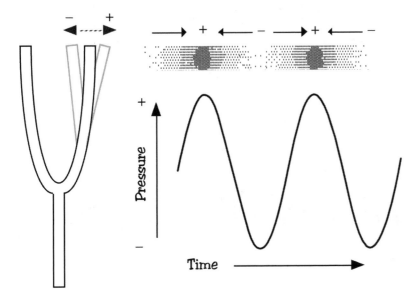

Fig. 5.9. *A tuning fork vibrates when struck, generating a sine wave.*

Frequency and Period

A sine wave is said to be *periodic*, which means that its waveform repeats exactly over time, cycle after cycle, and therefore has very predictable and measurable characteristics. The *frequency* of a periodic wave is a measure of the number of cycles that it completes in one second. This is directly related to the vibrational motion of the source. For example, a motor running at 1200 rpm, or 20 rotations per second, will generate a fundamental frequency of 20 Hz. (The traditional unit for frequency, cycles per second or *cps*, was replaced by *hertz*, or *Hz* for short.)

Figure 5.10 shows the relationship between frequency and the notes on a piano. The entire range of audible frequencies from lowest to highest is generally given as 20 Hz to 20 kHz for humans, although this is just an average. The actual audible range for a given individual will depend on age, type of exposure to sound over time, genetics, and any number of other factors. It is tempting on an intuitive level to equate frequency with *pitch*. Pitch is our subjective perception of frequency, and might be described as the sensation of a sound being "high" or "low," "shrill" or "deep." Frequency is the objective measure of cycles per second. While there is a strong link between perceived pitch and frequency, this relationship is not as completely straightforward as it might at first appear. More on this in a later chapter.

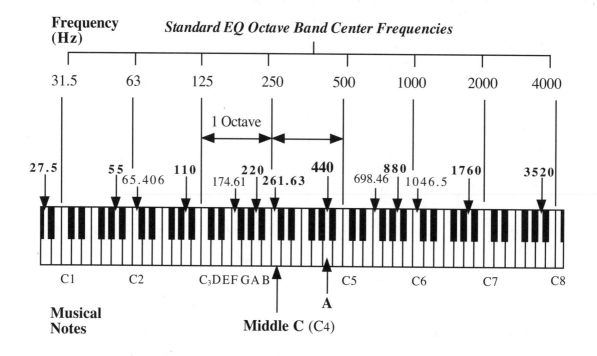

Fig. 5.10. *The relationship between frequency and musical notes on a piano keyboard. An octave represents an exact doubling of frequency. (Note that the low-band EQ center frequencies are an approximation of exact octave doublings.)*

Figure 5.11 shows the properties of a progressive periodic waveform. The *period* of a repeating waveform is simply the time it takes to complete one cycle. This is usually measured from one crest to the following crest in the wave, although it can be taken from any two points that are *in phase* in adjacent cycles. The *phase* of a periodic wave refers to its current position with respect to the completion of a full cycle, and is measured in degrees. A full cycle would represent 360°, as with one full rotation of a circle. One half-cycle would measure 180°, and so on. Thus, the term *in phase* implies occupying the same relative position in time within a given cycle, which also implies coinciding *amplitudes* (or levels) for like-waves. (The term *amplitude* is used to describe maximum displacement, whether the element in question is vibration, air pressure, or electrical voltage.)

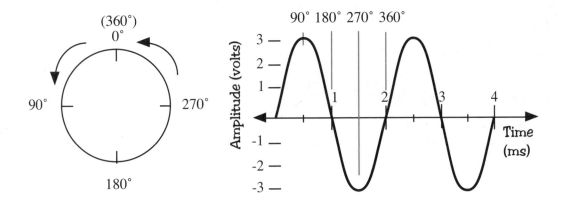

Fig. 5.11. *The phase progression of a periodic wave, in degrees*

In the Studio

Phase

Phase has significant implications, particularly when recording using more than one microphone. The phase of the signal captured by each microphone will depend on the position of the microphones with respect to the source. When out-of-phase signals are combined, frequency cancellations occur that may distort the sound of the source signal, causing audible loss of high, mid, or low frequencies. Thus, special care in the placement of multiple microphones and in monitoring the resultant sound (checking it in both stereo and mono) is crucial. This allows us to take advantage of constructive summations (full sound) and avoid unpleasant destructive cancellations (thin or unnatural sound).

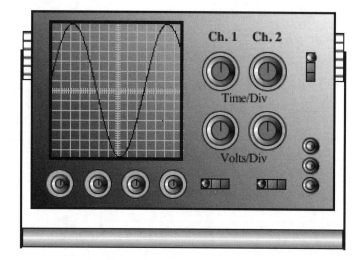

Fig. 5.12. *An oscilloscope displays electrical waveforms as a function of volts over time.*

It can be helpful to have a sense of the duration of cycles for different frequencies, particularly when dealing with delay, phase cancellation, and when doing audio testing and troubleshooting. A useful tool for measuring audio in the recording studio is the *oscilloscope* (figure 5.12), which displays waveforms as a function of amplitude (in volts) over time (in milliseconds). While one is unlikely to use it during an actual recording session, it is crucial when testing equipment and ensuring that all equipment performance is optimized and up to spec. Types of measurements may include amplitude, frequency, period, phase, distortion, etc. The period of a sound wave can be measured using an oscilloscope, which displays a graph of the waveform as in figure 5.13. The sine wave in figure 5.13 has a period of 2 milliseconds. Knowing the period of a sound wave also allows us to calculate the frequency of the wave displayed by using equation 5.1.

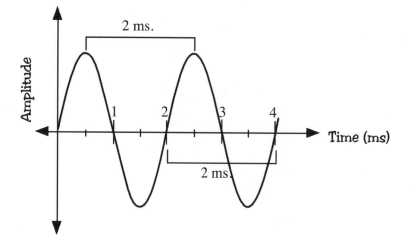

Fig. 5.13. *Measuring the period of a sine wave*

$$f = 1/t$$

again, f = frequency and t = period (time)

Eq. 5.1. *Used to calculate the frequency of any periodic wave*

Thus, a wave whose period is 2 milliseconds (0.002 s.) has a frequency of $\frac{1}{0.002}$, or 500 Hz (which would be perceived as a slightly flat C above middle C). A quick way to solve this fraction without a calculator is to simply multiply both top and bottom (*numerator* and *denominator*, respectively) by 1000. This gives us $\frac{1000}{2}$ = 500. (Anything can be done to solve a fraction as long as the same thing is done to both the numerator and denominator of the fraction.) Electronic tuners use period to generate frequency readouts.

Alternatively, if the frequency of the wave is known, we can simply calculate period using the same equation, rewritten as equation 5.2.

$$t = 1/f$$

where t = period and f = frequency

Eq. 5.2. *Used to calculate the period of any repeating (periodic) wave*

Therefore, the period of a 1 kHz (1000 Hz) tone is equal to $\frac{1}{1000}$ of a second, or 1 millisecond. If you are unsure of the unit to use, simply write in the units of all variables in the equation and simplify the units along with their values. Here for example:

$t = \frac{1}{f}$ cycles/sec = $\frac{1}{1000}$ cycles/s = $\frac{1s}{1000}$ cycles = $\frac{0.001\,s}{cycle}$.[6]

Since we know that period refers to the completion of a single cycle, we can leave out *cycle* when expressing our answer, and simply say t = 0.001 s, or t = 1 ms.

Notice that period and frequency are *reciprocals* (exact inverses of each other), so as frequency increases, period decreases proportionally, and vice versa. This makes sense since a higher frequency implies that more cycles need to fit in the same amount of time (1 second); so each individual cycle must therefore take up less time. You can think of frequency as cycles per second, and period as seconds (or a fraction thereof) per cycle.

6. This operation results from the rule that 1 divided by a fraction is equal to the inverse of that fraction: $\frac{1}{(a/b)} = \frac{b}{a}$. Thus, $\frac{1}{(1000\ cycles/s)} = \frac{s}{1000}$ cycles.

A note here on the use of variables in equations. We use equations to express truths about how certain physical properties change with respect to other physical properties. By using variables such as x and y (or in this case t and f), we are able to plug in, at any time, the values for the current situation being observed and find the result. The choice of which variables to use is somewhat flexible, but is generally made so as to remind us easily of the properties being expressed. While certain conventions exist, the main concern when setting up equations should be to fully disclose what the chosen variables represent, and to use a distinct variable for each property. While this may seem like an obvious point, it is an important concern when we are faced with simultaneously expressing properties such as power, pressure, period, etc. Here we have chosen to use t (*time*) for *period*, saving p for *pressure* and W or P for *power*.

Any periodic sound wave will have a recognizable pitch closely related to its measurable frequency. A plucked guitar string naturally vibrates in several modes simultaneously, all of which are even multiples of the simplest mode or motion—the *fundamental* (figure 5.14). (A *vibrational mode* is the natural pattern of vibration that an object exhibits when struck. The simplest mode, or fundamental, exhibits the fewest back-and-forth motions per second.) This results in a single audible pitch. If you were to lightly place a finger on the vibrating string in just the right spot, you would damp out (or *mute*) only the primary mode (fundamental) while allowing the upper modes to continue to ring out. Other placements would damp out more modes, resulting in different remaining modes and resultant pitches. This is often referred to as playing "harmonics."

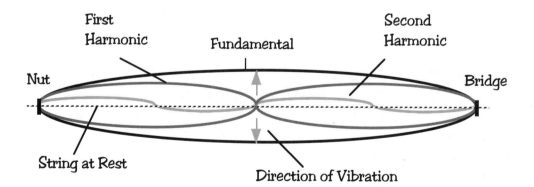

Fig. 5.14. *A plucked guitar string simultaneously vibrates in several modes, which are exact multiples of the fundamental mode. This yields the sensation of a single distinct pitch.*

Non-periodic sounds, whose cycles do not repeat exactly over time, are harder to describe as having a distinct pitch. A bell, for instance, often can be heard to produce several distinct, non-musically related (*non-harmonic*) pitches simultaneously. This is due to the coexistence of several non-related vibrational modes in the bell. A snare drum usually does not produce any distinct pitch unless it is specifically tuned to do so, because it contains a greater number of independent non-harmonically related vibrational modes. It may have one particularly strong resonance or ring that stands out from the rest of its sound. This ring is usually unwanted and often treated and removed before recording. The more random a sound's sonic makeup, as with the snare drum, the more it begins to sound like noise rather than a pitched signal. The waveforms of non-periodic signals appear more random than pitched signals as well (see figures 5.15 and 5.17).

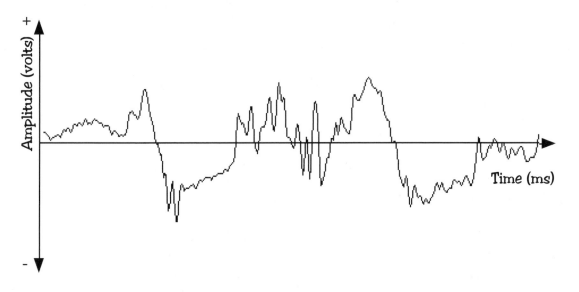

Fig. 5.15. *A non-harmonic sound wave, such as a snare drum being struck, is made up of several unrelated vibrational modes.*

Most individual musical sounds that we deal with, however, are periodic in nature, and therefore, have the same basic characteristics as a sine wave. For this reason, and because of its innate simplicity, we tend to use the sine wave to help us in discussing sound in general.

Wavelength

The *wavelength* of a sound wave is a measure of the distance that sound will take to complete a single cycle. It is important to have a general sense of the wavelengths of different frequencies as this directly impacts the sound quality captured with different microphone placements, as well as the effect of various acoustical treatments on sound in the studio. Specifically, it impacts how we deal with absorbers, diffusers, and baffles in the studio to control and contain sounds most effectively, as well as modify the sonic characteristics of the room itself. Like period, wavelength is usually measured from crest to crest. However, unlike period, wavelength is affected by the speed of sound, since the greater its speed, the farther it will travel in the same amount of time (e.g., 1 second). In general, we can consider the speed[7] of sound in air to be a constant at 1130 ft/s or 344 meters/s at 20° C (68° F). Although this is affected by temperature and humidity changes, in the studio these are generally not a significant factor. In outdoor live sound reinforcement, on the other hand, they can become an issue.

Wavelength is represented by the Greek symbol λ (*lambda*), and can be calculated using equation 5.3.

$$\lambda = c/f$$

where c = the speed of sound, and f is the frequency.

Eq. 5.3. *Used to calculate the wavelength of any periodic wave*

Thus, the wavelength of 1 kHz (1000 Hz) is $^{1130}/_{1000}$ or approximately 1.1 ft.

Again, to find the proper unit of measurement, include the units throughout the operation: (1130 ft)/(1000 c), the seconds cancel out in the numerator and denominator (1130 ft/s)/(1000 c/s), and we are left with 1.13 feet/cycle. We can leave *cycle* out, since wavelength implies the distance for a single cycle. The wavelength of A440 is $^{1130}/_{440} \approx 2.6$ feet. The wavelength of a kick drum *fundamental* (lowest frequency) of 60 Hz would be $^{1130}/_{60} \approx 19$ feet! This puts the first pressure apex at 4.75 feet, which incidentally, is not a bad place for a mic to pick up strong low end from the kick (combined with a close mic to capture the beater hit). This is also one of the reasons that low frequencies are problematic in small rooms. Baffles are ineffective in stopping them, as these long wavelengths simply wrap around the obstacle and continue on their way. Further, if there is not a natural outlet for them in the room, such as a *bass trap* (low-frequency absorber), they have nowhere to go and tend to build up uncontrollably, creating an overall "boomy" sound.

7. While the terms *speed* and *velocity* are often used interchangeably, there is a distinction. *Speed* is the rate at which something travels without regard to its direction of travel. *Velocity* implies both rate and direction. Thus, a car traveling at a speed of 55 miles/hr would be said to be traveling southeast at a velocity of 55 miles/hr.

Incidentally, if this same sound (1 kHz) were traveling in water, where it travels about four times as fast, its wavelength would be four times greater, or approximately 4.5 feet. An electrical signal traveling down a wire has a much longer wavelength since it travels essentially at the speed of light (186,000 miles/s). Note that in each case, the frequency and period do not change; only the wavelength does.

For a better sense of wavelengths of sound in air, refer to table 5.1. Note how small the higher-frequency wavelengths are, such as those found in cymbals. For this reason, very small changes in mic placement can have a dramatic impact on the sound captured—again, particularly when combining multiple microphones.

Sound Wave	Freq. (approx.)	Wavelength in Air
Lowest audible frequency	≈20 Hz	56.50 ft.
Kick drum fundamental	≈60 Hz	19.00 ft.
Concert tuning note (A440)	440 Hz	2.57 ft.
Vocal sibilance ("s")	≈5 kHz	0.23 ft. or 2.70 in.
Cymbal "sizzle"	≈16 kHz	0.07 ft. or 0.85 in.
Highest audible frequency	≈20 kHz	0.05 ft. or 0.68 in

Table 5.1. *Some common sound waves with corresponding frequency and wavelength*

In the Studio

A baffle or *gobo* used in the studio to isolate one sound source from another will only be effective at blocking frequencies whose *wavelengths* are smaller that the dimensions of the baffle. For instance, a 4 ft × 4 ft baffle will not effectively block any frequencies below F = 1130/λ = 1130/4 = 287.5 Hz. For this reason, it is a good idea to try to put low-frequency sound sources, such as bass guitar amps, in a separate isolation booth whenever possible.

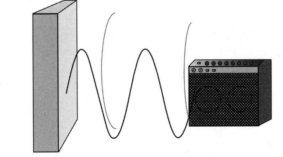

Amplitude (Pressure)

The *amplitude* of a sound wave is closely related to how loud it sounds. Very generally, we can say that we perceive amplitude as loudness, in the same way we perceive frequency as pitch, with some important caveats. We might also call it the "strength" of the wave. There are a number of different ways to describe and measure amplitude. If we look back at figure 5.8, we have a physical model of simple harmonic, or sinusoidal, motion. We described the amplitude of the motion in *distance traveled away from point of rest*. We might call this *displacement amplitude*.

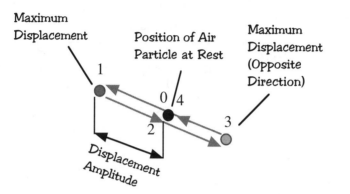

Fig. 5.16. Amplitude represented as the displacement of air particle. Moving consecutively through positions 0–1–2–3–4 represents one cycle in the vibration of the air particle.

This also describes what actually happens with air molecules when disturbed by a sound wave. Because a stronger sound wave causes a proportionally greater displacement, this might represent a way to measure a wave's amplitude if there were a practical method for finding the maximum distance each vibrating particle of air had traveled away from its steady-state position (figure 5.16).

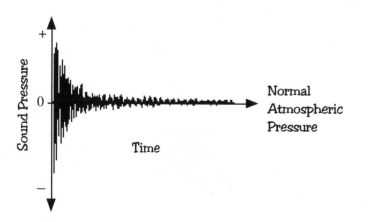

Fig. 5.17. Graph of sound measured as sound pressure over time for a complex sound (drum hit). The signal's amplitude varies greatly as it decays.

Fortunately, there is a simple alternative. Microphones can be used that respond directly to *pressure* changes in the air around them. All *omnidirectional* microphones work in this fashion, and this is the type of microphone used in a *sound level meter*. The greater the compression caused by a sound wave, the greater the resultant increase in the pressure of air, above normal atmospheric pressure. The type of visual representation in figure 5.17 is typical of the way software-based hard-disk recording programs display recorded audio signals. This visual representation greatly facilitates graphic digital editing.

The microphone responds to this change in pressure amplitude and generates a proportional change in electrical voltage.[8] Therefore, we generally use *pressure* to describe the amplitude of acoustical sound waves. The microphone is what we would call a *transducer* because it converts (transduces) one form of energy (acoustical pressure) into a different form of energy (electrical voltage).

But what exactly is pressure? In general terms, pressure is a measure of the amount of *force* exerted on a particular object over a specific unit area, such as a square inch or a square meter. Anytime you push or pull on something, or pick something up, you must exert a corresponding amount of force on that object. Lifting a five-pound book would require 5 lbs. of force, or approximately 23 *newtons* (named after Sir Isaac Newton). The newton is the metric unit for force (*N*), where about 4.5 N is equal to one pound of force. Pressure is simply a measure of the force that is distributed over the surface area of the object. Mathematically, pressure can be expressed or calculated using equation 5.4.

$$p = F/S$$

where p is pressure, F is force and S is surface area.

Eq. 5.4. *Used to calculate or express sound pressure*

Atmospheric pressure is generally given as 14.7 lbs/in^2. This represents the amount of force that holds air particles together, and that air exerts on everything around it. In metric terms, atmospheric pressure is given as 10^5 N/m^2. (Note that we are converting square inches to square meters.) This pressure is also known as "*one atmosphere.*" The variations in pressure resulting from sound (or resulting *in* sound, depending on your perspective) are minuscule by comparison. In fact, a pressure of 0.00002 N/m^2 (or 2×10^{-5} N/m^2)[9] above atmospheric pressure is what

8. Voltage is the electrical equivalent of acoustical pressure and will be discussed further in chapter 6.

9. We employ scientific notation to help us represent very large and very small numbers easily and concisely. Scientific notation always follows the form $n \times 10^X$ where n must be a number greater than or equal to 1 but smaller than 10 ($1 \leq n < 10$). Thus, 250,000 becomes 2.5×10^5, while 0.0000736 is written as 7.36×10^{-5}. The power, or exponent, of ten represents how many times ten has been multiplied by itself: $100,000 = 1 \times 10 \times 10 \times 10 \times 10 \times 10 = 10^5$. A negative exponent means that rather than multiplying, we are dividing by 10 as many times. Thus, $0.001 = 1 \div 10 \div 10 \div 10 = 10^{-3}$.

we generally consider the softest sound that we can hear under the best of circumstances. This is known as the *threshold of hearing* or *threshold of audibility*. Sound pressure this low is outside of most people's experience, as noise levels in our environment exceed this level considerably. A pin drop generates a pressure about three times greater (or approximately 0.00006 N/m^2). The loudest sound that we endure (clearly, quite subjective) is only about 20 N/m^2. This pressure is called the *threshold of pain* or *threshold of feeling*, where a sound is so loud that it takes on more of a feeling sensation than strictly a hearing one. Rock concerts can produce sound pressures in this realm, and any sustained listening at this level virtually guarantees some resultant hearing loss. A jet engine also generates similar pressures as far as 100 meters away, necessitating mandatory hearing protection for all runway personnel. These reference pressures define the *limits of audibility* for the human ear.

While these pressure variations are minuscule when compared to baseline atmospheric pressure, they are in fact quite vast when compared to one another. In fact, our hearing is easily the most sensitive and fine-tuned of our senses, with a range of measurement (in power) of about a trillion to one. As we begin to form a better idea of the limits of our senses in their ability to capture the world around us, it is helpful to define those limits. With respect to our hearing, we might call this the *audio window*. Use table 5.2 as a quick preliminary reference. It is useful to begin to recognize these various units and reference measures in order to be able to make more sense of equipment spec sheets, as well as to be able to follow discussions on sound in various contexts.

Atmospheric Pressure = 14.7 lbs/in^2 $\Rightarrow$
1 Atmosphere = 10^5 N/m^2 (5 atm = 5 × 10^5 N/m^2)
Threshold of Audibility = 0.00002 N/m^2 (or 2 × 10^{-5} N/m^2)
Threshold of Pain ≈ 20 N/m^2 (above atmospheric pressure)

Table 5.2. *References for atmospheric pressure, and limits of audibility (in sound pressure)*

In different disciplines or contexts, the units used for these basic references are sometimes different. Thus, you might see the threshold of hearing represented as 0.0002 (2 × 10^{-4}) *dynes/cm^2* or *μbars* (*μbar*, or microbar = 1 millionth of a bar), or again 0.00002 (2 × 10^{-5}) *pascals* (*Pa*), which is equal to 20 μPa. Note that *Pa* is equivalent to *N/m^2* and that *10 dynes/cm^2 = 1 Pa*. Don't let these different units scare you off; they all represent the same thing. But it is worth recognizing them

Threshold of Audibility
2×10^{-4} (0.0002) dynes/cm^2
2×10^{-4} (0.0002) μ bars
2×10^{-5} (0.00002) Pa
20 μPa
2×10^{-5} (0.00002) N/m^2

Threshold of Pain [10]
200 dynes/cm^2
200 μbars (or 0.2 millibars)
20 Pa (20,000,000 μPa)
20 N/m^2

Table 5.3. *Alternative reference units for limits of audibility (in sound pressure)*

and understanding what they represent when you encounter them. You can use table 5.3 as a quick reference.

The threshold of audibility is an important element, as it is most often used as the reference to which all other sound levels are compared. In the context of music and studio recording, we tend to speak less of sound pressure directly, and concentrate more on sound pressure level, or dB SPL, with 0 dB SPL being the threshold of audibility and 120 dB SPL the threshold of pain.[10] A wise moderate level for monitoring in the studio is between 80 and 90 dB SPL.

Amplitude (Peak vs. RMS)

Besides using a microphone and sound level meter, we can also use our oscilloscope (figure 5.12) to view and measure the amplitude (as well as period) of a waveform in the electrical realm, whether reproduced via a microphone or generated by an electronic instrument. The display is read by setting a value for time (*timebase*, in microseconds or μs) and amplitude (*sensitivity*, in volts) per subdivision or display square. The wave's amplitude would be given in volts, but may be calculated in several distinct ways.

Perhaps the simplest type of amplitude measurement, called *peak amplitude*, is found by measuring the highest point above zero reached by the wave in a given cycle. The peak amplitude of the wave in figure 5.18 is 3 V. (For a discussion of *voltage* see chapter 6.) The *peak-to-peak amplitude* of the wave is found by measuring the difference between the highest and lowest points in a given cycle, which will be equal to twice the peak amplitude for any periodic wave. For the wave in figure 5.18, the peak-to-peak amplitude is 6 V.

10. Note—Throughout the book, we have chosen to use 120 dB SPL as our reference for the threshold of pain, which yields the numbers above. This is consistent with numerous past publications. Some have argued that the threshold of pain is really closer to 130 dB or perhaps even 140 dB SPL. However, given the somewhat subjective nature of this reference, coupled with the well-known phenomenon of hearing loss particularly associated with the high decibel levels of music in the recording and sound reinforcement fields, we have deliberately chosen to stick with the 120 dB figure. Fortunately, most recording engineers now understand the wisdom of monitoring at reasonable levels, both from a health as well as a creative perspective.

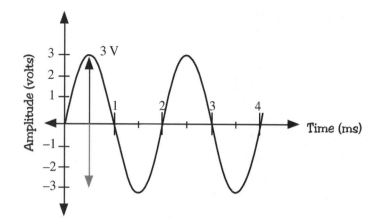

Fig. 5.18. *Measuring the amplitude of a sine wave*

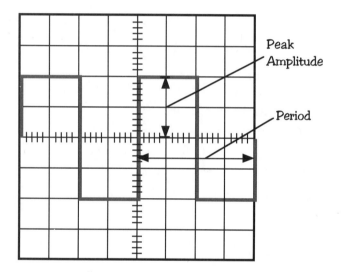

Fig. 5.19. *Measuring amplitude and period from a scope display. If sensitivity is set to 0.5 V/subdiv., the above wave has a peak amplitude of 2 × 0.5 = 1 V. Given a timebase setting of 0.5 ms/subdiv., the period of the above wave is 4 × 0.5 = 2 ms. Frequency = $^1/_{0.002}$ = 500 Hz.*

To measure peak amplitude using the display on an oscilloscope, we would simply count the squares (or fractions thereof) along the *y* or vertical axis occupied by the wave above the zero *x* axis (horizontal), and multiply this value by the value set per subdivision (square) at the *sensitivity* control. For the signal displayed in figure 5.19, if the sensitivity were set at 0.5 V/subdivision (square), the peak amplitude would measure 2 × 0.5 = 1 V. If the *timebase* were set at 0.5 ms/subdivision, the period of this signal would be 4 × 0.5 = 2 ms. The frequency of the wave would therefore be $f = ^1/_T = ^1/_{0.002}$ = 500 Hz.

Given two similar sound waves, the one with the greater peak amplitude will sound louder. However, given two different waveforms, the correlation between peak amplitude and actual loudness or power of the sound wave becomes less obvious. For example, take the square wave and a sine wave in figure 5.20, each with a peak amplitude of 3 V. (Note that both of these signal are synthesized and do not typically occur in nature, but are very useful as test signals.) The square wave will sound significantly louder than the sine wave because it spends virtually all

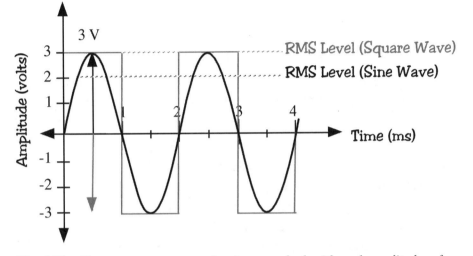

Fig. 5.20. *Given a square wave and a sine wave both with peak amplitudes of three volts, the square wave will be significantly louder-sounding.*

of its time at its maximum or peak amplitude. The same is true of musical signals. Transient signals, which don't spend much time at peak level (such as acoustic piano), sound less loud than similar signals of equal peak value but greater sustained level (distorted guitar, for instance).

So, how can we measure sound waves in a way that more closely correlates amplitude with loudness or power? The most effective method is called *root-mean-square* or *rms*. Rms level is calculated by taking a large number of samples of the sound wave at regular intervals, squaring the samples to remove negative values, adding up all the squared values, dividing the sum by the total number of samples, and taking the square root of the result.

Algebraically, this is written as equation 5.5:

$$V_{rms} = \sqrt{\frac{(S_1)^2 + (S_2)^2 + \ldots (S_N)^2}{n}}$$

Eq. 5.5. *Calculating rms level for any waveform, where s = sample amplitude and n = the total number of samples taken*

Rms is a very precise type of average level that correlates closely to the power inherent in a sound wave and therefore to apparent loudness. For continuous sine waves, rms amplitude is more easily calculated from peak amplitude. The relationship is as follows:

$$V_{rms} = V_{peak} / \sqrt{2} \quad or \quad V_{peak} = \sqrt{2} \times V_{rms}$$

This can also be written:

$$V_{rms} = 0.707^* \times V_{peak} \quad or \quad V_{peak} = 1.414^* \times V_{rms}$$

(*Note that $1/\sqrt{2} = 0.707$, and $\sqrt{2} = 1.414$)

Eq. 5.6. *Calculating rms from peak level and vice versa (for continuous sine waves only)*

Therefore, our sine wave with a peak amplitude of 3 V would have an rms value of $3 \times 0.707 = 2.121$ V_{rms}. In contrast, the 3 V square wave from figure 5.20 would have an rms value of 3 V, since every sample taken would have a value of 3 V. Note that the rms-to-peak calculations above are valid for continuous sine waves *only* and may not be used for any other waveforms. These are useful since power measurements should always be based on rms voltages, while peak voltages are more easily read from the oscilloscope display.

If we zoom in on a complex wave such as the drum hit from figure 5.17, the signal would look like the wave pictured in figure 5.21. With music signals, particularly percussive signals such as these, there is typically a much greater difference between the peak value and the rms value than with the sine wave. This difference between peak and rms (or average) level is called the wave's *crest factor*. In general, the more percussive or *transient* the sound, the greater its crest factor. For these waves, the rms level can be calculated using equation 5.5, and circuits exist whose sole function is to measure rms level in this way. Again, this is useful because rms amplitude correlates more closely to the perceived loudness of an audio signal as well as directly to its inherent power. Acoustical pressures, given in N/m^2 are always rms values. The difference between peak and rms level is an important issue, especially with respect to metering.

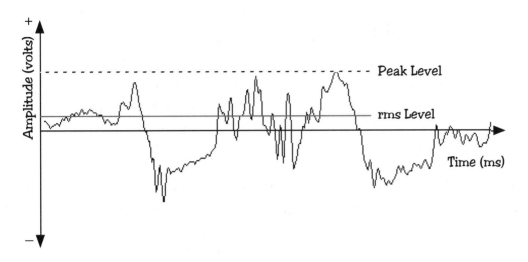

Fig. 5.21. *The typical relationship between peak and rms level for a complex wave such as a snare drum signal*

In the Studio

Meters in the recording studio can either display average or peak level (or both). Classic VU meters display average level (akin to rms) to correlate more closely to perceived loudness. However, this also means that the actual peak of the signal may be much (as much as 15 dB) higher than the level shown on the meter (watch for the peak LED to light up). Since the peak of the signal is what tends to distort when passing through audio equipment, tran-

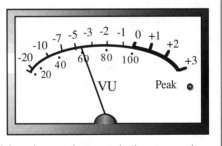

sient signals with strong attacks, such as kick and snare drums and other percussion, should be kept lower (as low as –6 or more) on the meters in order to avoid distortion, particularly if recording to analog tape.

Complex Sound (Fourier)

Eighteenth-century French physicist Jean-Baptiste Joseph Fourier (1768–1830) proved (mathematically) that all periodic waves can be broken down into individual sine waves. Furthermore, these sounds that we call musical are made up of sine waves that are exact multiples of the fundamental. The fundamental, or lowest frequency, determines the pitch that we hear, as well as the period of the sound wave, while the harmonics, or multiples of the fundamental, determine the timbre or tone color of the complex wave. More specifically, the relative amplitude and phase of the individual harmonics determine the overall wave shape and resulting timbre.

In musical terms, we often refer to the musical tones generated by an instrument above the principal note played as *overtones*. The fundamental, or principal note, is also known as the first harmonic, the first overtone would be the second harmonic, and so on (figure 5.22). As a general rule, higher harmonics within a sound wave contain less energy than the lower harmonics. Certain vintage instruments such as Stradivarius violins are prized largely for the patterns of overtones and resultant rich timbre that they generate. (One could argue, of course, that the exorbitant cost of such instruments is due at least in part to the fact that they are so old and few in number, in addition to their undeniable sonic prowess and masterful construction.) Vintage pieces of audio equipment, such as classic tube-based microphones, preamps, and compressors, are prized in much the same way for the particular tone-color or sonic stamp they impose on signals by generating and adding additional harmonics. Software models of such vintage equipment, in the form of DAW plug-ins, try to recreate these patterns through mathematical algorithms generated from studying these devices' sonic characteristics.

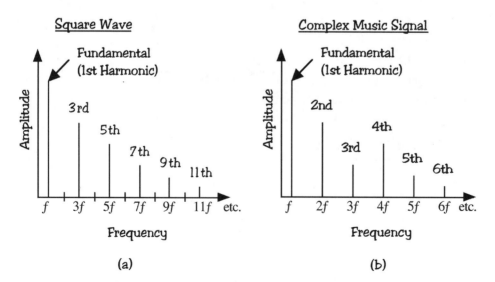

Fig. 5.22. *Graphical representations of harmonic content of (a) a square wave with infinite odd harmonics and (b) a complex music signal*

Let's look at harmonics and timbre more closely. Given, as an example, a piano and guitar each playing note A440, both instruments generate frequencies 440 Hz, 880 Hz, 1320 Hz, etc. The two notes have the same pitch, but will of course sound different in timbre. This difference in timbre is largely due to the difference in amplitude (and phase) of the various harmonics generated by the two instruments. In fact, the relative amplitudes of the harmonics generated is very much dependent on how each instrument is played, as well—soft or loud, for instance. In the hands of a skilled musician, a musical instrument becomes extremely expressive, with the ability to reproduce a wide range of varying tone colors or timbres.

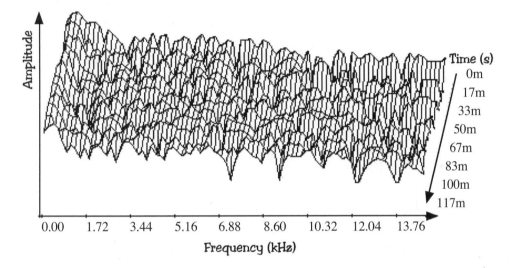

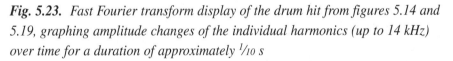

Fig. 5.23. *Fast Fourier transform display of the drum hit from figures 5.14 and 5.19, graphing amplitude changes of the individual harmonics (up to 14 kHz) over time for a duration of approximately ¹/₁₀ s*

Thanks to the processing power of computers, we now have the ability to analyze sound waves using a process called *fast Fourier transform*, or FFT. This process allows us to display the wave as a three-dimensional graph; the axes are amplitude and frequency over time (figure 5.23). This display gives us a very clear picture of the harmonic makeup, or frequency spectrum, of the complex sound wave, as well as how it develops over time. Each contour represents a snapshot in time of the relative energy at each frequency within the sound's spectrum. By following the change in amplitudes from the back to the front of the graph, we can track the envelope of the sound at various frequencies. For instance, the low frequencies seem to sustain (remain strong) while the highest frequencies decay more quickly.

Fourier (Additive) Synthesis

The idea that periodic sounds can be defined by the frequency and amplitude of the fundamental plus the harmonics leads to the conclusion that we can actually reconstruct any periodic wave by combining the appropriate harmonic sine waves at their respective levels. This is the basis for a technique called *additive synthesis*, which is used in certain electronic synthesizers to create or recreate sounds. In this type of sound design, a series of oscillators in the synthesizer are tuned to various harmonic frequencies. Their respective amplitudes are then adjusted until the desired timbre has been achieved. In addition, a device called an *envelope generator* allows the user to define how the sound begins, sustains, and ends.

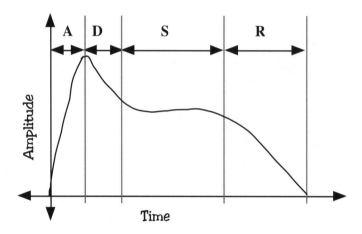

Fig. 5.24. *The envelope of a sound wave, shown as ADSR—attack, decay, sustain, release—describes how the sound begins, sustains, and ends with respect to overall amplitude.*

ADSR

The *envelope* of a sound, often referred to as *ADSR* (attack, decay, sustain, and release), describes the sound's overall amplitude change over time (figure 5.24). In fact, the attack portion of a signal contributes a great deal to its apparent timbre. This is probably due to the fact that during the attack, the envelopes of the individual harmonics are changing rapidly (figure 5.25). Our hearing, as perhaps all of our senses, is such that we tend to focus on changes rather than steady states, so this early portion of the signal is especially rich in information for our ears. In fact, an interesting experiment is to paste the attack of one instrument onto the sustain of a different instrument. Upon playback, these edited sounds are most often identified, even by trained listeners, as the instrument belonging to the attack portion of the signal.

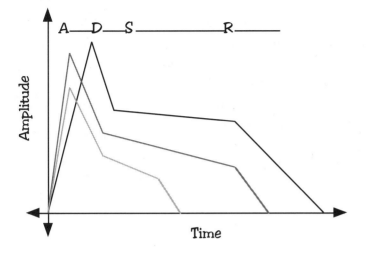

Fig. 5.25. *The simplified envelopes (ADSR) of the first three harmonics of a complex periodic wave. The most active amplitude information lies in the attack portion.*

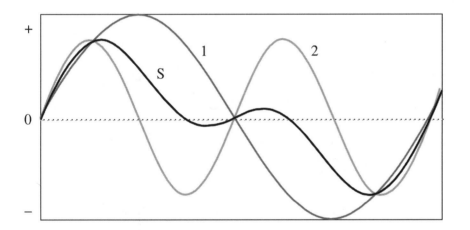

Fig. 5.26. *The waveform resulting from the sum of the first and second harmonics of a complex wave*

Combining Sound Waves

As we have seen, complex waveforms are the result of the summation of individual sine waves. To see how this happens, let's consider the first three harmonics of a 100 Hz complex wave. The fundamental, or first harmonic, would be 100 Hz, the second is 200 Hz, and the third, 300 Hz. The sum of the first and second harmonic can be found by simply adding the discrete amplitudes of the two waves at any given point and graphing the result as in figure 5.26. The waveform resulting from all three harmonics would be found in a similar manner as in figure 5.27.

Notice that the wavelength and period of the complex wave are the same as that of the fundamental. Also notice that the contours of the complex wave follow closely the contours of the harmonics. The greater the amplitude of the harmonics, the greater the corresponding deviations in the complex wave. Thus, if a wave has significant upper harmonic activity, it will exhibit a more jagged overall waveform (figure 5.28). Alternatively, a complex wave with very little upper harmonic content will have a relatively smoother wave shape. For instance, compare the waveforms of a bass guitar signal (little upper harmonic content) with that of an acoustic piano (great upper harmonic content) in figure 5.29.

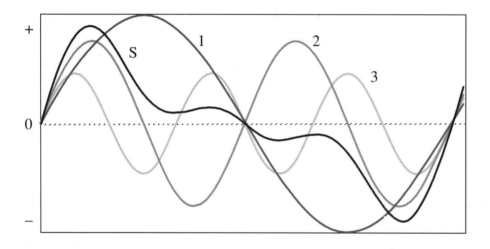

Fig. 5.27. *The waveform resulting from the sum of the first, second, and third harmonics of a complex wave*

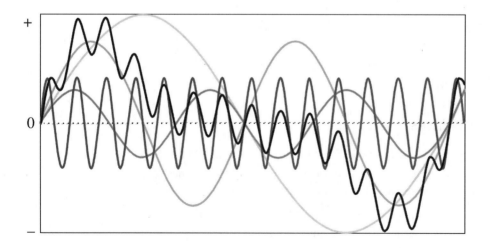

Fig. 5.28. *The same sound wave as in fig. 5.27, but with the addition of a strong 14th harmonic component*

This summation of individual sine waves to form complex waves applies to the addition of multiple complex waves as well—for instance, the combined signals of two microphones on a single source, or two sources picked up by a single microphone. In either case, the resulting signal will be a point-by-point summation of the discrete amplitudes of the two waves where they meet at the mic(s). Again, minute changes in placement can yield dramatic differences in resultant sound.

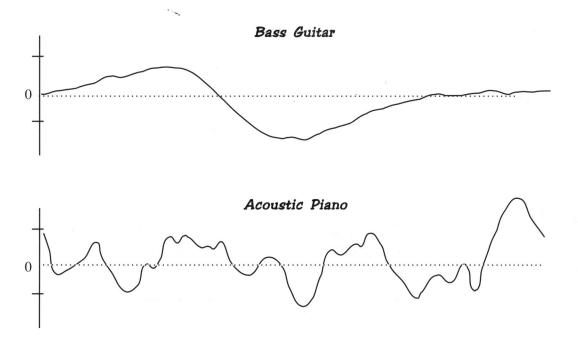

Fig. 5.29. *Complex waveforms compared: bass vs. piano*

Common musical signals are simply more complex summations of different frequency harmonics. These generally yield more complex waveforms than those shown in figures 5.27 or 5.28. Every musical signal that we hear and record sounds the way it does due in large part to the pattern of amplitudes of its harmonics. In the process of recording and mixing, equalizers are often used to bring out or to minimize different portions of a signal's frequency content. For instance, to bring out more low-end chest-thumping "oomph " in a kick drum signal, we might boost the fundamental around 50 or 60 Hz. Or to bring out the high-end "sizzle" in the cymbals, we might try to boost around 16 or 18 kHz. It is vital to develop a strong sense of the harmonic makeup and frequency range of various musical sounds in order to be able to make these tonal decisions and adjustments. To gain a clearer understanding of how frequency and harmonic content apply to some familiar musical sounds, refer to figure 5.30.

	20 Hz	31.5 Hz	63 Hz	125 Hz	250 Hz	500 Hz	1 kHz	2 kHz	4 kHz	8 kHz	16 kHz	20 kHz

Piano — 27.5 Hz ... 4.2 kHz

Vocal — 82 Hz ... 1.2 kHz ... *presence "s"*

Strings — 38 Hz ... 700 Hz ... 3.2 kHz

Woodwinds — 60 Hz ... 1.6 kHz ... 4.5 kHz

Brass — 44 Hz ... 700 Hz ... 1.5 kHz

Bass Guitar — 41.2 Hz ... 700 Hz ... 1.5 kHz

Kick Drum — 40 Hz ... *beater attack* 1 - 3 kHz

Snare Drum — 60 Hz ... 1.2 kHz ... *snares*

Cymbals — 130 Hz ... 1.2 kHz

Subjective	"Warmth"	"Body"	"Presence"	"Bite"	"Sizzle"

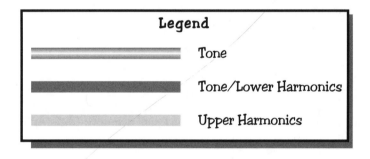

Legend

Tone

Tone/Lower Harmonics

Upper Harmonics

Figure 5.30. *Frequency range chart of instruments and their harmonics, accompanied by the subjective contribution of a frequency range to a sound's character*

PROJECTS

1. Calculate the fundamental frequency of a sound whose period is 5 ms; calculate the period of the concert tuning note A440.

2. A vocal being recorded bounces off the music stand, and the reflection reaches the mic, along with the direct sound, after an additional 2 ft. of travel. (a) What is the delay time of the reflected vocal? (b) What frequency(s) will be canceled, and what frequency(s) will be reinforced? (Hint: when delay equals period, a wave is essentially back in phase with itself.) (c) What do you do about it?

3. What are the wavelengths of 20 Hz and 20 kHz (the limits of audibility) in air?

4. How large a baffle would you need to effectively block sound down to 150 Hz?

5. Does the exploding guitar amp in the forest make a sound? Explain.

Chapter  Basic Audio Theory
Ohm's Law

One of the most misunderstood and often (unnecessarily) intimidating subjects in the field of recording is electrical theory: voltage, current, and impedance, and how they interact to make audio equipment work the way it does. This is probably due in part to the fact that electricity—the force that fuels electronics—is a largely invisible process, and as such, it holds a certain aura of mystery. For many, there is something seemingly magical about the whole thing. However, an understanding of the topic is not only within everyone's grasp but also essential for safe and proper setup and operation of any recording system. In this chapter, we will try to shed some light on the subject and begin to demystify the process.

Electricity

Because electricity is an invisible process, analogies to similar but more visible processes are helpful to our understanding. A common analogy for electrical current is the flow of water. Electricity is the flow of electrically charged particles, called *electrons*, through wires and circuits. By controlling that flow in specific ways, we can get it to do all kinds of work for us. In order to get any kind of flow, there must exist pressure in the line, similar to water pressure in a pipe system or hose—no pressure, no flow. This pressure, called *voltage*, is initially provided by the power company at a main generator, which raises the voltage above a "zero" voltage reference level, known as *ground potential*.

Voltage is also called *potential difference* because it is a measure of the difference in electrical potential (pressure) as compared to a zero ground potential, just as water pressure is measured above ground level. The water company's pumping station raises water to a storage tank or reservoir above ground level and gravity does the rest. The greater the level above ground level, the greater the potential difference, and therefore, the greater the pressure. Figure 6.1 shows electricity presented as a water supply system. (One of the major differences here is that gravity provides pressure in water systems, while gravity has no impact on the flow of electricity.) Because of the difference in water levels, pressure to equalize forces the flow to the right. As water current may be measured in gallons-per-minute (or hour) of flow, *current* is a measure of how many electrons flow past a certain point on a circuit each second. As with water, electrical current is created when there is pressure caused by a difference in potential or level above *ground*. The greater the difference in levels, read *voltage*, the greater the potential for water (or electrons) to flow.

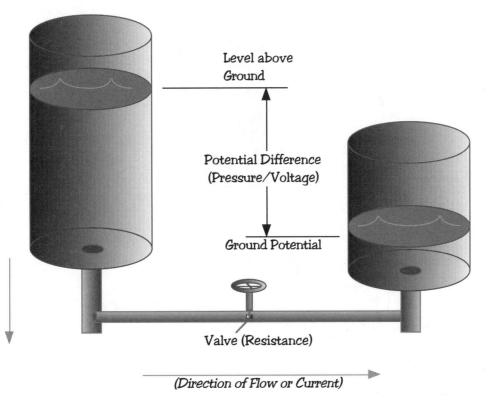

Fig. 6.1. *Schematic of a water system as analogy for electrical circuits*

However, the valve located in the center of figure 6.1 also has a say in determining how much current will exist.[11] This valve is analogous to *resistance*, which is a measure of the electrical resistance to the flow of electrons through a circuit. All elements have a certain amount of internal resistance, measured in *ohms* (Ω). Elements that present very little resistance to the flow of electrons, such as the copper wire used in telephone and some audio cables, are called *conductors*. Certain specialty cables even use gold-plating, which is meant to improve conductance as well as to resist corrosion. Elements that present a higher resistance, such as those used in mic pads and mic trims, are called *resistors*. As discussed previously, level controls such as mic trims use variable resistors to precisely control the amount of resistance presented to a signal, and therefore its eventual level. Materials that effectively block the flow of electrons, such as the plastic or rubber coating around audio cables, are called *insulators*. Combined use of these elements

---

11. Strictly speaking, water and electrons *flow*, while current simply exists; current does not flow.

within a circuit or audio system allows us to move electrons around in a controlled manner, the way pipes and valves control the flow of water (or the way traffic lights and signs control the flow of traffic).

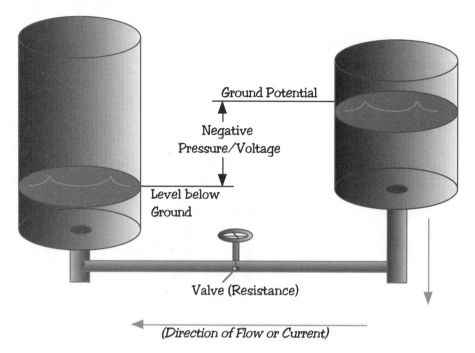

Fig. 6.2. *If the voltage becomes negative with respect to ground, the current reverses direction.*

Notice that the direction of flow through the pipe (or wire) is determined by the potential difference (voltage) with respect to ground. As long as it is above ground, the flow will be pulled to equalize pressure towards ground. If it falls below ground, flow is forced in the opposite direction (figure 6.2). This reversal in the direction of current is precisely what happens with *alternating current* (AC), or if the leads on a battery are reversed. Strictly speaking, the figure above only depicts *direct current* (DC), the type of current provided by battery power. A battery[12] is set up with two electrodes—one positive, one negative—separated by a chemical called an *electrolyte*. The negative pole contains an excess of electrons as compared to the positive pole. Because of this difference in potential, measured in volts, there is pressure for electrons to travel back to the positive pole to equalize. We take advantage of this natural tendency by connecting the battery to a circuit, thus making a connection between the two electrodes through the connected device (figure 6.3). Electrons flowing through the device on their way from one pole to

12. What we colloquially refer to as a *battery* is technically a *chemical cell*. Several cells together constitute a battery.

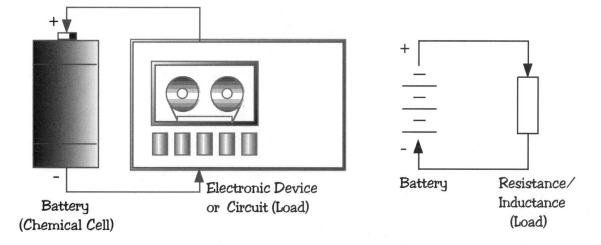

Fig. 6.3. *DC power provided by a battery; current flows in one direction from the negative to the positive pole (a), although it is typically represented as flowing in the opposite direction in circuit schematics and electrical discussions (b)*

the other will do the work needed. The batteries used in a portable CD player, for example, as well as in some microphones, provide the *electromotive force* (EMF) to generate the desired action (spinning the CD, for instance).

The direction of electron flow: a clarification needs to be made here about the direction of flow of electrons. There are two main particles that hold a charge: the positively charged proton and the negatively charged electron. An element containing an equal number of each is at equilibrium and carries no charge. An excess of electrons causes an element to be negatively charged, while a deficiency of electrons causes it to be positively charged. If two elements in close proximity have different charges, there will be an attraction and pressure to equalize. Because protons are hard to move while electrons are relatively light and more easily transferred, discrepancy in charge, or potential difference, causes electrons to flow from the negatively charged to the positively charged element. Thus, on an atomic level, flow of electrons is always in a direction from negative to positive.

However, by convention, in electrical circuits electricity is described as flowing in the opposite direction, from positive to negative. This convention dates back to Benjamin Franklin, who postulated the existence of an "electric fluid" that flowed from an excess of fluid (positive) to a deficiency of fluid (negative), much like our initial water analogy. To this day, electrical engineers and electricians alike consider the flow of electricity to be from positive to negative, and represent it as such in discussions and schematics. While we recognize how this departs from reality, for our discussions here, we will stick with convention. Ultimately, as long as one is consistent, the actual direction of flow is somewhat inconsequential.

This setup is akin to putting a waterwheel across the flow of a river flowing back to the ocean. Altitude above sea level causes the water to flow, and in so doing, it turns the waterwheel. By connecting the waterwheel to a motor or other device, it can now do whatever work we need done (churn butter or generate power in a hydroelectric plant, for instance).

The device connected presents a resistance to the flow of electrons on their travel from one pole to the other. (An element that heats up, such as the tungsten filament in a light bulb, is called a *resistance*, while a device that uses current and magnetism, often to run a motor, is called an *inductance*.) This is called the *load* on the current provider (the battery here). The lower the resistance, the greater the load, because more current is drawn from the source. Current passing through a resistance always generates heat. In fact, *power* is actually a measure of heat dissipation. The greater the current, generally, the greater the power, and therefore the greater the heat generated. High-current audio devices such as consoles, amplifiers, and computers, as well as tube-based outboard gear, generate a great amount of heat. For this reason, most of these devices include a design scheme for keeping the device cool, such as vents, fans, or heat sinks (the fins on a power amplifier chassis, for instance). It is extremely important to leave plenty of space around such gear so as not to block the air circulation; such blockage could lead to excessive heat buildup and eventual circuit and system failure. Always follow manufacturer recommendations for gear placement and spacing.

Ohm's Law

The specific behavior of electrons within a circuit can be predicted through a series of simple equations stemming from *Ohm's Law*, named after Georg Simon Ohm, a nineteenth-century German physicist. Understanding Ohm's Law is the key to any proper sound-system design and setup, from something as simple as connecting an amplifier to a pair of speakers, to designing a full-blown permanent-install distributed sound system. A lack of understanding here will prove frustrating in the inability to predict and explain the interaction of various devices with each other, with respect to levels, metering, and distortion.

Ohm postulated that the flow of electrons through an element is related to the internal resistance of that element. He also found specifically that doubling the length of a given element, such as a copper wire, through which the current must travel, doubles the resistance, while doubling its thickness cuts the resistance to one-quarter its former value. This observed relationship leads to the most basic statement of Ohm's Law, which allows for the calculation of the resistance of any element based on the current passing through a circuit, given a specific potential difference (voltage) across it:

$$R = V/I$$

where R = resistance, V = voltage, and I = current (intensity)

Eq. 6.1. The most basic statement of Ohm's Law, used to calculate resistance from voltage and current

Ohm's Law predicts that if we put 1 V of electrical pressure across a 1 Ω (ohm) resistance, it will generate 1 A (amp) of current, and this setup will result in 1 W (watt) of power (figure 6.4). The *ampere* (or "amp" for short—named after André Marie Ampère, a French scientist) is the unit used to measure current, where 1 A corresponds to approximately 6.3 billion billion (6.28×10^{18}) electrons passing a given point on a circuit in one second. The *watt* is the unit used to measure power, which represents the amount of work being done or energy consumed (or heat dissipated) by the circuit: 1 W = one joule (unit of energy) per second. In the most general sense, power also translates to loudness. All things equal, the greater the power, the louder the signal.

$$1 \text{ Volt} \Rightarrow 1 \text{ Ohm} \Rightarrow 1 \text{ Amp} \Rightarrow 1 \text{ Watt}$$

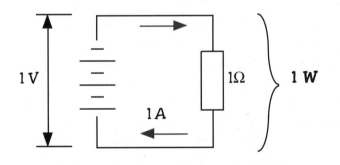

Fig. 6.4. The most simple application of Ohms Law: 1 V across a 1 Ω circuit will cause 1 A of current and generate 1 W of power

More important, Ohm's Law demonstrates that if one of these elements is modified, the others will change in predictable fashion. As we shall see, it allows us to understand what happens to our audio signal as it passes through each device, as well as from device to device—for instance, when we connect a bass amplifier head to different speaker cabinets. This relationship can be summed up in the following equations, an expanded statement of Ohm's Law:

$$\text{(a) } P = IV$$

and

$$\text{(b) } V = IR$$

where P = power, I = current, R = resistance, and V = voltage

Eq. 6.2. To calculate power from current and voltage (a), or to calculate voltage from current and resistance (b)

These equations tell us that power generated by a device or circuit is a product of the amount of current through it and the voltage across it (6.2a), while the voltage across a resistance is equal to the current through the resistance times the total value of the resistance (6.2b). As an example, if we have a 1 V signal generating 0.5 A of current, the resulting power output will be P = (1)(0.5) = 0.5 W. If this signal is fed through a power amplifier on the way to a speaker, and the current is increased to 3 A (a power amp basically functions as a current multiplier), the output power of the signal (all other things being equal) would be P = (1)(3) = 3 W. However, the signal voltage would also likely be boosted by the amp to perhaps 50 V, which would yield P = (50)(3) = 150 W. If more power is needed, then either the current or the voltage must be boosted. The power needed will depend on the task at hand. Though 100 W may be plenty to fill an average living room with sound, it would be completely inadequate for a dance club. The louder the needed signal and the larger the space, the more power required. Typical live sound applications need power in the tens of thousands of watts.

While we often may not know the exact current of a given signal, we could also calculate power given only voltage and resistance. This is most helpful when dealing with amplifiers (voltage) and speakers (resistance/impedance). We simply rework the above equations accordingly:

$$V = IR \text{ so } I = V/R$$

therefore

$$P = IV = (V/R)V$$

Result:

$$P = V^2/R$$

Eq. 6.3. To calculate power from voltage and resistance

So, given a 20 V signal across an 8 Ω load (such as a speaker), the resulting power would be $P = (20)^2/8 = 50$ W. This last equation demonstrates an important fact: power changes exponentially as the square of voltage. Assuming a constant resistance, a change in voltage yields an exponential change in power. By multiplying current as well as boosting voltage, a power amp is very effective at generating power gain.

We could also find power, given current and resistance, by substituting as follows:

$$P = IV \text{ and } V = IR$$

therefore

$$P = I(IR)$$

Result:

$$P = I^2R$$

Eq. 6.4. *To calculate power from current and resistance*

In the Studio

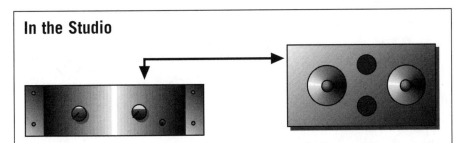

What is the implication of connecting an amp rated to deliver up to 250 W into 8 Ω, to a 4 Ω speaker instead, for instance? (The Ω, in this case, represents *impedance*: the total resistance presented by the speaker at a measured frequency.) The speaker with the lower impedance will present less of an obstacle to the flow of electrons and will therefore draw greater current from the amp. Provided that the amplifier is able to provide said current, half impedance/resistance means double the current. Since P = IV, doubled current (I) means doubled power (P), assuming no change in voltage (which is generally the case as most modern amplifiers are constant voltage devices). This would theoretically yield increased maximum output of 500 W into 4 Ω. Actual output power will often be less than this (say 400 to 450 W) due to restrictions in current-generating capability of the amp. More dramatically, if the amp is not rated to handle a 4 Ω load, the increased current can lead to blown fuses in the amp, thermal shutdown, or worse yet, failure of internal parts.

Voltage (V)	Resistance (R)	Current (I)	Power (P)
1.00 V	1.00 Ω	1.00 A	1.00 W
2.00 V	1.00 Ω	2.00 A	4.00 W
4.00 V	1.00 Ω	4.00 A	16.00 W
0.50 V	1.00 Ω	0.50 A	0.25 W
1.00 V	2.00 Ω	0.50 A	0.50 W
1.00 V	4.00 Ω	0.25 A	0.25 W
1.00 V	0.50 Ω	2.00 A	2.00 W
1.00 V	0.10 Ω	10.00 A	10.00 W
1.00 V	1.00 Ω	1.00 A	1.00 W
3.00 V	1.00 Ω	3.00 A	9.00 W
1.00 V	0.20 Ω	5.00 A	5.00 W

Table 6.1. *Charting the effect of changing voltage or resistance on current and power. Increased voltage yields increased current and exponentially increased power; increased resistance yields decreased current and power; increased current results from either increased voltage or decreased resistance.*

Thus, if we have a signal generating 0.5 A of current through a 600 Ω circuit the resulting power will be $P = (0.5)^2(600) = 150$ W. As long as we know two of the four values (voltage, current, resistance, or power) we can calculate the other two using the equations above. The ability to manipulate these values is obviously critical in electrical engineering, electronics, and audio-equipment design. Even as a recording engineer or musician, however, it is useful to have a strong sense of how these values interact, particularly when dealing with matching speakers or headphones to amplifiers, or putting together a recording system.

To get a better idea of how these properties interact within a circuit or device, or between devices, refer to table 6.1. We start with Ohm's basic setup of 1 V–1 Ω–1 A–1 W. First, consider what happens when we vary the voltage. As voltage increases, current increases proportionally, and power increases exponentially; as voltage decreases, current decreases proportionally, and power decreases exponentially. Remember that voltage represents pressure. Greater pressure causes increased flow (current), and hence a greater amount of work done (power). Again, loosely, more power means louder (and louder is, of course, better).

Next, let's consider resistance. As we decrease resistance, more electrons can flow and more power is generated. As we increase resistance, the current will drop and therefore less power will be generated. For example, the power of a "hot" mic signal that is distorting the mic preamp could be reduced by inserting additional resistance in the form of the mic pad circuit. A pad might also be used when feeding a tiny stereo (1/8-inch) headphone output (meant to drive the small speakers in headphones with around 100 mW) into a regular line input, although generally, line inputs have a wide enough dynamic range to handle the slight boost in voltage from such a source.

Finally, consider current. The two ways that we can increase current is by either increasing the voltage (pressure) or decreasing the resistance (or both). Hence, increasing either voltage or current, or decreasing resistance will each result in increased power, all other things being equal.

Impedance

Strictly speaking, only pure *DC* (direct current) circuits can be described as having pure resistance. Most of our audio systems have *impedance*, a frequency-dependent kind of resistance found in *AC* (alternating current) circuits. Impedance is akin to resistance but contains an additional component, called *reactance*. While resistance is constant, relatively speaking, reactance (and as a result, impedance) varies with frequency. Thus, any statement of impedance should technically be accompanied by a statement of associated frequency to be fully accurate.

AC refers not only to AC power but also to audio signals. Audio signals are usually electrical analogs (copies) of acoustical signals. As we discussed, while these signals are complex and do not follow simple sinusoidal motion, they do alternate continuously in a positive and negative direction. Thus, when discussing audio proper, we speak of impedance rather than resistance. Ohm's Law still holds true, as long as we accept that we are considering one frequency (as is the case with speakers, where the impedance is given as a single number—8 Ω for instance—for nominal impedance at one characteristic frequency).

Ohm's Law can be restated in these cases as $Z = V/I$, where Z stands for impedance, and takes the place of resistance R. It is helpful to think of impedance as a type of resistance encountered with AC and audio signals. For most of our discussion here, we just deal with resistance, although we take some liberties in using the two somewhat interchangeably. Impedance will be discussed further in the next chapter.

All of the equations stemming from Ohm's Law are summed up in a useful reference nomograph (figure 6.5). The principal parameters of voltage (V, or E for electromotive force), current (I), resistance (R) or impedance (Z), and power (P or W) are each located in one of the center quadrants of the circle. To solve for a given parameter, simply find that parameter in the center of the chart, and the associated equations can be found in the same pie quarter. Just find the equation that uses the parameters for which you have a given or measured value and solve for the center value.

Resistances/Impedances in Series

We have explored what happens to current and voltage with respect to one resistance, but what if we have several resistances in the circuit? Such a case might involve connecting more than one PA (public address) speaker—technically an impedance or load—to a single channel of a power amplifier. (For this and future examples, we may equate speaker impedance with resistance. While this is not entirely accurate, the same basic rules apply.) The result depends on whether those resistances (or impedances) are wired in series or in parallel. With two resistances *in series*—that is, one after the other along the same connection—the resistances add, such that total resistance is the sum of the individual resistances (figure 6.6). Because the current has only one path through which to travel, both resistances will receive the full current.

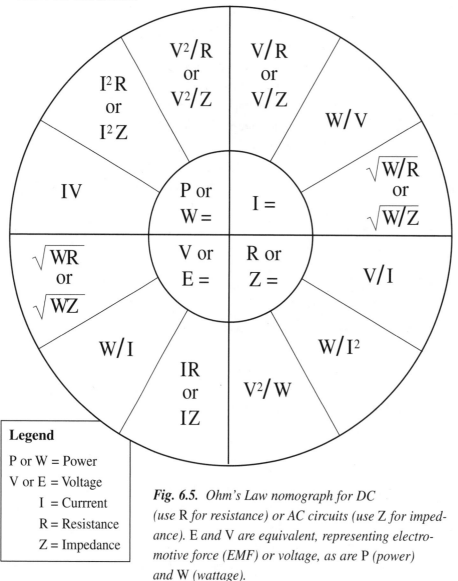

Legend

P or W = Power
V or E = Voltage
   I = Currrent
  R = Resistance
  Z = Impedance

Fig. 6.5. Ohm's Law nomograph for DC (use R for resistance) or AC circuits (use Z for impedance). E and V are equivalent, representing electromotive force (EMF) or voltage, as are P (power) and W (wattage).

The voltage, on the other hand will be divided between them, the greater resistance receiving the greater voltage drop across it. Note the voltage at the different points marked in the circuits. Also note that we measure voltages *at* specific points, and potential differences *between* two points; both are measured in volts. We also measure *voltage drops* across resistances (or loads)—drops that are equal to the potential difference between the two points on either side of the resistance.

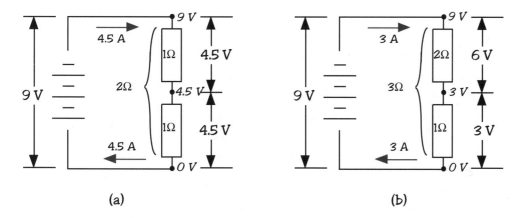

(a)   (b)

Fig. 6.6. *Resistances add when in series; each resistance will see the full current, while the voltage divides between them. The greater resistance receives the greater voltage.*

To calculate the voltage drop across each resistance, simply apply Ohm's Law to each resistance individually. Thus, for the 2 Ω resistance in circuit 6.6(b), we get V = IR = 3(2) = 6 V. For the 1 Ω resistance, we get V = 3(1) = 3 V.

An alternate way to think through this is to see that the voltage drops will be proportional to the ratio of the resistances. In other words, 2/3 of the total resistance will receive 2/3 of the total voltage. Thus, we could divide the resistance in question by the total resistance to get the ratio, and multiply the result by the total voltage to get the voltage drop across the resistance in question (equation 6.5).

$$(R_n / R_T) \times V_T = V_n$$

where R_n = one resistance of several in series, R_T = total resistance,
V_T = total voltage and V_n = voltage drop across the resistance in question

Eq. 6.5. *To calculate the voltage drop across one resistance of several in series*

Looking again at the same circuit (figure 6.6 b), the 2 Ω resistance receives 6 V because $^6/_9$ (resistance ratio) = $^2/_3$, and $^2/_3(9\text{ V}) = 6$ V; the 1 Ω resistance receives 3 V because $^3/_9 = ^1/_3$, and $^1/_3(9\text{ V}) = 3$ V. This last type of calculation is probably most useful when the resistances form a simple ratio with respect to the total voltage, allowing for simple and immediate mental calculation. Otherwise, it makes more sense to use Ohm's Law directly.

Resistances in Parallel

By contrast, resistances (or impedances) that are wired in parallel each receive the full voltage. This is because each is connected to both the 9 V and 0 V rails of the power supply. Therefore, the potential difference and resulting voltage drop across each resistance must be the same, the full 9 V, regardless of the value of the individual resistance. However, because the electrons have more than one path to take, the current divides (figure 6.7). What's more, because there are now multiple paths for the flow of electrons to take, the total current is increased. This is akin to opening an extra lane on a clogged highway. The more lanes, the greater the flow of traffic. Rather than adding resistance, the total resistance is actually decreased with each additional load wired in parallel. Thus, the total resistance will be less than any individual resistance taken alone.

In the Studio

Impedances in Series

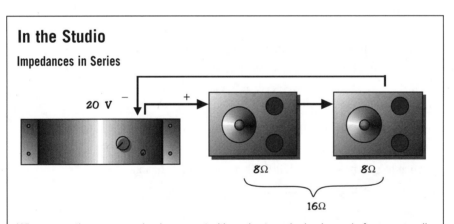

When more than one speaker is connected in series to a single channel of power amplification, the resulting total impedance is a sum of the individual impedances. Thus, two 8 Ω speakers in series yield a total impedance of 16 Ω. Increased impedance means reduced current, and thus reduced power. With a 20 V source, I = V/Z = 20/16 = 1.25 A of current. P = IV = 1.25 (20) = 25 W into 16 Ω. Each speaker receives full current, but only half the total voltage. This is not the most efficient setup, but it can allow for multiple speakers to be powered by a single channel of amplification. Some acoustic power can be regained by acoustically coupling the cabinets, placing them side by side, or even better, one on top of the other.

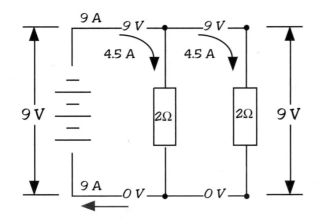

Fig. 6.7. *When resistances are wired in parallel, each resistance receives the full voltage, while the current divides between the resistances; also, there is increased current since there are multiple paths for electrons to flow. If the resistances are of equal value, total resistance will be the value of an individual resistance divided by the total number of resistances.*

So, how do we calculate the total resistance in this case? Let's consider the circuit in figure 6.7. Because the two parallel resistances are of equal value, we can simply take the value of the resistance (2 Ω) and divide by the total number of resistances (2). Result: 2/2 = 1 Ω total resistance. Mathematically, we can express this relationship as follows:

$$R_T = R_v/N$$

where R_T = total resistance, R_v = value of the individual resistance, and N = the total number of parallel resistances

Eq. 6.6. *To calculate total resistance for a circuit with several resistances of equal value, wired in parallel*

Alternatively, we know that Ohm's Law can be applied to each resistance individually. This allows us to calculate current through each resistance as follows:

$$I = V/R$$
$$= 9/2$$
$$= 4.5 \text{ A}$$

Having 4.5 A through each of the two resistances means that the total current is (2) 4.5 = 9 A. Now that we have total voltage and total current, we can calculate total resistance using Ohm's first law:

$$R = V/I$$
$$= 9/9$$
$$= 1 \text{ Ω}$$

But what if the resistances are of all different values? In this case an alternative equation can be used to calculate total resistance as follows:

$$1/R_T = 1/R_1 + 1/R_2 + 1/R_3 + \ldots 1/R_n$$

where R_T = total resistance, $R_1 \ldots$ = value of each individual resistance,
and n = the total number of parallel resistances

Eq. 6.7. *Alternative equation to calculate total resistance for a circuit with several resistances of any value, wired in parallel*

In the Studio

Impedances in Parallel

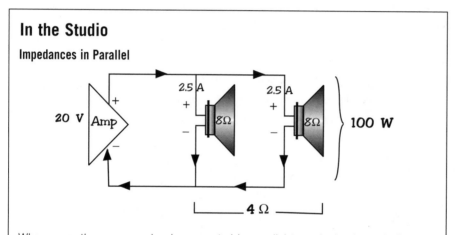

When more than one speaker is connected in parallel to a single channel of power amplification, the resulting total impedance is actually reduced. With equal impedances such as the 8 Ω speakers above, total impedance $(Z_T) = (R_v/N)$, i.e., the impedance value divided by the total number of impedances = $^8/_2$ = 4 Ω for the speakers.

Reduced impedance means increased current, and thus increased power. With a 20 V source, I = V/Z = $^{20}/_4$ = 5 A of current. P = IV = 5(20) = 100 W into 4 Ω . Each speaker receives full voltage, but only half the total current. This can be an acceptable way to gain additional power from a single power source, but only if the power amp is able to provide the needed current to drive the greater load.

One must be careful, however, when splitting a source such as a microphone into two parallel paths, to access an outboard preamp, for instance. Such a source cannot drive the increased load and current, which will simply lead to a greatly deteriorated signal. For this reason, a patch point that allows direct access to a mic signal before the preamp must be fully normalled; patching out will interrupt the original path. To split a mic signal to two separate destinations, a special splitting transformer must be used.

This equation can be used regardless of the values of the various resistances. If the resistances are different, such as in figure 6.8, we can use equation 6.7 to get $1/R_T = \frac{1}{1} + \frac{1}{2} = \frac{3}{2}$. To flip a fraction—in this case $1/R_T$—take the reciprocal of both sides: therefore $1/(\frac{1}{R_T}) = 1/(\frac{3}{2})$ or $R_T = \frac{2}{3}$ Ω.

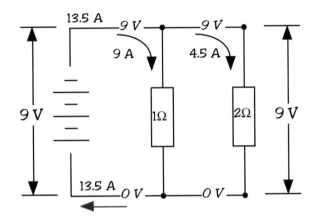

Fig. 6.8. When resistances of differing values are wired in parallel, each resistance gets the full voltage, while the increased current divides between the resistances according the value of the total resistance: $\frac{1}{R_T} = \frac{1}{R_1} + \frac{1}{R_2} + \frac{1}{R_3} + ... \frac{1}{R_n}$ or $R_T = (R_1 \times R_2)/(R_1 + R_2)$. The smallest resistance receives the greatest amount of current.

Alternatively, to find total resistance, we can use the following equation:

$$R_T = (R_1 \times R_2)/(R_1 + R_2)$$

where R_T = total resistance, R_1 = value of resistance 1,
and R_2 = value of resistance 2

Eq. 6.8. Alternate equation to calculate total resistance for a circuit with several resistances wired in parallel

In this example, we get $R_T = (1 \times 2)/(1 + 2) = \frac{2}{3}$ Ω total resistance. If there were more resistances, we would simply continue this process in pairs using our current result ($\frac{2}{3}$ Ω) as the next R_1.

Now that we have the total resistance in the circuit, we can calculate total current using $I = V/R$. Result: $I = 9/(\frac{2}{3}) = 9 \times (\frac{3}{2}) = 13.5$ A. To find how much current each resistance receives, we simply apply Ohm's Law to each:[13]

13. We could also find the ratio of one resistance to the other, and multiply the total current by the reciprocal ($\frac{1}{x}$) of that value. In other words, in our example circuit, R_2 is two times the value of R_1 and therefore receives half as much current as R_1. Thus, of the total 13.5 A, R_1 receives 9 A, and R_2 receives half as much, or 4.5 A.

$$I_1 = V/R_1$$
$$= \frac{9}{1} = 9 \text{ A}$$
$$I_2 = V/R_2$$
$$= \frac{9}{1} = 4.5 \text{ A}$$

Because parallel wiring schemes are more flexible than series schemes, they are used for AC receptacles and lights. In a series scheme, any disconnection or interruption will disrupt the entire circuit. A parallel wiring scheme allows for some lights or outlets to be used while others on the same circuit are not currently in use. However, this also means that the more devices that are plugged in, the greater the load will be on the electrical supply source. Calculating the total current drawn is a simple matter of adding up the individual current ratings of the various connected devices (total current equals the sum of individual currents through parallel loads).

Electrical outlets are rated to handle a certain amount of current; exceeding this rating introduces certain dangers. Specifically, high current means more power, and more power means more heat. This is why a 100 W bulb shines brighter (and hotter) than a 75 W bulb; it is drawing more current. Exceeding the rated current handling capacity of any electrical system, whether it be an outlet or an amplifier, puts a strain on that system, and can lead to system failure, or worse, fire. Again, this is why connecting a 4 Ω speaker to an amplifier output rated for a minimum load of 8 Ω is dangerous for the amp. The greater load draws twice as much current from the amp, and if the wiring is not rated to sustain this kind of current, the circuits will distort or even melt (or, more typically, the amp will blow fuses, which are easily replaced, or go into thermal shutdown to protect itself).

Series-Parallel

An alternative to series or parallel is a scheme called *series-parallel*. This has often been employed in situations where many devices must be fed simultaneously, such as with distributed ceiling speakers in a department store or possibly large PA installations. The idea here is to provide even sound distribution over a large area, without the sound being very loud in one area near speakers and less loud far from speakers. Series-parallel combines the current and voltage characteristics of both series and parallel to offset each other and effectively power several loads simultaneously from a single power source.

Consider the setup in figure 6.9a. Given an amplifier rated to deliver 50 W per channel when connected to an 8 Ω load (speaker), if we connect two 8 Ω speakers in series to a single output channel of the amp, the total load will increase to 16 Ω (series resistances/impedances add), the current will be cut in half, as will the power (25 W) resulting in the output signal being less loud. On the other hand, if we add

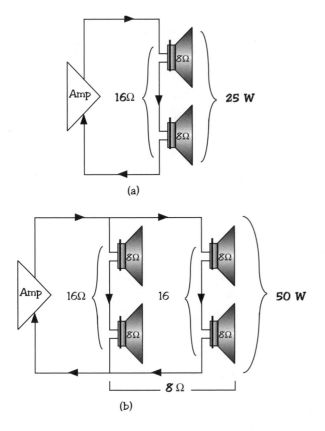

Fig. 6.9. *When speakers are connected in series (a), loads add, and power and current are diminished proportionally. In series-parallel (b), full power is maintained by offsetting drop in current from the series connection, with proportionally increased current from the parallel connection.*

two more 8 Ω speakers in series with each other, but in parallel with the first two speakers (figure 6.9b), the total resistance will now be 16/2 = 8 Ω. (Remember that $R_T = R_v /N$ when the parallel resistances are of equal value.) Total power goes back to 50 W, but we are now powering four speakers instead of just one from the single amplifier channel without overtaxing the amplifier.

Of course, no added power has magically been created.[14] Each individual speaker is only getting one fourth the available power, but the technical load requirements have been adhered to while meeting the practical requirement of powering multiple speakers from a single amplifier channel. Series-parallel schemes have fallen into disfavor for live sound reinforcement applications because, as it turns out, they have an adverse effect on the *dispersion characteristics* (the angles at which the sound spreads out) of loudspeakers.

14. *The law of conservation of energy* tells us that energy can never be created or destroyed; it can only be converted into a different form of energy. Thus the power "lost" by adding a second speaker in series is not lost at all, but merely converted into additional heat energy due to increased resistance/impedance.

AC Electrical Circuits

The conditions discussed so far are very straightforward for simple DC circuits, but somewhat more cloudy in AC systems, such as AC power or audio signals. The water analogy works well for DC because the water is always flowing in the same direction. By contrast, AC is called alternating current because it is continuously reversing direction, first forward and then backward. Let's return to our water system analogy for a moment, and take a closer look at what happens in a simple circuit such as a light. Electricity is supplied by the power company, arrives at the studio, and is distributed to the outlets and light switches via "hot" (or +) wires, much like the main pressurized water supply pipes of the plumbing system. The wires themselves are made of highly conductive material (such as copper), which present low resistance to the flow of electricity. In order to prevent electrons from escaping, all wires are coated with non-conductive insulating material (plastic or rubber, or in older wiring, paper), which keeps the flow confined to the prescribed path of wires and junctions (receptacles, lights, etc.).

When a light switch is turned on, it is akin to a faucet being opened (figure 6.10). Electrons flow from the hot wire through the light bulb's filament and cause it to heat up and glow, thus producing light. Once the electrons have passed through the light bulb, their potential drops to zero, the way the water from the faucet loses its pressure as it drains out of the sink and eventually back to the sewer. The electrons drain back to the power plant via a second wire, the neutral (or –) wire. At this point, even though the current has lost its voltage, it still has amperage, as it heads back to the power plant at ground potential.

Thus, the circuit (the light) forms a send-and-return loop from the power supply and back again. The switch either interrupts this loop (off or "open") or completes the loop (on or "closed"). For electronic devices to work, the loop is necessary. Electrons must be able to pass *through* the device to do their work, just as water must pass through the waterwheel for it to spin. Thus there must always be both a send (hot) wire and a return (neutral) wire for current to exist. In the case of speakers, you will notice that for the speaker to work, both the positive feed and negative return wires must be connected. All audio cables have at least two internal conductors for the same reason.

Keep in mind, however, that this is AC. Here, our water analogy falls apart slightly, because no sooner has the flow begun, than it reverses course and heads in the opposite direction back down the hot wire (figure 6.11). This is akin to reversing the leads on a battery, or exchanging the positive and negative wires feeding a speaker. AC performs this reversal 120 times per second. (Imagine trying to paddle down a river changing course 120 times per second!) The potential therefore continually shifts with respect to ground, first positive and then negative. Every

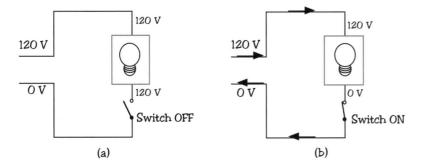

Fig. 6.10. *A simple electrical system such as a light, consists of a current loop from the hot (+) lead of the power supply, through the light, and back through the neutral (–) wire. Notice that the voltage at the other end of the light goes from a 120 V potential (a) to 0 V potential (b) when the switch is turned on to complete the circuit.*

time the current goes through a forward motion followed by a reverse motion and back again, we call this one *cycle*.

Because AC goes through this full cycle 60 times per second, we say that AC has a frequency of 60 cycles per second, or 60 Hz. It also follows a pure sinusoidal

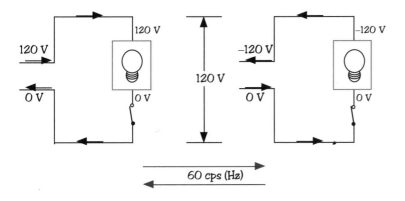

Fig. 6.11. *AC current reverses direction 120 times per second (60 full cycles) as the sine wave voltage shifts from +120 V to –120 V. Notice that in either case, the potential difference is still 120 V.*

path or waveform. AC power is carried via high voltage lines, but arrives at most outlets through a series of step-down transformers, at a potential of 120 V (240 V in Europe). Thus, AC is an electrical sine wave (figure 6.12) with a measured amplitude of 120 V_{rms} and a frequency of 60 Hz (240 V_{rms}, 50 Hz in Europe). For this reason, when AC finds its way into audio lines, it sounds like a low hum.

In contrast, audio passing through speaker wires is less predictable, traveling in a complex pattern of back and forth motion. As electrons move first forward and then backwards through the loop, the speaker's diaphragm mimics this electron motion and recreates the original acoustical waveform.

Because equipment is designed to work with this precise input voltage, outlets must comply with this precise specification, ± 5% (114–126 V). Any over- or under-voltage situations beyond about 105 V and 130 V can actually damage equipment.

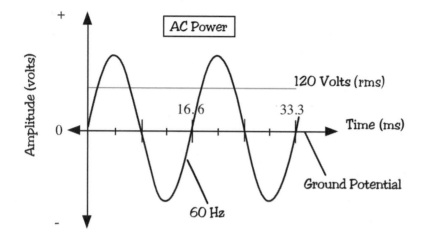

Fig. 6.12. *AC power in the US is a 120 V, 60 Hz sine wave. All AC power outlets must fall within these specifications, ± 5%. More than 130 V and less than 105 V can damage equipment.*

Some equipment does allow for operation with either European or US voltage, often via a switch on the back panel. Sometimes, this switching is done automatically. The device senses the voltage input and makes the necessary internal circuit switching. Such is the case with most computers.

While the current present at the power outlet is 15 A at a potential of 120 V, most audio devices, and most devices in general, need much less current and voltage internally to function. For this reason, the first stage in any audio device is typically a step-down power transformer stage which brings the voltage down to around 9 V and the current typically to below 1 A. Most currents, in fact, are measured in milliamps (mA or 1/1000 A); 1 A is a relatively large amount of current.

The step-down transformer can either be wired inside the device's main chassis with the rest of the electronics, or it can take the form of a "wall wart" power transformer (figure 6.13), which plugs right into the wall outlet. The advantage of the wall wart is that it keeps the transformer (and its strong magnetic fields) away from the sensitive internal electronics. The disadvantage is obvious to anyone who has had to use one. They are bulky, take up too much space in a power conditioning strip, and because of their weight, do not stay tightly seated in a regular outlet. We will explore the use of transformers for audio further in the next chapter.

Fig. 6.13. Typical "wall wart" power transformer employed by some audio equipment. Typical values for voltage and current are 9 V and less than 1 A.

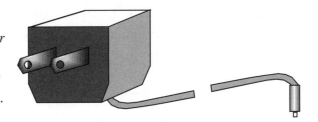

In addition to stepping down the voltage and current, the power transformer also includes a *rectifier*, which converts AC to DC (figure 6.14). It does so using an arrangement of *diodes*, elements that only allow electrons to flow through them in one direction. The rectified AC is then smoothed out using a *smoothing capacitor* connected in parallel. A *capacitor* is an element that has the capacity to hold a charge. When the voltage is high, the capacitor charges up. As the voltage decreases the capacitor discharges, and in so doing maintains a more consistent voltage level. Audio devices (and other electronic devices as well) require DC internally to function. This is one reason that low-power devices can be either battery operated (DC) or plugged into an AC outlet using a power transformer. Why then do we need to generate AC power at all, if we are just going to convert it to DC to power devices internally? The short answer is that DC is more complicated and expensive to generate on a large scale. And even on a small scale, devices such as power amplifiers require more current than batteries could easily or practically (read cheaply) provide—not to mention that batteries tend to run out at the most inopportune times, as in the middle of the perfect lead vocal take.

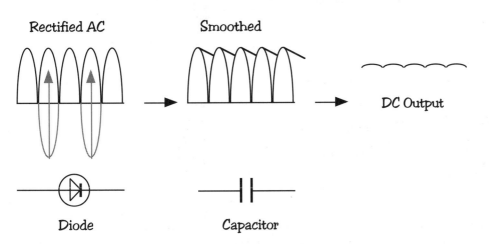

Fig. 6.14. AC to DC conversion process following the power transformer stage. The rectifier converts the negative portion of AC using diodes, and the smoothing capacitor smoothes the DC output to minimize ripple.

Grounding

In addition to the hot and neutral wires, AC wiring also contains a third wire: the *ground wire* or *safety ground*, which is like having an additional drain present as a safety measure in case of a short circuit or other faulty condition (figure 6.15, a–d). If, for instance, the internal electrical insulation of a device, such as a compressor or other outboard device, were to break down and the hot wire were to come into contact with the chassis (outer casing), that device could become a serious shock hazard (b).

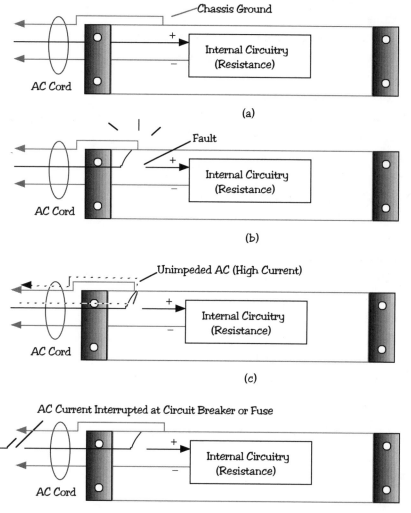

Fig. 6.15. *The function of the third wire (safety ground) in an AC connection is to drain any stray electrons or current safely to ground (a). One such situation would be caused by a fault in the hot (+) wire making the chassis of a device "live" and dangerous (b). The chassis ground forces a short circuit condition (c); the resulting high current trips the circuit breaker (d).*

However, as long as there is a ground wire connected to the chassis (called chassis ground—the typical scenario in audio equipment), any current present on the chassis would be immediately drained to ground (c).

Under this condition, because the current has managed to bypass the main resistance elements (load) of the device, there would be virtually no resistance to the flow of electricity. This condition is called a *short circuit*. The sudden high current would invariably burn out or "blow" a fuse (figure 6.16), or trip a circuit breaker at the main breaker panel (both safety mechanisms), thus interrupting the circuit and averting danger. The newly non-functioning circuit would now also alert the operator to the faulty condition (figure 6.15d).

Figure 6.16 shows a typical fuse, incorporated in the circuitry of many pieces of both audio and non-audio equipment. The purpose of the fuse is to provide an easily replaceable "weakest link" to the system. The fuse is made of a thin filament of low-melting fusible alloy encased in glass. In the presence of high current (typically more than 15 A), the alloy filament will melt, thus creating a gap in the circuit and preventing the high current from damaging sensitive and less easily replaced internal electronics of the device. If a circuit breaker or fuse is repeatedly being blown or tripped, the offending equipment should be checked and serviced for possible faults. Some audio equipment has fuses built in, although it is often incumbent upon the user to insert them in the circuit, such as between high-current amplifier outputs and monitor (speaker) inputs, in order to protect the speaker drivers from sudden transient spikes.

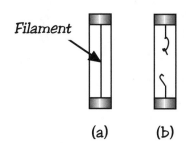

Fig. 6.16. *(a) Typical fuse used to protect equipment from short circuits or sudden spikes. A very thin filament (wire conductor) enclosed in a glass casing acts as the "weakest link" in your system. If any short-circuit or other high-current situation should occur, the filament will melt first (b), cutting off the flow of electricity and protecting the equipment's internal wiring. A fuse is cheap and easily replaced.*

The ground wire makes its connection via the third prong in a three-prong receptacle or outlet (figure 6.17). This safety feature is the primary reason that "lifting" (removing or breaking) the ground connection for AC power is a dangerous practice. When this is absolutely necessary, due to a two-prong outlet and a three-prong device, make sure to use an adapter that also allows for a ground connection to be made via the screw plate (figure 6.18). In two-hole outlets, the receptacle box (including the screw plate) is itself grounded via the conduit shield or ground wire. This is like "chassis ground" for the receptacle. New devices employing a two-prong AC cord are wired and insulated internally in such a way as to allow for proper internal safety isolation, according to strict UL certification. UL, or Underwriters' Laboratories, Inc., is an independent US electrical standards testing organization—like the CSA in Canada—which clears equipment as being in compliance with the National Electrical Code. Electronic or electrical devices not bearing these symbols, particularly older two-prong devices, should be viewed with extreme caution and generally avoided.

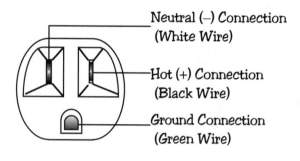

Fig. 6.17. *Standard US 15 A 120 V receptacle. The neutral prong is slightly longer and wider than the hot, to ensure proper AC phase.*

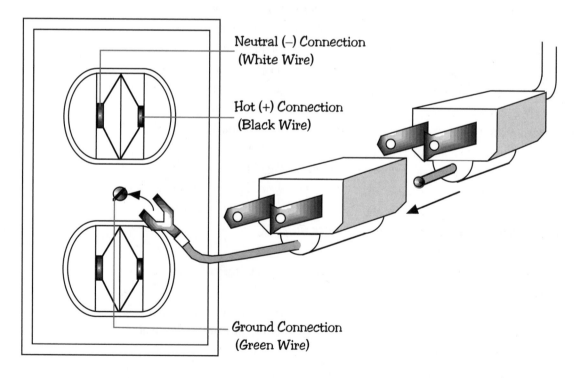

Fig. 6.18. *Use of a proper ground-lift adapter is crucial to maintain safety ground integrity when using a two-hole outlet for a device equipped with a three-prong plug.*

To verify correct wiring and proper ground, you can use a plug-in receptacle tester, or for better precision and increased information, use a *volt-ohm meter*. Touching the two leads to different points in the circuit should yield the results shown in figure 6.19. There should be about 115 V potential difference between the hot and neutral legs, and the neutral should be at earth ground potential (0 V). The plate screw should also demonstrate proper grounding (0 V) by showing no potential difference with either the neutral or the earth ground. With two-hole outlets, the same tests can be performed, using the plate screw as the ground contact point. In lieu of a volt-ohm meter, small plug-in testers are available that identify correct wiring or potential problems. However, while these may be useful in spotting improper wiring, they tell the user nothing about the voltage present.

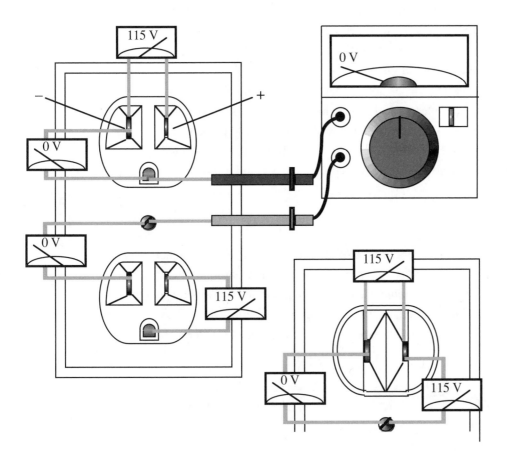

Fig. 6.19. *Using a volt-ohm meter to check for proper outlet wiring*

Earth Ground

So, what exactly is "ground?" Fundamentally, it is exactly as the name implies: a connection to the earth. The earth itself is essentially a large spinning magnet (which explains why compasses work as well as they do), whose poles are, literally, the North and South Poles. As such, it serves as the perfect receptacle for all stray electrons and current. Dangerous electrical conditions become even more dangerous when you are in contact with water or bare (moist) earth because of the conductive nature of both. This is one reason you do not want to be standing in the middle of a golf course during a lightning storm (besides being all wet and alone). Like water, electricity seeks the path of least resistance; earth ground is there to ensure that *you* do not become that path. All electrical ground connections make their way eventually to the earth either via a metal rod hammered into the (moist) ground somewhere, or by contact with water pipes, which naturally come into contact with the earth (figure 6.20). For this reason, the safety ground connections in a studio or house are called *earth ground*.

Because of the increasing use of non-conductive PVC (polyvinyl chloride) rather than metal piping, the latter method may no longer always be safe. The water meter, for instance, is often isolated using lengths of PVC piping to protect water company personnel from the potential of electric shock. It is always a good idea to have an electrician check all electrical connections in the studio for proper earth ground.

Signal Ground

In audio systems, ground also refers to a "zero" reference to which audio signal amplitudes or voltages can be compared and by which they are measured. This is most often referred to as *signal ground*. Generally, signal ground has a physical electrical connection to earth ground, but this is not always the case. The implications of earth and signal ground will be explored further in the next chapter.

PROJECTS

1. Test the outlets in your studio to confirm that they are properly wired and grounded. Which outlets are on the same circuit? Is there anything else on these circuits, such as a refrigerator or air conditioning machine? Can the way you use these circuits be optimized to reduce your system noise?

2. Locate your electrical service panel. How many amps can the circuit(s) handle? How many amps are currently being used by your equipment?

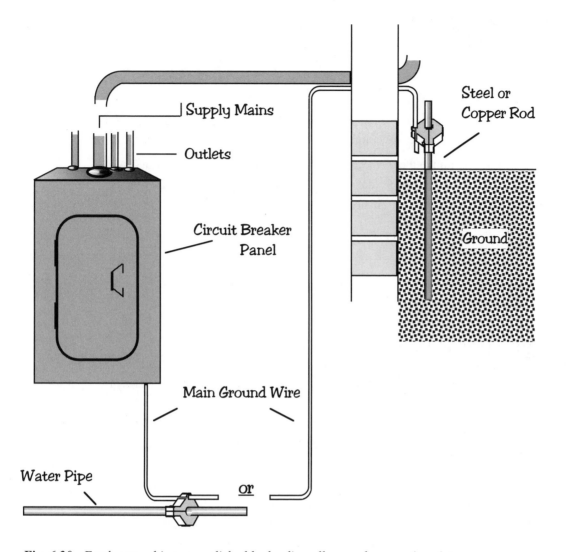

Fig. 6.20. *Earth ground is accomplished by leading all ground connections into contact with the earth, either (a) via a water pipe, or (b) (preferred) via a steel or copper rod hammered deep into the ground. For this to be effective, the soil must remain moist for proper conductivity.*

Chapter **7** Advanced Audio
Interconnections

Now that we have a better sense of audio and electrical theory, as well as signal flow in the studio and through the recording console, we can look more closely at the implications of interconnecting different pieces of audio equipment throughout the recording studio, and more specifically, what happens to our audio signal.

Impedance

Every device within an audio signal flow has both an input and an output impedance. The *output* or *source impedance* (Z_{out}) is the total opposition that a device presents to the flow of electrons passing from it and drawn into the receiving device. The *input* or *load impedance* (Z_{in}) is the total opposition that a device presents to the flow of electrons it is drawing into it, and into which the source device would be looking. When we connect one device to the other, we say that the output of the source device has a certain internal source impedance, while the input of the destination device presents a certain load impedance to the source device and signal. The voltage (V), current (I), and resulting power (P) can be calculated as usual, using Ohm's Law and factoring in the impedance (Z) at hand.

As we saw in the last chapter, impedance is one of the basic technical descriptors that differentiates speakers or headphones (as well as other equipment), and is a piece of information that is easily accessible when purchasing such equipment. Speakers are meant to be matched up to an appropriate amplifier based upon both power handling capacity as well as impedance. Given a loudspeaker rated at 8 Ω (the most common) nominal impedance, then, how much current will be drawn from a power amplifier if the power output is 400 W? To review, $P = I^2Z$; so $I = \sqrt{(P/Z)}$ (we get this by dividing both sides by Z and taking the $\sqrt{}$ of both sides) $= \sqrt{(400/8)} \approx 7.07$ A. What signal voltage would generate 400 W of power? $V = IZ = 7.07 \times 8 = 56.6$ V. If the same amplifier is now connected to a 4 Ω speaker, the power would jump to $P = V^2/Z = (56.6)^2/4 = 800$ W. As expected, cutting the load impedance in half will double the power, as long as the amp can supply the necessary current. Exactly what current are we dealing with now? $I = \sqrt{(P/Z)} = \sqrt{(800/4)} = 14.14$ A. The voltage at the output of the amplifier (assuming it is a modern constant-voltage amp) will remain the same, as long as the impedance does not fall below a specified minimum value.

As we also saw in the last chapter, impedance Z is different from resistance R in that it is not a constant, but rather varies with frequency. Specifically, it is made up of both resistance and *reactance*, a frequency-specific opposition to electrical flow in AC circuits. Reactance takes the form of both *inductance* (L), where opposition increases with increasing frequency (also called *inductive reactance*), and *capacitance* (C), where opposition is decreased for high frequencies and increased for low frequencies (also called *capacitive reactance*). A winding or coil represents inductance and can be called an *inductor* (figure 7.1a). (A motor is also properly called an inductance, as opposed to a resistance, as it consists largely of windings.) An inductor naturally presents lower opposition to low frequencies and a greater opposition to high frequencies. Inductances generate electromagnetic fields that can in turn induce currents in nearby cables and conductors. This process, known as *inductive coupling*, can be the source of noise and signal degradation within an audio system, and is a good reason for the use of balanced connections to reject such outside interference.

A capacitor is an element that consists of conductors (usually small metal plates) separated by non-conductive material, generically called *dielectric*, and has the ability to store a charge (figure 7.1b). It naturally presents a greater opposition to low frequencies and a lower opposition to high frequencies. Inductors, and to a greater extent capacitors (or *caps* for short), are the elements used to carefully control the flow of electricity through audio and other electronic devices to make them work. Also, because of the properties listed above, these elements can be used in conjunction with resistors to create filters such as low-pass (R-C) and high-pass (R-L) filters, as well as EQ circuits in general. However, other similarly configured conductors, such as the insulated conductors and/or metal shield within an audio cable, can unintentionally exhibit the same characteristics as a capacitor or even a filter. Also, electrostatic noise can induce noise in the audio cable through *capacitive coupling*. For this reason, care must be taken when choosing cables and configuring any audio system.

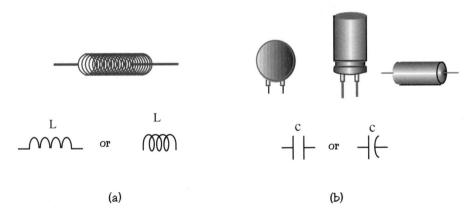

Fig. 7.1. *Inductor with schematic representation (symbol) below (a); capacitor with schematic representation below (b)*

Devices that are *transducers*—that is, which transform signals from one form of energy to another—are often called *reactive*, because they consist of reactive elements such as coils (e.g., microphones, electric guitar pickups, loudspeakers) and capacitors (e.g., condenser microphones). Because of the characteristics mentioned above, they are particularly sensitive to the impedance of the input they are driving. The latter can have an important effect on their frequency response, particularly if there is an impedance mismatch.

Figure 7.2 shows the characteristic impedance curve of a loudspeaker. For most audio devices, impedance rises with frequency above a certain point, and often also has sharp anomalies around the resonant frequency of a particular device. Because impedance varies with frequency, we generally consider just one frequency, sometimes called the *nominal* impedance. This is usually the lowest impedance above the *resonant frequency* of the device. Resonant frequency is the characteristic or natural frequency at which an element or device vibrates most easily and vigorously. We are mainly interested in the lowest impedance because this will determine the current supplying needs and requirements of the source device (in this case, the amplifier).

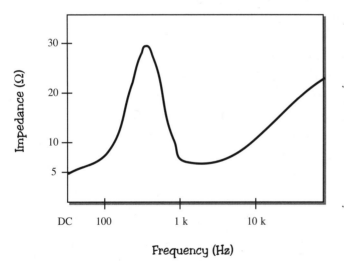

Fig. 7.2. *Typical impedance curve (with respect to frequency) of a loudspeaker with a nominal impedance of 8 Ω. Impedance curves of amplifiers will generally be flatter.*

On the other hand, modern *solid state* (transistor-based) amplifiers are designed such that the *voltage* from the source remains constant regardless of the load impedance, as long as the latter does not dip below the specified range. This fact is a good reason for the more recent use of *dBu* instead of *dBm* as the nomenclature for electrical levels. While the voltage (dBu) is predictable and constant, the power (dBm) may not be, and is in fact likely to change depending on the impedance.

Remember that Ohm's Law states that:

$$P = V^2/Z$$

Thus, assuming a constant voltage, halving the impedance will double the power.

Alternatively:

$$I = V/Z$$

so halving the impedance will double the current; and since

$$P = IV$$

double the current yields double the power.

However we look at it, halving the load impedance doubles the current (and thus the power) drawn from the source device, ignoring for the moment any real-world current or power-supply restrictions. For this reason, returning to our amp and speaker example, an amp rated to provide 100 W when connected to an 8 Ω speaker should be able to provide close to double that power (200 W) into a 4 Ω speaker. Paradoxically, this decrease in impedance is actually considered an *increase* in the load, because it represents a more taxing situation for the current-supplying source device. Thus a *load* is *increased* from 8 to 4 Ω, and *reduced* from 4 to 8 Ω.

Matching vs. Bridging Impedances

Before the days of solid state equipment, when most gain stages were tube-based, all impedances were matched at 600 Ω. Tubes themselves have a very high internal impedance, and necessitate the use of input and output transformers to step the impedance down to 600 Ω. An impedance of 600 Ω was the impedance of choice in audio equipment and installations mainly because the telephone company used 600 Ω to terminate all their lines. Therefore, it was assumed that all professional equipment, including studio equipment, must use 600 Ω. In fact, this is only neces-sary in the case of very long cable runs (such as phone lines) to minimize signal degradation. To this day, 600 Ω is considered the informal cut-off point between so-called *high-impedance* or hi-Z (above 600 Ω) and *low-impedance* or lo-Z (below 600 Ω) equipment. Low impedance is the standard output for professional equip-ment, which rarely exceeds 200 Ω and is often as low as a fraction of an ohm.

While the old *matching* scenario for studio connections has certain advantages, it is not very efficient. About half of the signal's power is lost in the transfer. What's more, outputs can not be easily split and sent to multiple destinations without using splitting transformers; otherwise, the signal is easily degraded. Because solid-state equipment can be made to have very low internal impedance, and provide constant voltage for a wide range of load impedances, the preferred connection standard is a *bridging* setup, where the load impedance is at least ten times greater than the source impedance. With this type of setup, the cable's own impedance contributes very little to the overall impedance, and very little signal power is lost in the transfer. Another tangible benefit of this setup is that several devices can now be wired in parallel without "loading down" the source device—that is, overtaxing the source device by drawing too much current from it. (Remember that resistances wired in parallel actually present *decreased* resistance to the source and therefore draw increased current from it.) Let's look at some typical studio connection scenarios. Keep in mind that audio fidelity is most often lost or degraded in the transfer of an audio signal from one device or gain stage to another. Therefore, proper connections with respect to level and impedance, as well as use of high-quality cables, are essential for good results.

A typical professional low-impedance microphone has a source impedance in the neighborhood of 50 Ω to 200 Ω. The microphone input to the console is generally rated on the order of 1.5 kΩ, or 1500 Ω, which yields approximately the 10:1 ratio called for in a bridging setup. Similarly, the console outputs, including sends, direct patch points, etc., are often as low as 100 Ω. Inputs to most professional gear to which you might be connecting these console outputs are in the 10 kΩ range and often far exceed even this figure. The general idea is that output or source impedances are made to be as low as practically possible. Input or load impedances are made as high as practically possible. Inserting an audio device violating this principle can lead to significant loss in level. The exception to this is in the case of very long cable runs in professional installations such as some live sound reinforcement or telephone lines, where lines are still generally matched at 600 Ω. This reduces buildup of noise in the line as well as a loss of high frequencies over such long runs.[15]

Another exception to the bridging rule are the old passive (non-amplified, non-powered) audio devices, such as a passive filter or a passive graphic equalizer (also properly called a "filter" set), which need to be matched in the classic sense at both the input and the output. Thus, a 600 Ω passive input must be fed from a 600 Ω

---

15. The two inner conductors, or a conductor and the shield, in a long, balanced (three-conductor) cable, can act as a capacitor. You'll remember that a capacitor consists of metal plates separated by an insulator. In parallel with the cable's normal resistance, this capacitance can form a simple low-pass filter (R-C—resistance/capacitance wired in parallel), which rolls off high frequencies.

source, and a 600 Ω passive output must be connected to a 600 Ω load for proper signal transfer. This is often accomplished via external input and output transformers.

Damping Factor

Damping factor, one of the basic specifications given to describe a power amplifier's performance, represents the amplifier's ability to effectively control the speaker it is driving. Technically, it is the ratio between a loudspeaker's input impedance and the amplifier's output or source impedance. For example, if an amplifier is connected to an 8 Ω speaker and has a damping factor of 500, we can calculate the source impedance to be 8/500 = 0.16 Ω. The higher the damping factor, the better the amplifier will be able to control the speaker cone motion, and the more accurate the resulting sound will be, all other things being equal. In the absence of a high damping factor, a speaker cone will tend to ring out or "overhang," even after the source signal has stopped. Because speakers have a very low load impedance (generally 4 Ω to 8 Ω), an amplifier's internal source impedance must also be made very low. Thanks in large part to transistors, this is a relatively easy task, where impedance can be made to approach or equal zero. However, because a speaker's impedance varies with frequency, the damping factor will also shift. For this reason, a better specification gives a range for damping factor as it relates to frequency, such as damping factor ≥ 500 below 10 kHz. Impedance in audio devices, including amplifiers, tends to rise at higher frequencies, so a drop in damping factor is to be expected.

Instrument Level

A peculiar situation arises with electrical instrument signals from a source such as an electric guitar or bass. While the level (usually somewhere between 100 mV and 1 V) falls within the general definition of "line level," unlike other line level signals it is a high-impedance source signal. The output impedance of a typical electric guitar runs in the order of 15 kΩ. This yields a signal power of $P = V^2/Z = 1/15,000 = 0.000067$ W or 67 μW. This low power source is incapable of driving even a modest load. What's more, because electric guitar pickups are reactive, the output calls for even higher load impedances than otherwise required for proper frequency tracking. A guitar amplifier is built to accommodate this type of signal via its ¼-inch high-Z input(s), and the acoustical output of the amp's speaker cabinet can then be miked as usual for recording or sound reinforcement.

However, sometimes it may be desirable to take the signal directly from the guitar without the amp's contributing sound, to take advantage of a software plug-in like Amp Farm, for instance. If the electric guitar is plugged directly into the line input of a console or mixer (10 kΩ), the impedance mismatch will result in a signal that is not only quite weak but susceptible to poor frequency response. The modest guitar signal with its microwatt-range power output is incapable of driving the load effectively. Furthermore, even modestly long guitar-cable runs are impossible because of the rapidly increased loss of signal, and increased gain requirements in turn mean increased noise. To exacerbate the problem, the guitar cable is unbalanced (discussed later in this chapter) and thus more vulnerable to outside noise and interference.

In this case, the preferred solution is to use a *DI* (direct injection) *box*. The DI box accomplishes several things. First, it presents the guitar output with the high-impedance bridging input that it needs to be properly loaded, on the order of 500 kΩ to 1 MΩ. Next, it transforms the audio signal by stepping down both the voltage and the impedance, which allows the signal to properly address the mic input to the console. Because the mic input presents a bridging load for the low-impedance DI output, the cable run can now be much longer (50 ft. or more) without too much loss of level. Finally, along the way, the DI also converts the signal from an unbalanced to a balanced signal, which is more immune to outside interference signals. The principal means for accomplishing all of this is a *transformer*. To understand how this is done, let's look more closely at how a transformer works.

The transformer has long played—and continues to play—an important role in audio. It is composed of three main elements: two coils or windings of wire called the *primary* and the *secondary*, and a metal core between them composed of plates or rings around which the coils of wire are wound (figure 7.3a). Note how the schematic representation of a transformer reflects this elemental construction (figure 7.3b).

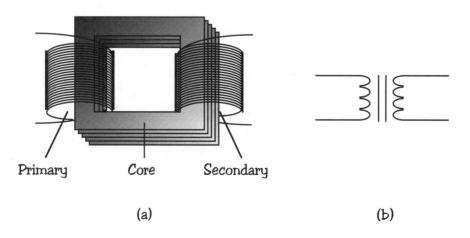

Primary   Core   Secondary

(a)   (b)

Fig. 7.3. *The main elements of a transformer include the primary and secondary windings, separated by a metal core (a). Schematic representation (symbol) for a transformer (b)*

The transformer uses electromagnetic induction to convert the signal in the magnetic realm during the transfer from primary to secondary windings. The signal passing through the primary winding generates an alternating magnetic field proportional the signal's voltage. That magnetic field in turn induces an alternating current in the secondary winding (through *inductive coupling*) without the two windings ever coming into physical contact. This allows for the signal to be changed in a number of ways. First, the voltage of the signal across the secondary will be proportional to the turns ratio between the primary and secondary windings. Thus, if the primary has ten times the number of turns of the secondary (a 10:1 ratio), the voltage across the secondary will also be ten times smaller. Additionally, the impedance of the secondary will be proportional to the *square* of the turns ratio. Therefore, given the same scenario of a 10:1 turns ratio, the impedance at the secondary will be 10^2 or one hundred times smaller than the impedance at the primary. Given a 20:1 turns ratio, the impedance at the secondary would be 400 times smaller, etc.

Let's examine how this works with our electric guitar signal. The typical turns ratio of a DI box transformer is in the neighborhood of 100:1 (100,000:1,000 turns). Let's assume an appropriately high impedance load of 1 MΩ (1,000,000 Ω) at the DI's input (and primary), and an average input voltage from the guitar of 500 mV (1/2 V). The voltage across the secondary would be 500/100 (input voltage divided by turns ratio) = 5 mV (i.e., a mic level signal). The impedance at the secondary would be 1,000,000/10,000 (input impedance divided by the square of the turns ratio) = 1,000,000/10,000 = 100 Ω, a low enough impedance to address the 1.5 to 2 kΩ console mic input. Also, since the signal has passed through a transitory magnetic stage, the signal at the secondary stage can easily be wired for a balanced signal at the output (and subsequent cable run).

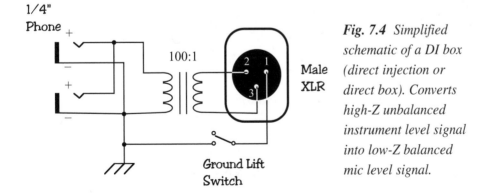

1/4"
Phone

100:1

Male
XLR

Ground Lift
Switch

Fig. 7.4 Simplified schematic of a DI box (direct injection or direct box). Converts high-Z unbalanced instrument level signal into low-Z balanced mic level signal.

Figure 7.4 shows a simplified schematic of a DI box. The input is in the form of an unbalanced ¼-inch phone jack, the output in the form of a 3-pin male XLR jack typical of a low-Z (impedance) microphone output. In addition, there is a second ¼-inch jack that allows for the guitar signal to be simultaneously routed to a guitar amplifier whose output will be picked up via microphone. This type of setup (figure 7.5) is very typical for recording both electric guitar as well as electric bass. The two signals (direct and miked amp) are routed through the console on two separate channels and then recorded either to two separate tracks for proper balancing during mixdown, or combined straightaway and recorded to a single track.

The benefit of this approach is that it takes advantage of the natural warmth and fullness of sound typical of the amp signal, and adds to it the clarity of attack and "edge" typical of DI signals. Possible disadvantages include more complex setup, leakage of the live amp signal into other instruments' microphones, and potential phase differences between the direct and mic signal leading to frequency anomalies when the two signals are combined. Some engineers prefer the simplicity of the DI, especially for electric bass guitar, and automatically record bass through a DI. Others complain of its thinness of sound and lack of character, and insist on recording bass through an amplifier/speaker cabinet (with or without additional DI signal).

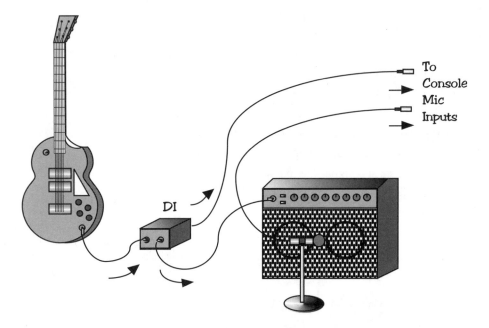

Fig. 7.5. *Using a DI box to record direct and amplified electric guitar simultaneously*

Another use for the DI box is to enable long guitar-cable runs onstage using two DIs (figure 7.6). A short ¼-inch guitar cable is plugged into a first DI. The low-Z balanced mic signal from the DI can now be run a good distance onstage, where it addresses a second DI. The cable connecting the two DIs must be specially wired with a female XLR connector on both ends in order to address both DI mic connections. The second DI now transforms the signal from mic back to instrument level, and can be plugged into the guitar amplifier as usual with another short ¼-inch guitar cable. Of course, going wireless is a nice solution as well.

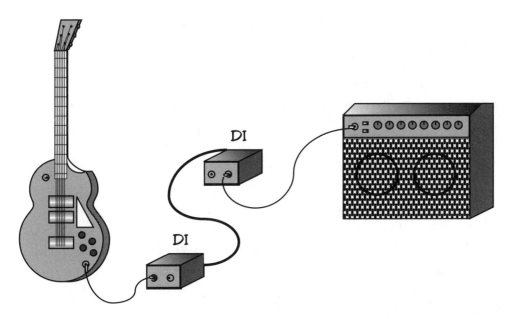

Fig. 7.6. *Using two DI boxes to facilitate a long guitar-cable run onstage*

Balanced vs. Unbalanced Connections

Interconnections between audio devices generally fall under one of two categories: *balanced* or *unbalanced*. The main difference between these, besides price, is that the balanced cable or connection has three separate conductors or signal paths, while the unbalanced has only two. In practical terms, balanced connections are more immune to electromagnetic noise and interference, and are more expensive. Unbalanced connections tend to be significantly less expensive but also more noisy. Let's look at why this is.

You will remember from the discussion about electricity in chapter 6 that all electrical/electronic devices need to have a send and return path for electrons to pass through the device in order for it to work. In the case of electrical connections, there must also be an additional connection or path for any stray current to be lead away safely and disposed of by draining to ground, hence the term *safety ground*. Balanced audio connections also have three paths, the *send* (+) path, the *return* (–) path, and the *signal ground* path. Thus, all balanced audio cables must have three conductors (figure 7.7). There are always two inner conductors that are individually insulated. These are surrounded by a third conductor called the *shield*, which is usually a braided metal. The job of the shield is to prevent external noise sources, particularly *electrostatic* noise resulting from electrical spikes and static around or within the audio system (from motors, lights, etc.), from penetrating the inner conductors and infiltrating the audio signal. Poor shielding and/or grounding can cause such external noise sources to enter the inner audio conductors through *capacitive coupling*. (The shield and an inner conductor or the two inner conductors act as two plates of a capacitor and noise signal is transferred and stored between them.) For this reason, the cable shield is sometimes called the *electrostatic shield*. Signal ground connections are usually made by making contact between the cable shield and the chassis of the device. The *chassis ground* connection is made by connecting the chassis to the *earth ground*, the electrical ground wire feeding the third prong of the AC cord (figure 7.8), as discussed in chapter 6. The shield is connected at both ends to ground, thus any induced currents are quickly drained away and the audio's integrity is protected.

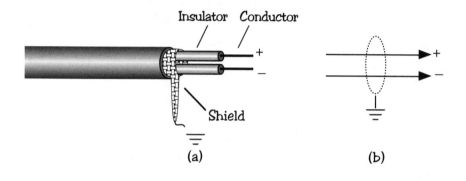

Fig. 7.7. *Dual-conductor audio cable, with two inner conductors and an outer mesh shield (usually balanced) (a). Schematic representation (b)*

In the context of signal flow, it is usually unnecessary to differentiate between these three types of ground connections; in fact, ground connections are often left out entirely. However, in the context of a schematic or electronic discussions in general, it is very useful to know whether we are dealing with signal ground, chassis ground, or earth-ground connections. For this purpose, several different symbols exist and may be used simultaneously (figure 7.9). Of course, the purpose of each of these—to intercept and carry away stray currents, whether for safety or audio integrity—is inherently the same, and the distinction is mainly a physical one. In fact, most often (though not always) a physical connection is made from signal ground to chassis ground and finally to earth ground for disposal, as pictured.

Cables used for balanced connections are called *dual conductor* cables, the shield path being considered separately from the two inner conductors. By contrast, *single conductor* cables used for *unbalanced* connections have only two possible paths: one inner insulated conductor and the shield (figure 7.10). This is done to economize on cost. However, it also means that the shield must pull double duty, acting as both the return path for the signal as well as the shield tied to ground. For this reason, it is easier for electrostatic and other noise to find its way into the audio signal.

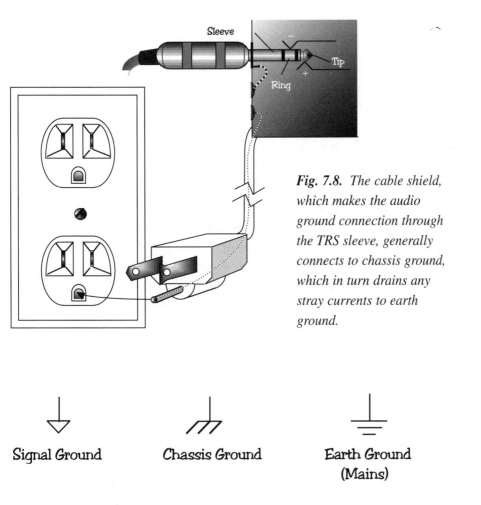

Fig. 7.8. *The cable shield, which makes the audio ground connection through the TRS sleeve, generally connects to chassis ground, which in turn drains any stray currents to earth ground.*

Signal Ground   Chassis Ground   Earth Ground (Mains)

Fig. 7.9. *Schematic symbols that may be used to differentiate between different types of ground connections within a circuit*

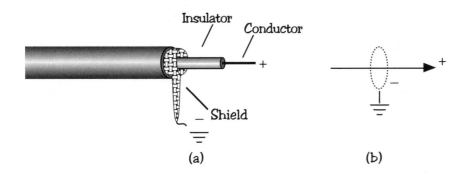

Fig. 7.10. *Single-conductor audio cable, with one inner conductor and an outer mesh shield for signal return path and ground (unbalanced) (a). Schematic representation (b).*

Cables and Interconnects

Audio cables can be terminated with whatever type of plug is needed to connect the devices in question. The most typical jacks used for balanced connections are either *XLR* (*ground-live-return*) plugs—also called *QG* for *quick ground* because pin 1, which connects to ground, makes contact first to eliminate pops and spikes that might result from slight differences in ground potential upon initial device connection—or ¼-inch *TRS (tip-ring-sleeve)* plugs (figure 7.11), also called *GPO* for *general post office* standard plug. These last can be differentiated physically from ¼-inch unbalanced phone plugs (*TS* for *tip-sleeve*) by the presence of an extra ring on the shaft of the plug, signaling the presence of the additional isolated conductor. The ¼-inch plug has largely been replaced in patch bay application by the smaller *Bantam* or *TT* (*tiny telephone*) balanced plug. In addition to the TS phone plug (figure 7.12a), unbalanced connections can also be made via RCA or *phono* (for "phonograph") plugs (figure 7.12b). While these cables resemble *coaxial* cables (termed "coaxial" because one conductor is physically inside the other—hence they share an axis), which are used for high-frequency video signals, they are not. Coaxial cables use a solid (or nearly solid) center conductor rather than multiple thin strands, and always have an internal impedance of 75 Ω to accommodate RF signal transfer. This type of conductor is also used for S/PDIF digital

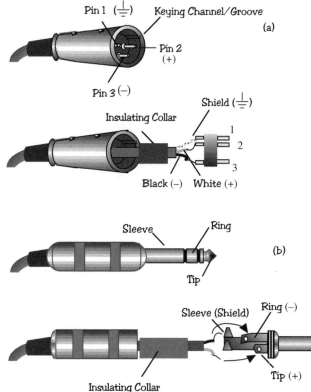

Fig. 7.11. (a) XLR and (b) 1/4-inch TRS plugs and standard wiring. Note that with XLR connectors, pin 1 is always shield/ground, but pin 3 is occasionally wired hot instead of pin 2, particularly in older US-made audio equipment. Check specifications to be sure. Also note the XLR's keying channel—a small notch that ensures proper pin alignment.

connections with RCA plugs, while XLR plugs are used for 110 Ω AES/EBU digital connections.

While RCA and TS connections are physically limited to being unbalanced (with the exception of floating-balanced connections, which have no direct connection to ground), since they have only two possible contact points, technically XLR and TRS plugs and jacks *can* be wired for either balanced or unbalanced operation. While one can generally assume these to be wired for balanced operation in all modern gear, some older gear does employ XLR connections for unbalanced operation. Always check the specifications to be sure. In addition, when making connections between balanced and unbalanced gear, a dual-conductor cable can be used and wired at either end with whatever plug is necessary to make the connection. However, it is always preferable to avoid combining balanced and unbalanced connections (although in practice, this is often difficult).

There is a frequent misconception that the terms *balanced* and *unbalanced* imply a level issue. It happens that consumer and semipro gear often employs unbalanced connections along with a lower operating level, but one does not necessarily follow from the other. As we know, this type of gear makes certain technical concessions in order to offer a more accessible price point. However, it is very possible to encounter gear operating at a +4 dBu pro operating level that employs unbalanced connections, as well as gear operating at –10 dBV semipro levels that

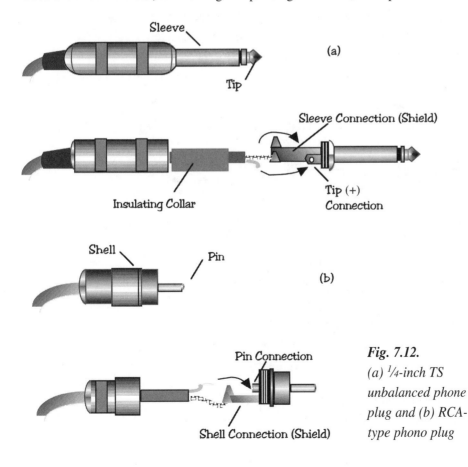

Fig. 7.12.
(a) ¹⁄₄-inch TS unbalanced phone plug and (b) RCA-type phono plug

163

employs balanced connections. Consumer hi-fi type gear almost invariably operates at consumer or (occasionally) semipro level and employs unbalanced connections, most notably RCA or phono plugs.

Active Balanced vs. Transformer Balanced

Despite the three separate paths found in balanced connections, it is possible for noise sources, especially shorter-wavelength high frequencies, to penetrate through the gaps in the shield and find their way to the inner conductors. A foil shield, because it it has no gaps, is more immune to this penetration. However, a foil shield is also less flexible and prone to tearing; therefore, it is less frequently used, except in the most permanent of installations, which are unlikely to be moved much and subjected to stress. *Snakes*, which are multiple mic- or line-level cables grouped in one outer sheath for neater installation, use foil shields to cut down on bulk as well as for their noise-rejecting superiority. For this reason, special care should be taken when handling these cables to avoid tearing the inner shield(s).

Even foil shields, however, are unable to reject *electromagnetic* noise, which enters the cable via *inductive coupling*. Magnetic fields, you will remember, result from coils or inductances. These fields are generated by coils in electric motors, AC power transformers, fluorescent lights, and particularly notorious, *SCR (silicon controlled rectifier)* dimmers, as well as *RFI (radio frequency interference)* from nearby radio stations. Unbalanced circuits are virtually completely at the mercy of such interference, helped only by sheer distance from the noise source. Fortunately, in balanced lines, even if interference penetrates the inner conductors, there is addi-

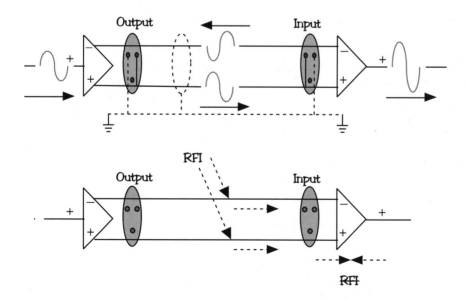

Fig. 7.13. *An active-balanced circuit uses differential amplifiers to protect against and cancel out induced noise and interference.*

tional protection afforded by balanced input circuits beyond any protection afforded by the shield. Balanced inputs can be in the form of either *active-balanced* or *transformer-balanced* circuits.

Active-balanced connections use differential amplifiers that yield the same signal on both conductors at the output but in opposite polarity (one positive, one negative). The signal travels down the cable and at the input the polarity of the negative conductor is reversed again by the differential amplifier (figure 7.13). What this means is that any interference that has been induced in the cable between output and input will be canceled out. This is because the interference will have been induced in equal phase in both conductors. Upon polarity reversal of the negative conductor, the two signals find themselves 180° out of polarity and cancel each other out, while the audio signal is put back in phase and reinforced. Another way to say this is that the differential amplifier only recognizes or passes differential signals, and cancels out common mode signals. In practice, the interference is not perfectly induced in both conductors, and thus, the rejection is not perfect either. To ensure the best cancellation possible, the cable's two inner conductors should be twisted for uniform induction of interference signals.

A *transformer-balanced* input is also called *transformer-isolated* because it physically isolates the circuitry that follows from induced currents in the cable (figure 7.14). The transformer, like the differential amp, yields identical signals of opposite polarity on the two inner conductors. The input transformer only passes differential signals, while common mode signals meet at the center of the transformer, and unless there is a center tap, cancel each other out. The circuit's effectiveness at rejecting interference is measured as *CMRR* (*common mode rejection ratio*), which is the ratio of the strength of interference signal induced to the strength of the interference signal passed by the circuit. For transformer-balanced mic-input circuits, this is generally in the 80 dB range for midrange frequencies. By contrast, active balanced circuits' CMRR are often in the 50 dB range, and under certain conditions, can fall well below this figure.

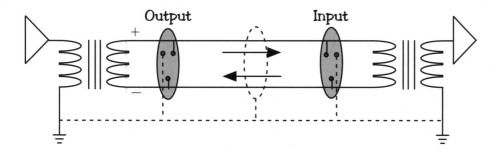

Fig. 7.14. *Transformer-balanced circuits only recognize differential signals and reject common mode signals.*

On the other hand, because of microtechnology, differential amplifiers can be built on *IC* (*integrated circuit*) chips, and even when built discretely, they take up very little space compared to transformers. For this reason, as well as for their general cost-effectiveness, active-balanced inputs and outputs are the most common type(s) of balanced connections found on recording or mixing consoles. Besides, high CMRRs are only really necessary on low-level microphone inputs, where interference is particularly damaging because of the high level of amplification necessary. The more the audio signal needs boosting, the more the interference signal will be boosted along with it. Line-level inputs can easily get by with CMRRs as low as 30 dB at key frequencies, since the interference signal will be relatively low in level by comparison. Additionally, transformers are accused of being prone to distortion from core saturation, particularly at low frequencies. Very good-sounding transformers are commensurately very expensive. That said, good-quality transformers can sound great, in addition to being significantly more immune to interference than differential amplifiers. These are some of the important considerations not just for the design engineer but for the educated musician and recording engineer when selecting audio equipment.

Ground Loops

While the use of balanced connections throughout a system considerably improves the system's immunity to external noise and interference, a poorly configured audio system allows for the possibility of a potential problem known as a *ground loop*. Ground loops arise when there is more than one path to ground within a circuit (figure 7.15). If there is even a slight difference in potential between the two connections to ground, as is often the case between different AC outlets or circuits, current will flow from ground through the shield in a loop. Outside noise interference is also easily picked up by the loop (like an antenna) and can be carried by the AC current. There is often a fair amount of noise current present on an audio device's chassis from the AC connection (see inset) that can be passed on to the cable's shield. As long as the entire system is balanced and individual equipment is internally grounded properly, the loop should not introduce noise into the audio lines. However, if the current is great enough, the resulting magnetic field can induce current in the inner conductors through inductive coupling. Also, if any portion of the system is unbalanced, the ground- and signal-return paths are shared, and the noise will infiltrate the audio line. This leads to the all-too-often-heard sound of AC hum in the audio line, easily identified as a low 60 Hz (or 50 Hz in Europe) drone. This can also happen if the signal path within a balanced piece of equipment is not properly isolated from the chassis ground, allowing for the noise signal to transfer from the ground to the signal path.

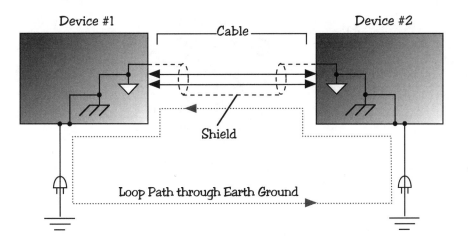

Fig. 7.15. *Ground loop formed between audio ground path through the audio cable's shield and earth (mains) ground path*

In the Studio
Dirty AC

Public AC generators have to provide a huge amount of power to many different destinations in order to power devices ranging from light switches to air conditioning units and refrigerators. Many of these are turned off and on frequently and generate all kinds of electrical spikes down the line. Therefore, most AC power is fairly "dirty" and full of noise besides the pure 60 Hz 120 V sine wave. For this reason, most recording studios and even some home audiophiles set up their own personal generators for a cleaner source of power, and hence a more pristine source for audio.

Taking things to an extreme, legendary mastering engineer Bob Ludwig, when setting up his new studio complex, Gateway Mastering in Portland ME, decided to run the entire facilities off of batteries supplying DC power to all audio equipment. This is the ultimate in clean! In fact, in the early days of electricity, DC was a competing scheme to AC for supplying power. The proponents of DC, including Edison, launched shrewd anti-AC PR campaigns by developing the electric chair to run off of AC, and then calling it "AC—the current that kills." DC was ultimately found to be an impractical and expensive way of providing electricity on a large scale. In your own studio, it is a good idea to keep all non-audio devices on a separate set of circuits, including light switches, dimmers, and especially air conditioners and refrigerators that cause large electrical surges and spikes when they kick in.

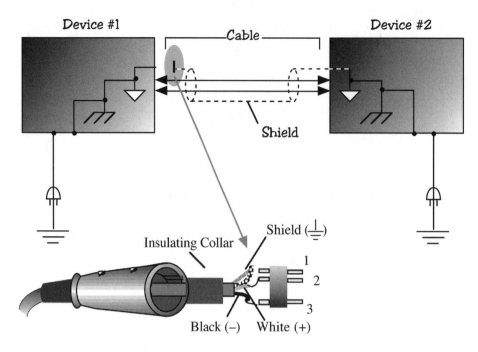

Fig. 7.16. *A ground loop can be eliminated by disconnecting the shield at one end of the cable (called a telescoping shield) connecting two devices together.*

Finding the source of a ground loop is often a tricky and time-consuming process, complicated by the fact that ground loops have the annoying tendency of coming and going without apparent explanation.

When the source of a ground loop has been located, however, a common remedy is to break the loop by disconnecting the shield from the output end of the balanced connection (figure 7.16), thus interrupting the audio-ground portion of the loop. While now unbalanced at one end, a connection configured in this way retains virtually all of the noise rejection capability of a fully balanced connection (the balanced input is what rejects most of the noise). A shield connected at one end only is called a *telescoping shield*. The ground lift switch on a DI and some other equipment serves the same purpose. The shield connection should only be broken in a balanced connection, since an unbalanced connection relies on the shield to carry the audio-return signal. Break this path, and you have broken the audio path itself. Never disconnect the chassis or safety ground, as this can lead to a hazardous condition as previously discussed.

A common solution to ground loops in professional studio installations is what is known as a *single-point ground* or *star-ground* setup (figure 7.17). In this case, one central device, usually the console, provides the main connection from signal ground to earth ground, and all other devices' signal grounds are tied to the console via dedicated ground wire(s) running from the equipment racks or power strips. (This wire is bundled closely with the audio lines to avoid the loop antenna effect.)

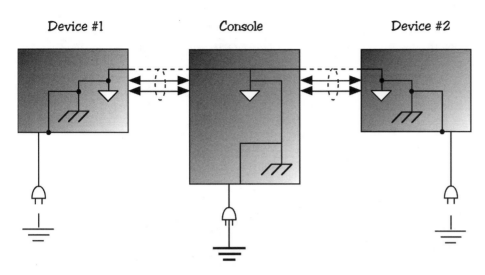

Fig. 7.17. *A star-ground or single-point ground setup typical of professional studio installations. Signal ground connects to earth ground at a single point, effectively eliminating the possibility of ground loops between earth and audio grounds.*

Because the direct connection from chassis ground to earth ground is lifted on each rack, the dedicated ground wire provides the safety ground through the console for all equipment in the rack(s) and therefore *must* be secure. As discussed in the last chapter, the presence of proper safety/earth ground connection throughout the studio is extremely important for safety reasons. Therefore, it is critical to have a professional oversee this type of installation. At the same time, this setup also ensures that there is only one physical connection to ground and therefore no possibility for the development of ground loops. A variation on this setup is to treat each equipment rack as an audio subset with a single-point connection between audio and earth grounds. Ground loops between racks can be prevented by using input isolation transformers between all racks and console inputs. This type of input is called *floating* or *floating-balanced* because the transformer completely isolates the signal ground from the earth ground (figure 7.18) by inserting a magnetic rather than purely electrical stage.

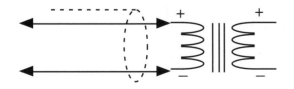

Fig. 7.18. *A floating transformer-balanced input*

This type of studio setup is usually not possible in live sound reinforcement installations, because of the larger distances involved between the main house mixing board and onstage amplifiers and other equipment, and the temporary and mobile nature of many installations. Beyond the nuisance of ground loops, a potentially hazardous situation arises in live installations from unreliable AC wiring as well as notoriously unreliable guitar amplifiers. If a performer's electric guitar is hot (+) because of a fault in the guitar amp, and that performer also touches a microphone whose chassis is grounded through the console (as is the case with virtually all microphones), AC current *will flow through the performer*, who has become the live guitar's path to ground. While it is a dramatic stage effect to have the lead singer/guitarist blown off the stage and land in the audience still smoking from the shock, frequent lead-singer replacements will put a strain on any band's longevity.

The presence of unwanted current can be due to a number of factors. Perhaps the amp's chassis has become connected to the AC neutral instead of ground (through a loose wire or design flaw) and the amp's AC plug has been inserted backwards, reversing the hot and neutral legs; or perhaps the AC supply system itself is wired backwards. Even without faulty wiring, the outlets at the console end of the room may have a very different ground potential than the outlets on the stage side of the room if there does not exist a direct electrical connection between them. Difference in potential means voltage, and voltage in a completed circuit means current. While this last type of situation generally yields a smaller non-lethal current, it can still result in an annoying shock for the performer. The best protection from this kind of scenario is to use an AC power isolation transformer on all AC feeds to onstage guitar and bass amplifiers. It is also a good idea to carry a simple plug-in outlet tester to ensure proper wiring of outlets before plugging in amplifiers.

Ground Loops in Unbalanced Gear

It is also possible to encounter ground loops in an unbalanced connection using single-conductor cables. Since the shield *must* be connected at both ends—it is not only acting as the ground connection but also as the signal-return connection—the two separate connections to ground can result in a ground loop between the two devices (figure 7.19). The only remedy in this case is to source the two AC connections from the same outlet, and to keep the two audio cables (if applicable) as short and as closely bundled together as possible. A large physical loop can act as a loop antenna and attract external noise into the loop with greater efficiency. Ground loops can also arise inside of an improperly designed piece of audio equipment. Again, there is no remedy short of having the device internally rewired.

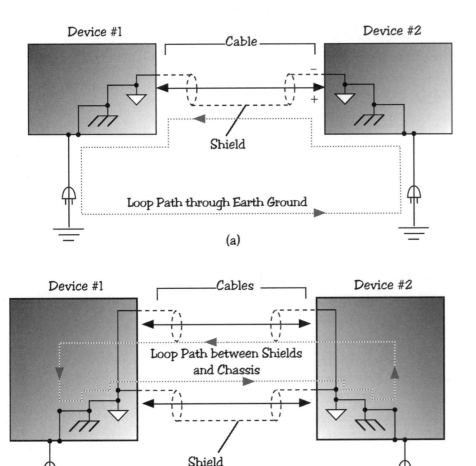

Fig. 7.19. *Ground loops in an unbalanced system can develop between a cable's shield connections to earth ground (a) or between the shields of two cables and chassis ground (b)*

System Noise Prevention

If a single-point ground setup is not possible or practical, there are some preventative measures that can be taken to reduce the infiltration of noise in a sound system. First, ensure that all gear is sourced from one set of outlets on the same circuit. Particularly avoid using outlets that are separated by a large distance (most likely tied to different circuits). This ensures that all devices will be referenced to the same ground potential, thus reducing the possibility of ground current that might otherwise result from a slight difference in ground potential. While all outlets are theoretically operating at the same voltage as well as ground potential, in practice, slight (and sometimes not so slight) differences are almost a given. The caveat to this solution is that the outlet(s) used must be capable of supplying the necessary current drawn by all devices. This usually requires dedicated higher amperage wiring for a studio installation. Home installations require special care in this regard, as most home wiring is not designed for very heavy loads. At best, over-taxing the system will cause a circuit breaker to trip; at worst the high current load can result in overheating and potential fire hazard, particularly with older wiring using paper insulation.

Use balanced lines and circuits whenever possible, and employ a telescoping shield wherever necessary. Rack-mount all outboard equipment using metal mounting rails. This ties all of the equipment chassis together to form a common shield against electrostatic fields. It also helps keep cables short, which helps reduce noise pickup. Avoid grouping line-level cables with mic-level cables especially over long runs, as this can lead to interference through *crosstalk*, and in extreme cases, feedback. Keep loudspeaker cables away from other audio lines, and keep AC power lines as far away as practical from all audio lines. Grouping same-level cabling (i.e., mic with mic and line with line), however, is quite beneficial in cutting down on ground loops and external noise pickup. Wherever mic, line, and AC cables must come into contact, try to keep them at 90° angles to minimize inter-action. Keep noise sources, such as motors in non-audio devices, or lighting dimmers, as far from the audio system as possible and connected to a different supply source, or at least a different leg of the power supply source. Dimmers may also be isolated using power transformers.

Choose high-quality cables with adequate shielding, and avoid overly flexing them, particularly snake cables with foil shields. Keep all power transformers and power amplifiers away from all other cabling and audio equipment, as these emit strong magnetic fields. In urban areas with very strong RF emissions from nearby radio stations, it is sometimes necessary to surround the entire sound system or studio with what is known as a *Faraday cage*. As with the shield, the purpose of the Faraday cage is to intercept all outside interference noise before it reaches any part of the sound system and drain it to ground. This solution is only implemented in extreme cases, as it is rather involved and extremely costly.

Proper gain staging and level (and impedance) matching, of course, is critical in making the most of the available dynamic range of the system. Avoiding unnec-essary or inefficient gain boosts can help minimize noise inherent in the system itself.

Tracking Down Noise

When trying to identify the source of noise in a system, logic and common sense go a long way. Sometimes verbalizing the troubleshooting thought process in the form of a logic flow (figure 7.20) can help, in the same way that a signal flow, once drawn out, can help crystallize one's understanding of the sound system—be it a console or the entire studio setup—especially as the system gets increasingly complex. In general, start as far as possible downstream (speakers, then amplifiers, then console, etc.). If the connection to a piece is removed and the noise persists, it must be originating further upstream in the studio signal flow. Also try to identify the *type* or *quality* of noise present. This can help to narrow in on the culprit(s). Distortion or hiss (amplified thermal noise) are usually the result of poor gain staging and level matching. Intermittent noise or crackling is usually the result of a faulty connection (cable or jack) or a dirty pot. Hum and buzz are usually the result of a ground loop, or of inductive coupling from a source such as a power amplifier's power transformer (or the power transformer in another piece of audio equipment) or from lighting dimmers.

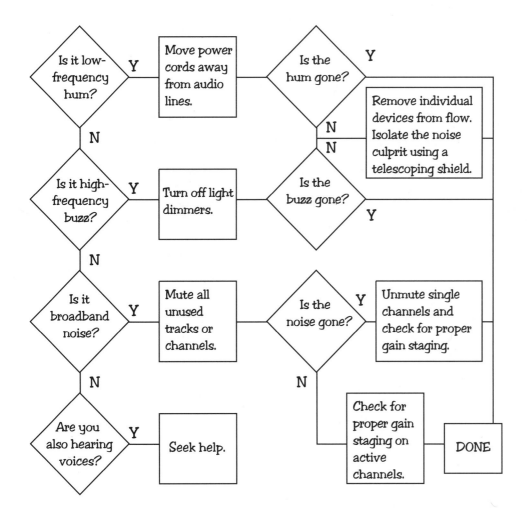

Fig. 7.20. *A troubleshooting logic flowchart using questions (diamonds) and actions (squares)*

Levels between Balanced and Unbalanced Gear

A professional line level of 0 VU corresponds to +4 dBm or 1.228 V$_{rms}$. As our signal passes through the console, and is patched through various pieces of outboard gear and recorders, the ideal is for it to remain within this average level range for best gain-staging and level maximization, taking into account the noise floor and point of distortion through each gain stage. Within analog multitrack and 2-track tape recorders, the level is boosted and regulated via transformers and amps to achieve a strong enough magnetic field for recording to tape, but the inputs and outputs are line level. Most other signal processing will occur at line level.

As we have seen, some outboard gear may be operating at a semipro level of −10 dBV. This means that an input signal coming from the console will have to be reduced so as not to distort in the device, and the output signal will have to be boosted back up to be within the same level range as other pro line-level signals. The result? A slight increase in noise added to the signal, resulting from the semipro device (figure 7.21).

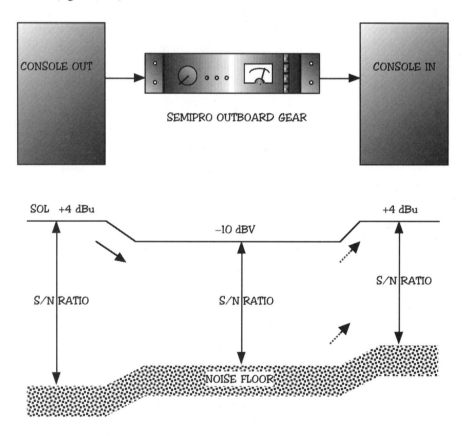

Figure 7.21. *Inserting semipro gear into the flow reduces available dynamic range by bringing the noise floor up. Semipro gear not only has a lower SOL (standard operating level) but tends to be inherently noisier as well (higher noise floor).*

Other devices, such as CD players, may also be operating at –10 dBV or an even lower –10 dBu consumer level. Again, if these signals are fed through the console, their output signal level will have to be boosted to match the level of other signals being monitored. There do exist interface boxes that facilitate the connection between semipro and pro gear in particular while optimizing level and impedance matching. However, while these are extremely handy, they will not magically correct for the fact that using semi-pro or consumer gear will generally mean a slightly (at best) more noisy operating system. Also, remember that unbalanced connections will also increase the probability of outside noise interference being added to the signal.

Cabling between Balanced and Unbalanced Gear

As previously mentioned, sometimes it is necessary to interface balanced with unbalanced gear. When connecting such gear directly, it is advisable to use a cable (easily modified) that facilitates the connection. In general, when unbalancing one side of a dual-conductor shielded cable, disconnect the shield on unbalanced outputs, but keep the shield connected on unbalanced inputs. If the plug being used for the input has only two contact points (e.g., TS), simply connect both the low side (–) and the shield to the same contact point (sleeve connection). Of course, on the balanced side, the shield should always remain connected, with the possible exception of a floating (untied to ground) transformer-balanced connection. And remember to properly label any modified cables for easy identification and proper implementation.

Another very common scenario typically found in semipro consoles is the use of a single output jack to serve both as a send and a return path for connection to an outboard (external) signal-processing device. This requires the use of a Y-cable with a TRS plug on one end splitting into two TS plugs on the other (figure 7.22). The TRS is wired unbalanced with the tip conductor wired to the send (effects device input) plug and the ring conductor wired to the return (effects device output) plug. Both paths share the same return and ground path via the shield.

Headphones also use a TRS connection in unbalanced configuration, using the two inner conductors for left and right channels respectively (figure 7.23). The shield is shared between the two paths for the return of signal and connection to ground. The headphones must be fed from a headphone amp to drive the speakers with power in the range of 100 mW.

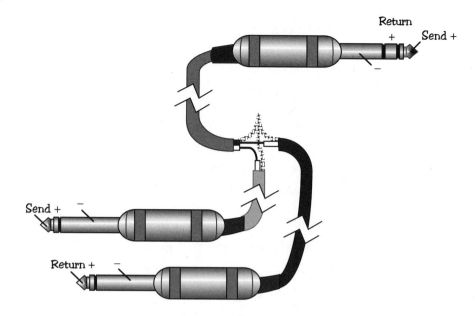

Fig. 7.22. *An insert Y-cable using a single TRS plug and jack for both effects send and return. Red usually means send.*

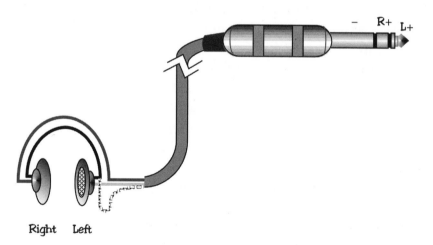

Fig. 7.23. *Headphones employ a TRS-terminated dual-conductor cable in unbalanced stereo configuration. The inner conductors carry the left and right signal respectively.*

Speaker Cables

Speaker cables are different from the single- and dual-conductor cables discussed so far in that they are unshielded. They carry two internal insulated conductors, one for the send (+) and one for the return (−) signal, but no shield (figure 7.24). Because of the higher power involved in driving speakers (potentially hundreds of watts rather than milliwatts), and due to the fact that the signal is not amplified

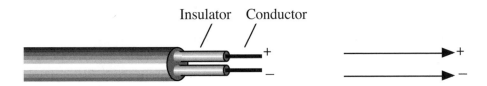

Fig. 7.24. *Speaker cables have just two inner conductors and no shield.*

further on in the audio signal chain, outside interference is not much of an issue and the shield is unnecessary. Furthermore, the presence of a shield can actually be detrimental to speaker performance, adding capacitance to the cable (not to mention cost). For this reason, it is important to use cables designated as speaker cables (electrical 18-gauge lamp or "zip" cord can work fine as well, as long as short lengths are used and signal power is not too high) and avoid using regular single- or dual-conductor shielded audio cables for this purpose.

The main consideration here is that the cable be of a large enough gauge to handle the high current drawn from the amp by the low impedance speaker. Wire thicknesses are accorded gauges according to the American Wire Gauge (AWG) standard; the lower the gauge number, the thicker the wire—so 12-gauge is thicker than 18-gauge. You may remember from Ohm's Law that doubling the thickness of a conductor reduces the resistance to one-quarter its former value, while doubling the length of a conductor doubles its resistance. The greater the resistance of the cable, the more power will be lost or dissipated in the transfer. The general idea, then, is to keep speaker cables as short as practical (under 15 feet, if possible) and relatively heavy-gauge. Whatever the length, equal cable lengths between channels is also important to help ensure proper phase alignment between channels. That said, the current over-marketing of specialty *hi-fi* (high-fidelity) or *audiophile*[16] speaker cable at astronomical prices should probably be viewed by most audio enthusiasts with some skepticism. The chart below (table 7.1) showing signal loss as a function of speaker impedance over 100 feet distance should put things into some perspective. Other than for live sound applications, most cable runs that we deal with in the studio are much shorter, and as long as reasonably thick and sturdy quality cable is used, signal loss is negligible. Of course, overall signal

16. An *audiophile* is any music enthusiast who appreciates and seeks out high-quality audio reproduction. The term *hi-fi*, most popular in the '70s and '80s, is generally used to refer to any home component stereo system. Ironically, most of these systems are anything but high-fidelity, often displaying uncontrolled bass response and lack of detail or imaging. While these have largely been supplanted by surround home-theater installations or computer setups with modest playback capabilities via small computer speakers, the term is still in use. *Audiophile* on the other hand, implies both home system and high quality. Of late, there has been more overlap between audiophile and professional studio equipment. The main difference in design criteria is that pro equipment must be able to sustain long periods of high-intensity work, and dare we say, abuse. It is therefore generally built more ruggedly for such sustained usage.

loss is not the only measure of a good cable. Poor quality cables can have a dramatic impact on audio fidelity, including poor frequency response, phase distortion, noise, even intermittent dropouts. In this respect, the quality of the connection is as important, if not more important, than the wire itself.

You will also notice from the chart that, as expected, increased load impedance results in proportionally lower loss of signal in the transfer itself, although it also draws less current (and power) to begin with.

Wire Gauge	Speaker Impedance		
	4Ω	8Ω	16Ω
#10	0.44 dB	0.22 dB	0.11 dB
#12	0.69 dB	0.35 dB	0.18 dB
#14	1.07 dB	0.55 dB	0.28 dB
#16	1.65 dB	0.86 dB	0.44 dB
#18	2.49 dB	1.33 dB	0.69 dB

Table 7.1. *Loss of signal power as a function of speaker gauge (and load impedance) over a 100-foot length of speaker cable*

Cable Impedances

There are specific audio functions and signal types that require specific cable impedances for clean and frequency-accurate transfer. Because of the very high-frequency content of video signals (in the megahertz, or MHz, range), 75 Ω coaxial cables must be used to ensure good high-frequency response and eliminate signal bounce-back and image smearing. This phenomenon tends to happen when electrical wavelengths approach cable length, as is the case with very high-frequency signals such as video or digital audio. These cables are generally terminated with *BNC* (*Bayonet Neill Concelman*, the push-and-turn type) connectors. Digital S/PDIF (Sony/Phillips Digital Interface Format) audio connections also use 75 Ω coaxial cables, typically with RCA (phono) connectors, for the same reason. Digital AES/EBU (Audio Engineering Society/European Broadcast Union) type signals should ideally be transferred via 110 Ω cables, which are typically terminated with XLR-type connectors (although one may encounter other types of connectors being implemented). Microphone cables are sometimes used erroneously because they are terminated with XLR-type connectors. This is not advised, as the incorrect impedance can contribute to blurring of the signal, called digital *jitter*. Refer to table 7.2 below for typical cable impedances and connectors. Most general-use cables vary greatly in impedance, according to length, gauge, and type of conductor used.

Signal Type	Cable Z	Typical Connector
Mic	30–90 Ω	XLR
Line (patch bay)	Varies	TT (TRS)
Guitar	Varies	¼-inch TS
Speaker (10 m)	>0.5 Ω	Bare wire, ¼-inch TS
Video	75.0 Ω	BNC, RCA (coax.)
Word clock	75.0 Ω	BNC (or embedded)
AES/EBU	110.0 Ω	XLR
S/PDIF	75.0 Ω	RCA (coax.)

Table 7.2. *Typical cable uses, impedances, and connector types*

PROJECTS

1. Review the cabling in your studio setup. Are like kinds of wires bundled together? Are power cables kept away from audio cables, or crossing in perpendicular fashion? Look for other opportunities to minimize noise in your setup. Neat and organized cabling will go a long way.

2. Take note of what balanced or unbalanced equipment is included in your setup. What is the operating level of each device? What is the output and input impedance? How do you interface unbalanced with balanced gear, with respect to both signal levels and cabling?

3. Review all of the digital audio connections in your setup. Are you using proper digital cabling?

The unit that we use most often to describe sound and signal levels is the *decibel*. You cannot spend more than ten minutes in any recording situation without someone referring to "dB" in one way or another, whether about recording levels, EQ adjustments, mic choices, or simply loudness in the studio or control room. Unfortunately, it is often poorly understood and consequently frequently misused. The more we understand about the decibel, the better chance we have of understanding and getting the most out of our sound recording equipment.

Origins

The decibel is used to describe gains and losses in signal power within an audio system, and the earliest of these was the telephone system. In the early days of telephony, gains and losses were not measured in dB but rather in *miles of standard cable* (*MSC*). The greater the distance in cabling, the greater the loss in signal power due to cable resistance. Measuring signal loss in this manner enabled the phone company to predict where booster amps were needed to bring the signal back up to acceptable levels. In 1929, in honor of Alexander Graham Bell (1847–1922), inventor of the telephone, and to recognize the work of the Bell Telephone Company, the *bel* and more precisely the *decibel* (1/10 bel) was adopted as the preferred unit for measuring changes in signal power.

Logarithms

Because the decibel is a logarithmic unit, to understand the decibel, we must first understand logarithms. A *logarithm*, or *log* for short, is the power—or *exponent*—to which we raise a certain number—or *base*. When we describe a change or progression as being "logarithmic," we mean that instead of progressing in a linear fashion, as in 1–2–3..., it progresses exponentially, for example 10–100–1000.... We could also express this particular progression as $(10)^1$–$(10)^2$–$(10)^3$. Notice that the base for each number stays the same—10—while the power, or exponent, changes. Expressing numbers using exponents allows us represent very large numbers or changes more easily. The same is true of logarithms.

Perhaps the most common logarithm, called—appropriately enough—a *common log*, uses 10 as the base, as in the example above. For instance, we could take the number 100, which equals (10)(10) or 10^2, and say that:

$$10^2 = 100 \text{ therefore } \log_{10}100 = 2$$

(or "the log, base 10, of 100 equals 2")

Notice that the $\log_{10}$ of the number 100 is the power to which the base (10) must be raised to equal 100, hence 2. Thus:

$$\log_{10}1000 = 3 \text{ because } 1000 = 10^3; \text{ and}$$
$$\log_{10}1 = 0 \text{ because } 1 = 10^0.$$

In this way, a very large change, such as from 1 to 10,000,000, becomes a relatively manageable change, from 0 to 7 on a logarithmic scale [from $\log_{10}(10)^0$ to $\log_{10}(10)^7$]. Such are the changes in signal or sound power that we are exposed to in music and audio, and this is, in fact, exactly how our hearing responds to these changes in level. An exponential change in power is perceived as a linear change in loudness. For this reason, the decibel is such a useful unit for describing levels.

We can express the concept of the logarithm more generally as follows:

If B is the base and P is the power to which we raise the base, then for a given number N:

$$\log_{B}N = P \text{ simply means that } B^P = N$$

In other words, $\log_{10} 100 = 2$ because $(10)^2 = 100$, where 10 is the base (B), 2 is the exponent or power (P) and 100 is the number (N) that results from B^P. It bears repeating that the "log" *is* the exponent. Alternatively, if $5^2 = 25$, then we can say that $\log_5 25 = 2$ where 5 is now the base. We could choose any number as the base for a logarithm. However, when dealing with sound, the base is always 10 since the decibel is, by definition, a base-10 logarithm. In fact, if you see a log expressed without a base, such as "log 100," you can assume the base to be 10 and the log to be a *common* log (table 8.1).

log 1	→	log 10^0	→	0
log 10	→	log 10^1	→	1
log 100	→	log 10^2	→	2
log 1,000	→	log 10^3	→	3
log 10,000	→	log 10^4	→	4
log 1,000,000,000,000	→	log 10^{12}	→	12

Table 8.1. *Common logs (base 10) from one to one trillion. This range approximates the range of our hearing with respect to power, from softest to loudest.*

Of course, there are many numbers that fall in between perfect powers of 10. Between $\log_{10} 1 = 0$ and $\log_{10} 10 = 1$ there is, for instance, $\log_{10} 2 = 0.301$ (rounded to the nearest thousandth). This means that you must raise 10 to the power of 0.301 to equal 2, or $10^{0.301} = 2$. To calculate logs such as these, we may simply rely on a scientific calculator to perform the logarithm by inputting the number and pressing the log function key. Table 8.2 lists some useful logarithms to know.

log 100.0	=	2.0
log 10.0	=	1.0
log 8.0	=	0.9
log 5.0	=	0.7
log 3.0	=	0.5
log 2.0	=	0.3
log 1.0	=	0.0
log 0.1	=	–1.0

Table 8.2. *Some useful common logs (rounded to the nearest tenth)*

Power and Intensity

So exactly how do logarithms relate to sound? If a guitar string is plucked, it will vibrate at a certain frequency and amplitude, and cause the air around it to vibrate similarly. As we saw in chapter 5, this vibration sets up regions of alternating compressions and rarefactions. If the guitar is plucked with greater force, it will vibrate at the same frequency but with greater amplitude, setting up regions where the air is more compressed and others where it is more rarefied. Ultimately, the vibrations will be picked up by our eardrums, and the greater amplitude will generate what we would call a "louder" sound.

It is important to make the distinction here between *loudness*, which is a subjective perception of the strength of a signal, and *intensity* or *power*, which are directly measurable entities. Specifically, *power* is a measure of the amount of energy generated or dissipated per unit of time, measured in *joules per second* (equation 8.1).

$$W = E/T$$

where W = power, E = energy (in joules), and T = time (in seconds)

Eq. 8.1. *To express or calculate power as a function of energy spent over time*

Power is usually given in *watts*, where one watt is equal to one joule per second. Thus a 50 W amp running at full power would use 50 J of energy per second.

$$1 \text{ W} = 1 \text{ J/s}$$

We can think of power as the amount of work that is being done by something. Since power is energy exerted over time, sound must have energy in order to generate power. That energy comes from the initial vibration that pushes and pulls on air particles. We could say that during a compression, the energy is temporarily stored, and then exerted on the next volume of air as it moves outwards. The greater the amplitude of vibration, the more compressed the air is, the more energy stored and then exerted, and therefore, the greater the power.

Intensity is a measure of the amount of energy passing through a specific *area* in one second, i.e., the amount of sound power spread over a given area, in *watts/m^2* (equation 8.2).

$$I = W/S$$

where I = intensity, W = power (in watts) and S = surface area (in m^2)

Eq. 8.2. *To express or calculate intensity*

In other words, while power refers to the energy inherent in a source, intensity is a measure of how that power is spread in the space around it. To get a better sense of the difference between power and intensity of sound, we can use the analogy of light. For instance, we use power, in watts, to refer to things like light bulbs. We know intuitively that a 75 W bulb will inherently produce less light (power) than a 100 W bulb.[17] We also now know that it will use less energy than the 100 W bulb, specifically 25 J per second less. This is a characteristic of the source itself and is linked to brightness in some way.

17. It is interesting to note that the power of sound in general is very small when compared to the power of common light sources. For instance, a very weak light source such as a night-light carries a power of ¼ W, or 250 mW (1000 mW = 1 W). By comparison, an average speaking voice only generates an acoustical sound power of about one microwatt (1 µw = 1/1,000,000 of a watt), while a very soft sound, such as a pin-drop, generates only a fraction of a microwatt. The loudest sounds that we are generally exposed to rarely exceed 1 W of acoustical sound power.

However, the brightness produced by each bulb is dependent not just on its power but also on its surroundings, such as the size of the room, the lightness of the paint on the walls, as well as the distance from which the brightness of the light source is being judged or measured. In this case, brightness is akin to intensity. By measuring the amount of power acting on a particular area, we can get a much better sense of how effective that power is in the particular space where it exists. Given our vibrating guitar string as a source, then, it will have a certain amount of inherent power; but its intensity will depend greatly on how far away we are standing from the source (and, if indoors, to a certain extent how reverberant the space is, as well).

Threshold of Pain	1	W/m^2
Rock Concert	10^{-1}	W/m^2
Average Conversation (1 m.)	10^{-6}	W/m^2
Pin-Drop	10^{-11}	W/m^2
Threshold of Audibility	10^{-12}	W/m^2 (0.000000000001 W/m^2)

Table 8.3. *Typical sound intensities within our range of hearing*

The typical range of intensities within our hearing is given in table 8.3. The threshold of pain, sometimes also called the *threshold of feeling*, is that intensity at which we begin to *feel* more than *hear* the sound, and where sustained exposure is sure to yield some permanent hearing loss. The *threshold of audibility*, also called the *threshold of hearing*, represents the softest sound that we could hear under the best of circumstances—perhaps in an anechoic chamber. It is outside of most people's experience.

Having made the distinction here between intensity and power, from this point on, we will use the two somewhat interchangeably. In the context of the recording studio, we are mostly manipulating signals in the electrical realm, where intensity takes a backseat to power. The signal is well-controlled and confined (hopefully!) while traveling down wires, and therefore we are not dealing with power over area (intensity), but just power. Intensity is mainly of interest in the acoustical realm where sound power spreads out through space in a relatively non-confined manner. In that particular context, intensity is generally more revealing than power.

Loudness

So, given our two guitar notes, the one with the greater amplitude will have more inherent power, exert more energy, and ultimately sound louder to us. But how is loudness different than power?

Because our hearing is logarithmic in nature, our ear is capable of responding to a staggering range of intensities, from infinitesimal to very large. If we were to compare our hearing scale to a weight scale, it would be akin to having a scale capable of accurately weighing anything from a feather to a thirty-story building. As we have seen, the difference between the softest and loudest sounds that we can hear—from the *threshold of audibility* to the *threshold of pain*—is on the order of one-trillion-to-one, or a range of 10^{12}.

By comparison, our eyes can generally only handle a range of about 10^3 from brightest to darkest in any given moment. (In fairness, the eye does adapt or recalibrate itself to different levels of brightness, so that dark objects at first unnoticeable become visible with extended exposure to a dark surrounding—at which point, of course, an otherwise moderate amount of light becomes blindingly bright.) Exposing the eye to a greater intensity could cause permanent damage, such as looking straight at the sun, or directly at the laser of an optical device, such as a CD or DVD player. (This is not to say that repeated or prolonged exposure to high sound intensities, such as those found at rock concerts or dance clubs, does not also induce permanent damage to hearing.)

Within this wide range of powers, our ear does not respond equally to equal changes in power but rather to equal *ratios* of powers. For instance, there is a 10 W difference from 10 W to 20 W, and again from 20 W to 30 W. However, the first level change, from 10 W to 20 W, will sound greater to us. We would need a change from 20 W to 40 W for the change to sound as great, and again from 40 W to 80 W, and so on. These changes would all sound like equal increments or changes of loudness because they each represent doublings of power—a ratio of 2 to 1.[18]

Similarly, it takes a tenfold change in power, or a power ratio of 10 to 1, to yield the impression of a sound being "twice as loud." Thus a 10 W sound would be perceived as being roughly twice as loud as a similar 1 W sound. But that same sound would need to be boosted to 100 W to sound twice as loud again.

18. To confuse matters considerably, the subjective impression of loudness is very dependent on the *frequency* in question, as well as the general level at which we are making loudness comparisons. As we shall see in chapter 10, our ears do not hear equally well at all frequencies at all levels. We will try to explore some of the approaches that have been taken to try to quantify loudness in an attempt to make it a somewhat less subjective entity.

Bels and Decibels

When we discuss a change in power, then, it is useful to express that change as a ratio on a logarithmic scale to better represent our *perception* of that level change. It is also convenient to avoid having to describe changes in power or intensity on the order of millions or millionths. Again, the unit for a ratio of powers was named the *bel*. In mathematical terms we could say that:

$$\text{Change of Power (in bels)} = \log_{10}(W_1/W_0)$$

where W_0 represents the power we start off with, or reference power, and W_1 represents the power that we end up with or that we are comparing to the reference. Thus, any tenfold change in power, from 1 to 10, or 10 to 100, would be expressed as $\log_{10}(^{10}/_1) = 1$ bel, since $\log_{10}10 = 1$. If we do the same with the range of our hearing from softest to loudest, we get $\log_{10}(^{10^{12}}/_1) = 12$ bels. On a logarithmic scale, then, the entire range of our hearing could be scaled to twelve steps, from one to twelve bels.

However, our hearing is also very sensitive, such that we can detect much smaller changes than one bel, which generally corresponds to a perceived doubling in loudness. Since the bel represents too coarse a scale, the *decibel* was agreed upon as the unit of choice when discussing levels. As its name implies, the decibel, or dB for short, represents one-tenth of one bel. Because it takes ten decibels to make one bel, our power formula now becomes equation 8.3.

$$\Delta \text{ Power (in dB)} = 10 \log_{10}(W_1/W_0)$$

where Δ means change, W_1 = new power, and W_0 = initial or reference power

Eq. 8.3. *Power formula to calculate or express a change in power, in decibels*

Our tenfold change in power becomes:

$$10 \log(^{10}/_1) = 10 \text{ dB}$$

and the dynamic range of our hearing, from softest to loudest sound, becomes:

$$10 \log(^{10^{12}}/_1) = 120 \text{ dB}$$

It is important to note here that, in a practical sense, this power formula (as well as other formulae presented here) is probably not going to be called upon or used in the heat of a recording session. However, it is very useful in helping us gain a solid understanding of how voltage or power changes, in watts or volts, relate to how we experience changes in perceived signal loudness. Once we learn to relate decibels to perceived loudness, then changes in wattage, for instance, become more meaningful. Once again, foundational understanding is the key to proper system setup and operation.

Note that we can also have negative dB, which would simply connotate a *decrease* in power. For example, if we were to halve the power we would get:

$$10 \log(\tfrac{1}{2}) = -3 \text{ dB}$$

A result of 0 dB does not mean that there is no sound, but rather that there has been no *change* in power or level.

Once we know that a doubling of power yields a 3 dB increase, and that a ten-fold change in power corresponds to a 10 dB change, we can quickly arrive at a number of similar correlations. For instance, "5 × power" is half as great as "10 × power." We know that 10 × power yields a 10 dB change, and that half the power yields –3 dB; therefore "5 × power" ⇒ 10 dB – 3 dB = 7 dB. What about "50 × power?" Well, 100 × power = 10 × 10 × power; for each tenfold change we add 10 dB, which here yields 10 dB + 10 dB = 20 dB; and "50 × power" is half of "100 × power," so we subtract 3 dB, which yields: 20 dB – 3 dB = 17 dB change. Keep in mind that these are all power ratios (50:1 or 100:1) and that *dB* always implies a *ratio* of powers. As we have seen, it is more useful to express changes in power as ratios rather than as absolute differences in power because our *ear* responds this way. Being able to make these quick translations from differences in power to differences in dB allows us to have a better sense of how equipment's technical specifications, such as amp power ratings, translate into audible reality, such as loudness.

For instance, let's say we are comparing two power amps identical in every respect save power rating: a 300 W amp and a 75 W amp. Assuming both amps are running at maximum output power, the difference in output signal power is 4 to 1. The resulting difference in dB, then, is 4 × power = 2 × 2 × power = +3 dB + 3 dB (add 3 dB per doubling of power) = 6 dB greater output power from the 300 W amp. Is this significant? A 6 dB change in level is fairly noticeable, although perhaps less than one might expect from such a large difference in power (not even twice as loud).

Of course, often the power ratio is not quite so easy to categorize. For instance, our two power amps from the example above might instead be rated at 160 W and 50 W respectively. This gives us a power ratio of 3.2 to 1. How, then, would we express the difference in output power between them in dB? We could simply plug that ratio into our power equation, and let our calculator do the rest:

$$\Delta \text{ Power} = 10 \log(\tfrac{3.2}{1}) = 5 \text{ dB}$$

Figure 8.1 summarizes the relationship between a change in power and the corresponding level change in decibels. It is important to emphasize that dB always implies level resulting from a power ratio. Note the need for a logarithmic scale to graph power change opposite a linear change in decibel level. Again, this is very consistent with our ear's perception of level changes. We could try to keep the power ratio scale linear on our graph to emphasize the logarithmic nature of the decibel scale, but we quickly run out of space (figure 8.2).

Conveniently, *1 dB* is about the smallest change of level that we can perceive under most circumstances in a quiet environment such as a studio. This is called the *just noticeable difference*, or *JND*. As we shall see, JND very much depends on frequency as well as on the level at which we are making level comparisons. (JND is closer to 0.5 dB in the midrange frequencies, for instance.) Outside the studio, we more often need a change of as much as *3 dB* in overall level to notice a difference.

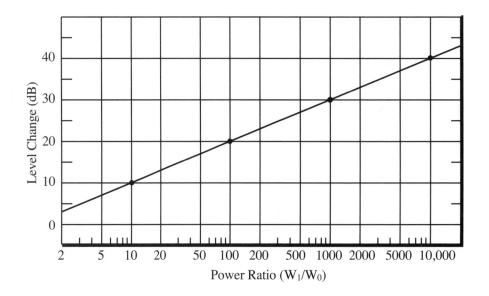

Fig. 8.1. *Relationship between power change or ratio, and level change in decibels*

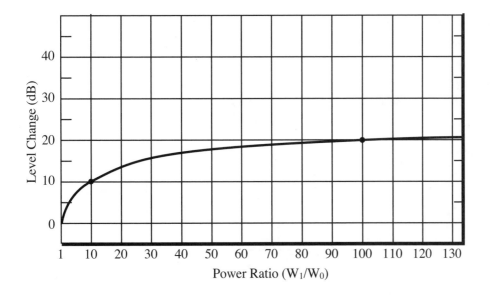

Fig. 8.2. *Relationship between power change or ratio, and level change in decibels, using a linear rather than logarithmic graphing scale.*

What of a doubling in power? Doubling represents a power ratio of *2 to 1*. We know that the log of 2 is 0.301, or simply 0.3 for ease of use. So, the ratio in dB is 10 times that, or 3 dB. Or again:

$$10 \log_{10} (2/1) = 3 \text{ dB}$$

Therefore, if we had two identical power amplifiers rated at 50 W and 100 W respectively, how much louder could one expect the 100 W amp to be, again assuming a perfect world with all things being equal (a rare occurrence, to be sure)? With both amps running at full power, the 100 W amp would be running at twice the power, which would make it 3 dB, or just noticeably, louder. How many watts would we need to sound twice as loud as the 50 W amp? We know that a 10 dB change is required to make something sound subjectively twice as loud, and we also know that a 10-to-1 power ratio corresponds to a 10 dB change. Therefore, we would need a 500 W amp (*10 x power*) to produce an output signal twice as loud as that produced by the same 50 W amp at full volume. Mathematically, this would be:

$$10 \log_{10}(500/50) = 10 \log_{10}(10/1) = 10 \text{ dB}$$

It is worth pointing out that the impression of something being "twice as loud" is quite subjective and somewhat hard to pinpoint. The 10 dB figure is really just an average arrived at by using test groups of average listeners. The more fine-tuned someone's hearing, the more sensitive that person will be to smaller increments of change. In fact, listening tests indicate that people with so-called "golden ears" are more likely to hear an increase of only 8 dB as being approximately "twice as loud." Figure 8.3 graphs the generalized relationship between change in power or intensity, change of level in decibels, and perceived change in loudness.

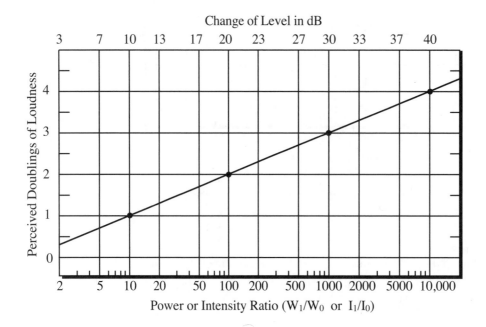

Fig. 8.3. *The relationship between change in power, change in dB, and average perceived change in loudness. Note that each tenfold change in intensity yields a level change of 10 dB and a perceived doubling of apparent loudness.*

Table 8.4 can be used as a quick reference. It summarizes average responses to, and importance of, level changes in dB.

10 dB	A perceived doubling of loudness; also 10 × power or intensity
–10 dB	A perceived halving of loudness; also power ÷ 10 ($^1/_{10}$ power)
5 dB	An obvious change in perceived level
3 dB	Smallest change perceived in most real-world environments; also, doubling of power or intensity
1 dB	Average JND (just noticeable difference) usually only perceived in a lab/studio environment with very low noise floor (1.3 × power) *(JND range is actually 0.5 – 3 dB depending on frequency)*

Table 8.4. *Importance of various changes in dB, with respect to both intensity and perceived loudness*

PROJECTS

1. Find the following base-10 logarithms without using a calculator: 10, 10^5, 4, $10^{-2.3}$, 8, 200, 0.0000002. (You may check your answers using a calculator.)

2. Express the following voltage or power changes in decibels: 2 × power, 2 × voltage, 5 × power, 100 × voltage, 15 × voltage, power ÷ 2, voltage ÷ 5, 50 W to 125 W, 120 V to 220 V.

3. Express the average dynamic range of human hearing (approx. 120 dB) as a power ratio.

4. A sound reinforcement system boosts a vocal from its original 10^{-4} W/m^2 up to 2×10^{-2} W/m^2. What is the system gain in dB? What is the system gain in power (W)?

Chapter ⑨ More dB
Sound Reference Levels

When we discuss "level," we are implying a signal level in *decibels*, which, as we saw in the last chapter, means a logarithmic ratio of powers or intensities. However, there are several different ways that we can express this level. You may have heard musicians or engineers refer to *sound pressure level* (dB SPL, or L_p). In acoustic circles, you will likely hear or read the terms *sound intensity level* (dB SIL) and *sound power level* (dB PWL or L_w). If you try to compare specifications or interconnect pieces of gear, you will encounter signal levels described in dBu, dBV, dBm, or even dBµ. So what does it all mean? Isn't *dB* always *dB*? The short answer is yes. But the form that signal level takes depends on the starting or reference point that is being used for the purpose of comparison. Let's take a closer look.

Sound Power Level (dB PWL)

As you may recall, in chapter 8 we found that the difference in dB between two powers was a logarithmic ratio, which could be expressed as follows:

$$\Delta \text{ Power (in dB)} = 10 \log_{10}(W_1/W_0)$$

where Δ means change, W_1 = new power, and W_0 = initial or reference power

Acoustically, this relationship is called *sound power level*, where the acoustical power of any sound is always compared with the following standard reference power: $W_0 = 10^{-12}$ W, or one picowatt (1 pW). (Note that a subscript of (0) implies that we are using a reference level.) We can express sound power level in dB using equation 9.1:

$$L_w = 10 \log(W_1/10^{-12})$$

Eq. 9.1. *Expressing an acoustical power as sound power level in dB*

As an example, the sound power level of an average conversation, which might generate one microwatt (1 µW) of acoustical power (0.000001 watt, or 10^{-6} watt), would be:

$$L_w = 10 \log \left(^{10^{-6}}/_{10^{-12}}\right) =$$
$$10 \log (10^6) = 10(6) = 60 \text{ dB}$$

This simply means that the conversation's 1 μW sound power is 60 dB greater than our reference power of 1 pW. Having a single zero reference allows us to compare all sounds to a single known entity, thus providing an intuitive sense of how loud various sounds are. In this case, the reference power, 10^{-12} W, corresponds to the *threshold of hearing*, or the softest sound within the average range of human hearing.

As previously discussed, *power* is a quality inherent in the source, a property of the source itself irrespective of its surroundings. For this reason, acoustical sound power is generally not referred to or used much in the studio, as we are generally more interested in how sound exists and interacts acoustically in the space around it. It is also a bit tricky to measure directly. However, you may see sound power level (dB PWL) referred to in speaker comparisons, for instance. (Conversely, electrical power is of interest to us, and is referred to often in this text.)

Sound Intensity Level (SIL)

Intensity is generally a more useful entity than sound power in that it is a measure of power (W) per unit area (m^2). Think of intensity as the acoustical strength of the signal. In acoustics, the level (in dB) of a given intensity is called *sound intensity level* (SIL). The reference intensity used is still the *threshold of hearing*, measured in watts per square meter: $I_0 = 10^{-12}$ W/m^2 (0.000000000001 W/m^2). Again, having one reference for all level discussions or measurements facilitates quick comparisons. Think of a pilot stating, "We are cruising at 30,000 feet." If there were no standard reference point, this statement would suddenly become untrue as soon as the plane passes over a mountain. What the pilot means is "30,000 feet *above sea level*," so variations in the terrain below are of no consequence (assuming that the plane is traveling high enough so as not to crash into anything).

Thus, when we talk of a sound intensity level (SIL) of 60 dB, we mean an intensity that is 60 dB greater than our reference intensity (10^{-12} W/m^2)—the softest sound that the average ear can detect. How can we find the intensity in question? Simply use our power equation from chapter 8, rewritten as equation 9.2:

$$SIL = 10 \log \left({}^{I_1}/_{10^{-12}} \right)$$

Eq. 9.2. *To calculate or express sound intensities as sound intensity levels (SIL)*

Plugging in our known variables, we get $60 = 10 \log (I_1/10^{-12})$. We are solving for I_1, so we must simplify the equation by "undoing" everything that has been done mathematically to I_1, working from the outside in. (When solving equations, you can do anything you choose, as long as you do exactly the same thing to both sides to maintain the equality.)

Step 1

Divide both sides by ten (to get rid of the 10):

$$60/10 = [10 \log (I_1 / 10^{-12})]/10$$

This yields:

$$6 = \log (I_1 / 10^{-12})$$

Step 2

Get rid of the log by taking the *antilog* of both sides. [Antilog is the inverse operation of log, just as division is the inverse of multiplication. Antilog simply means 10^x, i.e., take the number you have (x) and raise 10 to the power of that number. For example, antilog $5 = 10^5$; or antilog $(-2) = 10^{-2}$. Inversely, log $10^{-2} = -2$.]

$$\text{Antilog } (6) = \text{Antilog } [\log (I_1 / 10^{-12})]$$

This yields:

$$10^6 = (I_1 / 10^{-12})$$

Step 3.

Multiply both sides by 10–12 to get I1 alone. This yields:

$$10^6 \times 10^{-12} = (I_1 / 10^{-12}) \times 10^{-12}$$

Answer:

$$I_1 = 10^{-6} \text{ W/m}^2 \text{ [19]}$$

(is 60 dB greater than 10^{-12} W/m²)

Of course, we could have guessed this, since every 10 dB represents a tenfold change in intensity; 60 dB represents six of these tenfold changes and is therefore 10^6 times greater in intensity than 10^{-12} W/m², i.e., 10^{-6} W/m².

As with our power formula from chapter 8, we are unlikely to be making these calculations in the heat of a recording session. It is useful, however, in helping us to understand where intensity levels come from and how they relate to what we hear.

19. Whenever you have to multiply or divide two equal numbers raised to a power, you can simply add or subtract the exponents. Mathematically, this would be summed up as follows: $a^x \times a^y = a^{x+y}$; and $a^x/a^y = a^{(x-y)}$. Thus, $10^6 \times 10^6 = 10^{(6+6)} = 10^{12}$; and $10^4/10^{-2} = 10^{(4-(-2))} = 10^{(4+2)} = 10^6$. On the other hand, $a^x/a^y = (a/y)^x$, so that $p_1^2/p_0^2 = (p_1/p_0)^2$.

Table 9.1 lists common sound intensity levels encountered within our range of hearing and their corresponding intensities.

Sound Reference	SIL (dB)	I (W/m²)	
Jet Engine at 10 m	150 dB	10^3	W/m²
Kick Drum at 1 ft	130 dB	10^1	W/m²
Threshold of Pain	120–130 dB	1–10	W/m²
Typical Rock Concert	110 dB	10^{-1}	W/m²
Subway	90 dB	10^{-3}	W/m²
Average Studio Control Room Monitoring Level	80–90 dB	$10^{-(4-5)}$	W/m²
Average Conversation	60 dB	10^{-6}	W/m²
Library	40 dB	10^{-9}	W/m²
Quiet Recording Studio	20 dB	10^{-10}	W/m²
Whisper at 1 m	10 dB	10^{-11}	W/m²
Pin-Drop	10 dB	10^{-11}	W/m²
Threshold of Hearing	0 dB	10^{-12}	W/m²

Table 9.1. *Typical sound intensity levels (SIL) and corresponding intensities within our range of hearing. SIL is always referenced to $I_0 = 10^{-12}$ W/m².*

Sound Pressure Level (dB SPL)

While sound *intensity* and *intensity level* are often used in discussions of acoustics, in the recording arts, we tend to use *sound pressure level* instead. "Level" always implies dB, and dB is always a reference back to a ratio of powers; but as long as we know the relationship between power and pressure (or voltage), we can use dB safely to refer to any of these.

As it happens, power is always proportional to the square of pressure, whether acoustic or electrical. Mathematically, we could write this relationship as:

$$\text{Power } \alpha \text{ (Pressure or Voltage)}^2$$

(α means "is proportional to")

Thus, a linear change in pressure or voltage yields an exponential change in power. As a ratio this would be:

$$(W_1/W_0) \; \alpha \; (p_1^2/p_0^2)$$

We could use this new information to derive a formula for calculating dB directly from pressures or voltages by substituting this new ratio into our power formula as follows:

$$\Delta \text{ Power (in dB)} = 10 \log_{10}(W_1/W_0)$$
$$= 10 \log(p_1^2/p_0^2)$$
$$= 10 \log(p_1/p_0)^2$$
$$= 20 \log(p_1/p_0)*$$

where Δ means change (of), W_1 and W_0 represent our two powers,

and p_1 and p_0 represent our two pressures.

*Rule: $\log N^x = x (\log N)$

Thus, to find the difference in level, in decibels, between two voltages or pressures, use this formula:

$$\Delta \text{ Pressure or Voltage (in dB)} = 20 \log_{10}(p_1/p_0)$$

where p_1 = the new pressure, and p_0 = reference or initial pressure.

Eq. 9.3. *To express changes in sound pressures or voltages, in dB*

When dealing specifically with sound pressure levels (dB SPL), our reference pressure is always the threshold of hearing, or 0 dB SPL, which corresponds to an acoustical pressure of 2×10^{-5} (or 0.00002) N/m² (or Pa), or alternatively 2×10^{-4} (0.0002) dynes/cm² (or µBars), or again 20 µPa.[20] Thus, when we speak of a sound pressure level of 40 dB SPL, we are referring to a pressure 40 dB greater than 0 dB SPL. To find that pressure, we can simply rewrite our pressure formula as Equation 9.4, and solve for p as follows:

$$\text{dB SPL} = 20 \log_{10} (p/0.00002)$$

where p_1 = the new pressure, and p_0 = reference pressure of 0.00002 N/m².

Eq. 9.4. *To calculate sound pressure levels from pressures, and vice versa.*

20. These pressures are all equivalent. Historically, in different disciplines and contexts, different units have been employed to express or measure the same entity. Do not let this scare you off; simply be aware that pascals (Pa) and newtons/m² (N/m²) are equivalent, and that µBars and dynes/cm² are equivalent and are $1/10$ as great as pascals or newtons/m².

Given a sound pressure level of 40 dB, the pressure would be:

$$40 \text{ dB} = 20 \log (P/_{0.00002})$$

Step 1

Divide both sides by 20:

$$2 = \log (P/_{0.00002})$$

Step 2

Take the antilog of both sides:

$$10^2 = 10^{\log(P/_{0.00002})} = P/_{0.00002}$$

Step 3

Multiply both sides by 0.00002:

$$0.00002 \times 10^2 = p$$

Answer: $p = 0.002 \text{ N/m}^2 \text{ (or Pa)}$

Thus, 40 dB SPL corresponds to a pressure of 0.002 N/m², which is 40 dB greater than our 0 dB reference pressure of 0.00002 N/m². Because our hearing correlates better to the logarithmic decibel scale than to a linear pressure scale, we tend to ignore pressures altogether, and instead refer directly to pressure levels in dB SPL (sometimes written L_p for *pressure level*). These always represent a pressure ratio with our reference pressure of 2×10^{-5} N/m². In fact, when we use a sound level meter, the integrated microphone is responding to pressure changes around it and gives us a meter reading in decibels, calibrated to our reference pressure of 2×10^{-5} Pa or 0 dB SPL. You will notice a close correlation between dB SIL and dB SPL. This is because both use the threshold of hearing as the point of reference (albeit expressed differently, as an intensity and a pressure, respectively). Therefore, a sound that is 50 dB above 0 dB SIL will also be 50 dB above 0 dB SPL. We will tend to use the latter.

We rarely measure pressure directly, but rather calculate it backwards, when desired, from pressure level readings. This tends to be done in acoustics rather than recording situations. Microphones are rated for maximum dB SPL; that is, how great a sound pressure level they can be exposed to before distortion. Typical ratings for modern dynamic microphones (and some condensers) are in the 140 dB range. This allows for close miking of very loud sound sources such as a kick or snare drum, or a cranked-up guitar amp stack. SPL meters in the studio also display levels in dB SPL directly. A smart average listening level in the control room is 80–85 dB SPL. This allows for sustained periods of listening without induced ear fatigue or, worse yet, permanent hearing loss. Some engineers monitor at much lower levels than even this, while occasionally checking at much louder levels for short periods of time (either for critical sonic evaluation, or sometimes just to impress a client).

Inverse Square Law

As you may recall from our discussion of sound in chapter 5, we found that sound spreads out from the source, as an ever-expanding sphere. Intuitively, we know that the further we get from the source, the lower the level will be. Figure 9.1 shows why. As we move away from the sound source, its inherent power is spread over a greater and greater area. Since intensity is a measure of the sound power passing through a given unit area, we can see that the intensity drops as a function of the growing area of the sphere. As we move further away from a sound source, its intensity (and perceived loudness) drops proportionally.

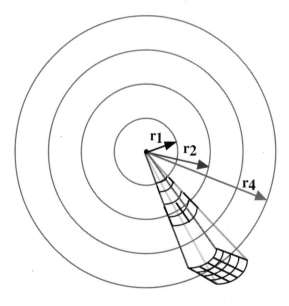
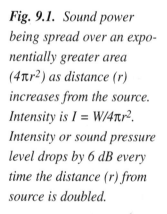

Fig. 9.1. *Sound power being spread over an exponentially greater area ($4\pi r^2$) as distance (r) increases from the source. Intensity is $I = W/4\pi r^2$. Intensity or sound pressure level drops by 6 dB every time the distance (r) from source is doubled.*

The intensity of a spherically spreading or *point* source can be expressed as $I = {}^W\!/_{4\pi r^2}$ ($4\pi r^2$ represents the surface area of a sphere). If we consider the spreading of sound as the surface area of a sphere $S = 4\pi r^2$, where r is the radius, we notice that every time we double the radius (or distance from the sound source), the surface area is quadrupled (r = 2, r^2 = 4; see figure 9.1). If the power of the source is spread over four times the area, each unit area will only have one quarter its previous intensity. This can be summed up in the following statement:

$$I \propto \sqrt[1]{r^2}$$

This is often referred to as the *inverse square law*, stating that the intensity (I) of a sound is proportional to ($\propto$) the inverse of the square of the distance (r) from the sound source. You may recall that a change in intensity, like a change in power, can be expressed as a level change in decibels using the following formula:

$$\Delta \text{ Power or Intensity (in dB)} = 10 \log_{10}(I_1/I_0)$$

In order to express the change in dB over distance, we could substitute r_0^2/r_1^2 for I_1/I_0 (since these two ratios are equivalent), which yields the following:

$$\Delta \text{ Level over Distance (in dB)} = 10 \log_{10}(r_0^2/r_1^2)$$

which simplifies as:

$$10 \log (r_0/r_1)^2$$

and further,

$$20 \log (r_0/r_1)$$

Thus:

$$\Delta \text{ Level over Distance (in dB)} = 20 \log (r_0/r_1)$$

To find how much the level drops over a doubling of distance, we simply plug in as follows:

$$\Delta \text{ Level over Distance (in dB)} = 20 \log_{10} (\tfrac{1}{2})$$
$$= 20 (-0.3)$$
$$= -6 \text{ dB}$$

Thus, for every doubling of distance away from the source, we get a drop in level of 6 dB.[21] Again, in general, we are considering sound pressure level, which is easily measured using a sound level meter, instead of intensity, which is more difficult to measure directly. In either case, the drop in *decibels* is the same, since dB always refers back to our power ratio.

How can we use the inverse square law to our advantage in the studio? When placing microphones, we know that close placement greatly boosts incoming level to the mic preamp, while distant placement requires increased gain from the mic

21. This assumes a perfect free-field condition with no absorption or reflection. In actuality, because of the absorptivity of the air (and the ground), level drops off somewhat faster than this outdoors. Indoors, the inverse square law only holds true for a relatively limited region (the free field) near the source where direct sound dominates over reflected energy. This will be dependent on how reverberant the room is.

preamp. Close miking is often used for rock and pop music recording because it allows for reduced leakage from proximate sources that are in the studio at the same time. Through close miking, the level of the primary source, say a snare drum, is boosted while the level of secondary sources, such as a nearby cymbal or tom, is reduced. Reduced leakage allows for more isolated treatment (EQ, compression, panning, etc.) and improved imaging of individual sound elements, as well as reduced chance of phase cancellations.

When individually miking proximate sources, such as several horns in a horn section, the distance between individual microphones should generally be at least three times the distance from each mic to its respective sound source. Known as the *3-to-1 rule*, this principle is based on the fact that the increased distance from each source to the more distant mics will mean reduced leakage of the non-principal sources into each mic. Each source will have greatest level at its principal mic, and significantly reduced level at each of the other mics, based on the inverse square law (as well as the rejection characteristics of the microphones' polar patterns). It is important to note that the 3-to-1 rule does not apply to stereo miking techniques.

Electrical Power and Voltage

As we have seen so far, when dealing with sound pressure levels, we use the 0 dB reference of 0.00002 Pa (or N/m^2) as a point of comparison. We can express this in shorthand, using the designation dB SPL (or L_p), which implies decibels above or below our reference pressure. Having a common reference allows us to quickly compare pressure levels, and using decibels to express this ratio helps us to correlate these levels to the way we hear.

This system of shorthand, using "dB" to represent a pressure as decibels above or below a standard reference pressure, is used for electrical powers and voltages as well. For instance, electrical powers are often expressed as dBm, where 0 dBm corresponds to 0.001 W, or one milliwatt (1 mW). Therefore, given a power of +6 dBm, we have a power that is 6 dB greater than 1 mW. Based on what we know about power and decibels, 6 dB represents two 3 dB increases, each of which represents a doubling of power. Thus, +6 dBm yields 0.001 W × 2 × 2 = 0.004 W, or 4 mW. We could also calculate this by plugging into our power formula as follows:

$$6 \text{ (dBm)} = 10 \log \left(\frac{W}{0.001} \right)$$
$$\frac{6}{10} = \log \left(\frac{W}{0.001} \right)$$
$$10^{0.6} = \frac{W}{0.001}$$
$$W = 0.001 \times 10^{0.6}$$
$$= 0.004 \text{ W}$$

Similarly, –10 dBm means a power 10 dB below 1 mW, which equals $\frac{1}{10}$ the power of 1 mW, or 0.0001 W. Or again:

$$-10 \text{ (dBm)} = 10 \log(^{W}\!/0.001)$$
$$^{-10}\!/10 = \log(^{W}\!/0.001)$$
$$-1 = \log(^{W}\!/0.001)$$
$$10^{-1} = {}^{W}\!/0.001$$
$$W = 0.001 \times 10^{-1}$$
$$= 0.0001 \text{ W}$$

Voltages can be treated similarly, generally referenced either to 0 dBV, which corresponds to 1 V, or 0 dBu, which corresponds to 0.775 V. As with acoustical pressure, to express voltage in decibels, we must take into account its relationship to power: power α (voltage)^2. This gives us:

$$\Delta \text{ dB} = 10 \log(W_1/W_0)$$
$$= 10 \log(V_1^2/V_0^2)$$
$$= 10 \log(V_1/V_0)^2$$
$$= 20 \log(V_1/V_0)$$

Now, given a voltage of +6 dBV, the voltage is 6 dB above 1 V. This gives us:

$$6 \text{ (dBV)} = 20 \log(V/1)$$
$$6/20 = \log V$$
$$0.3 = \log V$$
$$V = 10^{0.3}$$
$$= 2 \text{ V}$$

Notice that a 6 dB change corresponds to a *doubling* of voltage. This should make sense if you recall that 3 dB represents a doubling of power, and 6 dB represents two doublings (or a quadrupling) of power. Since $P \, \alpha \, V^2$, doubling the voltage quadruples the power, which indeed corresponds to a 6 dB increase.

Let's quickly apply this logic to some other voltage ratios. What would 10 × voltage be?

A 10 × voltage = $(10)^2$ × power = 10 dB + 10 dB = 20 dB. (Remember that 10 dB represents a tenfold change of power.) A 5 × voltage would be half of this;

half voltage = –6 dB, therefore 20 dB – 6 dB = 14 dB. A 20 × voltage = 2 × 10 × voltage = 6 dB + 20 dB = 26 dB. Get it? (Reminder: we can *multiply and divide powers and voltages*, but we must *add and subtract dB*. If you find yourself multiplying or dividing dB, you are doing something wrong.)

Understanding these dB references for voltage and power and being able to easily move back and forth between dB and voltage or power is key to being able to interpret equipment specifications as they relate to levels in the studio, as well as to use measurement and test equipment to ensure proper setup and function. For a summary of when to use the *10 log* versus the *20 log* decibel formula to find the difference in dB between two values, refer to table 9.2.

Use 10 log	Use 20 log
Power (W_1/W_0)	Voltage (V_1/V_0)
Intensity (I_1/I_0)	Sound Pressure (p_1/p_0)
	Distance (D_0/D_1) or (r_0/r_1)

Table 9.2 *Use as a reference for when to use 10 log vs. 20 log to calculate the difference in dB between two entities*

Origins of 0 dB Reference Levels

Table 9.3 summarizes some commonly used 0 dB reference levels. Why so many different reference levels? There is a history and reason behind each of these references. For instance, traditionally, audio systems have followed the model of the phone system, which has often led the way in most things concerning audio. The phone system was originally built using 600 Ω as the standard impedance on all its lines. It happens that an average unamplified conversation generates about 0.775 V_{rms} across a load impedance of 600 Ω, which results in approximately 1 mW of power. This yields the referenced 0 dBm = 1 mW, and 0 dBv = 0.775 V across 600 Ω. *VU (volume unit)* meters were originally calibrated in dBm, and designed such that an electrical signal level of 0.775 V_{rms} would deflect the needle to a reading of 0 *VU* (read, 0 dBm). This represents what is known as *standard operating level*, or *SOL*. For now you can think of standard operating level (SOL) as an optimum average signal level. As long as our signal is humming around 0 VU, it is great enough to be well above the system's noise floor, yet low enough in level to avoid distorting.

0 dB Reference Level	Corresponding Value
0 dBV	1 V
0 dBv*	0.775 V across 600 Ω
0 dBu	0.775 V
0 dBμ	0.000001 V (1 microvolt, μV)
0 dBm	0.001 W (1 milliwatt, mW)
0 dBW	1 W
0 dB SPL	0.0002 dynes/cm^2 (or μbars) 0.00002 Pa 20 μPa 2×10^{-5} N/m^2
0 dB SIL	10^{-12} W/m^2

Table 9.3. *Commonly encountered 0 dB reference levels.*

* 0 dBv is arcane and no longer in common usage.

Since most systems no longer use 600 Ω but rather much higher load impedances, 0 dBv has been replaced by 0 dBu = 0.775 V, where the *u* stands for "unloaded" (which basically ignores the load, or assumes a very high load impedance or "open" circuit). An added resistance was also placed in series with the VU meter such that a greater level of 4 dBu is needed to deflect the meter to a reading of 0 VU. This level has become the standard operating level for most professional equipment, and corresponds to a voltage of 1.228 V_{rms}.[22] (In many broadcast systems, 0 VU = +8 dBu, or a voltage of 1.947 V_{rms}.)

While dBu and dBm are no longer strictly equivalent (since the link of 600 Ω between them no longer exists), the two units are often used interchangeably. Thus, you will see professional standard operating level of 0 VU equated to both +4 dBm and +4 dBu. In this case, read "dBm" as referring to the voltage 0.775 V, rather than the power traditionally tied to this unit. Strictly speaking, in this instance, only the dBu reference is correct, but old habits die hard.

Meanwhile, when dealing with power at typical loudspeaker levels, 0 dBm is too small a reference to be practical, so instead we use dBW, where 0 dBW = 1 W.

---

22. To calculate this, simply plug the value into our voltage formula as follows:

$$+4 \text{ (dBu)} = 20\log \left(\frac{V}{0.775}\right)$$
$$\frac{4}{20} = \log\left(\frac{V}{0.775}\right)$$
$$10^{0.2} = \frac{V}{0.775}$$
$$V = 0.775 \times 10^{0.2}$$
$$= 1.228 \text{ V}$$

Thus, 3 dBW means a power 3 dB greater than 1 W, i.e., 2 W (remember that +3 dB means double the power). And 20 dBW would be 10 × 10 × 1 W = 100 W (10 × power for every +10 dB, remember?).

While dBW is an electrical reference, there is occasion when we want to discuss acoustical power—for instance, with respect to the efficiency of a loud-speaker (ratio of acoustical output power to electrical input power), or to rate a source for noise-generating potential. Acoustical power is also used to calculate reverberation time and estimate the sound pressure level of a known source in a room. As we saw at the start of this chapter, the unit *dB PWL (L_w)* while not often used, is such a reference, where 0 dB PWL = 10^{-12} watt (1 pW) acoustical power. As loudspeakers are notoriously inefficient, there is no direct connection between the electrical watts and acoustical watts, or between dBW and the acoustical dB PWL. As an example, given an input of 100 W, or 20 dBW (dBW = 10 log($^{100}/_1$) = 20), a direct radiator loudspeaker that is 3% efficient would output three acoustical watts (3/100), which is actually quite loud. This could be stated as dB PWL = 10 log (3/0.000000000001) = 125 dB PWL at the source! Sound power level is different from both sound intensity level (SIL) and sound pressure level (SPL) in that it is a characteristic of the source itself and does not take into account environmental factors.

But why complicate our lives with dB when we can simply list powers and voltages as actual signal levels in volts and watts and pascals? The simple answer is that by describing levels in dB, we are referencing everything back to how we hear and experience level changes. Once we have learned precisely how dB relates to how we hear, level changes in voltage and power expressed as dB make a lot more sense. An increase in power from 50 W to 100 W is equivalent to an increase from 1000 W to 2000 W. Both represent a doubling of power, which is a 3 dB change, i.e., a slight increase in perceived loudness (although the greater increase in watts will be significantly more expensive to pull off!). Thus, the phrase "a 3 dB change" is inherently more meaningful that "a 50 W change."

One potential for confusion arises, however, when we interface gear referenced to differing standard operating levels. For instance, most semipro audio gear is built around a SOL of –10 dBV. Invariably, in a home or project (and even professional) recording studio, this gear will be interconnected with professional audio equipment operating at a SOL of +4 dBu. Connecting a semipro DAT or CD player to the input of a professional console will yield an average level that is lower than other signals passing through the console. Ideally, in a permanent installation we would like all signal levels coming up to the console to fall within the same level range, so boosting the output from the CD is desirable, but by how much? It is tempting to say by 14 dB (the difference between –10 and +4); however, this would only be true if they were both referenced to the same 0 dB reference (dBu, for instance).

In this specific instance, we need to figure out first what the actual voltage is that is being represented by each SOL, and then find the dB difference between these two voltages:

Step 1

Find the voltage represented by −10 dBV, where 0 dBV = 1 V:

$$
\begin{aligned}
-10 \ (dBV) &= 20 \log \left(\tfrac{V}{1}\right) \\
\tfrac{-10}{20} &= \log V \\
-0.5 &= \log V \\
V &= 10^{-0.5} \\
&= 0.316 \ V
\end{aligned}
$$

Step 2

Find the voltage represented by +4 dBu, where 0 dBu = 0.775 V:

$$
\begin{aligned}
4 \ (dBu) &= 20 \log \left(\tfrac{V}{0.775}\right) \\
\tfrac{4}{20} &= \log \left(\tfrac{V}{0.775}\right) \\
0.2 &= \log \left(\tfrac{V}{0.775}\right) \\
10^{0.2} &= \tfrac{V}{0.775} \\
V &= 10^{0.2} \times 0.775 \\
&= 1.228 \ V
\end{aligned}
$$

Step 3

Find the difference in dB between these two voltages:

$$
\begin{aligned}
\Delta \ dB &= 20 \log \left(\tfrac{1.228}{0.316}\right) \\
&= 20 \log (3.886) \\
&= 20(0.59) \\
&= 11.8 \\
&\approx 12 \ dB
\end{aligned}
$$

Thus, the output of the CD would need to be boosted by 12 dB to bring it up to professional line level. A consumer CD player operating at the usual −10 dBu, on the other hand, would have to be boosted the full 14 dB (the difference between +4 and −10 dBu) to bring it up to pro line level. The implications of this will be explored further in chapter 11.

PROJECTS

1. Find the following voltages or powers: +10 dBu; –8 dBV; + 4 dBm; –10 dBW.

2. An outdoor sound reinforcement setup is known to produce 115 dB SPL 4 ft. from the source. What will the sound pressure level be 20 ft. away? 100 ft. away? 1 mile away?

3. Find the difference (in dB) in output power potential between a 50 W amp and a 450 W amp (all other things being equal). Is this significantly louder?

4. What sound pressure level corresponds to a pressure of 1 Pa? 2 N/m^2? 10 $dynes/cm^2$?

5. Given an input signal power of 150 W, what will be the acoustical output power, in dB PWL, from a speaker with a 2% efficiency rating? What will be the output sound pressure level (in dB SPL) 4 ft. away, if the speaker is rated to produce 90 dB SPL at 4 ft. given a 1 W input? [Hint: first find the difference in dB between rated and actual input power; then, assume the same dB difference at the output.]

Chapter **10** Psychoacoustics
Relating dB to What We Hear

The Audio Window

A change of 1 dB is generally considered the smallest average change in level that we can hear (JND—"just noticeable difference") in a controlled environment, 3 dB (double the power) is a more real-world JND, and a 10 dB change (10 x power) in level sounds "twice as loud" to the average listener. The softest sound we are theoretically capable of hearing corresponds to a sound pressure of 0.00002 Pa (0 dB SPL), and the loudest somewhere between 20 Pa and 200 Pa (120 to 130 dB SPL). These levels represent the human *threshold of hearing* (or *audibility*) and *threshold of pain* (or *feeling*) respectively.

With respect to audio frequency, we only hear frequencies between about 20 Hz and 20 kHz. A given individual may be able to hear frequencies below or above these extremes, and age is a very important factor in determining one's limits of audibility. In fact, most adults do not hear much above 16 kHz, and our sensitivity, especially to high frequencies, drops off dramatically with age.

Figure 10.1 shows what we might term our "audio window"—that portion of sound that we can safely deem within the bounds of human hearing. Of course, there is plenty of activity in the frequency spectrum below and above these limits, which we might call "infrasonic" and "ultrasonic," respectively. These are especially important in the animal kingdom, where ultrasonic frequencies are emitted and received by many species as a means of both communication and hunting. Bats emit ultrasonic "squeaks" for sightless navigation and to locate prey. They accomplish this by monitoring the reflections resulting from these sound waves bouncing off of surrounding objects. We have adapted this techniques for our own purposes in the use of *sonar* (*so*und *na*vigation and *r*anging), where ultrasonic waves are reflected off of underwater objects to reveal their location and distance.

There is also much energy in the frequency spectrum above our hearing range that does not fall under the category of sound at all. These waves consist largely of electromagnetic radiation rather than acoustical energy, and as such, have unique properties. For instance, like light, electromagnetic waves are not subject to the resistance of air in the way that acoustical waves are. Rather than traveling at the speed of sound (1130 feet/second), they travel at the speed of light: approximately 186,000 miles/second (or about 300,000 kilometers/second). Similarly, electromagnetic waves can travel through a vacuum and therefore can be projected into space. You may recall from our earlier discussion that sound needs an elastic medium (such as air or water) through which to propagate. Although electromagnetic waves in general fall outside of the realm of acoustics, they are quite relevant to the study of audio technology.

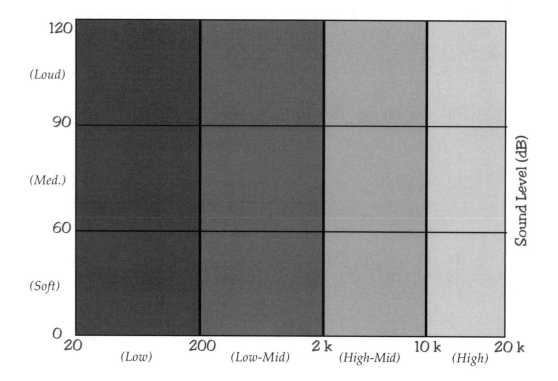

Fig. 10.1. The "audio window." Our limits of audibility with respect to both level and frequency.

Some commonly used wave frequencies or frequency ranges, both acoustic and electromagnetic, are listed in table 10.1, along with their functional application in audio technology.

Frequency	Application
0 Hz	DC voltage, battery power, control voltage
60 Hz (50 Hz Eu.)	AC line voltage
20 Hz–20 kHz	Audible audio frequencies (approximate)
44.1, 48, 88.2, 96 kHz	Standard audio sampling frequencies
30 kHz–30 MHz	LF, MF, HF: radio frequencies
38 kHz	FM radio stereo subcarrier
67 kHz	FM radio "storecast" subcarrier
560–1600 kHz	AM radio carrier frequencies
88–108 MHz	FM radio carrier frequencies
30–300 MHz	VHF: cell phone, TV, radio, wireless mics
300 MHz–5.8 GHz	UHF: TV, wireless mics, cordless phones
3–300 GHz	Satellite communication, microwaves, radar
300 GHz–400 THz	Infrared light, fiberoptics
400–750 THz	Visible light

Table 10.1. *Commonly used frequencies and their respective audio-related functions*

Fletcher-Munson Equal Loudness Contours

As suggested in the previous chapters, intensity level does not directly or consistently translate to subjective loudness. Instead, we have to carefully consider the *frequency* in question, as well as the starting level at which judgments are being made. The relationship between level, frequency, and loudness perception is of particular importance to anyone interested in recording or mixing music.

The particular question of how frequency affects the relationship between intensity level in decibels and subjective loudness has been carefully studied and quantified by psychoacousticians, perhaps most-notably Harvey Fletcher and Wilden A. Munson. These researchers found that, at low to moderate levels, we hear low frequencies very poorly. The same is true to a lesser extent at high frequencies. We are most sensitive by far to midrange frequencies, particularly in the range of 1 to 5 kHz.[23] This also means that at low and high frequencies, we need a greater change in intensity level to perceive a change in loudness (JND), compared to a smaller change necessary in midrange frequencies. At the same time, a tenfold change in power or intensity below 100 Hz sounds more like a tripling rather than a doubling in subjective loudness.

As overall intensity increases, our hearing tends to flatten out, such that we are more equally sensitive to low, midrange, and high frequencies. Think of what this means for monitoring music at various levels. When doing a mixdown from multi-track, or 2-track mastering, our impression of the frequency content of the mix will change dramatically at different listening levels. When monitoring at low levels, our perception of bass frequencies (and, to a lesser extent, very high frequencies) will be greatly diminished, and we may end up boosting with bass EQ to compensate[24]—possibly leading to a bass-heavy mix. On the other hand, monitoring at very high volumes may make us overly aware of low frequencies. By not feeling the need to accentuate bass frequencies in the mix, we may end up with a mix that is bass-light at more moderate volumes (listen to some hard rock mixes from the '70s to hear the result)—not to mention the fact that extended exposure to high sound pressure levels will precipitate the onset of permanent hearing loss, particularly at high frequencies.

The data of intensity vs. frequency is represented in what are called *equal loudness contours*, often referred to as *Fletcher-Munson curves* (figure 10.2). In an attempt to quantify subjective loudness, the unit of phons has been used, where a loudness level in *phons* is equal to the loudness level of a 1 kHz tone of the same number of decibels. In other words, a 100 Hz tone with an intensity level of 30 dB has a subjective loudness level of only 10 phons, meaning that it only sounds as loud as a 10 dB-1 kHz tone. In fact, all points falling on a given phon level sound equally loud, hence the name equal loudness contours. Note how much greater the intensity level must be at low and very high frequencies for the subjective loudness to be equal to that of midrange frequencies. For instance, we can see that a 57 dB-50 Hz tone, a 29 dB-500 Hz tone, and a 40 dB-8000 Hz tone will all sound equally loud since they all fall on the "30 phons" contour. All three sound as loud as a 30 dB-1 kHz tone. By definition, the loudness level of a 1 kHz tone in phons is equal to its intensity level in dB—a 40 dB-1 kHz tone has a subjective loudness

---

23. This is due at least in part to internal resonances in the ear canal. Interestingly enough, it also corresponds to the range of intelligibility for human speech, where plosives such as p's and t's exist. These sounds play an important role in helping us to decipher and distinguish words from each other.

24. This is the function of the "loudness" switch that is found on most stereos, car radios, etc. It boosts low frequencies, and to a lesser extent high frequencies, to compensate for the effect described by the *equal loudness contours* when listening at low levels. It restores the impression of a balanced mix with respect to frequency content, particularly low frequencies.

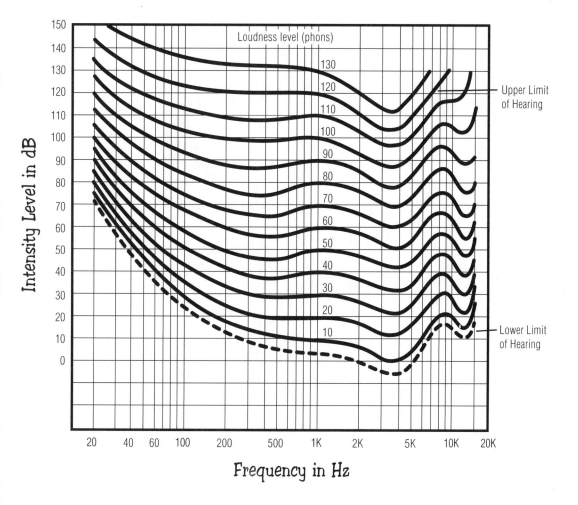

Fig. 10.2. *Fletcher-Munson equal loudness contours, where loudness level is measured in phons. Loudness level in phons is equal to the loudness of a 1 kHz tone of the same number in decibels.*

level of 40 phons. In a recording situation, you may notice that a low-frequency instrument such as a bass guitar or cello, while registering the same level on a meter as another instrument such as guitar or piano, will tend to sound less loud, particularly when they are all monitored at lower volumes. These contours explain why.

The information gathered in the equal loudness contours has led to the development of weighting scales used for level measurements, particularly noise measurements. Weighting scales allow for more low-frequency (and to a lesser extent very high-frequency) noise, based on the idea that we do not hear as well in these frequency ranges and are therefore less bothered by noise in this frequency range. A sound level meter (figure 10.3) that uses weighting scales inserts a resistance network before the meter, such that low frequencies (and very high frequencies) register at a lower level on the meter. This weighting is intended to correspond more closely to how we perceive the sound source. The three weighting scales—A, B, and C weighting—are meant to be used for different ranges of noise or sound level. A-weighting (dBA) uses a filter that greatly reduces the level reading of low frequencies (–39 dB@31.5 Hz) as well as highs (–7 dB@16 kHz). A-weighting (dBA) should be used principally for low-level measurements, since at low levels, we hear very poorly in the low-frequency range. C-weighting (dBC), on the other hand, has virtually no low-frequency correction (–3 dB@31.5 Hz), and should be used for measuring loud sound sources. B-weighting (dBB), which is intended for use with medium-level sounds, is rarely used. The designation dBLin (linear) indicates that the measurement is unweighted. For a complete list of weightings, refer to Appendix A.

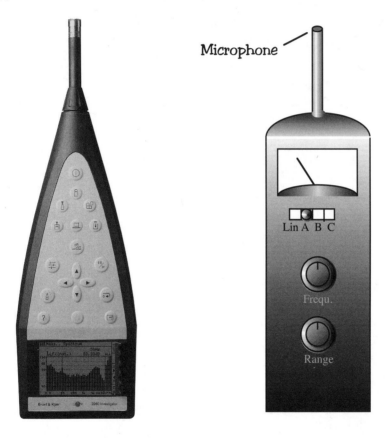

Fig. 10.3. *Sound level meter with weighting filters and spectum analysis (Courtesy Brüel & Kjær)*

How might understanding the implications of these loudness curves affect the recording engineer or the recording musician's approach in the studio? Perhaps the best approach is to apply the awareness of how our hearing works to our monitoring practices. Some mix engineers monitor at a consistent, moderate level, while occasionally checking at very low and very high levels (as well as on different speakers) to ensure that the mix holds up in different monitoring situations. Loud levels, while not advisable for making level or balance decisions, can be helpful in making critical EQ, timbre, and ambience (reverb, etc.) decisions. Other engineers have learned, through experience, how to interpret what they hear at a certain level, and use that level as their reference for all mixes—to extrapolate appropriate levels of bass, for instance. It is also very valuable to keep some CDs that you know intimately readily available as a reference point, to check low- and high-frequency content in particular.

Effect of Frequency and Initial Level on JND

For a complete picture of the subjective impression of *loudness*, we also must consider the initial level at which we are making level comparisons. Consider figure 10.4 (just noticeable difference—JND). At low listening levels, a greater change in decibels is needed for us to perceive an equal change in level (larger JND). As overall level increases, we become increasingly sensitive to changes in level (smaller JND). It is helpful to think of 1 dB as the average "just noticeable difference" in level, but we can see that it actually varies, from about 0.5 to 1.5 dB. Also note that these results are achieved in a controlled listening laboratory environment. As mentioned previously, the real-world average JND is closer to 3 dB.

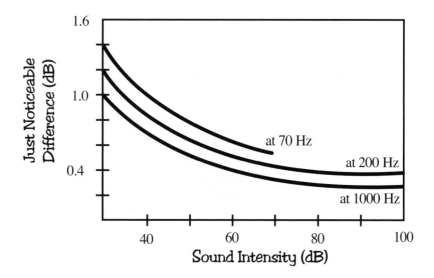

Fig. 10.4. Just noticeable differences (JND) in decibels for different frequencies, as a function of intensity level (after Backus, 2nd ed.)

Effect of Duration on Perceived Loudness

While less important than level and frequency, the duration of a sound can also have an impact on our perception of its loudness. This is mostly true for sounds of short duration. As you can see in figure 10.5 (effect of duration on loudness), a sound that lasts less than a few tenths of a second seems less loud than the same sound with the same intensity level but of longer or continuous duration. Remember, of course, that different sounds of the same peak level vary wildly in perceived loudness, depending on their average or rms level. Measured sound intensity and pressure levels are always rms values.

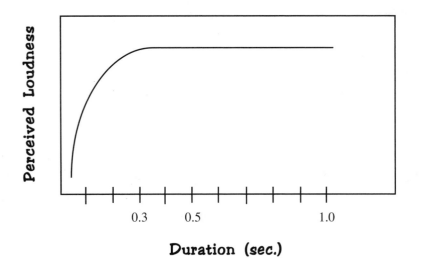

Fig. 10.5. *Effect of duration on perceived loudness. For sound durations of less the a few tenths of a second, perceived loudness is diminished (after Hall, 2nd ed.).*

Effect of Level on Pitch

We stated earlier that a sound's frequency is closely related to its pitch. However, we notice that given two sounds of the same frequency, the louder one actually sounds slightly sharper or flatter in pitch, depending on frequency. This is particularly true of pure tones. In general, increase in intensity yields a slight increase in pitch for high frequencies and a slight decrease in pitch for low frequencies. This is a subtle effect, and less pronounced for complex sounds than for pure tones. On the other hand, it helps to understand the difference between *frequency*, which is the objective description of a sound wave's cycles per second, and *pitch*, which is our subjective perception of a signal's quality of being high or low.

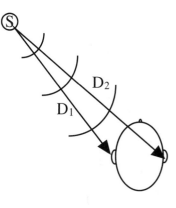

Fig. 10.6. *A sound source located to the left of a listener (viewed from above) is closer (D_1) to the left ear than to the right (D_2). Therefore, sound waves will reach the left ear with greater intensity.*

Localization

There are several factors that help us to determine where a sound is coming from. We depend on subtle differences in the sound that arrives at each ear—differences that the brain has learned over time to interpret and translate into the localization of the sound source. Understanding localization not only helps ensure that we follow proper monitoring practice, but is also essential for proper use of stereo miking techniques and reproduction of stereo (or even surround) sound fields.

Look at figure 10.6 and consider a sound originating from the left side of the head. Notice that the sound has to travel farther to reach the right ear. Based on the inverse square law, we can expect that because of the added distance, the intensity will be slightly lower at the right ear than at the left. More important, at high frequencies, the head itself acts as a baffle, preventing high frequencies from effectively reaching the far ear (figure 10.7). This shadow effect will contribute to the lower intensity at the right ear, as well as create a timbral or spectral difference in the sound reaching each ear.

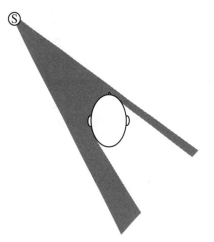

Fig. 10.7. *The shadow effect of the head on high frequencies reaching the far ear. The intensity of high frequencies arriving at the far ear will be further attenuated.*

Lower frequencies, however, with their longer wavelengths, will not be effectively blocked by the head. Instead, they will *diffract* (bend) around it (figure 10.8) and reach the far ear essentially undisturbed and unattenuated. At these lower frequencies, then, the brain must rely more on different cues for localization, namely *phase* or timing cues. Again, because of the added distance, the sound will reach the far (right) ear slightly later in time than the closer (left) ear and at a later point in its phase cycle (figure 10.9). This slight delay and phase difference at lower frequencies is interpreted by the brain as necessarily resulting from a left-oriented sound source.

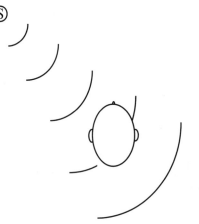

Fig. 10.8. *At low frequencies, diffraction (bending) of sound waves around the head precludes any shadow effect. Intensity will not be further diminished at the far ear.*

Thus, for complex sounds, which generally cover a whole range of frequencies, the brain uses a combination of intensity, spectral, and timing cues to determine the location of various sounds. These pieces of difference information between the two ears are called *interaural cues*.

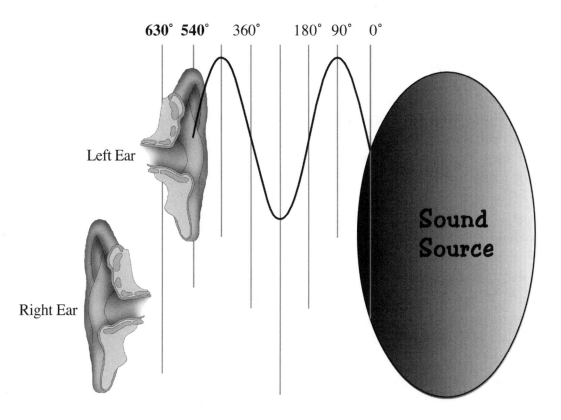

Fig. 10.9. *Phase difference, at the listener's left and right ears, of a lower frequency (around 500 Hz) originating from a source at the left of the listener. The brain uses this phase difference at lower frequencies to determine the sound source's location.*

Stereo Miking Techniques

These observations about human localization lead us directly to how we use microphones to capture a stereo sound field, and reproduce sources as they appear in their acoustical space. Since our ears respond to *intensity* and *time (phase)* cues for localization, our stereo mic setups must be carefully configured in such a way as to do the same.

Coincident Pair (Intensity Stereo)

Coincident miking techniques, also known as *intensity stereo*, use the intensity differences of sound arriving at two mics to recreate the stereo field. By angling two directional (typically *cardioid*) microphones between 90° and 180° away from each other, each mic will pick up principally the source it is aimed at while rejecting to a certain extent sounds that arrive off axis. At the same time, the capsules of two microphones are aligned along one plane such that all sounds reach both mics at the same time. This virtually eliminates any phase differences at the two mics. The advantage of doing this is that mono compatibility is realized—otherwise, phase differences yield frequency cancellations in the electrical realm, particularly when summed to mono. The disadvantage of coincident schemes is that the lack of phase cues can yield a less dramatic or convincing sense of stereo separation and placement.

The earliest stereo coincident miking scheme was the *Blumlein* pair (figure 10.10), developed by BBC engineer Alan Blumlein during the 1930s. It consists of two coincident bidirectional (figure eight) mics placed at a 90° included angle

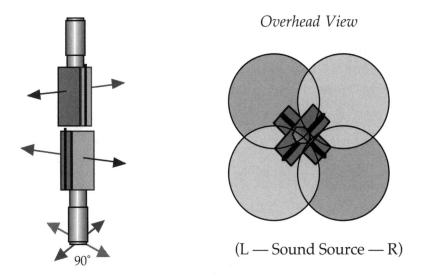

Overhead View

(L — Sound Source — R)

90°

Fig. 10.10. *Blumlein coincident stereo mic pair, using two bidirectional mics*

from each other, and 45° off-axis from the source. Each mic is sent to its own track or channel and panned hard left and right. The Blumlein scheme is especially well-suited to recording in a nice sounding acoustic hall, where it takes advantage of the mics' rear pickup pattern to pick up hall ambience in addition to the direct sound.

Similar setups using different directional mic pairs (cardioid or hypercardioid) are simply referred to as "X-Y" pairs (figure 10.11) and range from 90° to 180° included angle, with the wider angles used for the less directional mics.

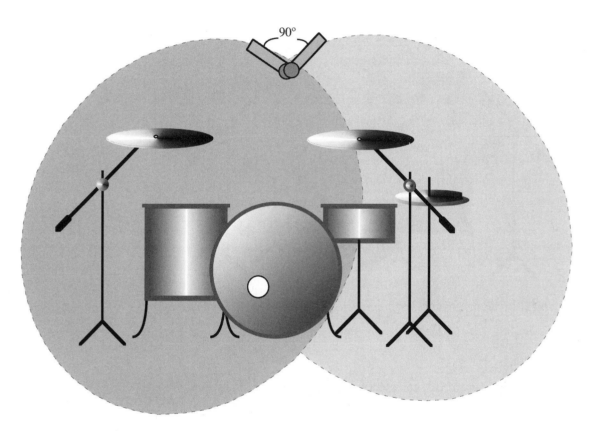

Fig. 10.11. X-Y coincident stereo mic pair, using two hypercardioid mics

Near-Coincident Pair

Near-coincident miking schemes introduce timing cues by spacing the mics slightly apart, typically about the width of a human head, with each mic essentially taking the place of one ear. One of the most common near-coincident schemes is *ORTF* (Office de radio-télévision diffusion française) named after the French broadcasting organization that developed it. It consists of two cardioid mics with capsules spaced 17 cm (6.69 inches) apart and a 110° included angle between them (figure 10.12). This scheme, meant to closely recreate the human listening experience, can be very dramatic and effective, as it captures both timing (phase) and intensity differences between the two mics. However, the result is by definition not phase coherent, and small adjustments in placement should be made to try to minimize phase cancellations when monitoring in mono. A variant on this scheme is the NOS (Nederlandse Omroep Stichting, the Dutch Broadcasting Foundation) near-coincident stereo pair, which calls for two cardioid mics spaced 30 cm (12 inches) apart, at an included angle of 90°.

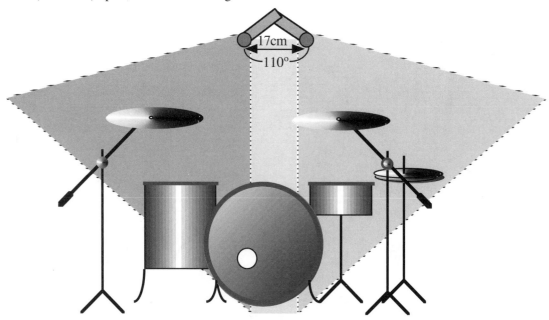

Fig. 10.12. ORTF near-coincident stereo mic pair, using two cardioid mics

Spaced Pair

A *spaced pair* (figure 10.13) consists of two identical mics of any kind, usually omni-directional, placed generally between 3 to 10 ft. apart, aimed directly towards the source. The farther apart the mics are, the more there will be the sensation of a "hole in the middle" of the sound field when reproduced. This is because sources falling in between the two mics will be greatly reduced in intensity coverage due to the inverse square law. Sources that are off-center will tend to "pull" dramatically left or right, yielding both an exaggerated sense of stereo separation as well as a hole left behind in the center image. The farther apart the mics, the more dramatic the effect.

One solution to this phenomenon is to place a third mic in the center between the spaced pair and blend it in to restore the center image. A three-spaced-omni technique, spaced 5 ft. apart, is often used by Telarc Records for their classical recordings. However, this solution brings with it the danger of introducing additional phase anomalies and cancellations. The greater number of mics used, the greater the possibility for phase cancellations. The advantage of using spaced omnis is that they have extended low-frequency response (compared to directional mics), as well as absence of off-axis coloration.

Fig. 10.13. Spaced pair using two cardioid or omni mics

Binaural

Taking the approach of recreating the human listening experience to its logical conclusion, the *binaural* recording system (figure 10.14) actually uses a dummy

head complete with outer ears (*pinna*) and an omnidirectional mic placed inside each ear canal. This yields perhaps the most dramatic and realistic recreation of the human listening experience using two channels. However, binaural recordings do not translate well to speakers and are best experienced through headphones.

Fig. 10.14. Binaural recording system using a dummy head (Courtesy Georg Neumann GmbH)

The Pinna

The binaural recording system takes advantage of an additional important element, besides phase and intensity, that contributes to the localization of sound—the *pinna* or outer ear. The signal that enters the ear canal is a result of the direct sound combined with high-frequency reflections off of the pinna (figure 10.15). This combination results in a series of notches in the frequency spectrum where the difference in distance between direct and reflected path equals one-half wavelength (or an odd-multiple thereof, such as ³⁄₂, ⁵⁄₂, etc.). Because these waves will be 180° out-of-phase when they combine, those particular frequencies cancel themselves out, resulting in a *comb-filtered* frequency spectrum (figure 10.16). As the position of the source or of the head changes, so does the difference in distance and the resulting frequency notches. Again, the brain learns over time to associate certain frequency spectra presented to the ear with visually or experientially observed sound source positions. In fact, given the proper conditioning we may be able to localize sounds even with only one ear. Small head movements are especially useful for helping with localization, presenting to the ear a rich array of continuously varying spectra for interpretation by the brain. The pinna's role is especially crucial in determining fore-aft (back-to-front) localization as well as localization on the vertical plane, where phase and intensity differences necessarily play a more limited role.[25]

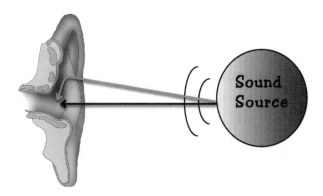

Fig. 10.15. *Direct sound and multiple reflections off of the pinna combine at the ear to create a comb-filtered frequency spectrum. The brain uses this spectral information to help determine the location of sounds, particularly along the vertical and fore/aft planes.*

25. Consider a sound arriving from behind the listener but located exactly equidistant from the two ears. The sound reaches both ears with equal phase and intensity, but its frequency spectrum will be quite different from an identical sound arriving from in front of the listener.

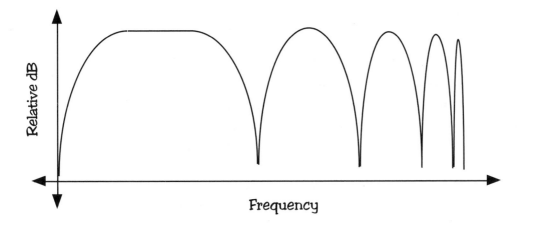

Fig. 10.16. The comb-filtered response resulting from the combination of direct sound and a single reflection off of the pinna. The actual response at the ear is greatly complicated by multiple reflections from different points on the pinna.

Haas (Precedence) Effect

A closely related principle in the theory of sound localization is the idea that we localize sound sources based on their first arrival time—a principle often referred to as the *precedence effect* or *Haas effect*. Studying the effects of sound in an indoor environment, Helmut Haas found that we are able to discern a sound source from among its many reflections generated in a closed indoor environment because of its earlier arrival time at the ear. The brain has been conditioned through experience to recognize that the shortest distance from a sound source to the ear is a straight line, and therefore the first arrival time defines the source of the direct sound. Any sounds reaching the ear later in time must necessarily be reflections of that initial sound source off of nearby objects or boundaries.

This principle holds true for sounds that occur within approximately 35 ms of each other (less for sounds with sharp attack). If the sounds are identical, or even similar (as is the case with early reflections), the later sounds will not even be heard, but will be lumped by the ear together with the first sound as emanating from the single source. Between approximately 35 and 50 ms, the additional sounds will be heard as added ambience or spaciousness to the original signal, but still localized with the initial signal. Beyond 50 ms, sounds will typically be heard as separate events emanating from their own source or direction.

Stereo Sound Reproduction

Effect of Localization on Music Reproduction

Localization has several important implications for the engineer in the recording studio, as well as for the music listener. First of all, consider stereo reproduction of music. We use two loudspeakers to recreate the illusion that sounds are spread evenly across the stereo sound field in front of us. This works only because the brain, when presented with equal information in both ears, visualizes a source coming from directly in front of the listener (since acoustically, this is the only condition under which equal information reaches both ears). The brain generates a *phantom image*, whereby the listener actually perceives the sound as originating from directly in front, as opposed to from the speakers located on either side (figure 10.17).

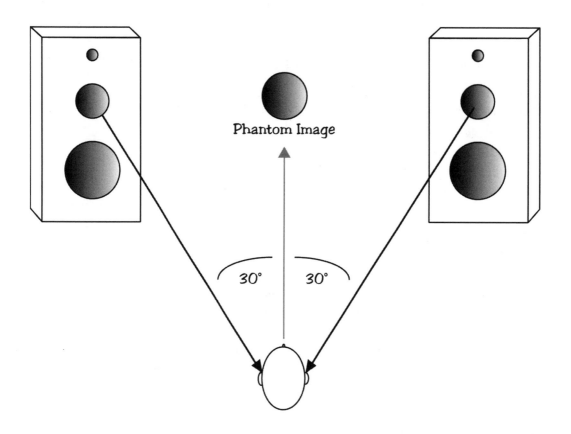

Fig. 10.17. *An identical signal coming from both speakers with equal intensity and time is perceived by the listener as originating from a phantom source located directly in front of the listener. This image called a* phantom image.

This psychoacoustic phenomenon of the phantom image is dependent on equal intensity, as well as equal arrival time, from both speakers. As we gradually adjust the relative level of a sound such that it becomes greater in one speaker than in the other, the phantom image shifts accordingly toward the louder source. A pan pot on a mixing console does just that. It adjusts the level of an individual signal sent to each channel, left or right, in inverse proportion. As the pan pot is turned to the left, the level is increased to the left channel while simultaneously being attenuated in the right. Thus, by using different amounts of panning left or right for different individual signals, we create the impression of sources being spread out evenly in front of us across the left/right horizontal plane (see boxed text).

What we must take into account, however, is that our brain's mechanism for localization based on *phase* or timing differences is also in effect. For proper imaging, then, whether mixing recorded music or simply listening back, we must ensure to occupy a listening position exactly equidistant from both speakers, on the so-called *median plane*. Any deviation from this listening position would cause sound from one speaker to reach our ears sooner than sound from the other speaker. Based on what we know about interaural phase cues, we would localize that sound to the speaker closest to us, and the perceived imaging would be skewed to that side. In fact, it only takes a deviation of about six inches from the median plane for a centrally panned signal to be perceived as coming entirely from one side (figure 10.19).

In the Studio

The Pan Pot

In order to create a smooth transition across the stereo field, the slope at which the pan pot transitions from left to right must be carefully controlled. One option is the so-called "constant power" pan pot. The slope of the pan pot is engineered such that each channel is reduced by 3 dB when the pan pot is in the center position. A signal panned to the center is sent equally to both speakers, but attenuated in each channel by 3 dB. Acoustically, these two signals combine in the power realm, and as we know, 2 × power = +3 dB. The result: constant power as we pan from left to right.

This sounds fine until we consider what happens if we monitor our signals in *mono* mode. When we select mono, the left and right channels are combined electrically in the voltage realm. You will recall that 2 × voltage = +6 dB, so that any centrally panned signal will be boosted by 6 dB. This means that in mono mode, the balance between signals will be greatly skewed towards center-panned signals, and the mix significantly altered. Back when mono playback was a main priority, pan pots were built to be constant-voltage by making the crossover point –6 dB (instead of –3 dB). Of course, under these conditions, all center-panned signals are weakened during regular stereo playback. The most common solution to this dilemma is a compromise between the –3 dB constant power and the –6 dB constant voltage crossover point. This yields a pan pot with a crossover point of –4.5 dB, with the center point only slightly attenuated in stereo and only slightly emphasized in mono (figure 10.18).

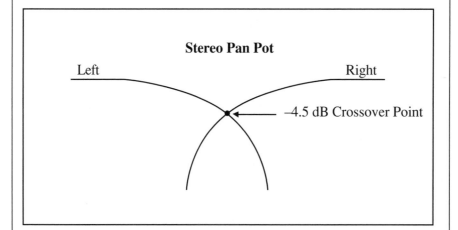

Fig. 10.18. *Stereo pan pot with the crossover point at center down by 4.5 dB. This represents a compromise between optimized mono (–6 dB center) and stereo (–3 dB center) playback.*

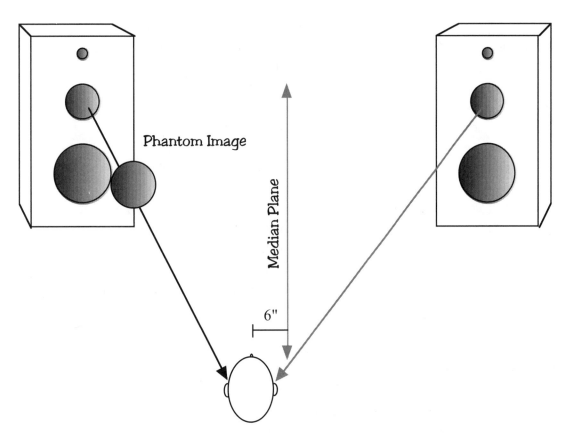

Fig. 10.19. *Phantom imaging will be skewed towards the closer speaker when the listener is not situated along the median plane. Deviation of as little as six inches would result in a center-panned signal appearing fully panned to the closer side.*

One way to ensure that we are on the median plane, in order to ensure proper imaging, is to check the mix in mono. When mono mode is selected for monitoring, all signals are sent in equal relative amounts to both channels. Under this condition, all signals should appear as a phantom image directly in front of the listener (assuming a properly calibrated monitoring setup with equal power level to both speakers). The engineer or listener need only adjust their seated monitoring position such that the above condition is met, and then mark the spot as a physical reference point.

Another important implication of localization cues arises when using delay as an effect during a mixdown. For instance, it is a common technique to create the illusion of a stereo source from a mono signal by panning the dry signal hard left, and panning a delayed copy of the same signal hard right. Because of the delayed attack times, we get the impression that the source is spread across the stereo sound field. However, if the delay is short enough, instead of creating a stereo spread, the delay merely creates a panning effect to one side. The effect is similar to that created by the listener being closer to one speaker than the other. Due to first-arrival-time localization (precedence effect), as well as phase and intensity cues, the brain will interpret the non-delayed signal as corresponding to the location of the direct source signal (first arrival time). As such, the signal will appear to be coming from just the one channel, as if it were hard-panned to that side. It would take a level increase of about 10 dB in the opposite channel to counteract the effect of the delay and restore the impression of a center-panned phantom image. (Remember that the brain uses *both* intensity *and* phase information for localization cues.)

The delay times that create such a panning effect are very much dependent on the envelope of the signal being delayed itself. The sharper the attack of a source signal, the easier it is to hear as a separate iteration, and therefore the shorter the delay that can be used without losing the impression of stereo spread. Table 10.2 lists some characteristic delay times applied to a signal that is sent to both left and right channels (speakers) but delayed in only one channel, and the resulting impressions of imaging on the listener.

Theoretically, it is possible to create pan pots that use delay or time difference instead of level difference between left and right channels to recreate different imaging positions across the stereo sound field. However, this is more problematic and not generally done, especially since the panning response varies with the percussiveness or transient nature of the signal passing through it. On the other hand, there exist 3D sound-effects signal-processing tools that use some of the psychoacoustic information discussed above to recreate the impression of a sound source coming from anywhere around the listener. By studying the specific phase and spectral information at the ear that results from sounds originating all around the listener, and then imposing such processing algorithms on a given input signal in the digital realm (*digital signal processing*—or *DSP*), sound designers have been able, with some success, to recreate "pseudo-surround" sound using just two speakers.

The more common method now is simply to create a surround-sound mix, using multiple channels instead of just two. The mix is then played back on an array of speakers situated all around the listening position. The most common of these is often referred to as "5.1" surround, which is comprised of left-, center-, and right-front channels (all full-frequency), as well as left and right surrounds. The ".1" refers to a sixth channel, a subwoofer channel, which only carries very low-frequency information (sometimes called the *LFE* or *low-frequency effects* channel), typically below 80 Hz. This channel is used to extend or enhance the low-frequency response and power of the system, and does not contribute to the surround effect itself.

Delay time	Resulting Impression
0 ms	Mono phantom image in center
> 0 to 10 ms	Sound source appears hard-panned to non-delayed speaker; listener unaware of other speaker output
10 to 30 ms	Impression of added "liveness"and increased volume; image still appears hard panned to non-delayed speaker
15 to 25 ms	Useful delay range for creating the impression of a stereo instrument in a mix from a mono source (delayed signal may need to be boosted slightly for an even left/right balance)
30 to 50 ms	Delay becomes noticeable as separate signal coming from the delayed channel speaker
> 50 ms	Obvious delay or echo from delayed channel speaker

Table 10.2. The effect on listener impression of sound-source imaging, produced by different delay times imposed on a signal sent to the left and right speakers

Masking

Another psychoacoustic effect that is of great importance in the process of recording and mixing is the effect of *masking*. To better understand this effect, we must first take a closer look at the ear itself and how it functions (figure 10.20). Sound is gathered at the outer ear aided by the *pinna*, enters the auditory canal (*meatus*), and causes the eardrum (*timpanic membrane*) to vibrate. These vibrations are amplified and transmitted through the middle ear by a series of three small bones called *ossicles* (hammer or *malleus*, anvil or *incus*, and stirrup or *stapes*) to the *oval window* at the threshold of the inner ear.

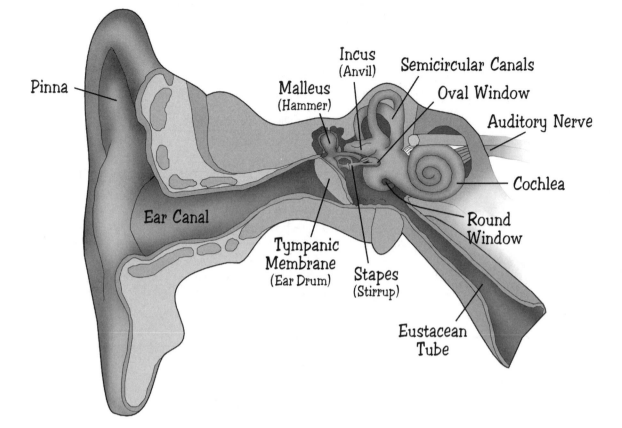

Fig. 10.20. Details of the anatomy of the human ear

Within the inner ear, vibrations at the oval window are transmitted into the cochlea, a tunnel curled up on itself in a spiral, much like a snail's shell. Figure 10.21 presents a simplified schematic of the ear with the cochlea as if it were unfurled. The cochlea is partitioned into two sub-chambers (*scala vestibuli* and *scala tympani*), which are filled with a fluid, the *perilymph*. The two chambers are connected by a small hole at the end of the partition called the *helicotrema*; the lower chamber is sealed off at the round window by another membrane similar to that covering the oval window. As the oval window is pushed in, the round window bulges out, and vice versa.

Within the cochlear partition itself is located the *basilar membrane* and the *organ of Corti*, which together make up the greater part of the sensory organ responsible for what we hear. The vibrations at the oval window cause pressure undulations in the fluid (perilymph) of the scala vestibuli. The resulting pressure difference in the two chambers sets the basilar membrane in motion. Because of the shape of the basilar membrane, which both narrows and thins gradually from base to tip, its stiffness varies accordingly (to a ratio of about 10,000:1). Depending on the frequency of the vibrations at the oval window, a certain region of the basilar membrane, corresponding to that resonant frequency, will be most greatly excited and undulate with the greatest amplitude.

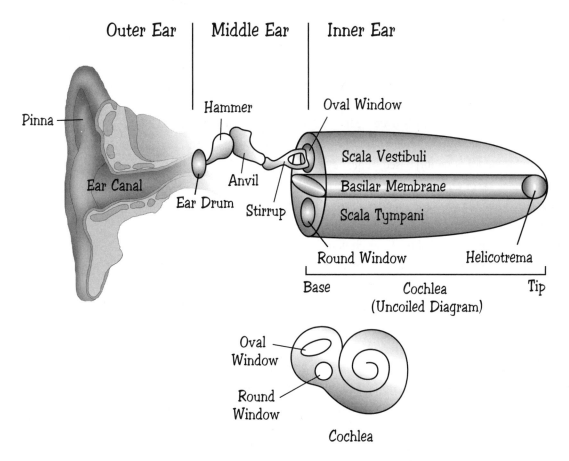

Fig. 10.21. *Simplified schematic of the ear, with the cochlea shown as if it were stretched out in a linear fashion*

When presented with a sine wave of specific frequency, the basilar membrane oscillates within a very limited region along its length, a region whose position is entirely dependent on the frequency of the tone. The lower the tone, the closer the oscillations will be to the tip, the higher the tone the closer the oscillations will be to the base near the oval window where the membrane is stiffest (greater stiffness, higher resonant frequency). Remember that resonant frequency is the frequency at which a physical entity vibrates most efficiently—its natural resonance. Natural resonance is dependent on both the mass and stiffness of the object.

The basilar membrane is lined with about 20,000 hair cells or receptors that pick up the motions of the membrane. These in turn are topped with tiny protrusions, called *stereocilia*. The hair-cell motions trigger adjacent nerve cells (or *neurons*) that send electrical impulses to the auditory nerve. These electrical impulses engage a feedback loop of two-way communication between the brain and the hair cells, whereby the identification of the region on the basilar membrane from which the impulses principally emanate is translated into the subjective impression of pitch. During this feedback loop, the brain hones in on the correct frequency by sending shut-off messages back through the auditory nerve to adjacent hair cells in order to get a more precise frequency reading. This process takes about 200 ms, and tellingly, we find that sounds of shorter duration are hard to identify as having pitch. Rather, the listener hears them as clicks devoid of any pitch or frequency-specific information, presumably because the ear/brain mechanism has not had the time necessary to analyze and hone in on the proper frequency.

From this theory of region-based frequency analysis or pitch identification, the so-called *place-theory of hearing* emerges as a possible explanation for the effect of masking. When the ear is presented with significant information within a specific frequency range, we find that lower level signals within that range will tend to be masked, or covered over, by higher amplitude signals within the same frequency range. It is as if the ear is not capable of processing both pieces of information equally and focuses on the one of greater amplitude (which it interprets as more important). One need only try having a telephone conversation during a noisy party to feel the full effect of masking, where shouting is often necessary to be heard over the din of background noise.

We can measure masking in terms of a *masking level,* defined by the intensity level necessary for a masked tone to be heard when in the presence of a masking tone of a certain intensity level. Figure 10.22 shows the masking level of a 415 Hz sine wave in the presence of a masking tone of different intensity levels and frequencies. We see that the level of the 415 Hz tone, in order for the tone to be heard, must be increased by the greatest amount when the masking tone is of the same general frequency. As the frequency of the masking tone differs from it by an increasing margin, the masked tone can be lessened significantly and still be perceived.

Masking is most apparent with signals of similar frequency content. However, it can occur with signals of different frequency as well. In these cases, the masking level must be significantly greater than the level of the signal being masked. Note the high level necessary for a masking tone to mask frequencies that lie in different ranges of the frequency spectrum, compared to the level necessary for masking within the same frequency range. For instance, given an 80 dB-1 kHz masking tone, the masked 415 Hz tone would only need to have a level of about 37 dB to be heard. The flip side of this observation is to note that the 80 dB-1 kHz masking tone would be able to effectively mask a 415 Hz tone of an intensity level of up to approximately 37 dB. Musically speaking, a loud flute might effectively mask a moderately loud piccolo, but probably not a timpani roll (except of the softest sort).

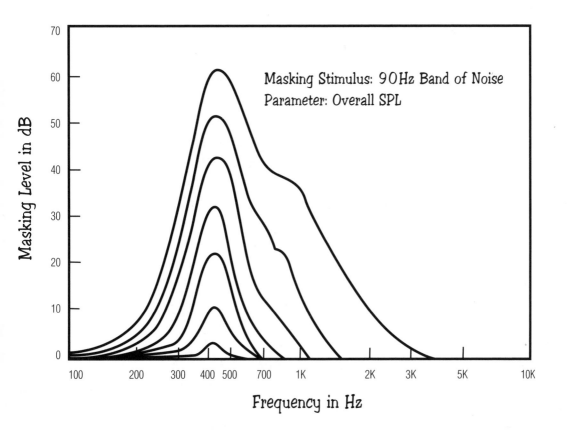

Fig. 10.22. *Relative levels (masking level—ML) needed for a masked tone of 415 Hz to be heard over a masking tone of different intensity levels (IL) (From Egan and Hake, 1950)*

Masking and the Mix Engineer

How does this apply to the recording studio? The way the multitrack recording process works, after an initial "basics" session where several instruments may be recorded simultaneously, we record, or overdub, individual instruments in succession on individual tracks. During the mixdown session, the engineer takes all of these individual tracks of instrument and vocal performances and blends them into one cohesive whole, in the form of a two-track stereo mix (or surround mix, in the case of "5.1"). The challenge is creating a mix in which all of the individual elements can be heard relatively well. This is dependent as much on frequency content as on level. Here is where the use of equalization (EQ) can become rather important in the creative process. Because of masking, if the mix contains too much activity in a given frequency range, the elements will appear to be "fighting" and will be difficult to distinguish.

For instance, the vocal track could easily be masked by an electric guitar if that guitar has significant information in the 1–5 kHz range, where speech intelligibility lies. Here, we use the term "masked" not to mean that the entire vocal disappears completely from the listener's ear, but rather that certain important portions of its frequency content are clouded over by the intruding or masking element (in this instance, the electric guitar). Remember that we are now dealing with complex tones made up of multiple sine waves as opposed to a single pure tone.

It is the job of the mix engineer, then, to ensure that the full spectrum of audible frequencies is well represented for the impression of a "balanced" mix (from a frequency perspective). This means that no two important elements within the mix are fighting for the same frequency range and listener's attention within that range. Some engineers are renowned for recording signals that do not sound particularly good when listened to in isolation, but when combined in the context of a mix have the uncanny quality of working extremely well together sonically. Thus, little EQ is ever needed for these sounds to work together. Ultimately, for most contemporary popular styles, the most important element is the lead vocal, followed closely by the drums. Any needed compromise will most likely be made in the supporting instrument tracks.

Interestingly, surround-sound mixes, where different instrument signals are distributed between five or more channels, seem to have an unanticipated advantage over stereo mixes. Besides creating a greatly enhanced sense of envelopment for listener, it seems that because of the expanded sound field, it becomes easier for the engineer to distribute signals, which might otherwise conflict with each other, between front and rear channels. This reduces the effect of masking experienced, as well as the need for EQ.

Use of Masking Theory in Audio Technology

The theory of masking has also been important in the development of certain audio technologies such as the Minidisc. This technology is dependent on the ability to store a great deal of digital information in a limited amount of space. To accomplish this feat, the system uses data compression algorithms (ATRAC in this case) to reduce the amount of data that must be stored (that is, recorded) for a given audio input signal. As part of the analog-to-digital conversion process, the input signal is analyzed spectrally to determine, based on our theory of masking, which portions of the signal we would actually hear. The system then simply discards any portions of the signal it deems would be effectively masked by other elements within the signal. This significantly reduces the amount of data needed to be recorded and therefore the amount of space taken up on the disc, allowing for a longer recording time on such a small medium. Other more recent "lossy" CODECs, as these data-crunching schemes are called, have improved on these original algorithms, including MP3 (MPEG Layer 3) and AAC.

PROJECTS

1. Use the localization information discussed above to properly calibrate your stereo (or surround) monitoring setup, taking special care with speaker angling and median plane listening position. Test your setup in mono mode.

2. Take any source signal, patch or send it through a digital delay, and pan the dry and delayed signals hard left and right respectively. Experiment with various delay times, as well as different source signals, and note the results. What delay times work well with what source signals to yield a pleasing "faux-stereo" effect? At what delay times does the effect shift from panning, to faux-stereo, to audible delay for each of these signals?

3. Using two identical microphones, try out various stereo miking techniques discussed (Blumlein, ORTF, spaced pair) on any source such as acoustic guitar, piano, etc. Note the differences in image width and accuracy, phase coherence and mono compatibility, evenness of left-right spread, "liveness," etc.. Experiment with changing the mics' polar patterns (omni, cardioid, hypercardioid) for each of these schemes and note the resulting changes in the above characteristics.

Chapter **11** The Audio Window
Relating What We Hear to the Gear

The Audio Window Revisited

Now that we have explored some of the capabilities and mechanisms of our hearing system, let's see what the implications are with respect to the recording equipment that we use in the studio. We have defined our hearing with respect to an "audio window" through which we experience sound on a level as well as a frequency basis. Based on what we have learned in chapter 10, we might revise figure 10.1 into a more detailed picture (figure 11.1), based in part on the Fletcher-Munson contours.

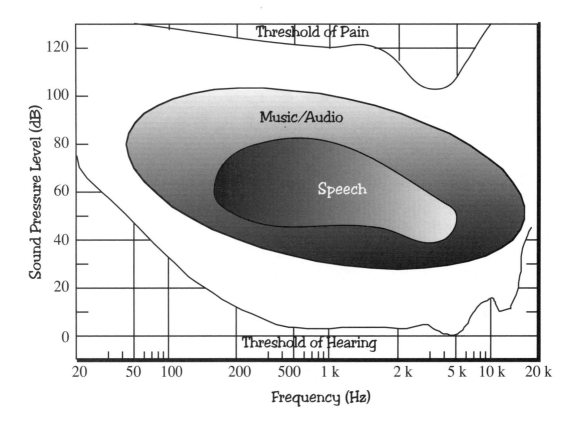

Fig. 11.1. A more detailed picture of our audio window. Most music does not exceed a range of level of about 75 dB from softest to loudest. Similarly, most recorded music does not contain much information above 18 kHz.

Audio systems generally are designed to try to capture and reproduce or transmit, unchanged, what we experience through our aural senses in the same way that visual systems, such as film, try to accurately capture and reproduce what we see. Reality, however, is stubborn in its reluctance to be captured, reproduced, or imitated. With this in mind, let's look at some of the limitations that we have to deal with in any audio system that we employ, as a means of learning how to get the most out of our music recording and reproduction setup.

Signal-to-Noise Ratio, Dynamic Range, and Standard Operating Level

All audio systems generate a certain amount of self-noise, i.e., noise inherent in the operation of the system when no input signal is present. This is called the *noise floor* of the system. For electronic devices, this noise generally consists of random motion of electrons, which typically sounds something like hiss, as well as a certain amount of AC current that has infiltrated into the audio lines, and sounds like a low hum or buzz. We could also use the term "noise floor" to refer to the background noise in a studio or performance hall. This could consist of noise from the heating, ventilation and air conditioning system (HVAC), buzzing from the lights, or leakage from noise sources outside the room such as traffic or adjacent performance noise. Obviously, these latter sources depend greatly on the time of day, and the most useful measurements of noise floor in that particular space would be made during the most typical times of use.

The noise floor of most systems is usually low enough to be masked when a music signal is passing through the system. However, it can become noticeable and problematic during low-level passages such as fade outs, or in classical music where there are very soft passages juxtaposed with very loud ones. A common measure of how noisy (or quiet) a system is, called its *signal-to-noise (S/N) ratio*, is the measured difference, in dB, between the noise floor (the level of noise in the system with no input signal present), and the system's *standard operating level (SOL)*. Standard operating level refers to the optimum average level recommended for the signal to pass cleanly through the system. The industry standard SOL for professional audio equipment is +4 dBu (or dBm) and is usually written 0 VU = +4 dBu. This means that a sine wave of 1.228 V_{rms} (+4 dBu) deflects the VU meter to its 0 VU reference position (figure 11.2). This represents a 100% modulation reading.

For a professional recording device, if we measured its noise floor to be –59 dBu, its S/N ratio would be given as 63 dB (the difference between –59 and +4). Does this mean that it can handle signals with a dynamic range (colloquially, range in level between softest and loudest passages) of less than 63 dB? Not exactly. On one hand, low-level signals must really be quite a bit higher than the noise floor to be usable as such. As signal approaches the level of the noise floor, the noise becomes too distracting, masking, and unpleasant.

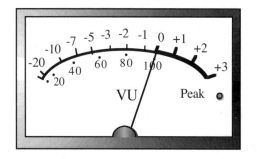

Fig. 11.2. The VU meter is meant to show the average loudness of a signal passing through it, in volume units (VU). Originally calibrated to dBm (rms), SOL of 0 VU corresponds to +4 dBu, or 1.228 $V_{rms,}$ for a continuous sine wave.

On the other hand, the SOL does not define the upper limit for level either. Instead, there is always extra level allowed above the SOL within the device before an input signal would overwhelm the system and be distorted. The true upper limit of our system, then, is the *point of distortion*, sometimes referred to as *maximum output level (MOL)*. The extra level allotment built into a device, between standard operating level and point of distortion, is called *headroom*. Typical headroom for a professional device is on the order of 20 dB. The range of levels that a given device can handle (record or transmit) effectively is called its *dynamic range,* the limits of which are defined by the noise floor and point of distortion respectively. Figure 11.3 sums up this relationship.

Why do we need so much extra wiggle room for our signal? There are two good reasons for this. First of all, as we know, music is not a continuous tone of predictable and constant amplitude, but rather a continuously variable complex signal whose amplitude as well as frequency content is constantly changing. If we set our recording levels based on a given passage, there is no guarantee that in the next moment our signal will be at the same level (although compressors are useful for ensuring that it will be close). The extra headroom allows for such swings in level from one moment to the next.

Perhaps more important, we know that the VU meter gives us an approximate (though not precise) reading of the *average* signal level in a given moment. It was originally designed to approximate the response of the human ear to loudness level of a complex signal. For a continuous sine wave signal, 1 VU increment corresponds to a 1 dB change, but for a complex music signal, the reading will very much depend on the signal's waveform, corresponding somewhat loosely to its average level and corresponding loudness.

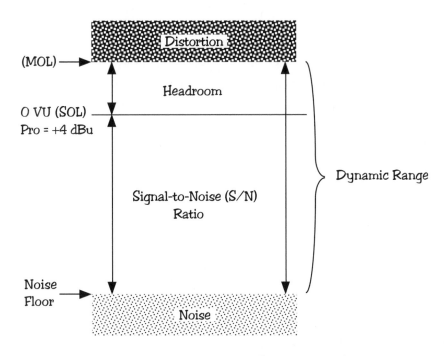

Fig. 11.3. A schematic of the operational levels that define an electronic system or device. We are always forced to work within the boundaries of our system—between noise floor at low levels and point of distortion at high levels.

However, the more significant factor in determining whether an audio system will be able to pass a signal cleanly is the instantaneous peak level of the signal. It is the peaks that cause distortion (or will be distorted, depending on your point of view). Because of the inertia (slow response time) of the needle, peaks hardly register at all on a VU meter; however, they still have the inherent ability to overdrive the system and distort. While the meter may be reading an average level of 0 VU, the peak level at that moment may be as much as 15 dB higher (figure 11.4). The difference between the average and peak level of a signal is called its *crest factor*.

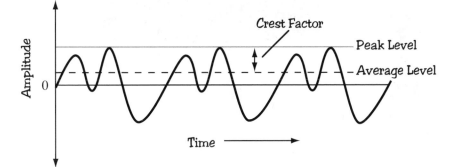

Fig. 11.4. The crest factor of a complex wave (here a bass guitar); the difference between its peak and average level can be upwards of 15 dB for certain percussive music signals. Note the smooth contour of the wave here due to limited higher harmonic content.

The extra headroom ensures that as long as our signal level is generally stable and "humming" around 0 VU, the signal will be passed cleanly without significant distortion. (I use the term "significant" here because there is always some measurable amount of distortion in any system. We are only concerned with that amount of distortion that is audible.) Even occasional forays into the red segments up to +3 VU should be safe from distortion.

Some VU meters do incorporate a small *LED* (*light emitting diode*) to warn us when our signal has reached a certain peak level close to the point of distortion (see figure 11.2), generally around 10 dB below clipping. But this kind of indication is rudimentary at best, and confusing at worst. As we shall see later, for digital recording, peak information is especially important. Once we overshoot a digital system's limits, we immediately go into full, unmitigated, and unpleasant distortion.

When comparing audio devices, a greater dynamic range implies the ability to handle larger swings in program (music/audio) level, from the lowest to the highest-level passages, without the signal either distorting or being buried in the noise floor. A lower noise floor implies a quieter device with less self-noise added to the audio signal. The SOL will indicate whether the device is operating at a pro, semipro, or consumer level (+4 dBu, –10 dBV, or –10 dBu, respectively). Generally, the lower the operating level, the more limited the dynamic range and S/N of the device.

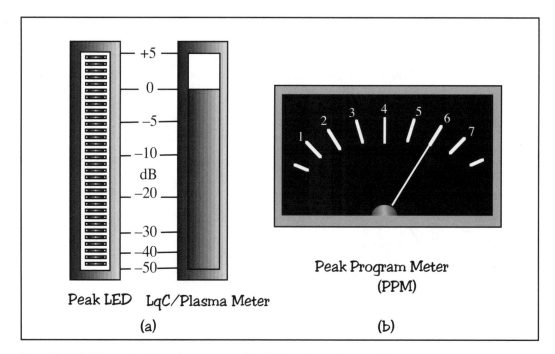

Peak LED   LqC/Plasma Meter

(a)

Peak Program Meter (PPM)

(b)

Fig. 11.5. Different Peak reading meters: Peak LED, Liquid Crystal, PPM; a reading of 6 on the PPM corresponds to 0 VU, and level changes are measured in increments of 4 dB.

Peak Program Meters

An alternative to the VU meter is the peak-reading meter, specifically the so-called *peak program meter* (*PPM*), which was developed in Europe around the same time the VU was being born in the US (figure 11.5b). The British version looks like a VU meter but has much faster ballistics and is calibrated on a scale from 1 to 7, where each segment corresponds to a 4 dB change (ranging from –12 to +12 dBu). PPM 6 represent a 100% reading referenced to +8 dBu or 1.95 V_{rms} (PPM 5 = +4 dBu; PPM 4 = 0 dBu). The 100% reading (PPM 6) corresponds to a 0 VU reading for program material (music), because the PPM is much more closely tracking the instantaneous peak of the signal.

Other peak meters exist, in different parts of the world and even different parts of the industry, which are calibrated to different levels. (For instance some equipment is calibrated for the broadcast SOL of +8 dBu.) For this reason, it is very important to know specifically what kind of meter is being used in order to be able to interpret the level readings properly with respect to noise and distortion. For example, imagine you are recording and monitoring levels using a peak meter with 0 referenced to +6 dBu (as is the case with a Nordic standard peak meter). If you treat this like a VU meter, you will not allow the level to exceed 0 by much. In actual fact, since the meter is showing you the peak rather than the average level of your signal, you would have at least 12 dB of extra headroom (and probably more) that you are not using. Your average level will be far below normal, resulting in a noisier recording.

Physically, the peak meter can also take the form of an LED bar graph whose resolution is dependent on the number of LED segments, or a liquid crystal or plasma display, which can have the advantage of an essentially infinite resolution (figure 11.5a). The numbering scale shown on this particular peak meter represents a *DIN* (*Deutsches Institut für Normung*, the German Institute for Standardization) peak scale where the 100% reading at 0 dB = +6 dBu or 1.55 V_{rms}.

Figure 11.6. shows the difference in ballistics between the peak program meter and the VU meter. Notice that for the same continuous signal, both meters will read the same level, but the peak meter resolves the level much faster (in 10–12 ms as opposed to 300 ms for a VU meter). For a non-continuous signal with a short transient duration, the resulting difference in level reading may be as high as 10 or 12 dB (unless digital, the peak program meter does not show *absolute* peak for a music signal either). The more percussive or transient the signal, such as a snare drum or clave, the greater the disparity. The difference between two meters' level readings of the same signal due to their difference in ballistics is called the *lead factor*.

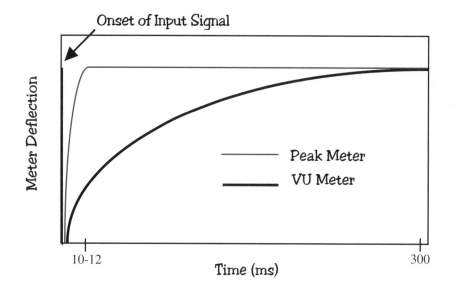

Fig. 11.6. *Comparison of peak vs. VU meter ballistics. Note the lag time (300 ms) on the VU meter's response to a transient signal (after Eargle, 3rd ed.).*

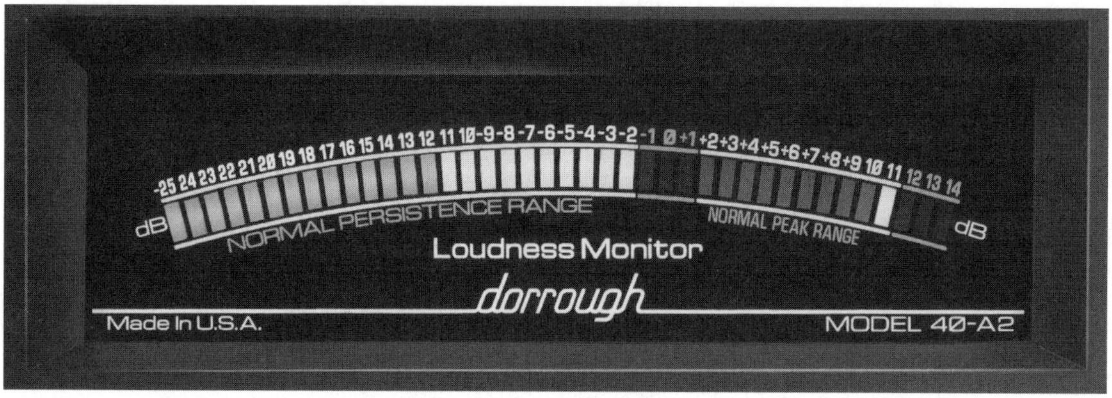

Fig. 11.7. *The Dorrough Loudness Meter, displaying average and peak levels simultaneously (normal persistence range vs. normal peak range). (Courtesy Dorrough)*

While the peak meter is inherently better at tracking peak signal levels, it does not correlate well with the actual power, and therefore the perceived loudness, of the signal. One advantage of the VU meter is that it does exhibit this correlation between movement or deflection and generally perceived loudness of the signal passing through it, and is therefore particularly useful for level-matching.

Perhaps a better alternative would be a meter that combines both average (VU) and peak level indication in a single meter system. Such a meter exists, called a *Dorrough Loudness Meter* (figure 11.7), which dynamically tracks both the average (mimicking the ballistics of a VU meter) and peak level of a signal simultaneously, with dedicated LED bar graph indications for each. However, the cost of putting such meters across every channel in a professional studio makes this option generally cost-prohibitive. There are other alternative metering schemes, and the advent of powerful computer processing opens up room for the interesting possibility of tracking multiple properties of the signal at once, using software-based metering programs. One must ask, however, how many different indicators the engineer can monitor usefully at once on a single display.

The VU meter's survival over the past sixty-plus years, and its continued use to this day is probably due in large measure to the fact that it is physically easy to watch, since its movements are slowed by the carefully controlled inertia of the needle. Peak-reading meters, by contrast, respond to every minute fluctuation in signal level, and while they are inherently more precise, they are often harder to read and fatiguing to track visually. In fact, engineers have learned over time to interpret VU meter readings and know what to expect and what levels to shoot for given specific input signals, such as kick drum or tambourine. One could say this is part of the art of the recording engineer. That said, especially given the overwhelming preponderance of digital audio equipment and digital recording media, perhaps it is time to give serious thought to the widespread adoption of an alternative metering system.

Digital Signal Metering

Digital recorders and other gear use a specific type of peak LED meter called a *full-scale* digital meter. The signal that registers on a full-scale meter is the analog voltage equivalent of the digital bit value (see chapter 14). The top of the full-scale meter is labeled "0 dB (FS)," meaning that the signal has reached full scale (all available bits are 1s), and the maximum voltage will be reproduced. For this reason, the input to a digital recorder is calibrated (using the input level pot or cal trim and an oscillator) such that an analog sine wave signal of +4 dBu (1.228 V_{rms}) will yield a reading of between –12 and –20 dB FS (figure 11.8). The most common calibration points for 0 VU are –16 dB FS and –18 dB FS, but this varies from studio to studio. The relationship between 0 VU on the console and dB FS on the full-scale digital meter establishes headroom in the digital recorder commensurate with that found in its analog counterparts. Headroom allows for sudden level changes in program material as well as for the difference between the peak and average or VU level of a signal. This also means, however, that since we are calibrating so that the signal will be consistently peaking at the top of the scale (to make use of all available bits for maximum resolution), the signal returning from the digital recorder may be somewhat "hotter" (greater in level) than other source signals, depending on what the full-scale voltage value of the device is (usually around 10 V).

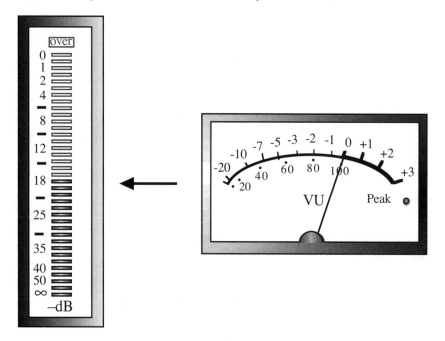

Fig. 11.8. *Relationship between VU and full-scale (dB FS) metering (for a continuous sine wave signal)*

Consumer and Semipro SOL

So far, we have only discussed SOL with respect to professional systems. However, we are often faced with interfacing professional with semipro and consumer gear. While standards become slightly more murky in this realm, there are certain elements that we can come to expect. For instance, SOL for semipro or consumer gear is often referred to as "–10" operating level. This begs the question, "–10 what?" The possibilities are generally threefold: –10 dBu; –10 dBV, or 10 dB below the professional level of +4 dBu; i.e., –6 dBu (4 dBu – 10 dB = –6 dBu). As a rule, consumer gear operates at a reference level of –10 dBu, while semipro gear will operate at either –10 dBV or –6 dBu. (Devices intended to straddle the divide between semipro and pro worlds often have a physical switch on the back allowing the operator to calibrate operation and metering of that device to either the "+4" or "–10" standard.) The two most common standards in the studio are +4 dBu (pro) and –10 dBV (semipro).

Does this mean that because the SOL is lower on semipro or consumer equipment, we therefore have more headroom? Not at all. What it means is that for cost reasons, the "consumer" device has been constructed with less expensive components, which are generally less capable of handling signals with high levels of current or voltage. In other words, the point of distortion will be reached sooner (that is, at a lower peak level). Yet we still need the same amount of headroom (or at least close to it). The only solution is to lower the standard operating level accordingly, hence the "–10 dB" reference. The situation is further complicated by the fact that cheaper components are also inherently more noisy (they generate more self-noise). Thus, not only have we lowered the point of distortion (and SOL) but we have also raised the noise floor, yielding a greatly reduced signal-to-noise ratio (as well as dynamic range). This is one of the reasons that consumer and semipro gear tends to sound noisier than bona fide professional gear.

Harmonic Distortion

We have already referred to the point of distortion, but what do we mean by *distortion*? Technically speaking, distortion is *any* change in the original waveform of the signal in question. Because an audio signal can be fully described as a graph of amplitude changes over time, the two types of distortions that can occur are either distortions in the timing of the wave or distortions in its amplitude. For now we will concern ourselves principally with the latter. In fact, when used casually, the term "distortion" usually refers to this type of distortion, specifically some form of *clipping*.

Clipping occurs when the amplitude of the input signal is too great for the device to handle. The upper portions (both positive and negative excursions) of the wave are either rounded off or drastically cut by the device, yielding a changed waveform (figure 11.9). The exact result of this, called *harmonic distortion*, will depend on the type of device in question. Solid-state devices tend to pass a signal relatively accurately as long as its level stays below the device's point of distortion, within the linear portion of its operating range. As soon as the level broaches this threshold, however, into the device's *non-linear* realm of operation, the onset of distortion is virtually immediate, and the wave is hard-clipped. This generates a waveform that resembles a square wave in the fact that its crests are flattened out.

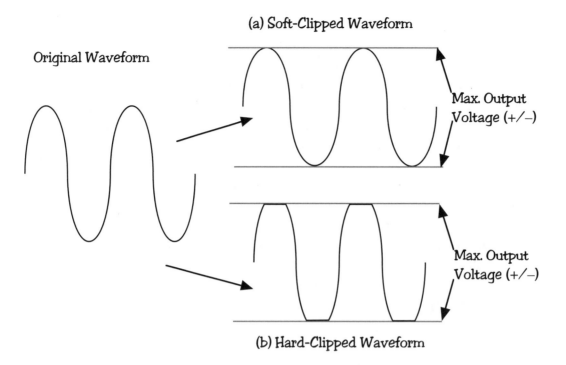

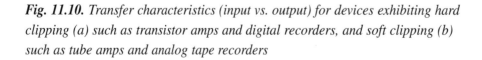

Fig. 11.9. Soft-clipping (a) and hard-clipping (b) distortion are both the result of input signal amplitude exceeding the limits or capability of the system or device.

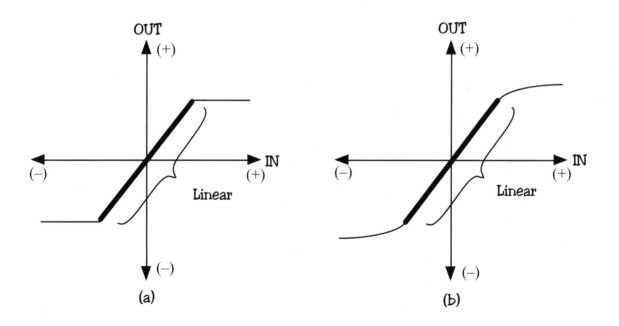

Fig. 11.10. Transfer characteristics (input vs. output) for devices exhibiting hard clipping (a) such as transistor amps and digital recorders, and soft clipping (b) such as tube amps and analog tape recorders

In doing so, it also generates the harmonic components of the square wave, notably *odd harmonics*. These harmonics represent distortion because they were not part of the original signal, and because of them the original waveform has been altered (or vice versa). Harmonic distortion is a type of *non-linear distortion* because the output signal is no longer proportional to the input signal. Digital devices will exhibit a very similar response, or *transfer characteristic*, with respect to an input signal (figure 11.10a).

By contrast, tube-based gear, which uses vacuum tubes instead of transistors for internal amplification, as well as analog tape, will start to gently distort before even reaching the so-called point of distortion, and subsequently eases into distortion gradually with increased input level. The resulting waveform is a rounded-off version of the original wave rather than a hard-clipped one, resulting in what we call *soft-clipping* or *s-curve* distortion. This type of response (figure 11.9b) tends to exhibit *even-order harmonic distortion*, where the distortion products generated are even harmonics of the input wave's frequencies. Even in this type of device, if we increase the input signal enough, we can force the system into hard-clipping as well.

How do we respond to these types of distortions, as listeners? In general, soft clipping is heard to be more musical and more pleasant than hard clipping, and is often referred to as sounding "warm," where hard clipping is said to sound "harsh" or "cold." This is one of the reasons that vintage analog tube-based equipment is in such high demand in the digital era, and commands such exorbitant prices. Tube-based guitar amplifiers are especially prized by guitarists to get that perfect distorted guitar sound because of their warm and rich sound. It is also the reason that many engineers still prefer to record to analog tape, and that analog tape still exists (although its days are perhaps numbered).

To understand why this is, let's look more closely at the harmonic series and the specific harmonics generated through harmonic distortion. You will recall that a harmonic is an exact mathematical multiple of the fundamental. Given a fundamental of 220 Hz, its harmonic series would be as follows:

Frequency (Hz):	220	440	660	880	1100	1320	1540	1760 etc.
Harmonic:	1st	2nd	3rd	4th	5th	6th	7th	8th
Pitch:	A	A	E	A	C♯	E	G	A

If we look at the harmonics in terms of pitches, we see that the first three odd harmonics above the fundamental A consist of E (fifth above A), C♯ (major third), and G (flat seventh). By comparison, the even harmonics are three A's (octave), and an E (fifth). Already, we see that the even harmonics are generally more consonant and reinforce the fundamental. This contributes to the "warm" sound that we associate with devices that generate this type of harmonic.

But why would the odd harmonic distortion sound harsh or unpleasant? The answer may lie in the fact that the frequencies and intervals of the harmonics generated are mathematically exact. The tuning system that we are accustomed to, which has been with us since the seventeenth century, is *equal-tempered* to allow for easy transpositions to and from any key while maintaining the same interval relationships within all keys. In order to accomplish this, since octaves are exact doublings, each of the twelve half-steps within the scale are made to be equal logarithmic subdivisions of the octave, based on the twelfth-root of 2 ($\sqrt[12]{2}$) or $2^{(1/12)}$. Mathematically, we can express the frequency (f) of any note within an octave as follows:

$$f = f_0(2^{n/12})$$

where f_0 = the starting frequency of the octave, and

n = the number of half-steps the note in question is above the starting frequency

Eq. 11.1. *Used to calculate the frequency of any note in our equal-tempered scale given the frequency of a common starting note such as f_0 = A440*

This means that we end up with thirds that are slightly sharp and fifths slightly flat from where they would be mathematically in a perfect tuning (*just-intonation*) system. While these lower intervals (thirds and fifths) generated by odd-harmonic distortion are not generally considered particularly dissonant, the distortion-generated, mathematically-exact harmonics are slightly out of tune. It is unclear whether we consciously hear this pitch difference, since it is probably below most measured JNDs of pitch (of course, the $\flat$7 seventh harmonic is *very* flat and especially "out" sounding). When taken as a group, however, it is clear that they are heard as unpleasant to most listeners' ears. What's more, these harmonics are less consonant and reinforcing of the original signal than the octave-heavy and "rich-sounding" even harmonics.

In addition to odd harmonics as a whole, it happens that higher harmonics are generally more bothersome than lower harmonics, as they become increasingly dissonant with respect to the fundamental. You will notice that a square wave, which is made up of infinite odd harmonics, sounds particularly edgy and harsh.

In the studio, one is likely to encounter and use both tube-based as well as transistor-based (solid-state) equipment. Understanding the distortion characteristics of each will help us to get the best results. Analog tube-based or tape-based devices are often prized for their "warmth" (read: even-harmonic distortion), and in order to elicit that sonic characteristic we need to drive them with generous input signal level. Very conservative input levels will not generally make the best use of this type of device. On the other hand, the best solid-state equipment is prized for its accuracy, precision of sound reproduction, and pristine sound. As long as the signal is well above the noise floor, there is no need to drive this device to the point of distortion. In fact, distorting this type of device generally yields signal degradation and a harshness of sound. It is generally a good idea to avoid this type of distortion unless this is precisely the sound that you are attempting to achieve.

Also, as with digital equipment, the onset of distortion is sudden, which is both a blessing and a curse. As long as the signal remains below the distortion point, it is completely clean and clear of significant distortion products. But cross that threshold and be prepared for unmitigated clipping. While it is dangerous to generalize, tube-based devices are often used on the front end of audio systems to imprint their sonic stamp on the signal, at which point the signal is recorded, often digitally, and an accurate transfer is sought thereafter. In the same way, analog tape is often used as an initial medium, to record drums and bass, for instance, after which point the tracks may be transferred to a DAW or other digital medium for overdubs and mix. The final mix is sometimes recorded back to analog (½-inch or 1-inch) master tape for a final polish.

Measuring Distortion

It is a good idea to be well aware of the point of distortion for each piece of gear within an audio system, and even better to be able to measure it, rather than simply rely on the spec sheet. The point of distortion depends on the device in question and the type of distortion it exhibits. For instance, because even-harmonic distortion is generally heard as inoffensive (and even pleasant-sounding) to the ear, we tend to accept more distortion from devices that generate mostly even-harmonics. Also, because these devices tend to ease into distortion, as opposed to the sudden onset exhibited by solid-state equipment, the point of distortion is harder to pinpoint. As an example, the point of distortion (MOL) for professional analog tape recording is defined as the point where 3% of the total output is made up of "third-harmonic distortion." It is agreed that more distortion than this becomes audible as obtrusive and unpleasant. In this particular case, we don't even concern ourselves with the percentage of even harmonics, which is surely greater than 3%.

How then would one go about measuring MOL or percentage of third-harmonic distortion? In order to determine the maximum acceptable recorded signal level, we can patch the output of the device in question to a spectrum or real-time analyzer, which directly displays the amplitudes of the various harmonics (figure 11.11). By applying a 1 kHz tone to the input of the device, we can monitor the output, including any harmonics generated by the device, at the output via the analyzer display. (If we were testing a tape recorder with a particular type of blank tape, we would need to be actively recording, while monitoring the output of the recorder from the playback head).

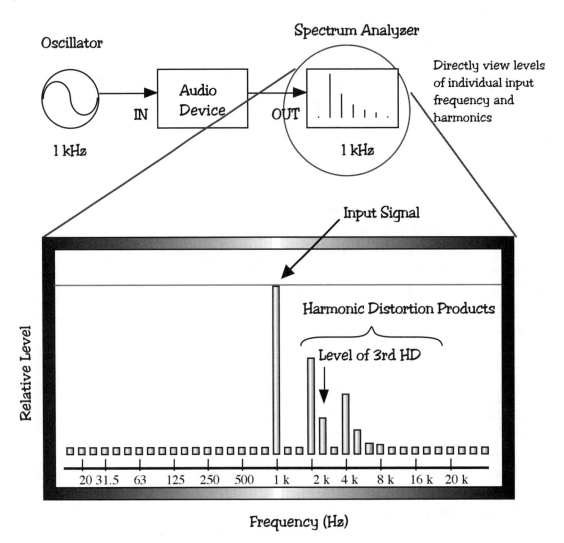

Fig. 11.11. *Test setup for measuring percentage of third-harmonic distortion generated by a device with respect to a specific input frequency at a specified input level*

We could then increase the input level to the recorder until the ratio of third harmonic to total output level would be 3:100, i.e., 3%. One advantage with this setup is that it negates possible contribution of noise to the distortion measurement. Because noise is broadband, the amount of noise energy in any one frequency band would be greatly limited and have a negligible impact on our measured level.

If our measured output level were in dB, how would we know when we have 3% third-harmonic distortion? If we realize that we are dealing with a voltage ratio (third-harmonic voltage vs. total output voltage), all we need to find is the dB difference that results from a voltage ratio of 3:100. This can be accomplished as follows:

$$\Delta \text{ dB} = 20 \log (^3/_{100})$$
$$= 20 \, [\log 3 - \log 100]$$
$$= 20 \, [0.5 - 2]$$
$$= -30 \text{ dB}$$

This result tells us that when the level of the third harmonic alone is 30 dB below the total output level, we have reached the point of 3% third-harmonic distortion. As a recording engineer, one would rarely need to go through such an experiment, except as a learning tool or to double-check stated performance. All blank tapes, as well as all recorders, are accompanied by recommended recording levels for accepted distortion specs.

Historically, different analog tapes, even within the same brand, have had different distortion specs. For this reason, each tape type must come with a recommended recording level calibration. As analog tape has improved over the years, its distortion specs have greatly improved as well (i.e., much lower distortion for the same input level). However, since *tape noise* has always been more bothersome than distortion in analog tape-based recording, the recommended input level has always been increased proportionally to yield the 3% third-harmonic distortion mark. Increasing the MOL in this way gains us a greater and more desirable S/N ratio.

Another common measure of distortion is *total harmonic distortion (THD)*, which is the percentage of the output signal made up of all distortion products. This is a typical spec for amplifiers, for instance. How would we go about measuring this? We could use the setup described above and simply add up the amplitudes of all of the distortion products. A better method involves applying a sine wave signal to the input of the device in question and patching the output through a *notch filter*, which effectively notches out or removes a specific frequency (or very narrow range of frequencies) from the signal (figure 11.12). If we set the filter to notch out the sine wave's frequency, and then measure the signal at the output of the notch filter, we are measuring everything that is left over besides the input signal, i.e., the distortion products.[26] We can then compare the two levels (total output signal vs. output signal with the 1 kHz signal removed) to find the percentage of THD at the output of the device.

It is important to recognize that the percentage of distortion is very dependent on the level of the input signal as well as the frequency in question. Thus, these two pieces of information must accompany any statement of distortion specifica-

---

26. This output signal also includes noise from the device. However, as long as the noise is more than 10 dB lower than the distortion products (which it should be most of the time, given a reasonably high input signal and a reasonably low noise floor), we can ignore it because it will contribute a negligible and immeasurable amount to the overall level.

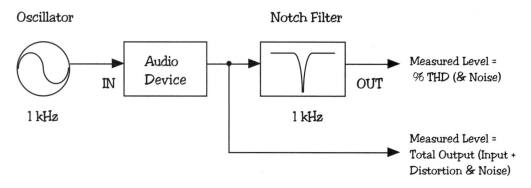

Fig. 11.12. *Test setup for measuring percent of THD generated by a device with respect to a specific input frequency at a specified input level*

tions—without them, the information is meaningless. Having a standard allows us to more easily make performance comparisons between similar devices. Unfortunately, even this does not ensure that comparisons using stated specifications will be easy or even possible. Did the tester in fact use a continuous signal or just an impulse? A sine wave signal, noise signal, or program material? Peak or rms values? Was the device loaded, and if so, how? You get the idea. While some standards exist, they are not necessarily adhered to. Very often, these basic testing conditions are not stated, and when stated, the conditions differ enough from product to product to make comparisons based on specification virtually impossible. This is another reason that while specifications are valuable to understand, they should be approached with caution and skepticism. Ultimately, it is better to test equipment oneself and to use one's ears. In the final analysis, if it sounds good, it is good.

For solid-state devices such as transistor-based amplifiers, the point of distortion is defined by the level at which output distortion suddenly jumps from a nominal and relatively consistent value, on the order of 0.1% THD, to a much greater value. For such equipment, we typically measure THD as opposed to third-harmonic distortion, since the majority of distortion products are objectionable. Figure 11.13 shows a graph of distortion with respect to input level for a typical solid-state amp. Note the sudden onset of distortion once the level broaches a specific threshold. For most professional devices, this corresponds to an input level of +20 to +24 dBu. Given a standard operating level of +4 dBu, then, we can expect that most professional gear will have a built-in headroom (above SOL) of between 16 and 20 dB. Again, understanding these distortion characteristics and measurement scenarios allows us to make optimum use of our audio and recording equipment, and if necessary, even test individual pieces to ensure proper operation and functioning.

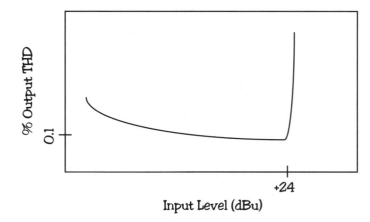

Fig. 11.13. *Graph of percent of THD at the output of a typical solid-state amp, with respect to input level*

Perhaps the simplest setup for determining the point of distortion for an amplifier is to inject a sine wave signal (typically 400 Hz) at the input and observe the output waveform on an oscilloscope (figure 11.14). At the first sign of deviation away from a sine waveform and towards a square wave, the output power can be measured using a volt-ohm meter. Again, the result should include input level, frequency, and load impedance connected to the amplifier's output(s) in order to be meaningful. Unfortunately, these are details routinely left out of specifications provided by manufacturers of audio equipment, making them all but useless for evaluating and comparing the performance of individual components without doing the testing oneself.

There are other types of distortion that can occur besides harmonic distortion. *Crossover distortion*, for instance, can occur in *push-pull* or *class AB-type* ampli-

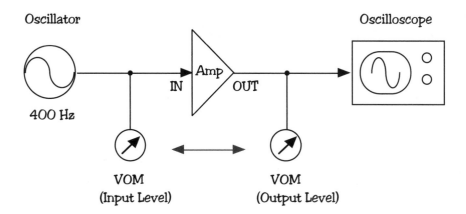

Fig. 11.14. *Test setup for measuring MOL of a solid-state amplifier*

fiers in which a separate power supply is used to generate each portion of a waveform—one for the positive and another for the negative. The transition between the two must be carefully controlled, or *biased*, for an accurate reproduction of the input signal. If the amp is malfunctioning, a bump or glitch can occur right around the crossover point (figure 11.15), such that every time a waveform crosses over from positive to negative and back again, distortion is introduced. This will happen regardless of input level, and tends to be worse at lower rather than higher levels. Crossover distortion can also occur in improperly biased analog tape recording. The easy way to differentiate between crossover and harmonic distortion is that harmonic distortion can be eliminated by reducing the input signal level; crossover distortion cannot. Equipment exhibiting excessive crossover distortion must be serviced (or perhaps recalibrated, in the case of an analog tape recorder).

Another type of distortion that may be encountered is *intermodulation distortion (IM)*. Low and high frequencies can occasionally interact and cause one or the other to modulate. This modulation generates new frequencies (sum and difference tones) that were not part of the original signal. IM is different from harmonic distortion as the distortion products are not harmonically related to the original input signal. For this reason, IM distortion generally sounds worse than harmonic distortion. Again, excessive IM generally needs to be addressed by a service technician.

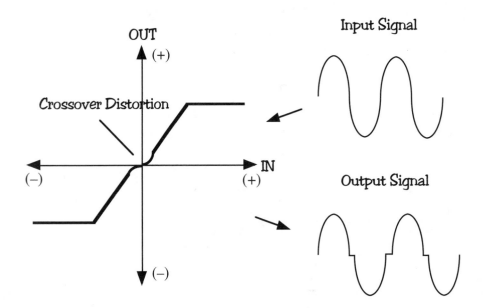

Fig. 11.15. *Transfer characteristic (in vs. out) of a device exhibiting crossover distortion, resulting in a distorted waveform*

Frequency Response

The *frequency response* of a device is a measure of its ability to reproduce an input signal accurately across the frequency spectrum. Frequency response gives us an idea of how well the device reproduces low, mid, and high frequencies, which helps us to predict how it will sound tonally or timbrally. For instance, a device with poor high-frequency response tends to sound dull, while one with poor low-frequency response may sound tinny or weak. We might also have a device that exaggerates the upper midrange frequencies, and may sound harsh or abrasive. These qualitative observations are subjective, but they are tied, at least loosely, to the objective measure that is the frequency response of the device.[27]

When measuring frequency response, we are comparing input to output signal. Most of the time, we would like to see a relatively flat response such that output is *proportional* to input within a specified frequency range. It is important to make the distinction here between *proportional* and *equal*. That is, certain devices are notoriously inefficient, such that a large input signal will generate only a small output signal. Such is the case with loudspeakers, where tens or even hundreds of watts of electrical power fed to the input typically yield but a meager few acoustical watts. (Most speakers, with the exception of horn-loaded speakers, are only 3–5% efficient at best.) But as long as the output is *proportional* to the input for all frequencies, such that changes at the input are reflected in *relative* fashion at the output, we have a linear transfer function, and the waveform will be reproduced fairly accurately. (It happens that loudspeakers are also very difficult to engineer with both a flat frequency response and a pleasing sound, and therefore are often the weakest link in our audio chain with respect to fidelity.)

How do we measure frequency response? Figure 11.16 shows a typical test setup. It consists of connecting a sine wave generator to the input of the device and measuring input versus output voltage at frequencies across the spectrum—typically every third of an octave.[28] We can then either chart the absolute gain at each frequency measured, or more typically, we can chart positive or negative gain at each frequency with respect to a reference frequency—typically 1 kHz. Response at 1 kHz is called 0 dB. If we are measuring the frequency response of an ampli-

27. It is important not to confuse *frequency response* with the *frequency content* of a sound source. We can describe signals as having a certain frequency range, defined by the frequencies that make up the signal, i.e., their frequency content. This is an inherent characteristic of the source related to its modes and amplitudes of vibration. Frequency response, on the other hand, can only refer to the ability of a *device* or transducer to accurately reproduce the frequency content of the sound source. A voice and a piano have a certain frequency range, and we can measure their frequency content; loudspeakers and microphones, and even our ears, have a certain *frequency response*.

28. A faster method might involve pink noise as a source, in which all octave bands are represented equally, but measurements would have to be in octave bands and would therefore be less precise.

fier, all frequencies will have a certain amount of gain, since that is the amplifier's job—power or voltage gain. In this case, a "flat" frequency response would consist of the same amount of gain for all frequencies within the stated range.

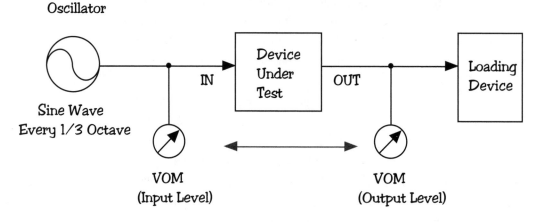

Fig. 11.16. Typical setup for frequency response measurements

Figure 11.17 shows a typical frequency response graph. The graph consists of decibel change at the output across the frequency spectrum (typically measured in third octave bands—that is, a measurement is made at every third of an octave frequency), as referenced to the output level at 1 kHz. Note that the 1 kHz measure appears as 0 dB regardless of the actual gain at 1 kHz, and all other frequency measurements here are referenced to the output level at 1 kHz. From the graph, we can tell that the device in question is relatively flat from about 150 Hz–3 kHz. It has a slight rise in response between 3 kHz–7 kHz, and a gradual drop-off in response below 150 Hz and above 7 kHz.

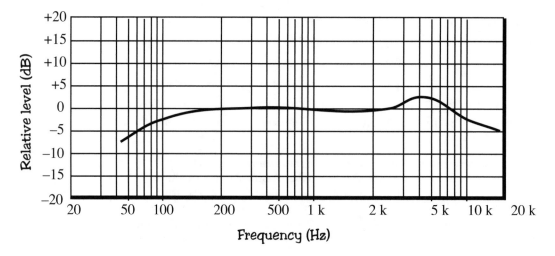

Fig. 11.17. Frequency response graph of a typical audio device (such as a micro-phone) plotted in decibels relative to a reference level (0 dB) at 1 kHz

However, rather than just stating the response as being flat from 150 Hz to 7 kHz, we can state an extended frequency response accompanied by a certain range of deviation from 0 within that range of frequencies. For instance, the above frequency response could be said to be flat between 100 Hz to 10 kHz (± 3 dB); or again, flat between 40 Hz to 20 kHz (± 5 dB; or +3 dB, –5 dB). This amount of deviation is on the high side for stated frequency response, but all of these statements are equally correct. However, notice that without the stated deviation, none of these statements is meaningful.

What is an acceptable range of frequencies across which a device should be "flat?" The most commonly stated (and perhaps overused) frequency response range is "20 Hz to 20 kHz," which is treated as something of a holy grail. Manufacturers often feel the need to fudge their specs in order to be able to print these numbers. As we have already seen, most adults are unable to strictly hear frequencies outside of about 30 Hz to 16 kHz or 18 kHz anyway, so an audio device reproducing frequencies above or below this may not necessarily be heard as superior (although audiophiles and recording engineers, at least those who try to protect their hearing, are often sensitive to frequencies beyond this range). At the same time, absence of high-frequency information above 18 kHz or 20 kHz does, in many cases, seem to be detectable.

In addition, it is arguable that for certain devices, such as amplifiers and mixing consoles, a much more extended flat frequency response range is required, because non-linearity in an upper frequency range can cause distortions within the audible range (such as *intermodulation distortion* or *IM*). Poor frequency response is, in fact, a type of amplitude axis distortion, whereby input amplitudes at certain frequencies are not reproduced correctly at the output, resulting in an altered waveform. Also, because of the advent of high-resolution digital recording systems (theoretically capable of capturing frequencies as high as 48 kHz or even 96 kHz (with 192 kHz sampling rates), extended frequency response is becoming more important for more devices. High-resolution microphones and loudspeakers, with stated frequency responses into the 30 kHz and 40 kHz range, are beginning to make their appearance. Even if one argues that we cannot hear in this upper frequency range, such extended response at least implies flatter response within the audible range. Ultimately only the listener can judge whether this is necessary or audible. Again, a healthy mix of subjective listening and objective measurement makes the most sense.

Of course, many other factors besides frequency response affect the quality of sound reproduced by an audio device. *Slew rate* or *transient response*, for instance, which measures an amplifier's ability to quickly respond to the onset of a sound (its transient or attack), can have a dramatic impact on the signal's accurate reproduction. As discussed previously, the attack portion of a signal plays a particularly important role in the identification of sounds and timbres. Obviously, frequency response measurements using continuous tones or pink noise have no way of taking the envelope of a musical sound into account.

For some devices, measuring frequency response is a little tricky. Consider, for instance, a microphone. In order to properly measure the frequency response of the microphone, we must know the level of the acoustical signal presented to it. The only way to know this is to measure it using a sound pressure level meter, which uses . . . a microphone. Furthermore, because the input signal is acoustical, it will be dependent on the frequency response and sensitivity of the loudspeaker reproducing the signal. How do we know the frequency response of the loudspeaker? We measure it, using . . . a microphone. You get the idea.

Once we have gone through this loop enough times, however, we start to get a good sense of what we are dealing with, and we have our ears to help confirm what we are measuring as well. We can then begin to establish reliable testing setups and equipment. We come to count on the fact that certain specific microphones and loudspeakers are known to have very good responses and can be used to accurately measure other devices.

When comparing equipment, all other things being equal, an extended frequency response with limited deviation (no more than 3 dB at any given frequency within the stated range) is desirable for properly reproducing the full spectrum of sound. You will notice, however, that two similar devices stating a frequency response of 20 Hz to 20 kHz may sound vastly different. This can be due in part to the fact that each manufacturer may have used a different setup perhaps with a different source test signal, or may not have included deviations in the specification. While published equipment specifications can be very misleading in this way, they can also give a general sense of predicted performance. (For instance, if a reputed microphone company claims a frequency response of up to 40 kHz, you can expect that the microphone will be very good at reproducing high frequencies, regardless of its actual high-frequency roll-off point.)

Discrepancies in sound are also due to the fact that, as discussed, many other factors come into play, such as distortion characteristics (IM, crossover distortion, or THD specs may be different) or transient response. Therefore, specs must be taken as a whole rather than on a piecemeal basis. The best approach is to use one's ears, perform objective tests oneself, and keep the test conditions consistent for all pieces of equipment being compared. Again, in the end, if it sounds good, it is good. Likewise, if it sounds bad, then it does not really matter how it measures (although measurements may help us figure out why it sounds bad, and hopefully correct the problem).

PROJECTS

1. Do a survey of the different metering systems within your studio setup. Pass a single signal (preferrably a sine wave) through each piece of equipment and determine the standard operating level (SOL) and point of distortion (MOL) for each using the techniques discussed. Which pieces sound pleasant when distorting and which do not? Use this information to find creative uses for distortion in your recordings.

2. Perform test recordings at different signal levels and note the result with respect to noise, distortion, and frequency response.

3. Perform frequency response measurements on the various components of your studio. How closely do the measured results correlate to your subjective perception of each device's sonic character or to the published specifications?

4. Using a sine wave signal, calibrate the digital components of your system for optimum average level and to establish the proper amount of headroom.

Chapter 12 Gain Structures
System Levels

It is worth looking at the entirety of our recording signal chain, and observing how levels are managed throughout, from initial input to final destination. Having this kind of overview allows us to maximize signal-to-noise and dynamic range throughout the system and come out with the cleanest possible signal. To this end, let's put together everything that we have been discussing about levels and gain stages into a single overall gain structure. *Gain structures* are views of all the level changes that occur throughout a system from initial input signal, through each transducer and gain stage, and to final output signal. Pay particular attention to points in the signal chain where an audio device's *sensitivity* comes into play. Sensitivity is a rating that describes the output level of an audio device, such as a microphone or a power amplifier, given a certain known input level. Given the same input signal level, a more sensitive device will yield a greater output signal. These points require a little more calculation in order to extract actual output level from rated sensitivity.

We will keep the signal chain in this example relatively simple, as follows: a single acoustic sound source, one microphone feeding a single console channel mic preamp input passing through the channel and monitor faders, master fader, control-room level, power amplifier, and loudspeaker (figure 12.1). Note that most of the manipulation of our signal happens in the electrical realm within our system. For this reason, it is important to have a firm grasp of electrical terminology and level measurement.

At each gain stage, we must be conscious of our audio limits—on the low end with the noise floor, and on the upper limit with the point of distortion. The goal, then, is to maximize the S/N ratio at each stage, so as to transmit our audio signal at optimum levels and ensure best audio fidelity or sound quality. This ratio can never be improved beyond the weakest link (barring noise-reduction signal processing), so one poorly managed gain stage can greatly reduce the overall performance of the sound system. The S/N ratio of the first acoustic stage is determined by the noise floor of the physical space being used to record or perform. Indoors, this would consist of noise contributed by the HVAC (heating ventilation air conditioning) system, buzzing from the lighting system, and leakage from external noise sources (adjacent performance spaces, street traffic noise, etc.). Noise at this stage can be minimized by moving microphones away from obvious noise sources and closer to the desired sound source being picked up.

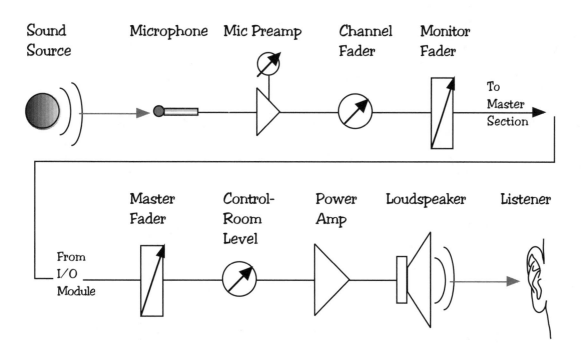

Fig. 12.1. Elements of a gain structure from acoustic input through console and
to acoustic output

The general approach to proper gain staging is to bring the channel fader to
unity gain—the point (marked 0) where the fader is neither boosting nor attenuating the signal passing through it—and then use as much of the mic (preamp) trim
as needed to bring the signal up to around 0 VU through the console and tape
machines. If recording to a digital medium, the signal level should peak as close
to 0 dBFS on the digital meter as possible without clipping. As discussed previously, more percussive source signals should be allowed to register significantly
lower on a VU meter, as they will be peaking quite a bit higher. Digital meters
should register the peaks accurately.

For the following discussion, please refer to the gain structure in figure 12.2.
The sound source is measured to produce 98 dB SPL, four feet away from the
source. The microphone used to pick up the signal is twelve feet away, so the first
step is to find the drop in level over distance according to the inverse square law.
(We are assuming a free-field environment with inconsequential reverberant contribution within the area under consideration.)

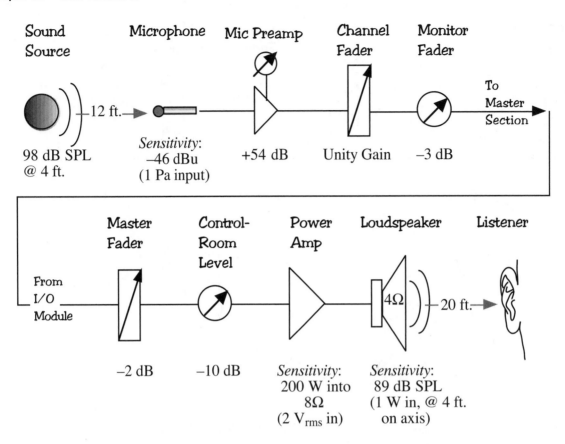

Fig. 12.2. *Example gain structure with sensitivities and level settings included*

Step 1

$$NR = 20 \log (D_2/D_1)$$
$$= 20 \log (^{12}/4)$$
$$= 9.5 \text{ dB}$$

The loss of signal over distance is 9.5 dB ≈ 10 dB from 4 ft. to 12 ft. For most applications, a fraction of a dB is insignificant, so we will merely round up or down to the nearest dB. Therefore, the sound pressure level at the microphone is 98 dB − 10 dB = 88 dB SPL.

Step 2

The microphone is rated such that a 1 Pa input yields an electrical voltage of –46 dBu. What we need to find is the corresponding voltage output given our actual input of 88 dB SPL. To do this, we must find the difference between 1 Pa (rated input) and 88 dB SPL. It happens that 1 Pa ≈ 94 dB SPL; thus, the difference between rated and actual inputs to the mic is 94 dB – 88 dB = 6 dB. Since our input signal is 6 dB lower that the rated input, our output will also be 6 dB lower than the rated output:[29] –46 dBu – 6 dB = –52 dBu.

Step 3

The mic signal feeds the mic preamp, which is set at the mic trim to boost the signal by 54 dB. This yields a level of –52 dBu + 54 dB = +2 dBu.

Step 4

Each consecutive gain stage will reduce or boost the voltage according to respective level setting. Thus, the voltage is unchanged at the channel fader, which is set to unity gain. The level is attenuated by 3 dB at the monitor fader, yielding –1 dBu, and by 2 dB at the master fader, yielding (–1 dBu) – 2 dB = –3 dBu. The control room level happens to be set to attenuate the signal by 10 dB, leaving us with a voltage of –13 dBu heading to the power amplifier and speaker(s).

Step 5

The power amp is rated to generate 200 W given an input of 2 V. Again, we need to compare our actual input with the rated input. There are two ways to do this. We could either find what voltage is –13 dBu and then find the dB difference between that and 2 V. However, converting 2 V to dBu instead will save us a step. Thus, dBu = 20 log (2/0.775) ≈ 8 dBu. Now we can easily compare rated vs. actual input, the difference being 8 dBu – (–13 dBu) = 21 dB. Again, we will say that a difference of 21 dB at the input yields a 21 dB difference at the output. Because our input signal is 21 dB lower than the rated input, to find our actual output, we need to find the power that is 21 dB less than 200 W. We do this by plugging in the known values into our power formula as follows:

---

29. An important point must be made here. We know that dB alone is simply a power ratio not tied to any specific level. A 6 dB change represents a doubling of voltage or a quadrupling of power. Therefore we can say that a change in dB at the input of a device will yield an equal change in dB at the output, regardless of whether it is expressed in dBu, dBV, or dB SPL. However, this is only strictly true if there is no difference in impedance between the input and output (which is rarely the case anymore). While impedance will not affect the voltage gain, it *will* affect the power gain ($P = V^2/Z$). For the purposes of this exercise, and because most input impedances and most output impedances each fall within a close range of values as a group, we will ignore the effect of impedance on power, with the exception of speaker impedance, and proceed as if all impedances are equal.

$$-21 \text{ dB} = 10 \log(P/200)$$

(Our reference power is 200 W, and we are looking for P.)

$$-21/10 = \log(P/200)$$
$$\text{antilog}\,(-2.1) = \text{antilog}\,[\log(P/200)]$$
$$10^{-2.1} = P/200$$

$$P = 200 \times 10^{-2.1}$$
$$= 1.6 \text{ W}$$

This would be our result if the amplifier were hooked up to to an 8 Ω load, as in the stated reference. However, you will notice that the speaker used is a 4 Ω load, which is half the resistance or twice the load. Assuming that the amplifier is capable of driving this greater load, half the resistance means double the power: $2 \times 1.6 = 3.2$ W into 4 Ω.

Step 6

The loudspeaker is rated to produce 89 dB SPL @ 4 ft. when fed 1 W of signal power. Our actual input signal power is 3.2 W. We must find the difference in dB between rated and actual input as follows:

$$dB = 10 \log (3.2/1) = 5 \text{ dB}$$

Therefore, our input is 5 dB greater than the rated input, which will yield 5 dB above the rated output: 89 dB SPL + 5 dB = 94 dB SPL @ 4 ft. If the signal were feeding two amplifier channels driving two separate speakers, the total power would be doubled. Acoustically, signals add according to their powers, which, in this case, means +3 dB, or a total of 97 dB SPL.

Step 7

The listener is 20 feet away from the speaker, so the signal will drop according to the inverse square law as follows:

$$\text{NR (for ``noise reduction'')} = 20 \log(20/4) = 14 \text{ dB}$$

This means that the sound pressure level at the listener would be 94 dB – 14 dB = 80 dB SPL.

If we were to draw a graphic representation of the gain structure with respect to level changes as well as noise floor, it would yield figure 12.3. The graphic assumes that the initial recording room's noise floor is the weakest link, and that gain staging is perfect such that no additional noise is added along the signal chain. Once the signal (along with ambient room noise) is recorded, the maximum possible signal-to-noise has been fixed. As long as each gain stage's noise floor is at least 10 dB below the signal's current noise level, there will be no significant additional noise contribution, and this will remain the signal-to-noise at the end of the signal chain.

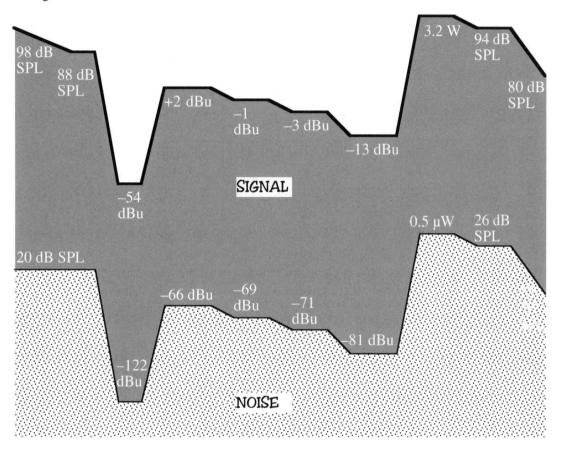

Fig. 12.3. Graphic representation of example gain structure as signal level over noise floor

Note that the signal-to-noise scenario can be improved upon initially, if we move the microphone closer to the source. Close miking is almost always necessary when doing basics for a multitracking session, in order to avoid significant leakage from other instruments playing simultaneously in the studio. During overdubs, it is possible and often desirable to record with the microphone further away from the source, assuming a good-sounding recording space. This allows for the instrument's overall natural sound to resolve before being captured, rather than focusing in on one particular area of the instrument's vibrational modes. In location classical recording, it is absolutely essential to use distant miking, in order to capture the overall ensemble, as well as the very important sonic contributions of the concert hall itself. Very little close miking of individual instruments is done in these situations. Individual instrumental sections do often receive spot miking, often in stereo pairs, as do soloists to enhance or bring out their sound within the overall ensemble.

PROJECTS

1. Calculate a gain structure as in figure 12.1, using the following specs instead:

Sound source:	102 dB SPL @ 4 ft.		
Mic sensitivity:	−52 dBu (1 Pa input)		
Mic preamp:	+60 dB	Monitor fader:	−5 dB
Channel fader:	Unity gain	Master fader:	−3 dB
Control room level:	−3 dB		
Power amp sensitivity:	250 W into 4 Ω (1 V_{rms} in)		
(8 Ω) Speaker sensitivity:	92 dB SPL (1 W in @ 4 ft.)		

2. Find all of the gain stages within your recording setup. Map these out in a gain structure; be sure to include any control that has an effect on level or volume.

3. Calculate a gain structure as in figure 12.2, substituting your own equipment's specs and sensitivity ratings. Use a sound source of your choice.

With the predominance of digital technology and digital audio recording, analog recording has been relegated to a specialty circumstance. However, it is still important to understand the analog world from whence we have come. Many of the conventions and ways of working in the digital realm have been borrowed from analog topologies. Most recording situations will, in fact, involve some combination of analog and digital gear. Analog recording is often used either in the initial or the final stage of a recording project (or both) so as to capture the natural "warmth" associated with it. So what is analog recording?

Analog Recording Process

All analog recordings involve capturing the continuous variations in sound pressure resulting from a sound wave in a fixed medium. We know that a microphone transduces the acoustical waveform into an electrical one, and the loudspeaker transduces the signal back from electrical to acoustical to reproduce the original acoustic sound wave. But in between these stages, the varying waveform needs to be stored, for reproduction at a later time.

Traditionally, this has been done in one of two ways. For decades, audio signals were mastered primarily to vinyl discs, where varying signal amplitude was captured and stored as variations in groove width or depth (figure 13.1).

Analog magnetic tape recording also looks to capture the signal's continuous amplitude variations, but stores them as variations in magnetic flux on tape. The tape consists of a *base*, usually a form of PVC (polyvinyl chloride) onto which a magnetic *slurry* is affixed. This oxide coating is made up of small, metal, needle-

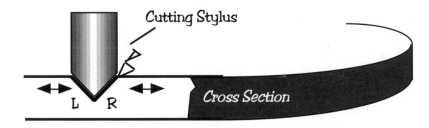

Fig 13.1. Analog recording to vinyl disc. Signal amplitude variations are recorded as variations in groove width.

like particles that have the ability to hold a magnetic charge, held together by a non-magnetic *binder*. The smallest particle capable of holding a charge is called a *domain*. The base also has a back-coating made of carbon fibers whose coarseness improves the winding characteristics of the tape.

Tape heads use coils to generate a magnetic field, through electromagnetic induction, which is proportional to the electrical signal fed at the inputs of the tape machine (figure 13.2). The front of the head contains a very narrow gap. By passing across this very narrow gap, the tape layered with oxide coating provides a path of least resistance for the magnetic field, which is concentrated at the gap. Positive and negative signal amplitude variations are recorded onto tape as regions containing positively or negatively charged magnetic particles (figure 13.3); the greater the signal amplitude, the greater the number of domains that are polarized in the same direction. The tape becomes a permanent magnet of sorts, with areas of varying magnetism. In contrast, blank tape has randomly oriented particles such that the sum magnetic flux on tape is zero. The erase head always precedes the record head for the purposes of recording over any previously recorded material (figure 13.4). The erase head re-randomizes the magnetic orientation of the particles so that it starts once again from a point of zero magnetism.

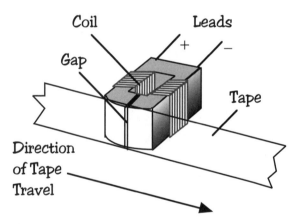

Fig 13.2. A coil in the record head generates a magnetic field when electrical current (the audio signal) passes through it.

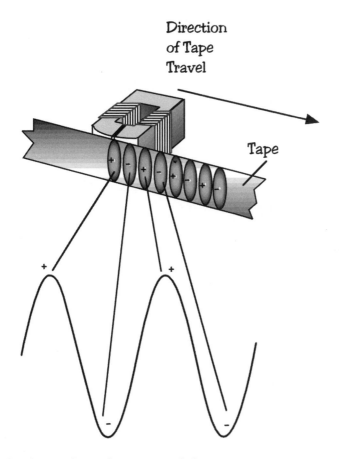

Fig 13.3. *An electrical waveform is recorded to tape as varying regions of positively and negatively charged magnetic particles.*

To get an idea of what the signal might look like once on tape, we can calculate the wavelength of the recorded signal as a function of the frequency of the input signal and speed of the tape as follows:

$$\lambda = c/f$$

where λ = wavelength, c = speed of tape, f = frequency of input signal

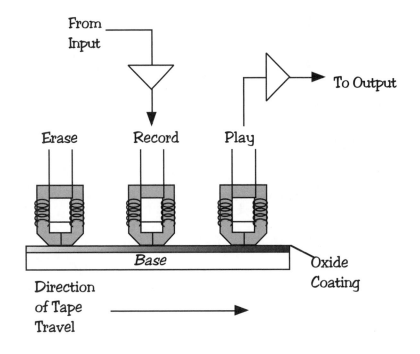

Fig 13.4. *The arrangement of heads in a 3-head tape machine*

Assuming a tape speed of 15 ips (inches per second), the wavelength of a 500 Hz tone would be $\lambda = 15/500 = 0.03$ in. Faster tape speeds, and proportionally longer recorded wavelengths, generally translate into reduced tape noise, and to a lesser extent, extended high-frequency response.

Upon playback, the process is reversed. The magnetic signal on tape becomes the source, which induces a current in the coil of the playback head and the electrical audio signal is reproduced. Notice that if the signal is monitored from the playback head during recording, there will be an audible delay, since the signal must travel on the tape from the record to the playback head before being fed to the output. The amount of delay is a function of the distance between the heads and the speed of the tape as follows:

$$T = D/c$$

where T = delay time between record and playback signals,
D = distance between the heads, c = speed of tape

Tape machines were often (and still are occasionally) used as delay devices, taking advantage of this unintended effect. Calculating the exact delay time at the output of the tape machine is useful for being able to more closely match delay time with song tempo during a mixdown, for instance. Given a one-inch distance between the heads and a tape speed of 15 ips, the resulting delay time would be T = 1/15 = 0.067 seconds (67 ms). Increasing or decreasing tape speed would allow us to increase or decrease the delay time in direct inverse proportion. To set up the effect, route an aux send to the input of the tape machine, and return the output of the tape machine back into the mix. Set the machine to repro (playback) mode, record enable, and record.

On the other hand, if the delay is not desired, during recording for instance, the output must be fed directly from the input signal (*source* or *input* mode), as in figure 13.5. In a multitrack machine, prerecorded tracks can also be monitored from their respective record head (*sel sync* or *sel rep* mode). Each track is associated with one head in the multitrack head stack. In this case, the record head in question acts physically in the same manner as the playback head. This is done so that the previously recorded tracks are in time with the live signals currently being recorded. Each prerecorded track is set to *sel-sync* (*selective synchronization*) mode, while new tracks are set to input mode. Upon mixdown, all tracks are set to *repro* mode to be monitored off the playback (or *reproduce*) head stack, which is optimized for playback.

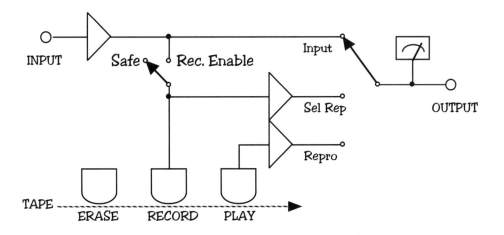

Fig 13.5. *One channel of multitrack machine set to input mode monitoring*

Analog Tape Alignment

Analog tape recording has survived for well over half a century (a full century, if you consider wire recorders) with continual improvements, and the basic principles have been adopted for digital tape recording. However, there are a number of inherent problems that have had to be addressed along the way. Professional analog recording involves a considerable number of regular adjustments in order to work properly. These must be understood by anyone interested in getting the most out of this medium.

Record Bias

To begin with, magnetic material does not like to be changed, and it resists an applied magnetic force so that the result is quite non-linear (output is disproportional to input). If we were to apply a changing magnetic field, as generated by an audio signal, to a stationary piece of magnetic tape and track the changing magnetism on tape, it would look something like figure 13.6. This is called a *hysteresis loop*, and is the reason that magnetic tape recording failed to work acceptably for the first four decades of the twentieth century. You'll notice that there is a lag between applied force (a) and the point where the magnetic material begins to respond. As applied magnetism is increased, the tape begins to change polarity accordingly until it reaches a point of *saturation* (b), where all domains have been magnetized. At this point, the tape is maxed out, and increasing applied force has

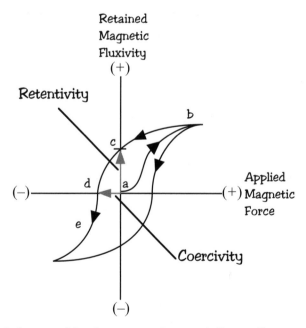

Fig 13.6. *Hysteresis loop resulting from magnetic material's non-linear response leads to distortion of input signal waveform.*

no further effect. As applied force (signal) is removed, the magnetic flux recorded on tape drops (c). The extent to which the tape retains its applied charge is called *retentivity*. The greater retentivity, the "harder" the material, and the better it is for recording.

As applied signal shifts from positive to negative polarity, the magnetism on tape is gradually forced back to a zero point (d), and then gradually towards negative polarity (e). The amount of force necessary to return tape to a point of zero magnetism is a measure of the tape's *coercivity*. Given a sinusoidal input, this pattern repeats, forming a loop response. The greater the loop, the greater the difference between applied signal and retained signal, the greater the distortion (read: change) of the original signal.

While the above description hopefully helps us to understand one of the basic problems with analog magnetic recording, in an actual magnetic recorder, this loop never really occurs because the erase head ensures that we are always starting from a point of zero magnetism. Instead, we get a *transfer characteristic* as in figure 13.7. It shares the same basic characteristics found in the hysteresis loop—namely lag around the zero crossing point as well as saturation. A transfer characteristic describes the relationship between input and output of an audio device. A *linear transfer characteristic* implies that the output is proportional (although not necessarily equal) to the input. With magnetic tape, the transfer characteristic yields significant *crossover distortion*. This means that every time the input signal approaches zero, either from the positive or negative side, it is not strong enough to generate any retained magnetism on tape at all. This results in a very distorted waveform.

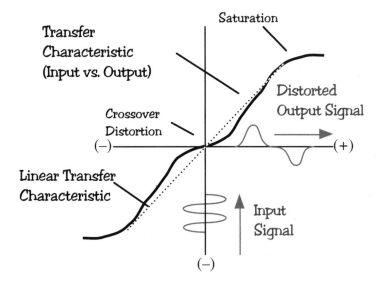

Fig 13.7. *Transfer characteristic of magnetic tape with no bias signal applied*

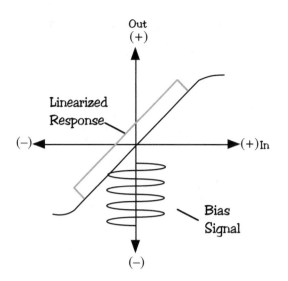

Fig 13.8. *Linearized tape transfer characteristic resulting from the addition of a high-frequency bias signal to the record head*

It was discovered, by accident, that if a strong high-frequency signal were added to the input signal applied to the record head, this crossover distortion could be overcome. By forcing the magnetic particles to shift very rapidly back and forth between positive and negative poles, the resulting response is averaged out, yielding a linear transfer characteristic (figure 13.8). This high-frequency sine wave signal (between 80 kHz and 400 kHz), called *bias*, is generated by a bias oscillator contained within the tape machine. Care must be taken in determining how much bias to add to the signal because, in addition to its linearizing effects, bias also has the potential to erase the signal from tape, particularly at higher frequencies. In fact, the bias signal is also fed to the erase head at a much higher level for the exact purpose of *randomizing* (erasing) the tape (figure 13.9).

The best method for setting bias is to feed a high-frequency sine wave signal (usually 10 kHz) to the input of the tape machine while monitoring the output level. As bias level is gradually increased, the recording process becomes increasingly effective, and more and more of the input signal will be recorded to tape. However, once the bias signal's amplitude broaches a certain threshold, it begins to have an erasing effect on the high-frequency signal, and the level at the output will begin to drop. It is generally agreed that the best compromise between low crossover distortion and good high-frequency response is the point where output level at 10 kHz has dropped by about 3 dB from its apex or highest point. This process is called *overbiasing*, and each type of tape comes with specific recommendations for the optimum overbiasing point (generally around 3 dB down @ 10 kHz, although the best overbiasing point in each case is generally found through practice and experimentation). By maximizing efficiency, overbiasing also has the happy effect of reducing noise as well.

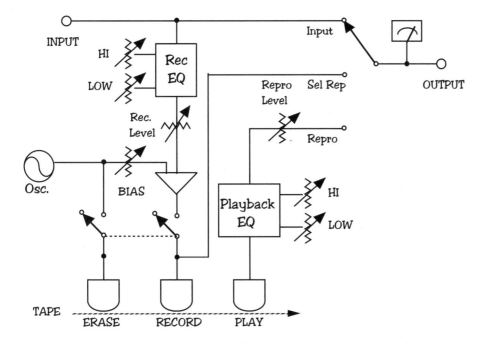

Fig 13.9. *Flowchart for one channel of a multitrack tape machine including bias signal flow and EQ circuit*

Playback EQ

The next problem that must be dealt with in analog tape recording is the fact that the playback head has very poor frequency response. Specifically, since the voltage across the playback head is proportional to the *rate* of change of flux across the gap, the output voltage level increases proportionally with frequency—by about 6 dB/octave. Therefore, the tape machine must include a playback EQ curve that compensates for this (figure 13.10).

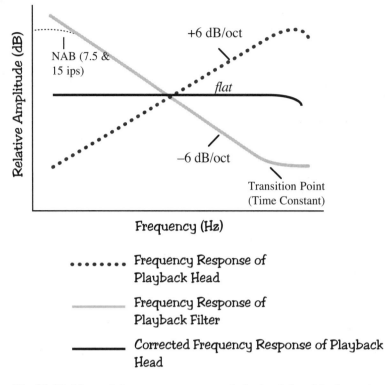

Fig 13.10. *Natural frequency response of playback head (voltage increases exponentially with frequency), requiring –6 dB/octave correction filter*

First, because different speeds yield different responses from tape, changing the speed on a recorder engages separate EQ circuitry. Additionally, there are several different playback EQ curve standards that have developed on different continents, and are defined by different high-frequency transition points, or *time constants*. Equalization is often expressed in terms of time constants represented by the following equation:

$$t = 1/2\pi f$$

where t = time constant in seconds, f = 3 dB transition point in Hz

The *IEC* (European standards committee) defined two standard playback EQ curves, optimized for use with 7.5 ips (70 μsec or 2275 Hz) and 15 ips (35 μsec or 4550 Hz). The *AES* (Audio Engineering Society, a US standards organization) standard adds a curve for 30 ips (17.5 μsec or 9100 Hz), and the NAB American standard is a compromise curve for use with both 15 and 7.5 ips tape speeds, which has both low (3180 μsec or 50 Hz) and high (50 μsec or 3180 Hz) frequency transition points. What this means is that it is critical that a recorded tape be accompanied by the EQ standard specification that was used for playback and recording calibration. Otherwise, the tape may not play back properly when mounted on a separate machine used for mixdown. The EQ standards must match.

You will notice from figure 13.10 that there is some high-frequency loss that is due to a number of factors, including *head-gap loss*. Head-gap loss occurs when the wavelength of the recorded signal on tape equals the gap length (figure 13.11). This yields an average magnetism of zero across the gap, resulting in zero output voltage. Fortunately, the gap length is engineered to be very small (as little as 1.5 μm), corresponding to frequencies upwards of 75 kHz at 15 ips and twice as high at 30 ips. However, the beginnings of gap loss do extend down into the top range of audio frequencies of interest and therefore must be dealt with.

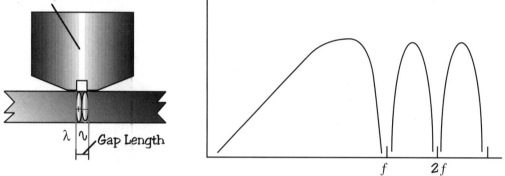

Fig 13.11. High-frequency loss at output of playback head with nulls where recorded wavelength = gap length, and at integer multiples of that frequency

Record EQ

The best way to compensate for high-frequency losses encountered in the recording and playback process is a technique called *pre-emphasis*. Pre-emphasis is the accentuation of certain frequencies in a signal (usually highs), by means of EQ, before it is recorded, in anticipation of those same frequencies being reduced by the recording itself. Pre-emphasis avoids having to boost high frequencies after the fact, as this has the effect of also boosting the noise from tape. Pre-emphasis can be used purely as a simple form of noise reduction as well, where certain frequencies are greatly boosted before recording and then attenuated after recording. (Care must

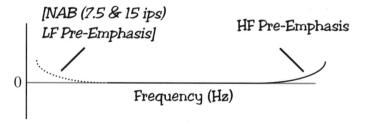

Fig 13.12. Pre-emphasis required at record EQ stage to achieve flat frequency response at output (following playback EQ curves)

be taken, however, as excessive pre-emphasis can lead to distortion.) The net result is unity gain for the audio frequencies and attenuation of the noise signal from tape.

Record EQ does just this, mainly focusing on high-frequency pre-emphasis, although NAB also calls for some low-frequency pre-emphasis at slower tape speeds (7.5 and 15 ips) for noise reduction purposes, to reduce the effect of hum from the motors (figure 13.12). There are no real standards here per se, but rather one must do whatever is necessary to achieve flat frequency response at the output of the machine given the playback EQ curve employed.

Alignment Procedure

In order to align the tape machine, we must have a known source. MRL (Magnetic Reference Lab) tapes are provided for this purpose. They contain tones carefully recorded in a laboratory environment at precise levels of magnetic fluxivity. A separate MRL tape must be used for each tape speed because of the different responses encountered at different speeds.

The basic process of alignment follows these steps:

Step 1

Assure that the tape path (tape guides, idler) and heads themselves are *demagnetized* (do not contain any residual magnetism from previous tape passes) using a head demagnetizer (degausser), as well as cleaned with appropriate solution in the direction of the tape path (left to right).

The tape heads must also be properly oriented for full contact with the tape. *Playback azimuth* is the principal adjustment to be made here, to determine that all tracks line up precisely (figure 13.13). This can be done using a high-frequency azimuth tone on tape fed to the two outermost tracks (1 and 24 for instance), the outputs of which are monitored on an oscilloscope for proper phase alignment.

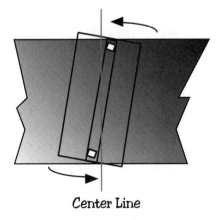

Center Line

Fig. 13.13. *Azimuth adjustment to ensure that all tracks line up perfectly, eliminating possible signal loss due to phase differences*

Step 2

Playback equalization. This is adjusted for each track such that the series of tones on the MRL tape play back with the flattest response.

Step 3

Playback level. Overall output level is calibrated using the reference level signal on the MRL tape, to yield a 0 VU reading on the tape machine's meter(s). Alternatively, if a higher output tape is to be used for recording, the level can be calibrated to a –3 dB reading on the meter, which will allow a 3 dB-hotter signal to register at 0 VU.

Once all playback adjustments have been made, the playback output can be assumed to be properly calibrated and can used for monitoring all record calibrations. These should be made with the blank tape that is going to be used for recording.

Step 4

Record Azimuth. Record a high-frequency tone (usually 15 kHz) to tape and monitor phase alignment as with play head calibration (repro mode).

Step 5

Bias level. Overbias as described earlier.

Step 6

Record EQ. Patch the console oscillator to the inputs and record a series of different frequency tones, adjusting record EQ for flattest response with particular attention to high and low end.

Step 7

Record Level. Adjust level trim so that output signal level equals input signal level (recorder operating at unity gain).

Reference Levels

So, how is the actual reference level for recording determined? Signal-to-noise and dynamic range issues are similar for magnetic tape recording as for other devices discussed so far. Because of the way magnetic tape approaches saturation gradually, as opposed to the sudden onset of distortion in solid-state amplifiers, for instance, the point of distortion is initially somewhat less clear. Due to the fact that analog tape harmonic distortion tends to generate less objectionable, even harmonics, a greater amount of distortion is deemed acceptable. The point that has been agreed upon as the point of distortion or *maximum output level (MOL)* is the level that generates 3% of third-harmonic distortion at the output in the midrange frequencies.

Recording levels are measured in *nanowebers per meter (nWb/m)*, which is a measure of the *surface fluxivity* on tape. The first standard that was arrived at and used as a reference for many years, called the *Ampex standard reference level*, measured 185 nWb/m @ 700 Hz, and is often referred to as "Ampex level." As tape formulations were improved to yield reduced amounts of distortion, the decision was made by recording engineers to increase the standard reference level to achieve the same distortion specs, but with improvement in signal-to-noise ratio. Noise, often called *tape hiss*, is a constant concern when recording to analog tape, and is generally deemed more objectionable than some tape overload distortion.

This trend led to the adoption of a new standard reference level of 250 nWb/m @ 1 kHz, which is about 3 dB hotter than 185. For this reason, it is often referred to as "+3 over 185," or simply "+3." An MRL tape meant for 185 calibrations could be used to calibrate for a 250-level tape by adjusting the output level to read –3 on the VU meter instead of 0. Newer so-called high-output tape formulations extended this level to +6 over Ampex (360 nWb/m), and even +9 (510 nW/m). Each time, the improvement comes at the low-level end with reduced tape noise. Note that in each case, the tape machine must be calibrated not only for level but for the specific type of tape to be used in the session.

Noise Reduction

Perhaps an even more important development in the life of magnetic tape recording was the introduction of noise reduction systems, notably Dolby A, and more recently, Dolby SR. Arguably, this single achievement helped analog magnetic recording survive in the face of the rising digital tide. Without noise reduction, the best analog tape recording boasts a maximum dynamic range of about 65 dB—a far cry from the 90+ dB possible with traditional 16-bit digital recording systems, not to mention the 144 dB theoretically possible from newer high-resolution 24-bit systems. Tape hiss and tape saturation have always been serious issues when recording to analog tape, where levels must be very carefully managed in order to avoid noisy passages, particularly during softer musical passages.

Most noise-reduction systems employed for analog tape recording are *double-ended*, which means that the process involves both an encoding and a decoding step (figure 13.14). The signal being recorded to tape is first passed through a noise reduction unit, which manipulates the signal going to tape. Upon playback, the signal must again be passed through the unit to be decoded, at which point the process is reversed and the signal is restored. In the process, the noise from tape is manipulated in such a way that it is significantly reduced. Almost invariably, the process involves some sort of *companding*—compression of the signal on input to raise the level of low-level signals, and expansion on output or playback to bring low-level signals back to their original level, thereby also reducing the level of noise from tape (figure 13.15). The main difference between the various noise-reduction schemes is in how the signal is manipulated. Following is a brief description of some of the major noise reduction systems.

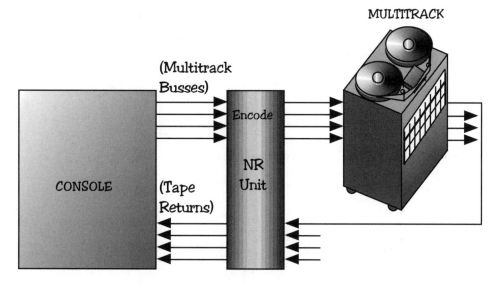

Fig. 13.14. *Double-ended noise reduction setup is inserted between console and recorder. This can either be in the form of a rack-mountable unit, or cards mounted directly in the tape machine.*

Dolby A

Introduced in the mid 1960s, this was the first professional noise-reduction system adopted industry-wide (though not the first available) for analog tape recording. It splits the signal into four different fixed-frequency bands, each with its own compressor, so that the modulation of the noise level does not occur all at once and is therefore relatively inaudible. Dolby A can be expected to increase dynamic range by an average of about 10 dB.

Dolby B and C

These consumer versions of Dolby NR were adapted for cassette tape recording and incorporated in the deck itself. Rather than having fixed-frequency bands, they employ sliding bands that adjust to the input program material, with greater high-frequency pre-emphasis for lower input signal levels, as well as an electronically controlled variable band-pass filter. While Dolby B, even when played back unde-coded, can actually sound acceptable (slightly compressed, with a boost in high frequency), C-type NR is more severe. It essentially consists of two Dolby B units in series, and results in increased noise reduction (about 20 dB average noise reduction).

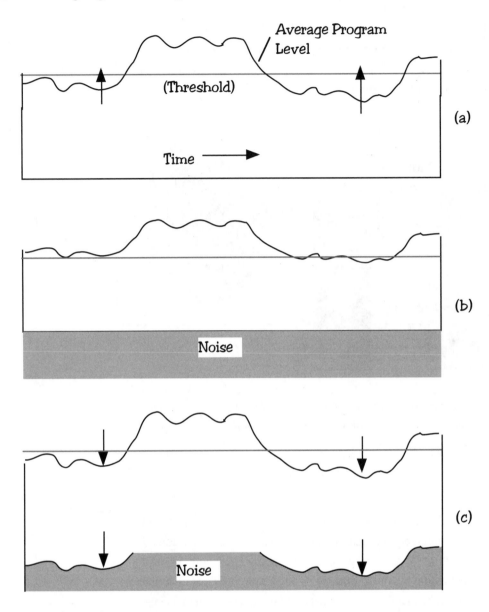

Fig. 13.15. Companding scheme for noise reduction at low signal levels yields increased dynamic range, although signal-to-noise remains the same. (a) Original signal average program level; (b) signal on tape following compression; (c) playback signal following expansion

dbx NR

This noise-reduction scheme, developed by dbx, is found in many semipro recorders such as multitrack cassette recorders, although both Type 1 (pro) and Type 2 (consumer) versions exist. Essentially, it consists of high-frequency pre-emphasis accompanied by full-band, up to 2:1 companding (compression on encode followed by expansion on decode). Contrary to the Dolby systems, dbx is sensitive neither to the frequency nor dynamic range of the input signal, but can provide up to 40 dB of noise reduction. However, in this system, high-level, low-frequency signals are often not able to mask the background noise.

Dolby SR (Spectral Recording)

Adopted in the 1990s, this complex system incorporates features of several earlier Dolby systems, including both *fixed* and *sliding* frequency bands. The intricate level-shaping that results yields up to about 24 dB of noise reduction in the most audible midrange frequency band. Coupled with newer high output formulation tapes, Dolby SR brings the dynamic range of the system within the realm of traditional digital recording, and even beyond in the midrange band ($\approx$110 dB @ 1 kHz), with virtually no audible adverse effects.

HX Pro (Headroom Extension)

This consumer-based system employed in cassette tape recorders is not, like the processes above, a noise-reduction system per se. Rather, it is a process that tracks the input signal looking for high-frequency content, and automatically adjusts the amplitude of the bias signal accordingly. Because high frequencies have some ability to self-bias, the system intermittently reduces the bias level, allowing high frequencies within the audio to bias themselves, with the net effect of increasing the headroom of the system.

Transport

Tape transport is, of course, a very important element in the accurate recording and reproduction of a signal, as recorded wavelength will translate into signal frequency ($f = \lambda/c$, where c = speed of tape). If tape speed is inconsistent, the recorded signal's frequency and resulting pitch will be mistracked. In the extreme case, given a signal recorded to tape at 15 ips and played back at 30 ips, its wavelength will be reproduced in half the original time, producing a signal with half the original period, or double the frequency. In addition to consistent speed, there must be consistent tape-to-head contact for proper recording and playback of the input signal.

The "modern" professional tape transport (figure 13.16) has been well-developed over the years to ensure consistent playback speed and tension. First, the *supply* and *take-up spools* (a, b) are driven by motors that turn in opposite directions. The take-up spool on the right has a more powerful torque, ensuring that tape motion during playback or recording is in the correct direction, while the weaker opposite torque of the supply spool ensures that constant tension is maintained. In addition, *tension arms* (d) help to monitor the tape tension and can release or engage to compensate for momentary tension surges.

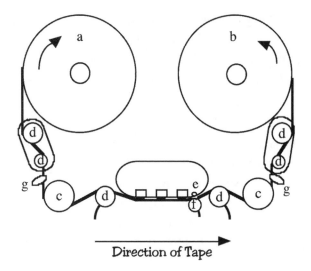

Direction of Tape

Fig. 13.16. *Modern tape transport, with supply (a) and take-up (b) reels, tape guides (c), tension arms (d), capstan (e), and pinch roller (f), and spring-loaded, motor-engaging guide arms (g)*

The key element to consistent speed is the *capstan* (e), which is tightly held against the tape by a rubber *pinch roller* (or *pressure roller*) (f) and is largely responsible for the precise speed of the tape across the heads. The capstan is driven by a *servo-controlled* DC motor, which is constantly self-monitoring and adjusting its speed (figure 13.17). "Servo-controlled" means that an output voltage signal is fed into a comparator and compared to a fixed reference (figure 13.18). The voltage at the output of the comparator is fed back into the motor, and depends on how the input and reference voltage compare. If V_2 is greater than V_{ref}, a negative voltage will be produced. If V_2 is less than V_{ref}, a positive voltage will be produced. In other words, if the motor is spinning too fast, the voltage will be reduced; if too slow, the voltage will be increased.

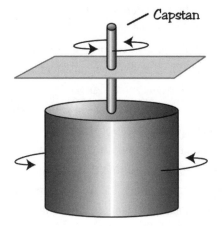

Capstan

Fig. 13.17. *Capstan on tape machine driven by servo-controlled motor*

In addition, there is a spring-loaded *guide arm(s)* (figure 13.16g) that engages the motors when tape tension is present and disengages them when there is no tension (if the tape has been spooled-off or has broken). It is of utmost importance that proper threading be followed both for proper functioning and to avoid undo stress on the sensitive elements of the tape path, which can easily become bent out of position and mistrack.

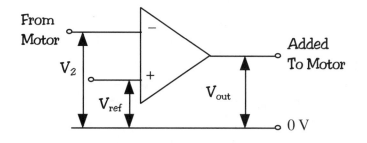

Fig. 13.18. *A comparator, used for servo-controlled DC motor driving capstan*

Needless to say, while the final result of quality analog tape recording can be glorious, the many adjustments required to make analog tape recording work properly are a daunting prospect for most smaller studios, complicated by the fact that calibrations should ideally be repeated before *every* session. Analog circuitry is notorious for getting out of alignment relatively quickly. These factors make digital recording a particularly appealing proposition. As we will see in the next chapter, however, digital audio has its share of obstacles to overcome as well.

PROJECTS

1. Look inside whatever tape player/recorder you have—even if it is just the cassette player in your boombox. Locate the various elements discussed, including heads, capstan, and pich roller. Clean and demagnetize the heads with proper cleaning solution and a degausser.

2. What bias controls and/or tape-type settings does your tape recorder have? What about noise reduction? Try recording 30 seconds of your favorite CD at each setting and compare the results. How do you explain the sonic differences? Which do you prefer?

Chapter **14** Digital Audio
Every Little Bit Counts

The idea of digital audio actually dates back to the mid-nineteenth century, and was formally described in a mathematical theorem in 1929 by Harrold Nyquist, a Swedish scientist, nearly half a century before its practical implementation would be possible. The key to understanding digital audio is understanding that all of the sonic information in a sound wave can be boiled down to amplitude changes over time. If we can find a way to capture enough information about the way the amplitude of a sound wave is continuously changing over time, we can accurately reproduce that sound wave. But what about frequency content? Remember that frequency is a measure of how often a sound wave completes a full cycle (compression and rarefaction) in one second, and a cycle is a pattern of amplitude changes that repeats. Thus, frequency is merely a function of amplitude. Recreate the amplitudes and you have recreated frequency content as well. Of course, this is easier said than done.

So, how much amplitude information is enough? As the *Nyquist theorem* demonstrates, we need at least two amplitude pictures, or "samples," per cycle to accurately capture and reproduce a simple wave. For a complex wave, then, we need a sampling frequency that yields at least two samples per highest component frequency cycle to accurately reproduce the wave. The actual implementation of digital theory, through the analog-to-digital (A/D) conversion process and digital-to-analog (D/A) reconstruction, can take a number of forms, and has a number of encountered problems to solve. Let's take a closer look at the process.

A/D Conversion

The basic function of the A/D convertor (figure 14.1) at the input stage of any digital device, as its name suggests, is to take the analog input signal and convert it to a digital data stream in which amplitude changes are represented by a string of binary digits. It does this by first capturing the continuously varying input signal as a series of stepped voltage levels, through a process known as *pulse amplitude modulation* (*PAM*). Amplitude modulation occurs when one signal (the *modulator*) causes another signal's amplitude (the *carrier*) to undulate in direct relation to the modulator's amplitude pattern (figure 14.2). Notice the amplitude pattern of the source signal being imposed on the overall amplitude pattern of the carrier signal being modulated. This process is used in many audio applications, including radio transmissions (AM) as well as analog synthesis.

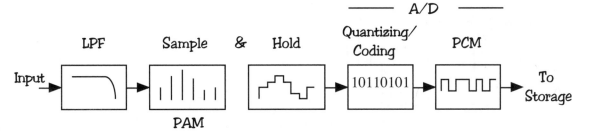

Fig. 14.1. *A/D (analog-to-digital) conversion stages at the input of a digital device*

In the case of digital audio, the signal being modulated by the input signal is a pulse wave (figure 14.3a) whose frequency is called the *sampling frequency*. The sampling frequency is also known as the *Nyquist rate*. As the input signal's voltage varies (figure 14.3b), the amplitudes of the pulses are modulated proportionally (figure 14.3c)—hence the term for the process, *pulse amplitude modulation* (*PAM*). This is akin to taking snapshots capturing the instantaneous level of the input signal at precise and regular intervals. The next stage in the A/D process is a *hold circuit* made up of a switch and capacitor (figure 14.4). You will recall that a capacitor has the ability to store a charge. For each sample to be taken, the switch is turned on and off, synchronized by a clock signal to the sampling pulse generator. The input voltage of the moment is captured and held in the capacitor just long enough to be measured and assigned a binary value. The capacitor then releases the voltage only to capture the next voltage of the moment, and so on. The result of the sample-and-hold circuit is a stair-stepped waveform (figure 14.3d), with each step representing the discrete instantaneous voltage of the original signal.

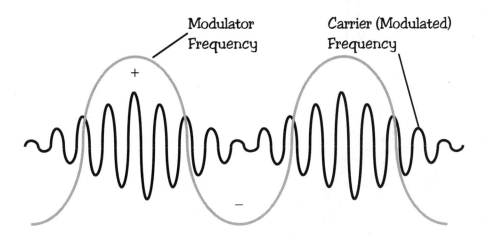

Fig. 14.2. *Amplitude modulation (AM)—input signal's (modulator's) amplitude continuously modulates the amplitude of the carrier frequency*

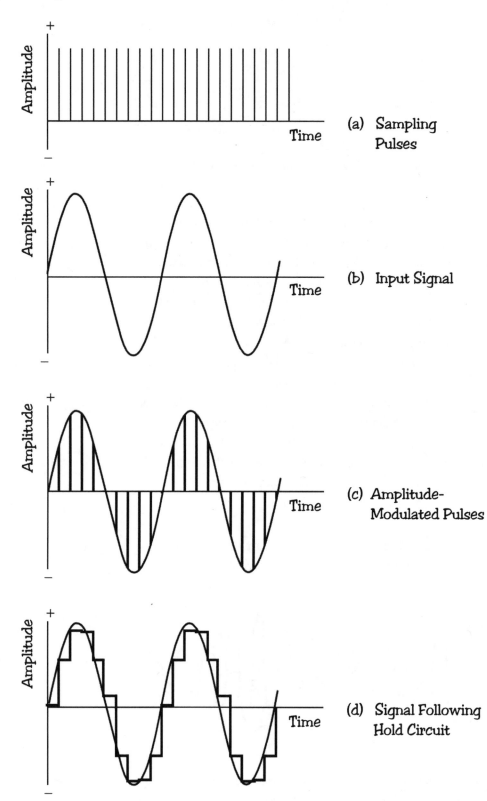

(a) Sampling Pulses

(b) Input Signal

(c) Amplitude-Modulated Pulses

(d) Signal Following Hold Circuit

Fig. 14.3. The sample-and-hold portion of the A/D process

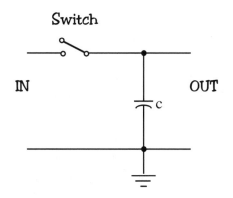

Fig. 14.4. *The hold circuit of the A/D process*

At this stage, the signal is still analog. The next step is to assign each of the discrete voltages a specific binary value, according to the total number of available bits in the system. This process is called quantization and coding. *Quantization* is the act of rounding a value up or down to the nearest available number. *Coding* is the process of writing that value in binary code. In a binary system, such as a computer or a digital audio recorder, information is represented as *bits* (*bi*nary dig*its*), which individually can only have one of two possible values—0 or 1 (hence the term *binary* meaning two). Larger numbers are represented by adding more bits. While each digit in the decimal number system represents a power of 10, each digit, or bit, in a binary system represents a new power of 2. The binary number 1011 is equivalent to the decimal number 11 because:

Binary number	**1**		**0**		**1**		**1**	=	
Bit weight	2^3		2^2		2^1		2^0	=	
Decimal value	8	+	0	+	2	+	1	=	**11**

The total number of different values that can be represented in a digital system is determined by the *bit depth* used by the system as described in the following equation:

$$N = 2^x$$

where N = total number of different values,
and x = the number of bits used in the system

Equ. 14.1. *Calculating available values based on bit depth of a digital system*

Thus, an 8-bit system is capable of representing $2^8 = 256$ different values. The standard specification for CD audio is 16-bit, which is capable of representing 2^{16} or 65,536 distinct values. New high-resolution systems, such as DVD-Audio, are theoretically capable of 24-bit resolution or 2^{24} = 16,722,216 possible values. The advantage of a higher-resolution system is that once we reach this next stage of assigning each voltage step a discrete binary value, the more possible values that are available, the closer the system can come to represent the true value of the signal level (or voltage) at each moment. The fewer bits available, the further the quantization circuit must round up or down to the nearest available value, and the more *quantization error* or *quantization noise* will be present in the signal. Quantization noise is a distortion (i.e., change in original signal) byproduct of the digital process, which is worse where fewer bits are available as more rounding off must be done. In fact, the theoretical signal-to-noise ratio of a digital system can be calculated in direct relation to the bit resolution of the system, as follows:

$$S/E = 20 \log(2^n)$$
$$= 20(n)\log 2$$
$$= 6.0206n$$

where S/E = signal-to-noise or signal-to-error ratio (in dB) of a digital system,
n = number of bits

Eq. 14.2. Calculating signal-to-noise ratio based on bit depth of a digital system

Another way to state this equation is to say that each additional bit improves system performance by about 6 dB. The *S/E* (*signal-to-noise* or *signal-to-error*) ratio is essentially equivalent to dynamic range in a digital system, since it defines the absolute lower and upper level limits that the system can handle or encode. A 16-bit system, then, is theoretically capable of a dynamic range of about 16×6 = 96 dB. A true 24-bit system is theoretically capable of 24×6 = 144 dB dynamic range performance. When working digital equipment into our overall signal flow and dynamic range considerations, we can either rely on the spec sheet for measured S/E or use the equation above (or mental calculation of $6 \times$ bit depth) to calculate approximately what can be expected. Real-world design considerations will bring this down considerably, although certain techniques, such as noise shaping, oversampling, dither, and 32-bit floating-point processing (as found in newer high-resolution hard-disk recording programs) can also help considerably.

Given the available bit values, how is a voltage assigned a number? This process, called *coding*, can take a number of different forms. The basic principle is illustrated in figure 14.5. Each momentary signal level (or step voltage) captured is compared to the available bit values and either rounded up or down to the nearest value. The more bits available, the smaller the difference between available steps, and therefore, the smaller difference between analog voltages the converter can

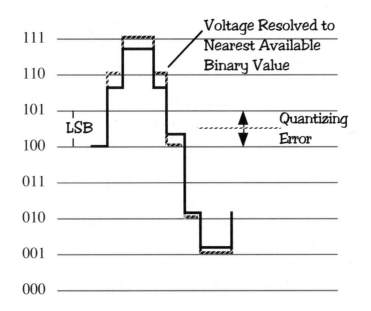

Fig. 14.5. *Quantization based on available bit values. Example of 3-bit system using offset coding (bipolar)*

resolve, called the *quantizing interval* or *least significant bit* (*LSB*). The LSB is the smallest or righthand-most bit in a digital word. The maximum error for a given voltage is always equal to one-half of the least significant bit, which would occur if the voltage were to fall exactly in between two available step values. The maximum error between two consecutive voltages, then, is equal to the least significant bit. The value of the least significant bit can be calculated based on the system resolution, as follows:

$$LSB = FS/2^n$$

where FS = the full scale, or
highest analog voltage value permitted by the system,
n = the number of bits

Equ. 14.3. *Calculating LSB value based on bit depth and MOL of a digital system*

Intuitively, this equation reinforces the fact that the greater the number of available bits, the smaller the potential for error, and the more accurate the coding (i.e., recording of the original input signal). Since digital systems move in steps rather than continuously varying voltages, the smaller each voltage step (LSB), the smoother and more accurate the waveform capture.

Thus, a 16-bit A/D converter with a full scale of 10 V would resolve input voltages from 0 to 10 V in steps of $10/(2^{16}) = 0.000015258789 \approx 153\ \mu V$ or 0.153 mV.

As you can see from the example above, low system bit-resolution, or alternatively, low input level, means greater error. In the example 3-bit system (figure 14.5), there are only eight available steps to which *all* input signal voltages must be resolved. The lower the input level, the further available bits are limited. You will also notice from the illustration that negative voltages may be represented by using the *most significant bit* (*MSB*) as a polarity indicator (1 for +, 0 for –). This is called *offset binary coding*, one of numerous binary coding schemes. Conversely, *two's complement* numbering system uses a MSB of 1 to represent negative values.

If the input signal level falls below half the LSB, it will be rounded down and not register at all. What if it goes above the full-scale level? Once the highest number has been reached, there is no way to represent any increase in level beyond that. Therefore, the signal will be clipped, yielding harsh-sounding digital distortion (figure 14.6). The degree to which this is objectionable depends on the duration of individual distortions. Very short peak distortions may go audibly unnoticed. Longer distortions are very harsh-sounding and objectionable, especially compared to equivalent analog distortion. Most digital audio systems have a specific criteria, such as a certain number of consecutive full-scale voltage readings. When the criteria is met, it triggers an "over" warning light to alert the user. Many mastering systems, such as the venerable Sony PCM1630, have a very strict limit on the number of "overs" that they will allow, even if they may be judged inaudible.

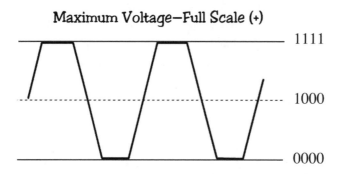

Maximum Voltage–Full Scale (+)

1111

1000

0000

Fig. 14.6. Digital hard clipping due to wave amplitude exceeding dynamic range of system

PCM

Now that each of our stepped voltages have been assigned a quantized value, the string of values must be recorded, somehow. The most common method has been a process called *pulse code modulation* or *PCM*. Like *pulse amplitude modulation* (*PAM*), PCM uses a modulated pulse wave to capture amplitude information; only this time, we are not recording direct signal amplitudes but rather numbers, which in turn represent signal amplitude values. Herein lies one of the great advantages of digital recording. A pulse wave, as a series of high and low voltages, can be used to represent a string of 0s and 1s in bit word patterns called *bytes*. Using the first half-cycle of our example waveform from figure 14.5, post-quantization, we might get a PCM stream as in figure 14.7. Notice that the pattern is high for 1 and low for 0. These pulse voltages make up the signal, which is carried down digital cables and recorded, either as magnetic polarity changes in the case of hard-disk or DAT recording, or as a pattern of physical pits on the surface of a CD or DVD.

What's the advantage? First, surface noise (such as tape hiss or record scratches) from the medium onto which the digital stream is stored is eliminated. An analog recording and playback system has no way to differentiate between the audio signal and any noise that has been added to the signal by the system. In digital recording, as long as there is a great enough level difference to distinguish between a 0 and a 1, the signal is recaptured perfectly, and all surface noise contributions are ignored. In addition, converting the signal to a string of binary numbers opens up the possibility of recording to a computer hard disk, digital signal processing (using algorithms to manipulate numbers for sonic effects), digital editing, as well as mathematical error-correction schemes to recover any damaged or corrupted audio.

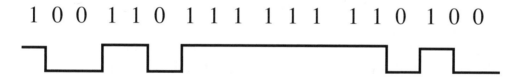

1 0 0 1 1 0 1 1 1 1 1 1 1 1 0 1 0 0

Fig. 14.7. PCM data stream resulting from quantized signal. High pulse represents a 1, low pulse (or no pulse) represents a 0. This represent a nonreturn-to-zero (NRZ) scheme where the pulse is held at the same level as long as there is no change in bit value.

But how can the post-quantization wave in figure 14.4 be equivalent to our input signal from figure 14.3, if we are missing all of the amplitude information occurring in between samples? The Nyquist theorem mathematically demonstrates that given two amplitude samples, there is only one sine wave that can possibly have those two particular amplitudes. In its practical implementation, consider a 20 kHz harmonic sine wave, captured by a 40 kHz sampling frequency. The resulting post-quantization signal resulting from the two samples generated per cycle would yield a 20 kHz *square* wave. Even if this were what we heard upon playback, it would sound like... a 20 kHz *sine* wave. The second harmonic of a 20 kHz square wave would be 40 kHz—already well above the audible range—and in fact, it has no real activity until the third harmonic, at 60 kHz. As we go lower and lower in frequency, we get more and more samples per cycle, yielding an increasingly smooth waveform. In fact, the reconstruction and smoothing process in the output stage removes the high-frequency harmonic distortions, which, even if inaudible, do have the potential to alter the waveshape.

Aliasing

We have said that the Nyquist theorem requires that the sampling frequency be at least two times greater than the highest audio frequency being captured. As long as we adhere to this rule, we are able to reconstruct the wave accurately. But what happens if we violate the Nyquist rule? If we allow frequencies higher than the Nyquist frequency (half the sampling rate) to enter our system, the result will be a type of distortion called *aliasing*. The violating frequencies will not be recorded, but instead, they will generate new frequencies, or aliases, which were not part of the original signal. (Think of an alias in the classic sense of the term—a pseudonym, as for an impostor masquerading as someone they are not.) We can find the frequency of the alias as follows:

$$f_a = f_s - f_v$$

where f_a = the alias frequency, f_s = the sampling frequency,
f_v = the violating frequency

Eq. 14.4. *Calculating aliasing frequency*

Thus, a 23 kHz signal allowed to enter a system with a sampling frequency of 40 kHz would generate an alias of $f_a = 40 - 23 = 17$ kHz. The higher the violating frequency, the lower in the audible range the aliased artifact. For this reason, the first stage in classic A/D conversion is a low-pass filter, called an *anti-aliasing filter,* which restricts the audio bandwidth to less than half the sampling frequency (figure 14.8). This ensures that no audio signals above the Nyquist frequency enter the system to begin with.

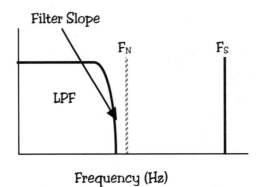

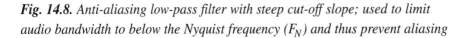

Fig. 14.8. *Anti-aliasing low-pass filter with steep cut-off slope; used to limit audio bandwidth to below the Nyquist frequency (F_N) and thus prevent aliasing*

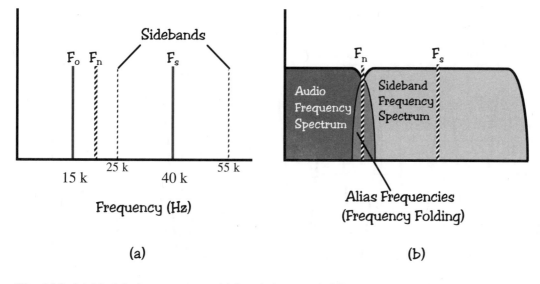

Fig. 14.9. *(a) Modulation generates sidebands (sum and difference tones). (b) When input frequency exceeds Nyquist frequency (F_N), sidebands fold or spill into audio range, yielding audible aliasing distortion.*

To better understand why aliasing occurs, let's take a closer look at the process of modulation that occurs in the *pulse amplitude modulation (PAM)* stage of the A/D conversion process. When one signal modulates another, sidebands are generated on either side of the carrier or sampling frequency. These sidebands are sum and difference tones; that is, carrier + audio, carrier – audio. A 40 kHz sampling pulse wave modulated by a 15 kHz sine wave would generate sidebands at 55 kHz (40 + 15) and 25 kHz (40 – 15) (figure 14.9a). If the audio bandwidth is allowed to exceed the Nyquist frequency, the resulting lower sideband would fold or spill into the audio range as audible aliasing distortion, which is completely unrelated musically to the original signal. The higher the violating frequency, the lower the alias (figure 14.9b).

A more familiar type of aliasing occurs in film, where consecutive still pictures recreate motion at a rate of 24 frames per second. This works well as long as the movements being filmed are relatively slow. Faster movements, notably spoked wheels spinning (e.g., stagecoach wheels in a classic Western), can become distorted because of too slow a frame rate. You will notice that as the wheel speeds up, it actually appears to begin slowing, gradually come to a stop, and eventually begin to spin in reverse. If the wheel rotations were ever to be perfectly synchronized with the frame rate (at 24 rotations per second), the wheel would appear to be completely motionless, having completed a perfect circle (360° rotation) between each snapshot. Frequency is simply a description of audio motion. When captured at too slow a rate (sampling frequency), the audio motion is reproduced incorrectly as a lower-frequency alias (figure 14.10).

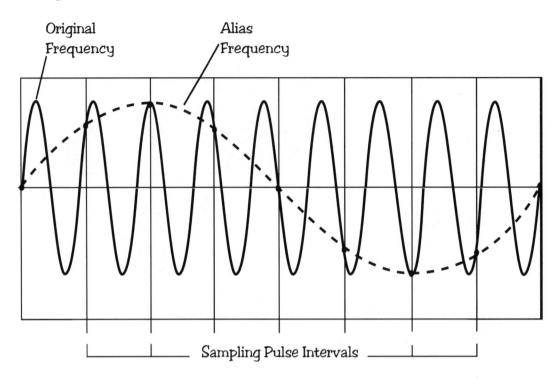

Original   Alias
Frequency   Frequency

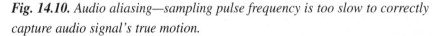

Sampling Pulse Intervals

Fig. 14.10. *Audio aliasing—sampling pulse frequency is too slow to correctly capture audio signal's true motion.*

The sampling frequency of a digital system, then, determines the upper limit of its frequency response. The higher the sampling frequency, the higher the possible frequency response. CD audio uses a sampling rate of 44.1 kHz (which can be traced back to the video origins of the first digital audio recorders, such as the Sony PCM-F1). The frequency response of CD audio is allowed to extend to 20 kHz, allowing for a bit of margin and the use of real-world (i.e., affordable) filters.

As discussed earlier, a digital system's bit resolution determines the system's signal-to-noise ratio or dynamic range. It also has an important impact on its faithfulness of reproduction as relates to resolution. This can be most easily related to the visual resolution of high-definition television compared to standard line resolution. More and finer scan lines (as well as techniques such as progessive scan in DVD players) mean a smoother image that more faithfully represents reality. In evaluating new high-definition audio formats capable of extended sampling frequency (96 kHz or even 192 kHz) and greater bit depth (24 bit), most observers (listeners) point to the fact that greater bit depth is a much more dramatic change than increased sampling rate when compared to *standard Red Book* CD audio (16-bit, 44.1 kHz). One might argue that higher frequency response is unnecessary due to the fact that most of us do not hear beyond 20 kHz. Clearly, more research needs to be done in this area. That said, increased word length or bit depth has quelled many if not most objections to the sonic character of digital audio, and has ushered in comparisons to the best aspects of analog: "warmth," "depth of field," and "accurate imaging," for instance.

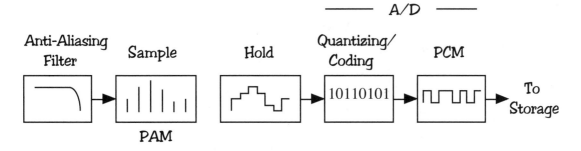

Fig. 14.11. Sequence of events in the A/D conversion process

A/D Block Diagram

Now that we have an understanding of the various processes involved in the analog-to-digital conversion stage, let's take another look at the simple block diagram describing the sequence of events (figure 14.11).

Because we are dealing with stereo audio for the most part, there will generally be two parallel channels with the same processing stages. The two signals are then *multiplexed*, allowing for two channels of information to be sent serially, as a single data stream. The actual data format contained in the PCM string will depend on the type of digital audio being recorded or transferred. In addition to the amplitude information, it will include parity information for error detection, redundancy codes (CRCC or Reed-Solomon) for error correction, track ID and timing information, user bits, etc. These follow strict specifications, according to whether the audio is being burned to CD (defined as *Red Book audio*), or transferred via AES/EBU or S/PDIF digital lines (see chapter 7). The specifics of each of these formats is beyond the scope of this text. It is useful to note, however, that two channels of non-data-compressed CD-quality digital audio corresponds to a data rate of 2 x 44.1 kHz x 16 bits ≈ 1.4 Mbits/s (1024 bits = 1 Mbit, since binary data works only in powers of 2), which translates into approximately 10 Mbytes/stereo minute of storage space (8 bits = 1 byte; 1024 bytes = 1 Mbyte). Because of the additional elements mentioned above, actual transmission rates will necessarily be higher than this, and will depend on the transfer protocol being used (AES, S/PDIF, etc.). As a general rule, standard compact discs are capable of storing 650 Mbytes of audio data. Of course, the greater bit depth and/or higher sampling frequency of high-definition audio yields a higher bit rate and greater storage space requirements.

Clock

Because of the unique complexity of the digital recording process, and the speed at which all of these individual steps must take place while perfectly synchronized within a very small margin of error, the issue of timing is critical. For this reason, all digital systems must incorporate a very accurate clock reference in the form of a quartz crystal-based oscillator. This clock, which carefully controls the A/D as well as the D/A processes, determines the sampling frequency for the device in question (figure 14.12).

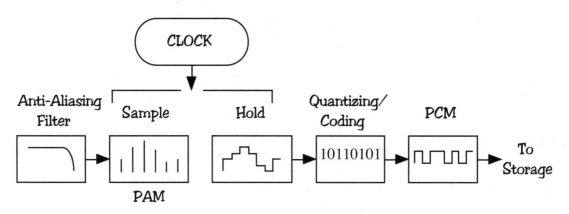

Fig. 14.12. A carefully controlled clock reference ensures timing accuracy and consistency in the A/D and D/A processes.

D/A Process

Upon playback, the coded audio must be decoded and the original waveform reconstructed. This is done essentially by a reverse A/D process (figure 14.13). Stereo channels are de-multiplexed, PCM code is decoded, and corresponding voltages are reproduced. (This can be done by having individual bit values switch on or off, corresponding to voltage supplies that are summed to produce the necessary voltage of the moment.) This yields a stair-stepped waveform, which is usually re-sampled to reduce the pulse widths (again, using PAM). To reconstruct the original waveform, the signal is passed through a low-pass filter, which removes the higher harmonics of the sampling pulses, as well as the modulation sideband images of the audio. This filter is identical to the anti-aliasing low-pass filter, but is called an *anti-image filter*. This step is essential for smoothing out the waveform and returning it to its original shape. Compare the frequency content of the reconstructed signal before and after final low-pass filtering (figure 14.14).

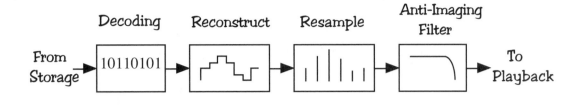

Fig. 14.13. *Sequence of events in the D/A conversion process*

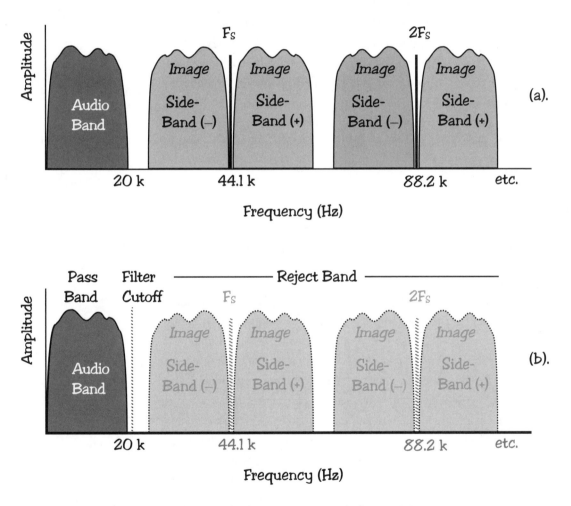

Fig 14.14. *Reconstructed audio signal's frequency content before anti-image filtering (a) and after (b)*

Interconnections—Word Clock

In order to transmit digital data from one device to another, timing accuracy and consistency must be maintained. This requires both a channel for data communication and common clock synchronization between the devices in question. This word-clock signal can either be embedded within the digital audio stream, or preferably, can be transferred via a dedicated BNC connection found on the back of most professional digital audio equipment. While word clock can be transferred from device to device in a setup with multiple digital devices, it is recommended that all digital devices within an audio system be clocked to the same source, particularly in a large setup. One device should be designated as the master clock source, and all others are configured to slave to that single device. Most digital devices can act as a clock master. However, ideally, a master clocking device should be incorporated in the system whose sole function is to provide a rock-solid timing reference and synchronization source for the entire system. The more accurate the timing reference, the less jitter and resulting noise and distortion is introduced into the signal. Master clock also facilitates quick one-step reconfiguration of the entire system (from 44.1 kHz to 96 kHz sampling rate, for instance).

Digital Cables

When transferring digital signals, it is also important to use cables with the proper impedance (110 Ω for AES/EBU; 75 Ω for S/PDIF) to handle the higher bandwidth of the digital data stream. (High data rate translates to high-frequency signal content.) Using non-specific standard audio cables can contribute to timing inaccuracies called *interface* or *transmission jitter*. Another common mode of digital transfer is via fiberoptics using a so-called *ADAT optical* (a.k.a. "lightpipe") connection. This is a fiberoptic cable consisting of a thin strand of glass or plastic through which an infrared light beam is passed. The light beam is modulated by the digital signal in the source device (the same way an RF radio wave is frequency-modulated by program material, and transmitted by the FM station) and demodulated at the receiving end to recover the data. There are many advantages with this type of transfer: we do not have to worry about cable capacitance or inductance, or about ground loops, since there is no metal involved; it is both safe and immune from interference of any kind; and it has an extremely wide bandwidth. Cables can also be quite long before the light signal begins to fade. We must be careful, however, not to abuse the thin (though flexible) fiberoptic cable. Also, over very long distances, as with phone company fiberoptic cabling, the light signal must be boosted at regular intervals.

Digital Signal Levels and Metering

Because of the inherent difference between digital and analog signals, we must take another look at interpreting and dealing with digital signals in our system. Signals entering and leaving digital audio equipment can be either analog or digital. As long as they are analog, having passed through the A/D and D/A process, we can treat them like any other signal. In the digital realm, however, the signal is generally of greater amplitude and frequency than other audio signals and thus require special treatment. Digital recording is sometimes called *saturation recording* because the magnetic tape (or disk) used is fully saturated; either + or – to represent 1 or 0 bits, respectively. This means that the recorded signal is at full possible amplitude at all times, which makes it particularly robust. Any tape used for digital recording has greater coercivity than that used in analog recording and is therefore more immune to accidental erasure from proximity to magnetic sources, such as loudspeaker drivers.

The signal that registers on a full-scale digital meter is the analog voltage equivalent of the digital bit value. The top of the full-scale meter is labeled 0 dB (FS), meaning that the signal has reached full scale (111111111111111) and the maximum voltage will be reproduced. For this reason, the input to a digital recorder is calibrated (using the input level pot or cal trim and an oscillator) such that an analog sine wave signal of +4 dBu (1.228 V_{rms}) will yield a reading of between –12 and –20 dBFS (figure 11.8); –18 dBFS is perhaps the most common calibration point for 0 VU. Again, setting up this relationship between 0 VU on the console and dBFS on the full-scale digital meter establishes headroom in the digital recorder proportional to that found in its analog counterparts. Also, remember that since we are calibrating so that the signal will be consistently peaking at the top of the scale to make use of all available bits, the signal returning from the digital recorder will generally be "hotter" than other source signals.

Complications with Digital Audio

While the theory of digital audio is brilliant (especially considering that those who first proposed it had no practical means of implementing or testing their mathematical theorem), there are some real-world problems in its early implementation that must be overcome.

Phase Shift—Oversampling

One of the first problems with the digital audio process is the use of *brick wall* filters with very steep slopes for anti-aliasing and anti-imaging purposes. Steep slopes are required to allow as much of the original audio band as possible, while fully rejecting any frequencies above the Nyquist frequency—first to protect against aliasing, then to remove harmonics and images that are byproducts of the process. The problem is that filters introduce *phase shift* distortion; the steeper the filter, the more phase shift is introduced into the signal particularly at high frequencies. Phase shift occurs when certain harmonics in a complex signal are delayed with respect to other harmonic components, thus distorting the waveshape and dulling the transients or attacks of the signal. High-frequency phase shift is the most common, since high frequencies as a general rule have the most trouble passing through circuit resistances. In the case of low-pass filters, resistance is greatly increased with increasing frequency, and phase shift increases proportionally as well. In addition, steep filters with a smooth band pass (limited ripple) are very difficult and costly to produce.

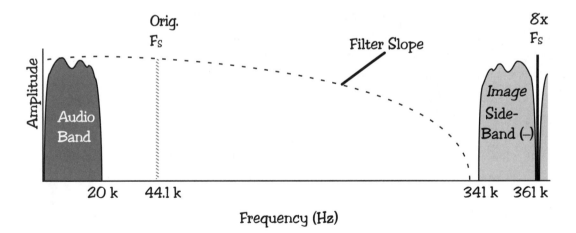

Fig. 14.15. D/A oversampling allows for a much gentler low-pass filter

The question, then, is how to do away with the brick wall filter altogether. One answer comes in the D/A process, where CD players, for instance, began to employ *oversampling*. Oversampling involves generating new samples in between the "real" samples to create an artificially higher sampling frequency. The higher sampling rate does not generate any new audio information, but it does mean that the sideband images will be shifted much higher in the frequency spectrum. For instance, a D/A converter with 8× oversampling would have sidebands around 361.3 kHz (the sampling rate) extending down to 361.3 kHz – 20 kHz = 341.3 kHz (figure 14.15). This creates a much greater difference in frequency between the audio cut-off frequency and the lowest sideband, and allows for the use of a lower-order filter with a much gentler slope. This technique virtually eliminates phase shift in the audio band from the D/A process.

However, we still have to deal with the phase shift introduced in the A/D process. Oversampling is also possible on this end. Typically, A/D oversampling is done at 64× the rate of standard sampling (2.8 MHz), but as little as one bit at a time. Perhaps the most common of such A/D oversampling methods is a 1-bit process called *sigma-delta* ($\Sigma\Delta$) *modulation*. Each bit simply records whether the current amplitude of the moment is higher or lower than the previous one. Our final digitized signal must be stored, however, so we cannot afford to keep the higher bandwidth generated by the process, if it is still to fit on the same limited medium. We must also end up with a data stream equivalent to that of traditional A/D converters. The traditional analog anti-aliasing filter is replaced by a digital decimation filter and digital low-pass filter, which produces at its output a PCM data stream with 16-bit samples at a rate of 44.1 kHz. Sample frequency is essentially traded for sample length. Because the digital filter operates in the digital realm, many of the problems, such as phase shift, encountered in analog filters are greatly mitigated.

Beyond the advantage of doing away with the cost and audio defects of steep analog filters, sigma-delta modulation also employs much simpler single-bit quantization and is fully integrated, doing away with external sample and hold circuitry. Also, because of the greatly increased frequency range of the initial modulation signal, the quantization noise is spread over the entire frequency range, most of which falls outside of the audio band. When the signal is filtered, most of the noise can also be removed. Additional digital *noise shaping* moves *in-band noise* (noise within the audible frequency range) from the most audible midrange frequency range (below 9 kHz) into a higher, less audible frequency range (above 16 kHz).

What does this mean for us in the studio? It means that digital audio equipment using oversampling A/D converters is an improvement over previous generations, in the reduction of phase shift, and to a lesser extent, quantization noise. This translates to cleaner, more faithful audio recording, all potentially at a lower cost. A block diagram for this type of oversampling A/D process is given in figure 14.16.

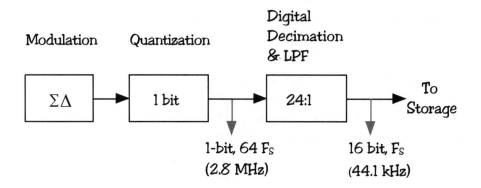

Fig. 14.16. *Oversampling A/D block diagram*

Dither

As we have seen, low bit depth generates quantizing noise because of greater error in matching the signal's true level of the moment. Low signal levels are always more problematic because of fewer bits available at the bottom of the scale. Where signal level falls below half the value of the least significant bit, quantization will round the level down and no signal will be recorded at all. However, there is a method whereby signal-to-noise performance and low-level resolution can actually be improved beyond the theoretical limit set by bit resolution. A pseudo-random noise signal called *dither*, with a level equal to half the least significant bit, can be added to the input signal. This has has two principal beneficial effects.

First, it ensures that if any audio signal is present at the input (i.e., points of lowest signal level), it will broach the necessary threshold and be rounded up and successfully encoded. Second, it randomizes the effects of quantization at low levels (figure 14.17). Without dither, a low level sinusoidal waveform will be grossly rounded up or down at regular intervals. Given the random nature of the dither signal, the quantization will also be randomized, crossing over the zero point at a more rapid rate. You'll notice that the rate is related to the waveform, however, and when averaged out over time, it yields a waveform much truer to the original. This has the effect of actually eliminating some of the quantizing error/noise that would otherwise be present.

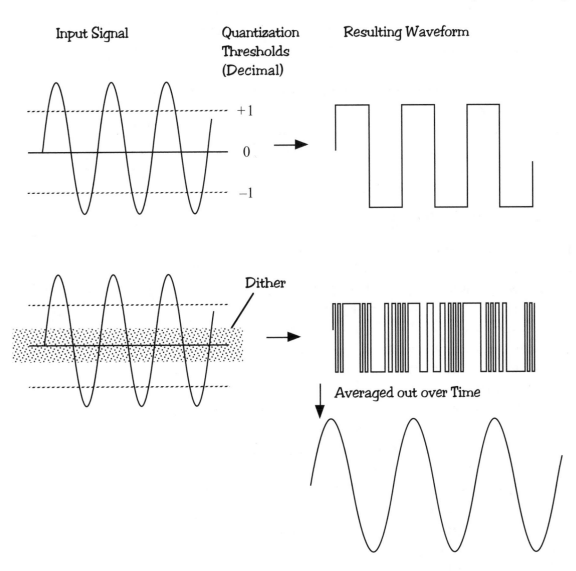

Input Signal   Quantization Thresholds (Decimal)   Resulting Waveform

Dither

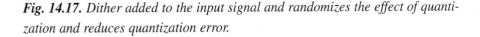

Averaged out over Time

Fig. 14.17. Dither added to the input signal and randomizes the effect of quantization and reduces quantization error.

In addition to being part of the A/D portion of any digital recording process, dither should also be used anytime a higher-resolution signal is bit-converted down to a lower resolution. This will ensure the best possible resolution in the final product. It is always best to work at the highest bit resolution possible, even when the final delivery medium is of lower bit depth. Not only does this ensure the best quality final product, but it also allows for the possibility of high-resolution archiving for future media. Already, we see that many digital recordings that were made during the first decade or two of the digital revolution were only mixed down, mastered, and archived to 16-bit. This precludes the possibility of remastering to take advantage of newer high-resolution delivery media such as DVD-Audio. In such cases, it would have been a good idea to archive to analog in addition to 16-bit digital, so as to maintain a better resolution and more extended frequency response than is possible using 16-bit PCM recording. As discussed in the last chapter, an analog recording captures a continuous waveform with essentially infinite resolution. (In reality, the resolution is limited to the finite number of domains that can be magnetized).

High-Resolution Audio

Recently, there has been a strong push for a high-definition digital medium to replace the venerable compact disc. *DVD-Audio* (*DVD-A*) uses a DVD (*Digital Versatile Disc*), which is similar to the compact disc but employs up to four separate layers for recording information. Improved laser technology also allows for smaller, narrower pit tracks. Together, these developments drastically increase the amount of storage space available on a single disc (approximately 18 Gbytes). DVD-Video, with its increased storage space, was initially adopted by the film/video industry, as well as for surround-sound music-only releases. While DVD-Video discs can boast high definition of up to 24-bit/96 kHz and up to eight channels of surround sound (at 16/48), the Dolby Digital (AC-3) data compression scheme that is typically used compresses the audio destructively (information is dropped out and left unrecovered), to make room for both the surround-sound (6-channel) audio and the video. DVD-Audio, on the other hand, uses the available space for non-destructively compressed true high-definition (24-bit, 96 kHz) surround sound. The specification also allows for the producer/engineer to use the available space as desired, allowing for a number of different sampling rates (up to 192 kHz) and word lengths (up to 24 bits). Otherwise, the methods used for A/D and D/A remain essentially unchanged.

An alternative to this method, however, is the so-called *Direct Stream Digital* (*DSD*) process, employed by Sony/Phillips's *Super Audio CD* (*SACD*). This approach looks to simplify the process by doing away with decimation and simply storing the high sample-rate 1-bit signal directly onto disc (figure 14.17). The resulting definition is comparable to that achieved by 24-bit 96 kHz sampling, but because of the reduced processing stages, the final result is said, by proponents, to be even more clear and faithful to the original signal. These discs are incompatible with ordinary DVD players, and can only be recorded and played back using proprietary Sony/Phillips DSD and SACD equipment. More players are introduced that support several formats, including some higher-priced universal players that include both DVD-A and SACD decoding. Only time will tell which of these formats will survive the rigors of the marketplace.

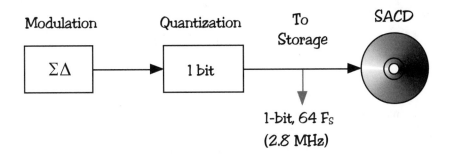

Fig. 14.18. Block diagram of the Direct Stream Digital process.

PROJECTS

1. Review the digital equipment in your studio setup. Create a flowchart including both digital audio and word clock connections (if separate). Do you have a master clock source? If not, what device is likely to be the master under most circumstances?

2. How much hard disk space would be required for 4 minutes of 24-bit stereo audio recording?

3. Do some test recordings at 16-bit and 24-bit resolutions. Compare the results and note the sonic differences. Do the same for sampling frequencies 44.1 kHz vs. 48 kHz (or 96 kHz, if you have the capability). Compare. Which yields a greater sonic difference: greater bit depth or extended sampling frequency?

4. If you have the necessary software, take your 24-bit recordings and burn them to a CD first with and then without dither. Compare the results.

Chapter **15** MIDI

Musical Instrument Digital Interface

Within our audio system, we may have many devices, such as keyboards, samplers, and even mixers, that communicate via *MIDI* (*Musical Instrument Digital Interface*). However, it is important to note, right from the start, that MIDI is *not*, nor does it carry, audio. In fact, one of the keys to understanding the function of MIDI within an audio or music system is the concept that MIDI connections do not carry any musical or audio signals. Rather, MIDI signals consist of data messages in a coded language, or *data communications protocol*, that allows MIDI-equipped devices to communicate with each other. The most basic type of communication is a *Note On* message sent to a sound-generating device (sound module or keyboard synthesizer), which tells it to play a particular note until it receives a *Note Off* message. *Sequencing* consists of recording strings of MIDI messages into a software program or *sequencer*, the way a composer would write the score to an orchestral piece, including information about note pitches and durations (in this case, note on and note off), loudness (*velocity*), instrumentation (*channel*), etc. The sequence can then be played back, causing the synthesizers, samplers, and sound modules or software synths to generate the actual audio or musical performance. MIDI communication can also be used to control virtual faders, pan pots, etc., in the virtual mixer of a DAW, via the physical controls of a MIDI-equipped digital mixer such as the Yamaha O2R or Tascam DM-24.

MIDI Connections

The MIDI specification (*MIDI 1.0 Detailed Specification*, 1983) consists of detailed requirements, for both hardware interface and data communications format, which a manufacturer must follow to be able to call their product a MIDI device. There are certain additional features that are optional and may or may not be included on a given device. All MIDI devices must include a MIDI-IN and MIDI-OUT port, and most devices also include a MIDI-THRU port. Figure 15.1 illustrates the rear panel of a typical MIDI device. Devices receive MIDI commands via the MIDI-IN port and send MIDI information out of the MIDI-OUT port. Information can also be patched through to a daisy-chained third device via the MIDI-THRU port. MIDI connections are made with MIDI cables using 5-pin male DIN plugs (figure 15.2). Audio connections are generally made via ¼-inch TS (or TRS) plugs. (The MIDI spec does allow for the use of XLR connectors instead, but this option is rarely used.) The MIDI cable itself is a twisted pair of dual-conductor shielded cables. The two inner conductors are wired to pins 4 and 5, while the shield is wired to center pin 2. As with balanced audio connections, the shield is used for connection to ground, via pin 2 in accordance with the MIDI specification. However, inside the receiving MIDI device (MIDI-IN) pin 2 does not make a connection to ground, so as to avoid ground loops. Pins 1 and 3 are not used at all under the current specification, but could be implemented in a later version of the MIDI Spec.

Fig. 15.1. *Rear panel view of a typical MIDI device*

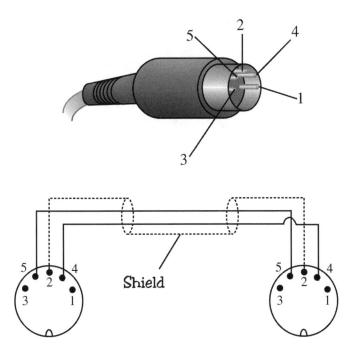

Fig. 15.2. *MIDI cable construction, using male 5-pin DIN plugs and twisted dual-conductor shielded cable*

MIDI Data

MIDI data communication is digital, with changes in current representing 0s (presence of current, sent via pin 4 from sending device) and 1s (no current present). Messages are transmitted *serially*, meaning that all bits are sent down a single pipeline (cable) one bit at a time, at a maximum rate of 31.25 kbaud or 31,250 bits per second. Bits are organized into 8-bit bytes, with an additional start bit (0) and stop bit (1) respectively before and after each word. Because MIDI data is transmitted without accompanying clock information (know as *asynchronous transmission*) and data may be transmitted at any time, the start and end bits help to organize the message and signal the start and end of each word. Upon receiving each start bit, the receiver adjusts the phase of its clock to match that of the sender, and the bits are then sent in order, beginning with the *least significant bit* (*LSB*) and ending with the *most significant bit* (*MSB*). The receiving device simply removes the start and stop bits and retrieves the actual data.

MIDI message bytes are grouped into *status* bytes (which begin with a 1) and *data* bytes (which begin with a 0). The first byte of a MIDI message, the status byte, identifies the type of message to follow and the MIDI channel number for the message. This is followed by one or two data bytes carrying the message data (note number, velocity, etc.).

To help describe MIDI messages, which can be rather long (given large binary numbers), MIDI spec sheets generally use the *hexadecimal* numbering system instead. This system uses powers of 16 instead of powers of 10 (decimal) or 2 (binary). In order for a single digit to have 16 possible values, the hexadecimal system uses 0 through 9 for the equivalent decimal values, and adds the letters A through F to represent decimal values 10 through 15. To represent decimal number 28, then, we would get:

Binary	1	1	1	0	0
Decimal weight	2^4	2^3	2^2	2^1	2^0
Decimal value	16	8	4	(2)	(1) = 16 + 8 + 4 = 28

Hexadecimal			**1**	**C**
Decimal weight			16^1	16^0 (1 × C = 12)
Decimal value			16	12 = 16 + 12 = 28

MIDI System Setup

Figure 15.3 shows a block diagram of the typical signal flow of a MIDI-equipped studio. Notice the differentiation between audio signal flow and MIDI signal flow. The use of a key or legend is essential for clarity in this type of flow.

MIDI flow originates from the keyboard controller, which may or may not have an internal sound engine. Note and controller (e.g., pitch bend) performance data is sent to the MIDI interface and routed to the computer, to be recorded into a sequence on the computer. The MIDI information is also routed through the sequencer using the program's MIDI-THRU function, back to the MIDI interface, and to the appropriate sound engines (sound modules, samplers and even the main keyboard controller). Each device responds to the input data and produces the appropriate sounds, notes, durations, loudnesses, etc., which are fed to the respective audio outputs. The audio can then be mixed, amplified, and sent to monitor speakers.

The main MIDI connections, then, are from MIDI-OUT of the controller to a MIDI-IN (often one of eight or more) of the MIDI interface. The MIDI interface provides a bridge between the MIDI devices and the computer, usually via a higher-speed USB (*Universal Serial Bus*—12 Mbits/s transfer rate) connection. All MIDI interfaces must perform buffering internally before feeding data to or from the computer. MIDI-OUTS (often eight to ten ports, although sometimes as few as one or two) of the MIDI interface are patched to the MIDI-IN of each sound module (including keyboard controller if it contains a sound engine). Connections between MIDI-OUT of sound modules and MIDI-IN of the interface are optional, but very useful as they allow for *patch dumps* from modules to computer. A patch dump uploads all information about the module's sound patches (how each sound has been constructed), including sound names and numbers, to the computer for use in the sequencer as well as other programs called *patch list managers* and *editors*. In this way, sounds can be organized and sound patch parameters can be edited and saved directly on the computer, and then downloaded back to the modules or synthesizers.

Again, NOTE ON and NOTE OFF messages do not contain any information about the sound to be produced itself. The same message sent to two different synthesizers will produce two completely different instrument sounds. A recorded sequence then must be played back through the same setup to produce the same results. An attempt to deal with this situation was the introduction of the General MIDI (GM) Addendum to the *MIDI 1.0 Detailed Specification*, a set of features that helps standardize performance from device to device. Specifically, it establishes 128 standard program numbers and corresponding instrument sounds, as well as a note-specific *Percussion Key Map*. A GM-compliant device follows this sound mapping such that a GM sequence will play back with the appropriate instrument sounds (specific timbres and methods of sound construction will vary from device to device) regardless of the setup used to create it. Thus, GM program 66 is always an alto sax sound (except on MIDI channel 10), and key 39 on MIDI channel 10 (reserved for GM Percussion Key Map) is always a hand-clap sound. With non-GM synths, program 66 could be any instrument sound at all.

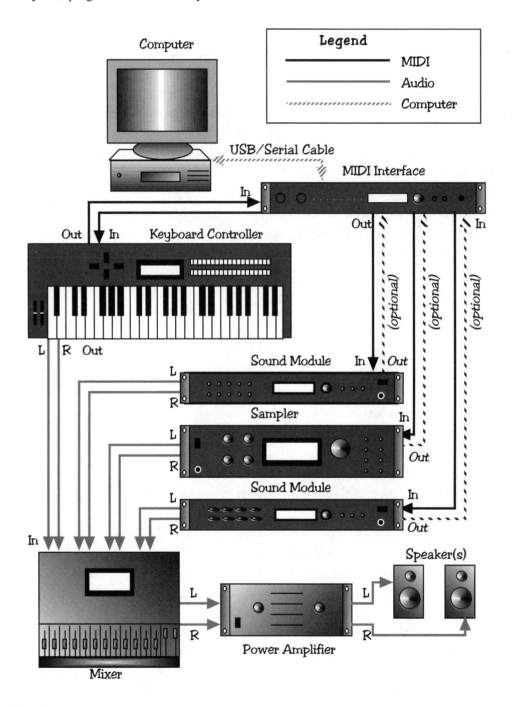

Fig. 15.3. *Typical MIDI studio setup. MIDI interface provides bridge between MIDI devices and computer.*

MIDI Messages

MIDI messages fall under two general categories: *channel* and *system*. Channel messages address only a particular MIDI channel and generally consist of *Note On/Off*, *Continuous Controller* (such as volume and pitch bend), and *program Change/Bank Select* messages (which allow the user to change patch sounds and banks on the fly during a sequence). These are all *Channel Voice* messages. There are also *Channel Mode* messages, which affect how a particular device responds to MIDI messages. While the original MIDI spec calls for four basic MIDI Channel Modes, the principal MIDI mode in use is *Omni Off-Poly*, which allows for maximum flexibility. (Multiple notes can be played simultaneously and address one specific device at a time.) In fact, most synthesizers use a newer *Multi Mode* setup that is not part of the original MIDI spec. It allows for a multitimbral instrument to use multiple Omni-Off/Poly modes, each addressing a different channel of the device which can now perform as several instruments in one. The MIDI spec allows for sixteen different possible MIDI channels, but this is further multiplied by using a multiport MIDI interface allowing messages to be routed a specific device on a given port (MIDI-OUT port 3, for instance), as well as a MIDI channel (sixteen channels per device).

Another important Channel Mode message is the *Local On/Off* message. Local Control gives a keyboard direct access to its internal sound engine (figure 15.4). During MIDI sequencing, Local Control should generally be turned off so that the keyboard may be routed exclusively to the sound engine of the moment, which may be an external or software-based sound module or sampler.

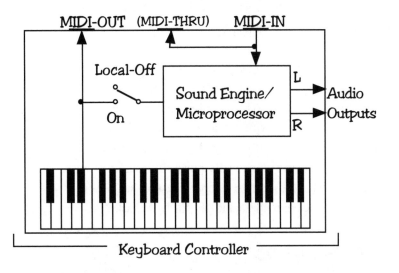

Fig. 15.4. Local Control gives a keyboard direct access to its own sound engine. Local-Off is generally used for MIDI sequencing.

System messages (which can be either *System Real Time*, *System Common*, or *System Exclusive*) address the entire device or system irrespective of MIDI channel. Examples of system messages include *Turn GM Mode On* (SysEx), *Song Select* (System Common), and *Timing Clock* (System Real Time). For further details on MIDI messages and message format, please refer to the *MIDI 1.0 Detailed Specification* and the "General MIDI (GM)" Addendum to the *MIDI 1.0 Detailed Specification*, which can be found at the MIDI Manufacturer's Association (MMA) Web site (www.midi.org).

Software Synthesis

As computer processing power increases, more and more is asked of the computer. *Virtual instruments*, that is, software-based synthesizers and samplers, are proliferating rapidly and offer some unique advantages with respect to flexibility, as well as smooth integration with DAW environments. In the instance where these devices are all computer-based, the signal flows described heretofore still apply, only they all happen within the computer. MIDI is still MIDI, and audio is still audio. Internally, the same MIDI messages are still sent from the sequencer to the virtual synth or sampler. The instrument must still receive those commands and its digital sound engine must produce the sound in the form of digital audio, regardless of how it is ultimately routed through the DAW. When using DSP processing in the form of TDM or RTAS (or other) plug-ins, it is the digital audio signal that is being processed with EQ, reverb, or compression, not the MIDI message. In fact, as systems become more integrated, it becomes all the more important to understand these fundamental signal-flow concepts in order to be able to effectively troubleshoot, as well as use, any system to its full potential. Remember that while MIDI messages consist of commands, ultimately it is the sound module or synthesizer (hardware- or software-based) that is responsible for generating the sound, or audio.

An important caveat as well: it is unwise to ask a computer to do too much at once. You may find it too taxing for the system to be recording multiple tracks of high-resolution digital audio into a DAW environment, while simultaneously playing back layers of samples and complex software synth patches all from the same computer. While each of these tools is individually powerful, each is also processor-intensive. It is often wise to have a separate computer just for sample or virtual synth playback, in addition to the computer dedicated for DAW tasks.

PROJECT

Review figure 15.3. Create a similar signal flowchart of your MIDI setup, including both MIDI and audio connections.

Chapter 16 Studio and Listening Room Acoustics
Where It All Begins and Ends

Thus far, we have mainly dealt with signals and audio systems directly. However, perhaps no single element has a greater impact on the overall performance of an audio system than the room in which it is recorded to or played back in. Whether dealing with a home stereo or surround-sound system or a full-blown recording studio and control room, it is critical to understand some of the ways in which sound and the listening environment interact.

Standing Waves (Room Modes)

One of the first acoustic phenomena encountered in an enclosed space is that of the *standing wave*. A "standing wave" occurs when the wavelength of an acoustical sound component has an exact mathematical relationship with a particular room dimension. The sound wave, upon reaching the wall, is reflected and superimposed back onto itself following an exact pattern of compressions and rarefactions. This pattern repeats as the sound wave reflects back and forth between two opposite surfaces. The net result is that the points of zero excitation (*nodes*) and maximum excitation (*antinodes*) always occur at the same physical location, as if the wave were standing still; hence the term "standing" wave (figure 16.1). This happens where the distance between two parallel surfaces is equal to half the signal wavelength, as well as at infinite multiples of this frequency. In the illustration below, distance = 1.5 × wavelength. A standing wave can be directly observed in a sealed plastic tube containing liquid with a loudspeaker driver at one end (figure 16.2). As the frequency of the sine wave signal fed to the driver is adjusted to correspond to the dimension of the tube's length as described above, stationary patterns of pressure form to displace the liquid, and the standing wave pattern appears.

Frequencies that correspond to standing waves in a given room, also called *room modes*, will have an exaggerated response. This can be particularly noticeable at low frequencies, where standing waves are fewer and farther apart in frequency. Room resonances can lead to a noticeable boost in amplitude response at certain low frequencies, yielding a "boomy" overall sound. At higher frequencies, multiple modes tend to blur the effect of any single standing wave and average out into a relatively even room response. The inclusion of absorptive wall treatments also minimizes the effect of standing waves at high frequencies, but has little effect on lower resonances.

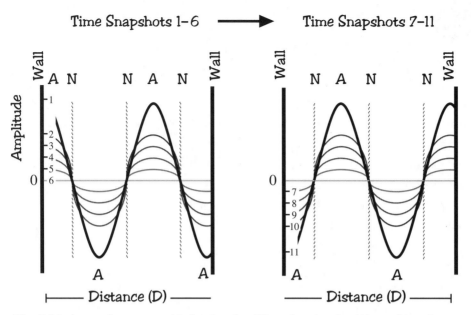

Fig. 16.1. *A standing wave with fixed nodes (N) and antinodes (A) resulting from a sound wave reflected back onto itself repeatedly in exact mathematical relationship [f = n(c/2D)] with the room dimension*

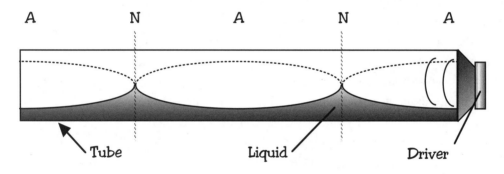

Fig. 16.2. *A standing wave resulting from a sound wave reflected back onto itself repeatedly in an enclosed tube partially filled with liquid*

Being able to calculate standing wave frequencies in a room, particularly at lower frequencies, allows us to deploy frequency-specific acoustic solutions such as bass traps or *membrane absorbers*. The frequency of a standing wave can be calculated based on the room dimensions as follows:

$$f = n(c/2D)$$

where f = standing wave frequency, c = speed of sound (1130 ft/s),
n = positive integers (1, 2, 3, 4 etc.),
and D = room dimension (length, width, or height)

This can be simplified as $f = 1130n/2D = 565n/D$. The first axial room mode, then, would occur at 565/D, which yields a standing wave where the dimension of the room = half the wavelength of the sound signal. Subsequent modes occur at multiples of this frequency. Given a room with dimensions L = 22 ft., W = 13 ft., and H = 10 ft., the axial room modes will occur at the frequencies listed in table 16.1.

L (22')	W (13')	H (10')
Frequ. (Hz)	*Frequ. (Hz)*	*Frequ. (Hz)*
25.68	43.46	56.50
51.36	86.92	113.00
77.05	130.38	
102.73		
128.41		

Table 16.1. *Standing wave frequencies corresponding to the first axial modes found in a small listening room with dimensions 22' x 13' x 10'*

These modes can also be displayed on a linear graph as in figure 16.3. This gives us a better visual sense of how the room modes are distributed. Individual modal bandwidths for most control-room-sized listening rooms are on the order of 5 Hz. In the example in figure 16.3, we note a potential problem near 55 Hz and another around 130 Hz, where there is an exaggerated amplitude response. There is also a substantial hole between 57 Hz and 77 Hz. This modal unevenness is nearly unavoidable in small spaces, and is usually compensated for by using a combination of low-frequency-specific absorption and room EQ—two channels of $\frac{1}{3}$ octave-band graphic equalizers placed before the system loudspeakers, and set to counterbalance the room and speakers' combined response for a flat net result. Severe modal problems, however, cannot be masked or overcome by EQ, which should only be employed for minor tweeks. The BBC (British Broadcasting Corporation) has determined that rooms smaller than 1,500 ft³ make for unacceptable broadcast studio rooms for this reason.

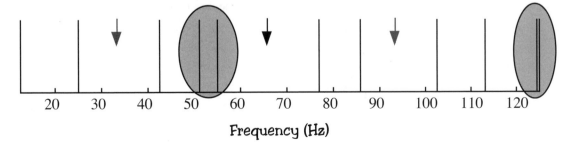

Fig. 16.3. *First axial room modes of example room. Overlap occurs around 55 Hz and 130 Hz, with substantial unsupported frequency holes in between.*

When designing new rooms, some studio and room designers subscribe to so-called "golden ratios" for room dimensions, because they tend to minimize room mode buildup and generate a more even spread, particularly at low frequencies. This is not a new idea, but rather dates back to the ancient Greeks. In the extreme, some musicians, when designing their homes, have taken into account the wavelength of the lowest frequency generated by their principal instrument, such as cello, in order to select room dimensions. While there is no single optimal ratio, there is perhaps a range of ratios that promotes more even (and desirable) distribution of room modes.

Standing waves can occur between any two boundary surfaces, including opposite walls, and ceiling and floor. Modes involving two parallel surfaces, called *axial modes,* tend to have the most energy potential (less reflection loss). However, room modes also exist involving two pairs of room surfaces (*tangential modes*) and even three pairs of surfaces (*oblique modes*). While it is possible to calculate these as well, it is more involved, and perhaps unnecessary, due to their lessened energy level. In fact, it is easy to dwell too much on room modes and overstate their importance on the overall sound of the room. It might be useful to calculate just the first few axial modes to identify any overt problem areas of modal superposition and frequency holes, perhaps up to 120 Hz, as in the example above. Membrane absorbers can then be used that are tuned to absorb the specific problem low frequencies. The situation is further complicated by the fact that actual room dimension is blurred by wall construction. Low frequencies pass through most surface materials (including drywall) at least partially, and are only fully reflected by more massive structural elements. For this reason, rooms with walls made of concrete tend to have more of a problem with low-frequency buildup.

A common path taken in studio design is the use of non-parallel walls and ceiling to diffuse standing waves. This solution is often impractical when dealing with an existing space and generally only applies to new constructions. Also, use of non-parallel surfaces *does not* eliminate room modes or standing waves, but simply spreads them out in a more evenly distributed fashion. It also makes them harder to calculate, as they all come to have the three-dimensional characteristic of oblique modes. However, by creating a whole spectrum of modal frequencies, this approach reduces the likelihood of superimposed standing waves on a given frequency and large unsupported frequency gaps in between. It also reduces the likely occurrence of *flutter echoes*. Flutter echoes are rapidly repeating echoes at high frequencies, which occur in small enclosed spaces between closely spaced parallel walls. Flutter echoes sound something like the rapid flutter of a bird's wings.

Perceived room response is also dependent on where the listener is situated in that room. Buildup of pressure, particularly at low frequencies, is most evident close to room surfaces. This is because sound is constantly trading off between velocity and pressure (figure 16.4). Points of zero pressure are the points at which the air particles are moving the fastest (greatest velocity), while points of maximum and minimum pressure are where the particles have been fully bunched together or stretched apart (stored energy) respectively. Since walls are not easily moved by sound, particle velocity at room boundaries is essentially zero, meaning that pressure is at its greatest. This is most evident at low frequencies because of the decreased number of, and increased distance (due to longer wavelength) between, points of maximum/minimum pressure (*antinodes*) and points of zero pressure (*nodes*). Looking at the first axial mode between two parallel surfaces, the resulting standing wave in any room will have antinodes (pressure buildup) at the surfaces, and a node in the center of the room. Figure 16.5 illustrates the simplest room resonances and resulting sound pressure pattern between two surfaces.

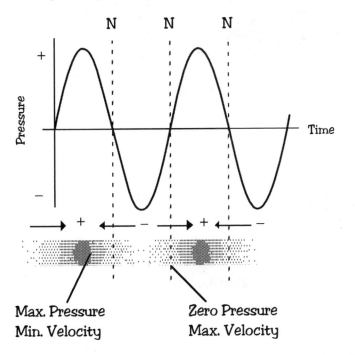

Fig. 16.4. *Points of maximum pressure in a sound wave represent points of minimum velocity; points of zero pressure are also points of maximum particle velocity.*

To test this, set up an oscillator tuned to a frequency whose wavelength is half or equal to one of your room dimensions. Then, using only one ear for most dramatic effect, walk around and notice where the signal gets the loudest and where the signal nearly drops out completely. These points will correspond to the antinodes and nodes, respectively. This simple exercise reinforces the fact that uncontrolled low-frequency standing waves cause unevenness in frequency response at different points in a room. Such unevenness presents a real challenge to critical listening and the accurate evaluation of the frequency content of a mix, for instance.

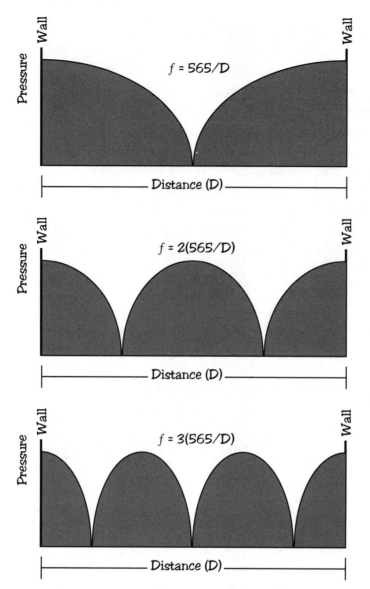

Fig. 16.5 *Standing-wave pressure patterns for first three axial modes between two room surfaces*

Speaker Placement

Because pressure builds up at room surfaces, and because this buildup is especially skewed towards low frequencies, it is generally advisable to avoid placing loudspeakers, particularly close-field monitors, directly against a wall. Speaker manufacturers often include recommendations for speaker placement, which usually call for placement away from corners (point of maximum bass buildup) and 2 to 4 feet away from the back wall. The exception to this rule is the speaker design that intentionally factors in wall-pressure effects as part of the speaker performance. Such a speaker must be placed accordingly for proper frequency response. While many recording studios employ in-wall soffited mounting for their large main monitors, the resulting exaggerated bass response can be misleading (although effective for impressing clients).

Subwoofers, on the other hand, often benefit from corner room placement, as their sole purpose is the reproduction of strong low frequencies (usually below 80 Hz). A useful approach for finding the perfect subwoofer placement is to place the subwoofer in the listening position. As signal is sent through the subwoofer, walk around the room, and try to identify that place where the bass sounds best (not necessarily the loudest). Once the position is identified, place the subwoofer there, and it will sound equally good to the engineer sitting at the listening position. A similar technique could be used for main monitor placement as well, although the angling and distance requirements for proper stereo imaging is much more restrictive.

Reflections (Reverberation)

Perhaps even more important than room modes to the overall sound of a room are its reverberation characteristics. *Reverberation* is the amalgam of reflected energy resulting from sound waves encountering obstacles (e.g., walls) and reflecting back into the room. In this case, sound waves behave a lot like light waves, where the angle of reflection equals the angle of incidence (figure 16.6). Sound reflects off of the wall and projects back into the room as if it were originating from a source on the other side of the wall equidistant with the actual sound source.

The process of *ray tracing*, now generally computer-generated, can begin to tell us how a given sound source (such as monitor loudspeakers) spreads out in an enclosed listening space. This technique has been used in concert halls to ensure proper spreading of sound to cover the entire seating area. Mirrors and flashlights can also be used in the space to visually mimic sound sources and reflections, and reflectors can then be positioned so as to ensure the best sound coverage and spread over the audience area. Both techniques are useful in the recording studio control room as well, to eliminate the presence of damaging early reflections at the listening position (figure 16.7), for instance. Once located, points of reflection can be treated, if necessary, with absorptive or diffusive materials. Notice the preferred positioning of monitor speakers behind, rather than on, the console bridge, so as to avoid direct reflections bouncing off the console face and towards the engineer's ears. Also note the splaying of the studio/control room window to avoid direct reflections back towards the listening position. Due to diffraction effects (discussed later), sound waves from the front of the speaker, particularly at lower frequencies, radiate backwards from the front edges of the speaker cabinets.

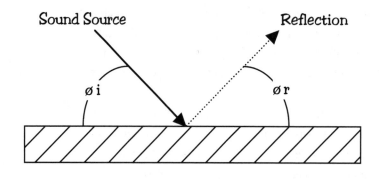

Fig. 16.6 *With sound waves, as with light waves, angle of reflection (ør) equals angle of incidence (øi)*

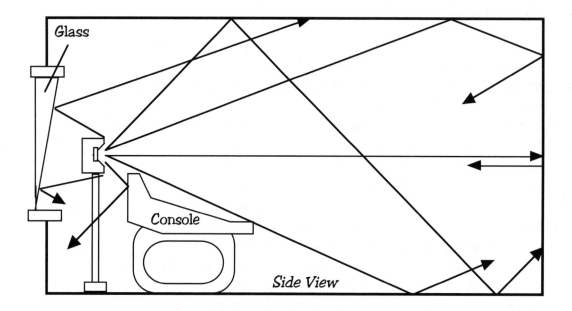

Fig. 16.7. *Ray tracing helps to understand how a sound source spreads within a listening room.*

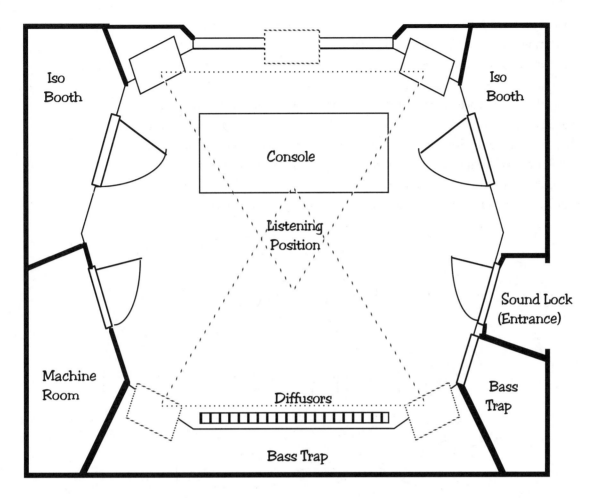

Fig. 16.8. *RFZ studio control room design, with possible 5.1 surround setup*

Control Room Design

Modern control room design often centers around a concept called the *reflection free-zone* (*RFZ*), which is an attempt to avoid direct or first-order reflections at the listening position by splaying front and side wall surfaces (figure 16.8). This is in contrast with the once popular *LEDE* (*live end dead end*) design, which looks to completely deaden the front end of the control room. Both are attempts to solve the same problem: preventing damaging early reflections from reaching the listening position. Strong reflected signals arriving at the listening position out of phase are damaging because they can combine with the direct signal and cause comb-filtering effects and other frequency anomalies.

To see why this is, let's look more closely at what happens when two similar sound waves (a direct signal and strong first reflection, or the same signal emanating from two loudspeakers, for instance) encounter one another other. Depending on where the listener is located, the waves will be heard to either combine constructively or destructively. With simple sine waves, this is easily observed because we are dealing with a single frequency and wavelength (figure 16.9). If the difference in path length to the listener between direct and reflected sound is equal to one whole wavelength (or integer multiples of it), the two wave-forms will arrive in-phase and combine constructively. On the other hand, if the difference in path length is equal to a half wavelength (or odd integer multiples of it: $\frac{3}{2}$, $\frac{5}{2}$, etc.), the waves will arrive 180° out-of-phase and combine destructively. If the waves are of equal strength, they will completely cancel each other out.

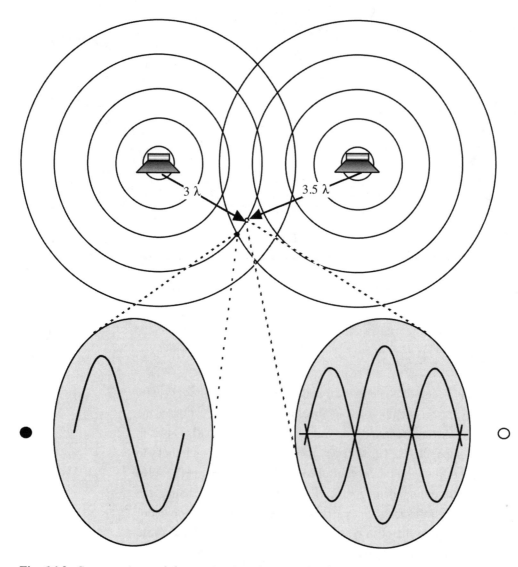

Fig. 16.9. Constructive and destructive interference. Circles represent compressions spreading out spherically from the source.

We do not usually hear the full effect because it is minimized by the fact that we have two ears, that indoors there are multiple reflections—each with different path lengths—and that we are usually listening to non-periodic complex music signals. However, to hear this effect more dramatically, patch an oscillator generating a 1 kHz sine wave signal to feed both speakers. Blocking one ear and moving your head only a short distance, you should be able to find points of constructive interference (maximum response = 2 × amplitude), and destructive interference (minimum response = 0 × amplitude). Complete cancellation will not be heard unless the test is performed in an *anechoic* (reflection-free) *chamber*, but the effect should be dramatic nonetheless.

With complex signals, the interferences are blurred but do occur for individual component waves, as above. The net result is that a strong reflection off of a nearby reflective surface can cause a comb-filtered response, where certain frequencies, at regular intervals, cancel out, leaving holes in the soundwave's frequency spectrum. Music stands are often covered with frictional material and/or repositioned so as to mitigate high-frequency phase cancellations at a nearby microphone (figure 16.10).

The same concern exists when multiple microphones are used simultaneously for several sources in the same space; during a basics session, for instance. Each source signal reaches separate microphones in different phase relationships. If the signals are then summed electrically, as happens in *mono*, phase cancellations *will* occur. As discussed previously, the *3-to-1 rule* tries to deal with this effect by ensuring that the distance between any two microphones is at least three times the distance from the microphone to the source (figure 16.11). Under these conditions, the inverse square law ensures that there will be a great enough difference in level between the two signals to avoid severe frequency phase cancellations (for total cancellation, the two signal amplitudes must be equal). In addition, use of directional microphones (cardioid, hypercardioid) further reduces the level of a signal arriving off-axis. The 3-to-1 rule does not usually apply to stereo miking techniques.

Fig. 16.10. *Sound reflecting off a music stand can combine with the direct sound at the microphone and cause a comb-filtered frequency response. The stand's surface can be covered with frictional absorbent to minimize the effect.*

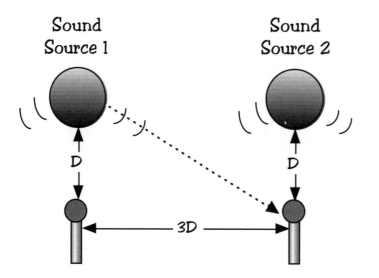

Fig. 16.11. *The 3-to-1 rule for minimizing phase cancellations when using multiple mics*

Reverberation Time (T$_{60}$)

Professor Wallace Clement Sabine of Harvard University is widely recognized for his work as the pioneer of listening room acoustics at the dawn of the twentieth century. He was the first to study the effect of reverberation on speech intelligibility in a room, and to devise methods of modifying a room's surface materials to alter reverberation characteristics (or to design a room with predictable listening characteristics from the onset). Specifically, he developed an equation to calculate reverberation time, based on the absorption characteristics and volume ($l \times w \times h$) of a room (equation 16.1). Reverberation time is defined as the amount of time it takes for sound pressure level in a room to drop by 60 dB once the sound source has stopped.

$$T_{60} \text{ (or } RT_{60}) = 0.05 \ V/A$$

where T$_{60}$ = reverberation time (s) , V = room volume (ft^3),
and A = total ft^2 of absorption (sabins)

Eq. 16.1 Sabine formula for calculating reverberation time

Total absorption (A) would be calculated by taking each surface material's absorption coefficient (α) and multiplying it by that surface's total area. The results are then added up and the final sum yields A. Mathematically, this gives us equation 16.2.

$$A = \Sigma \ S\alpha$$
$$\text{i.e., A} = S_1\alpha_1 + S_2\alpha_2 + ... + S_n\alpha_n$$

where Σ means "sum" or "summation of," S = surface area (ft^2),
and α = absorption coefficient (energy absorbed/energy incident)

Eq. 16.2. Formula for calculating total room absorption

Common building materials have absorption coefficient ratings for a range of frequencies that are measured in a testing lab using Sabine's formula or a close variation. Absorption coefficients are a ratio of the energy absorbed to the energy incident (amount of sound energy hitting the surface material under test), and thus have a possible theoretical range of 0 (no energy absorbed) to 1 (all energy absorbed).

Figure 16.12 is a graphic representation of the reverberation characteristics typical of a concert hall. Notice that reverberation time (T$_{60}$) is measured from the point that the sound (usually an impulse waveform) stops, to the point where the sound has decayed in the room by 60 dB. If the noise floor of the room masks the final decay of the reverberation above the –60 dB point, the –60 dB point can be extrapolated from the slope of the decay.

Because of the short delay times involved, early reflections from the nearest surfaces are usually not heard as distinct echoes but rather are psychoacoustically grouped or *fused* with the initial signal and contribute to its perceived timbre. Reverberation decay, which is the amalgam of multiple room reflections, is generally perceived as a diffuse wall of sound beginning some time after the initial signal. The delay between the initial impulse and the onset of reverberation, called *predelay*, is heard quite audibly in larger concert halls, as the delay time is long enough for the two signals to be perceived as separate. In fact, all other things being equal, predelay time is a good aural cue as to the size of a room. The use of predelay in artificial reverb units greatly enhances the realism of the effect.

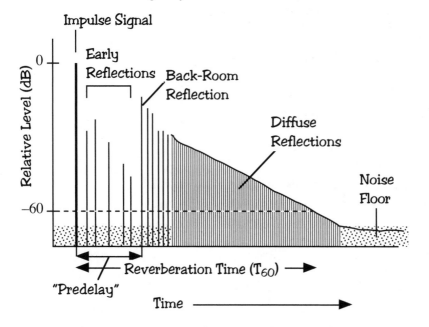

Fig. 16.12. *Graphic representation of room reverberation and calculation of reverberation time (T₆₀).*

The *Sabine formula* works well for most regularly shaped (i.e, rectangular) rooms with normally reflective surfaces, but is less well-suited for more absorptive rooms, such as certain recording studios, control rooms, and anechoic chambers. In these cases, a slightly more complex equation, known as the *Norris-Eyring formula*, has been suggested (equation 16.3).

$$T_{60} = 0.05 \ V/-S \times 2.3 \log(1 - \bar{\alpha})$$

where T_{60} = reverberation time (s), V = room volume (ft³),

S = total surface area (ft²),

and $\bar{\alpha}$ = mean sound absorption coefficient = $\Sigma \ S\alpha/\Sigma S$

Eq. 16.3. *Norris-Eyring formula for calculating reverberation time in very absorptive environments*

However, because most published material coefficients are based on the Sabine formula, it is probably advisable to use the first (Sabine) formula even in these instances. In any case, when designing a new music room or studio, using either formula would help to predict anticipated reverb times based on the room volume and type of materials planned to finish the room surfaces. Target reverb times are a key factor to take into account for the intended purpose of the space. As a general rule, shorter times are desirable for the purpose of speech intelligibility, while longer reverberation times are helpful for a natural blending of acoustic music. Reverberation times of greater than two seconds should generally be reserved for large spaces (>100,000 ft^3) where live orchestral music is to be performed, while reverberation times of 0.5 seconds or less should be reserved for recording or broadcast studios intended mainly for speech recording. Multipurpose spaces must necessarily compromise, although it is possible to build reversible or rotatable surfaces to alter the reverberation characteristics of a space according to the need of the day.

Reverberation time is frequency-specific, and should be measured and given for one frequency band. Sabine's original work looked only at the room response for 512 Hz. If frequency is not specified, one can assume that the frequency in question is either 500 Hz, 1 kHz, or an average of the two. Optimum reverberation time in this frequency range obviously varies greatly depending on the sound source, as well as the function and the size of the room being used. The larger the room, the longer the expected reverberation time, all other things being equal.

Control room reverberation must be especially carefully controlled, since critical listening decisions must be made in the context of recording and mixdown in particular. Direct sound from the speakers must not be masked or blurred by overly strong room contributions. However, the room must not be completely dead (no reflections) either, as the reproduced signal will begin to sound very unnatural. Room ambience plays an important part in achieving natural sound from loudspeakers even when the recorded music already contains artificial and/or natural reverberation.

Room Treatment

How can a listening room be modified to improve its sonic characteristics? We know from Sabine's work that adding absorptive material can alter the reverberation time and perhaps damp out unwanted reflections. But what type of absorption, and where? There are three basic types of absorbers: frictional, flexural, and resonant. *Frictional* absorbers are mainly effective at absorbing higher frequencies, and work by allowing air particles to pass through them. In doing so, the particles rub against the absorber and sound energy is converted to heat energy. For this to work the absorber must be porous. Elements that are fuzzy, such as fiberglass insulation, thick drapes, or carpets are generally good frictional absorbers. A good test is to blow through the material. If air can pass through, it is probably an effective frictional absorber. Naturally, frictional absorbers are *not* good sound isolators for the very same reason.

The thicker a given frictional absorber, the more effective it will be, particularly improving performance at lower-midrange frequencies (125 to 500 Hz) where it is not naturally very effective. However, a frictional absorber will be even more effective if spaced away from a surface rather than applied directly to that surface. If you recall, the point of maximum pressure is always at room boundaries, which means that the point of maximum velocity is ¼ wavelength (λ) away (figure 16.13). Since frictional absorbers work mainly on particle motion, not on pressure, they will be most effective when placed where the air particle motion is greatest. A complex wave, such as a music signal, is made up of multiple frequencies, each with its own wavelength, so precise ¼ λ placement is impossible and impractical for lower frequencies. Spacing the absorber about 3–6 inches away from the surface is a good rule of thumb, and can be expected to significantly improve absorption performance in the 250 to 500 Hz range.

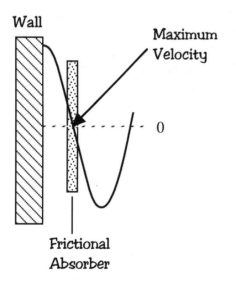

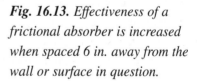

Fig. 16.13. Effectiveness of a frictional absorber is increased when spaced 6 in. away from the wall or surface in question.

Locating the points needing absorptive treatment can be as simple as aligning a light source (laser pointer, or even flashlight) with the tweeter (high-frequency driver) of the loudspeaker. The light source can be rotated in any direction along its axis to mimic sound spreading spherically. The higher the frequency, the more sound will beam straight ahead rather than spreading spherically. Using a small mirror on nearby reflective surfaces, look for mirror placements where the light source reflects directly onto the listening position. (Having someone sit in the engineer's chair is a good idea.) These are the spots that could benefit from absorptive treatment. An even simpler method for use in the studio is to use only a mirror. The person sitting in the engineer's chair looks out for mirror placements where the speaker tweeter's visual reflection becomes visible. As discussed, similar techniques have been used in concert halls to properly position sound reflectors. Shining lights on the reflectors allows the design team to adjust multiple ceiling reflectors for uniform sound coverage throughout the audience seating area.

Flexural absorbers are materials that flex in response to stimulus, and by moving with the source absorb some of its energy. Plywood, gypsum board (GWB or drywall), and glass are all flexural absorbers, and tend to be effective at lower-midrange frequencies (125 to 500 Hz). In contrast, massive structures, such as a concrete foundation, do not flex at all and are very poor at absorbing any frequencies. They do make good sound transmission isolators for the same reason. Flexural absorbers tend to be very reflective at higher frequencies.

Finally, *resonant* absorbers, sometimes called *bass traps* as well as *Helmholtz resonators* (named after Hermann von Helmholtz, 1821–1894), are effective at very specific narrow-bandwidth, low-frequency absorption. These can be an effective tool for dealing with problematic low-frequency standing waves, especially in smaller spaces. The resonant absorber consists of an enclosed volume of air tuned to a low frequency, with gaps or openings that allow low-frequency sound energy in. The air inside acts like a type of spring on the columns of air entering the slots. The cavity can also be filled with frictional absorbent, with the effect of widening the bandwidth of effective absorption to more generally absorb a group of low frequencies, at the expense of maximum absorption at the center frequency. Corner placement is often the most effective to release low-frequency pressure buildup in the room.

An easier alternative to the classic Helmholtz-type bass trap is the *membrane absorber*, which uses a flexural absorber, such as a large thin sheet of plywood, on an enclosed box with no openings. It can also simply be mounted on a wall and encased. The effective absorption or resonant frequency is a function of the thickness or density of the panel and the depth of the airspace behind it, as follows:

$$f_o = 170/\sqrt{(m(d))}$$

where f_o = resonant frequency (Hz), m = surface density of panel (lb/ft^2),
and d = depth of airspace (in)

Eq. 16.4. *Equation for calculating absorption or resonant frequency of a panel membrane absorber*

Various surface densities are widely published and available for common building materials. Surface density of any material can also be easily found by weighing a piece of known area, 1 ft^2, for instance. Given a commonly used ¼-inch plywood panel (m = 0.74 lb/ft^2), installed 6 inches from the wall, the resonant frequency would be $f_0 = 170/\sqrt{(0.74(6))} = 80.68$ Hz. For lower-frequency absorption, the panel would be installed further out from the wall. Thicker material could also be used although generally speaking, thinner panels are more effective absorbers, as they are more likely to flex in response to sound stimulus. Preconstructed membrane absorbers in the form of various-shaped boxes can also be purchased that are pretuned to various frequencies. These can be hung from the ceiling, serving both an acoustic and aesthetic function.

Diffusion

While absorption can be an effective tool, we must be careful not to abuse it. This type of reflection control quickly leads to a very unnatural sounding space. The extreme of this is the *anechoic chamber*, which is used for speaker and microphone testing. This type of room is completely absorptive down to fairly low frequencies (around 150 Hz) and sounds unlike any other real acoustical space. While it is very useful for testing purposes, it is *not* a pleasant listening environment. In designing or treating a real listening room, acousticians like to say that they only have a certain number of sabins (units of absorption) to work with. The goal is to try to find alternatives to absorption until absolutely necessary, and then to use absorption sparingly.

Fortunately, there is another powerful tool at our disposal, namely *diffusion*. The idea behind diffusion is the scattering of sound from a single strong discrete reflection to a broad array of lesser reflections spread in many different directions (figure 16.14). This has the net effect of spreading sound evenly throughout the room while eliminating audible discrete echoes, which can blur or destructively combine with the direct sound. The *quadratic-residue diffuser* dates back to the 1970s when Dr. Manfred Schroeder developed it for use in concert halls. Diffusers come in all sorts of shapes and sizes and have found a welcome home in recording studios and other music listening spaces (among the most successful have been the RPG Diffusers, developed by Dr. Peter D'Antonio). The frequency range down to which a diffuser will be effective is directly related to depth of the cavities or irregularities. The longer the wavelength, the less even a surface must be to diffuse the sound wave. Thus, the small patterns and irregularities on some of the acoustical treatments that are sold must be taken as purely aesthetic (not an unimportant consideration) but non-diffusive. Other diffusers include *phase grating* and *fractal* diffusers.

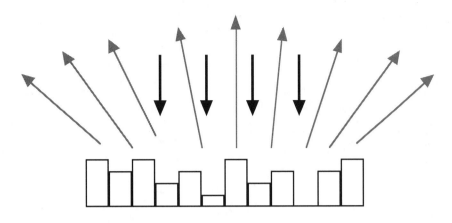

Fig. 16.14. *A diffuser scatters the incident sound wave, spreading energy out more evenly and eliminating strong discrete echoes.*

Diffusion is generally most effective at the back of the listening room, since that is the surface that will be receiving the brunt of the direct sound wave from the speakers. Diffusion can also be effective in conjunction with absorption to the sides as well as above the listening position. Because speakers generate significant energy that radiates from behind the speaker, strong absorption behind, potentially coupled with diffusion, is usually a good idea. Interestingly, *lateral reflections* (reflections from the side walls) have a significant impact on the sense of spaciousness and width of the stereo image. The amount of absorption used here must therefore be carefully chosen. Ideally, this should be done through listening tests to model the space for best results with different types of music. Figure 16.15 gives one possible approach to acoustical treatment for a typical home-studio control-room environment. This should only be taken as a starting point and cannot be generalized to all possible listening environments. Whenever possible, it is highly recommended to consult with an acoustician, especially in the design of new structures or to solve existing problems.

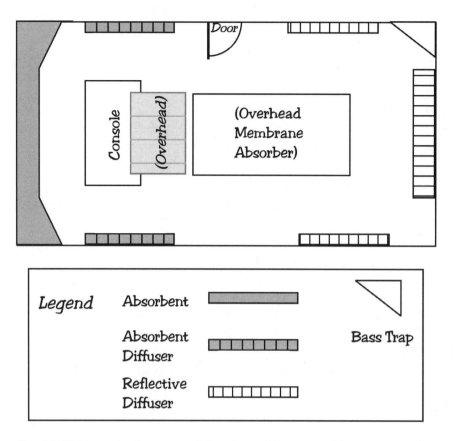

Fig. 16.15. Example placement of absorbers, diffusers, and bass trap in a home-studio-type control room

Sound Isolation

A completely different, although equally important, consideration for a studio environment is that of sound isolation. For critical listening purposes, the noise floor of the room itself must be low. For recording purposes, any stray noises will be picked up by the microphones, which cannot tell the difference between wanted and unwanted sound. Sound isolation to prevent unwanted sounds from entering the studio will be equally effective at keeping sounds in the studio from escaping to the outside and becoming a nuisance to neighbors. The principal tool for sound isolation is *mass*. Sound transmission occurs when the vibration of air molecules from a sound source causes vibrations in building structures, such as walls, ceilings, and floors. Those vibrations in turn cause the air on the other side of the structure to vibrate, and the sound wave is transmitted. A massive structure, by being unmovable, helps prevent the transmission of sound from one space to an adjacent space. The *mass law* states that for every doubling of mass, we can expect approximately a 6 dB improvement in sound isolation, or 6 dB decrease in sound transmission.

Materials and building constructions are actually rated for sound isolation ability in *TL* or *transmission loss*, which is a ratio in dB between energy incident and energy transmitted. The higher the TL, the better the isolation. A construction with a TL_{500Hz} of 35 dB means that it was capable of attenuating a signal by 35 dB in the 500 Hz band in a lab environment. We can restate the mass law by saying that a doubling in mass will result in an approximate 6 dB *increase* in TL. Additionally, high frequencies are much easier to stop than low frequencies. This is why the neighbor's music always sounds "boomy." Like reverberation and absorption, transmission loss is frequency dependent. The mass law states that a doubling of frequency also results in an approximate increase in TL of 6 dB. Conversely, if TL = 40 dB at 500 Hz, we can expect the TL at 250 Hz to be about 6 dB lower, or 34 dB.

Of course, exact results will vary from material to material, but the general tenet holds true: greater mass helps, and lower frequencies are more difficult to control. What this means is that adding sound absorption materials, such as acoustic foam tiles, inside a room or studio, will do little to keep sounds from entering or leaving the studio, particularly low to mid frequencies. This modification will change the quality of sound inside the room, by absorbing high frequencies and reducing reverberation time, but will do nothing to increase sound isolation from nearby noises. For this we need massive structures, such as concrete walls, or additional layers of GBW.

Closely related to TL, *STC* (*sound transmission class*) is a single-number rating (in dB) covering the TL performance of a construction between 125 Hz and 4 kHz. This allows for quick comparison of several construction options in their ability to isolate against sound transmission. It is important to note that STC does not give any indication of TL performance for low frequencies.

The problem with mass is that it is not always practical. Following the mass law, to improve the TL performance of a 1-foot-thick concrete wall by 6 dB, its thickness would need to be expanded to 2 feet! Fortunately, there are some ways to cheat mass. For instance, we can create a structure that makes it hard for vibrations to pass from one side of the wall to the other. One of the most effective of these is the *double-wall partition* (figure 16.16), which completely physically isolates one side of the wall from the other, making it very difficult for sound wave vibrations to pass through the structure. Properly constructed, including 9-inch insulation fill, this type of partition can yield an STC of close to 60 dB! Care must be taken to ensure that no part of one wall, including the insulation, comes into contact with the other wall. Use of metal studs instead of wood generally improves performance by about 5 dB.

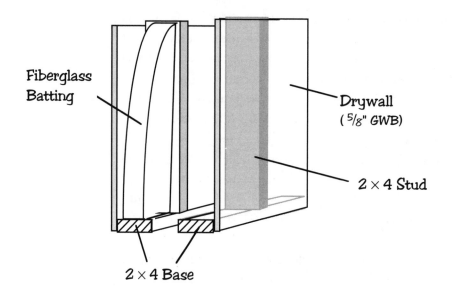

Fig. 16.16. Double-wall partition construction

Less effective but somewhat more space- and cost-effective alternatives for wall construction include a *staggered-stud partition* (figure 16.17) and a partition with a resilient channel strip running between the studs and drywall; both means of physically isolating one side of the wall from the other.

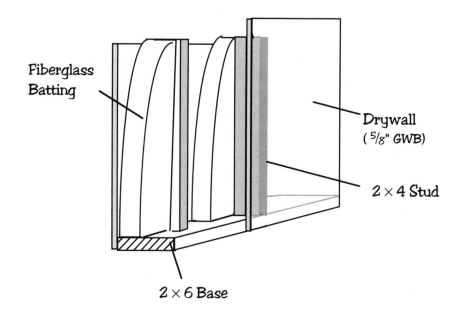

Fig. 16.17. Staggered-stud partition construction

Similar construction principles underlie the dual-paned studio glass used to separate the control room from the studio. The panes are separated by a volume of air with an air-tight seal, and vibrations of the glass panes are damped by rubber mounts on either side. The panes themselves can be multilayered, separated by a sheet of translucent damping material.

Baffles

Within the recording studio, it is often necessary to isolate sound sources from each other. This allows for effective individual miking, recording, and signal processing of instruments that are being played simultaneously in the context of a multitrack recording session. Strong leakage signals, unless intended as part of a concerted global approach to recording, can contribute to unfocused sound, phase cancellations, and poor imaging. *Baffles* or *gobos* are constructed and used to help create pockets of isolation within the studio. Baffles are constructed of plywood or other flexural absorbers for the inner layer, then covered or filled with a frictional absorbent, such as foam or insulation (figure 16.18). This yields a barrier that is both effective against transmission as well as absorbent across a wide frequency range. (Remember that frictional absorbent alone is a very poor isolator.)

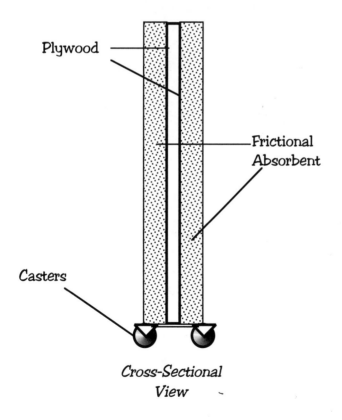

Fig. 16.18. *Baffle construction as seen from the side*

In order to be effective, the baffle must break the line of sight between the two sound sources/microphones and must be impervious. In fact, two of the factors that have the greatest impact on the effectiveness of a baffle or sound barrier are the extent to which it breaks the line of sight between sound source and receiver, and how close it is to the sound source or receiver (distant mic). In general, the closer the baffle is to the element being isolated (either sound source or remote microphone), the better. To increase the effectiveness of the baffle, it can be stood on its side for full contact with the ground. While the casters are useful for moving the baffle around the studio, the gap that they create between the floor and the bottom of the baffle create a *flanking path* for sound transmission. This can greatly reduce the effectiveness of the baffle. Alternatively, once in position, the gap can be filled in with a packing blanket. Packing blankets are also useful for covering open piano lids to increase isolation and diminish leakage from other instruments into the piano mics positioned over the strings.

The baffle also needs to be large enough in dimension to prevent *diffraction*. Diffraction is the bending of a sound wave around an obstacle or object (figure 16.19). This happens whenever the wavelength of a signal is greater than the dimensions of the obstacle. The lower the frequency, the longer the wavelength and the more easily diffraction will occur. A 4 ft. × 4 ft. baffle will not have much effect on any frequencies whose wavelengths are greater than 4 ft., i.e., $f < c/l = 1130/4 = 282.5$ Hz. In fact, for a baffle to be truly effective, it should be twice as long as it is high, to prevent *end-run diffraction* on either side of the baffle. To be effec-

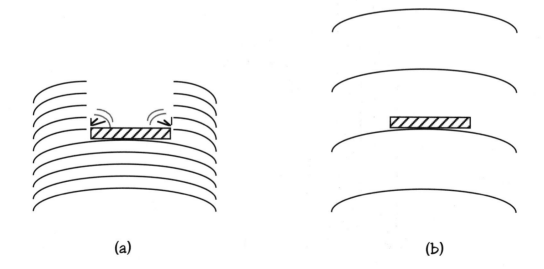

(a)   (b)

Fig. 16.19. *(a) High-frequency sound wave with short wavelength is effectively stopped, creating a shadow effect (with only slight redirection of highs into shadow region). (b) Low-frequency sound wave with long wavelength diffracts around obstacle and continues unaltered on its path.*

tive down to 282.5 Hz, then, the baffle should ideally be 4 ft. × 8 ft. Reflectors used specifically to redirect sound towards an audience, in a concert hall, for instance, must have dimensions 2 to 4 times greater than the wavelength of the frequency of interest for effective reflection. It is interesting to note that there is some redirecting of sound even at high frequencies from the top edge of the baffle back into the shadow region, as if from a new sound source.

Diffraction is also a large part of the reason that microphone placement can have a large effect on the resulting timbre of the recorded signal (figure 16.20). High-frequency components (wavelength or λ < opening) of the musical signal tend

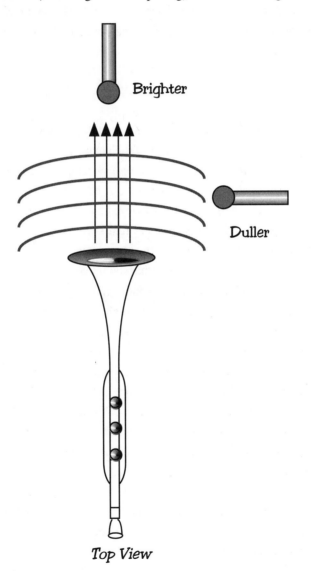

Fig. 16.20. *High frequencies tend to beam straight ahead while lower frequencies diffract and spread spherically.*

to beam and project straight ahead, while lower frequencies (λ > opening) diffract around the opening and spread more spherically. Thus, placing a microphone to the side of the sound source will capture a duller or "mellower" sound, while a microphone placed directly in front will capture both low and high frequencies equally, resulting in a brighter, "edgier" sound. Of course, when close miking a sound source, small changes in mic position also have a significant effect on timbre because the mic is in the source's nearfield. Therefore, it will pick up only a specific area of the source's vibrational patterns. To capture the full and natural effect of the source, the mic should be moved back away from the source (2 to 3 ft. is a good starting point) where its overall sound has had a chance to resolve. This assumes that the nature of the room, as well as the absence of proximate sources, allows for such treatment.

Noise

In addition to dealing with isolation from noises outside of the studio, we must also deal with noises originating from within. One of the most problematic noise sources for studios is the *HVAC (heating ventilation air conditioning)* system, particularly fan noise. The bad news is that quiet ventilation systems can be expensive, and small performance gains increase cost exponentially. However, a properly planned and professionally installed high-efficiency system can often save money in the long run. While the details of ventilation noise and treatment is outside of the scope of this book, there are some common-sense guidelines that should be kept in mind.

First and foremost, avoid feeding both studio and control room with the same air duct, as this allows sound from one room to bypass the high-TL wall and bleed into the adjacent room through the ductwork, largely unattenuated. At the very least, ensure that the two vent openings are as far apart from each other as possible, at opposite ends of the rooms. Also, high air velocity and air turbulence translate into increased ventilation noise level. Doubling air velocity, from 500 ft./min. to 1000 ft./min., for instance, is capable of increasing noise by up to 20 dB. Therefore, it is preferable to avoid small duct sizes, as well as right-angle bends and dampers located close to the vent openings, all of which contribute to increased noise from air turbulence. A good rule of thumb for air velocity: if it feels breezy, the airflow velocity is too high. Some fans have adjustable speeds, and it is generally preferable to slow the fan down rather than closing dampers. In fact, dampers can contribute considerably to air turbulence noise, and are often better replaced entirely with more sonically-transparent thin netting. Attenuation of noise in the duct itself can be increased by using absorptive duct lining, as well as specially designed silencers. External duct treatment may also help.

An additional caveat: ventilation provides a path for *sound*, as well as air, to enter and leave the studio, potentially compromising the isolation so carefully gained through effective wall construction. Again, as with many studio design desicions, it is often more cost-effective in the long run to consult with a professional ahead of time, rather than trying to correct problems encountered as a result of poor planning. At the same time, the greater understanding one has of the underlying issues and principles, the better communication and collaboration can be achieved when working with said professionals towards a common goal.

PROJECTS

1. Measure your studio and/or control room. Calculate the first four axial modes for each dimension (side walls, back and front walls, and floor to ceiling), and plot them on a linear chart. What are the problem frequency areas?

2. Play a frequency-swept sine wave and/or music through your speakers, and listen to the response. Do any frequency ranges seem to be overemphasized? How closely do they correspond to your finding from project 1?

3. Experiment with different speaker placements for smoothest response in the room, keeping in mind proper angling and distance from listening position. Once they have been positioned optimally, look for opportunities to treat nearby surfaces with difussive or absorptive material. (Try using a flashlight at the speaker position, and using a mirror to find reflection paths to the listening position.)

Appendix **A** Reference

Reference Units

Base Unit Value	Compares	Equivalent Value
0 dBu (a.k.a. 0 dBv)	voltage	0.775 V (600Ω/1 mW)
0 dBV	voltage	1 V
0 dBm	electrical power	1 mW
0 dBW	electrical power	1 W
0 dB SIL	electrical power	10^{-12} W (1pW)
dB PWL (L_w)	electrical power	10^{-12} W
0 VU (pro)	effective voltage	+4 dBμ = 1.228 V_{rms}
0 dB SPL (L_p)	sound pressure	0.00002 N/m^2 0.00002 Pa (20 μPa) 0.0002 dynes/cm^2 0.0002 μBars
1 atm	atmospheric pressure	14.7 lbs/in^2 10^5 N/m^2

Prefix	Symbol Value	Corresponding Value *Exponential*	Corresponding Value *Fractional*	Unit Example	Unit Name
deci	d	10^{-1}	$^1/_{10}$	dB	decibel
milli	m	10^{-3}	$^1/_{1000}$	ms	millisecond
micro	μ	10^{-6}	$^1/_{1,000,000}$	μV	microvolt
nano	n	10^{-9}	$^1/_{1,000,000,000}$	nWb	nanoweber
pico	p	10^{-12}	$^1/_{1,000,000,000,000}$	pF	picofarad
kilo	k	10^3	1000	kHz	kilohertz
mega	M	10^6	1,000,000	MΩ	mega-ohm
giga	G	10^9	1,000,000,000	Gbyte	gigabyte
tera	T	10^{12}	1,000,000,000,000	THz	terahertz

Appendix A Reference

Calculations

Δ Power (dB)	$10 \log(W_1/W_0)$
Δ Intensity (dB)	$10 \log(I_1/I_0)$
Δ Voltage (dB)	$20 \log(V_1/V_0)$
Δ Pressure (dB)	$10 \log(p_1/p_0)$
NR over distance	$20 \log(D_1/D_0)$ or (r_1/r_0)

Period	$t = 1/f$	where f = frequency
Frequency	$f = 1/t$	where t = period
Wavelength	$\lambda = c/f$	where c = speed of sound, f = frequ.
Speed of sound in air:	*$c = 1130$ ft/s or 344 m/s*	
Sound Pressure	$p = F/S$	where F = force, S = surface area
Power	$W = E/T$	where E = energy, T = time
1 W = 1 joule/s		
Intensity	$I = W/S$	where W = power, S = surface area
	$I = W/4\pi r^2$	for spherical spreading
Note Frequency	$f = f_0(2^{n/12})$	where f_0 = starting frequency,
		n = # of ½ steps above f_0

Power	$P = IV$	$P = I^2 R$	$P = V^2/R$
Voltage	$V = IR$	$V = P/I$	$V = \sqrt{PR}$
Resistance	$R = V/I$	$R = P/I^2$	$R = V^2/P$
Current	$I = P/V$	$I = V/R$	$I = \sqrt{(P/R)}$

where P or W = power, E or V = voltage, R = resistance, I = current

Calculations

Resistances in Parallel	$1/R_T = 1/R_1 + 1/R_2 + ... + 1/R_n$ *where R_T = total resistance,* R = one resistance of several in parallel, n = total number of resistances

Sound Indoors

Reverberation Time (Sabine Formula)	$T_{60} = 0.05 \ (V/A)s$ *where V = room volume (ft^3),* A = total ft^2 of absorption (sabins) *(use 0.16 for metric units)*
Total absorption	$A = \Sigma S\alpha$ (i.e., $A = S_1\alpha_1 + S_2\alpha_2 + ... + S_n\alpha_n$) *where Σ means sum or summation of,* S = surface area (ft^2), α = absorption coefficient (energy absorbed/ energy incident)
Norris-Eyring Formula	$T_{60} = 0.05 \ V/[-S \times 2.3 \log(1 - \bar{\alpha})]$ *where V = room volume (ft^3),* S = total surface area (ft^2), $\bar{\alpha}$ = mean sound-absorption coefficient = $\Sigma S\alpha/\Sigma S$

Common Frequency Ranges and Applications

Frequency	Application
0 Hz	DC voltage, battery power, control voltage
60 Hz (50 Hz Eu.)	AC line voltage
20 Hz–20 kHz	Audible audio frequencies (approx.)
44.1, 48, 88.2, 96 kHz	Standard audio sampling frequencies
30 kHz–30 MHz	LF, MF, HF: radio frequencies
38 kHz	FM radio stereo subcarrier
67 kHz	FM radio "storecast" subcarrier
560–1600 kHz	AM radio carrier frequencies
88–108 MHz	FM radio carrier frequencies
30–300 MHz	VHF: cell phone, TV, radio, wireless mics
300 MHz–5.8 GHz	UHF: TV, wireless mics, cordless phones
3–300 GHz	Satellite communication, microwaves, radar
300 GHz–400 THz	Infrared light, fiberoptics
400–750 THz	Visible light

Sound Level Measurement Weighting Factors

Octave Band Center Frequency (Hz)	A-Weighting Factor (dB)	C-Weighting Factor (dB)
31.5	–39	–3
63.0	–26	–1
125.0	–16	–3
250.0	–9	0
500.0	–3	0
1k	0	0
2k	+1	0
4k	+1	–1
8k	–1	–3
16k	–7	–9

Safe Noise Exposure Levels/Durations (Based on OSHA recommendations)

Duration Per Day (Hr.)	Sound Pressure Level (dBA)
8.0	90
6.0	92
4.0	95
3.0	97
2.0	100
1.5	102
1.0	105
0.5	110
0.25 or less	115

Appendix **B** Bibliography

Anderton, Craig. *Electronic Projects for Musicians.* New York: Amsco, 1980.

Asimov, Isaac. *Understanding Physics.* New York: Barnes & Noble Books, 1993.

Backus, John. *The Acoustical Foundation of Music, 2nd Ed.* New York: Norton, 1977. (ML 3805.B245 A3 1977).

Ballou, Glen M. *Handbook for Sound Engineers: The New Audio Cyclopedia 2nd Ed.* Carmel, IN: Sams, 1991.

Bartlett, Bruce. *Stereo Microphone Techniques.* Boston: Focal Press, Butterworth-Heinemann, 1991.

Bohn, Dennis A. *Pro Audio Reference.* Mukilteo: Rane Corporation, 2002.

Borwick, John. *Sound Recording Practice 4th Ed.* Oxford: Oxford University Press, 1996.

Cooper, Jeff. *Building a Recording Studio 5th Ed.* Calabasas, CA: Synergy Group, 1996.

Crowhurst, Norman H. *Basic Electronics Course.* Blue Ridge Summit, PA: TAB Books, 1972.

Davis, Don and Carolyn Davis. *Sound System Engineering 2nd Ed.* Boston: Focal Press, Butterworth-Heinemann, 1997.

Davis, Gary and Ralph Jones. *Sound Reinforcement Handbook 2nd Ed.* Milwaukee, WI: Hal Leonard, 1989.

Eargle, John M. *Handbook of Recording Engineering 3rd Ed.* New York: Van Nostrand Reinhold, 1996.

Eargle, John M. *The Microphone Handbook.* Plainview, NY: Elar Publishing, 1982.

Egan, J. and Hake, H. *Journal of the Acoustical Society of America,* 22, 622, 1950.

Egan, M. David. *Architectural Acoustics.* New York: McGraw-Hill, 1988.

Everest, F. Alton. *The Master Handbook of Acoustics 3rd Ed.* New York: TAB Books, McGraw-Hill, 1994.

Everest, F. Alton. *Critical Listening and Auditory Perception.* Emeryville: Mix Books, 1997.

Everest, F. Alton and Mike Shea. *How to Build a Small Budget Recording Studio from Scratch...With 12 Tested Designs 2nd Ed.* Blue Ridge Summit, PA: TAB Books, 1988.

Hall, Donald E. *Musical Acoustics 2nd Ed.* Pacific Grove, CA: Brooks/Cole, 1991.

Hoover, K. Anthony. *An Appreciation of Acoustics.* Sudbury, MA: Cavanaugh-Tocci Publishing,1991.

Joel, Irv, Jerry Bruck, and Albert B. Grundy. "An Audio Timeline." *Pro Sound News*, September, 1997.

Pohlmann, Ken C. *The Compact Disc Handbook 2nd Ed.* Madison, WI: A-R Editions, Inc., 1992.

Pohlmann, Ken C. *Principles of Digital Audio 4th Ed.* New York: McGraw-Hill, 2000.

Porter, John Paul. *Basic Wiring.* New York: Time-Life Books, 1996.

Roederer, Juan G. *The Physics and Psychophysics of Music: An Introduction 3rd Ed.* New York: Springer-Verlag, 1995.

Rossing, Thomas D. *The Science of Sound.* Reading, MA: Addison-Wesley, 1983.

Rumsey, Francis and Tim McCormick. *Sound and Recording: An Introduction 3rd Ed.* Oxford: Focal Press, 1997.

Rothstein, Joseph. *MIDI: A Comprehensive Introduction 2nd Ed.* Madison, WI: A-R Editions, 1995.

Tremaine, Howard M. *Audio Cyclopedia 2nd Ed.* Indianapolis: Sams, 1979.

White, Glenn D. *The Audio Dictionary 2nd Ed.* University of Washington Press, 1995.

Woram, John M. *Sound Recording Handbook.* Indianapolis: Howard W. Sams & Company, 1989.

Index